Charting
Chicago School Reform

Charting
Chicago School Reform

Democratic Localism as a
Lever for Change

Anthony S. Bryk
Penny Bender Sebring
David Kerbow
Sharon Rollow
John Q. Easton

Westview Press
A Member of the Perseus Books Group

Copyright © 1998 by Westview Press, A Member of the Perseus Books Group

Published in 1999 in the United States of America by Westview Press, 5500 Central Avenue, Boulder, Colorado 80301-2877, and in the United Kingdom by Westview Press, 12 Hid's Copse Road, Cumnor Hill, Oxford OX2 9JJ

A CIP catalog record for this book is available from the Library of Congress.
ISBN 0-8133-2319-3 (hb).   ISBN 0-8133-6625-9 (pbk).

The paper used in this publication meets the requirements of the American National Standard for Permanence of Paper for Printed Library Materials Z39.48-1984.

10   9   8   7   6   5   4   3   2   1

In memory of a good friend

John Kotsakis

Dedicated unionist and educator
Committed to advancing the professional capacities of teachers and
expanding learning opportunities for children in Chicago

Contents

Tables and Figures

Figures

Preface

With little training or advance planning, educators, administrators, and parents began in 1989 to implement local control in the Chicago Public Schools. The election of the first Local School Councils thrust new authority and resources into the hands of parents, community residents, and school professionals. Not surprisingly, confusion surfaced about the new roles for parents and educators at the local level and the proper function of the central office in a decentralized system. Would parent-led Local School Councils govern democratically and provide responsible guidance to their schools? Would schools change as a result of local control? Would this change in governance eventually affect how teachers taught? Would the central administration sufficiently loosen its hold over schools to allow them to utilize fully the opportunities afforded by this landmark reform legislation? Ultimately, would any of this have a positive effect on students and their learning?

It was in this context that the Consortium on Chicago School Research was born. As an independent affiliation of researchers from universities, advocacy groups, and the school system, the Consortium initiated a program of studies to examine the implicit theory behind decentralization, and how it was actually unfolding in elementary schools. In addition, other groups, such as the Center for School Improvement at the University of Chicago, the Chicago Panel on School Policy, and the North Central Regional Educational Laboratory, also were mounting studies.

This book represents a synthesis of what we learned from the first four years of Chicago school reform. In addition, the last chapter focuses on the unfinished business of that reform. We discuss the additional changes needed at the school site and district level if decentralization, Chicago-style, is to result in broad and deep improvement in learning opportunities for children. The lessons embedded here are of great significance to urban school districts most everywhere.

The topics we address in this book run the gamut, from governance and politics, to school organization and teaching practices, to the role of the central office. We rely on multiple methods, drawing on fine-grained case studies conducted over time, surveys in hundreds of schools, classroom observations, and interviews with principals, teachers, students, and Local School Council members. The experiences of two of our authors (Anthony S. Bryk and John Q. Easton) working in the school system's central office provided additional insights. Consequently, this book represents a unique blend of the expertise and research, professional, and personal skills that the authors collectively bring. It has been a genuine collaboration, much like that of musicians playing in a jazz quintet. Each individual plays a distinctive theme on his or her instrument, but it is the group as a whole that produces the full score.

In terms of individual contributions, Bryk created the overall conceptual framework for the book and was the primary author of Chapters 1, 6, and 7. He also provided analytical and editorial guidance to the other authors. Chapter 7 draws, in large part, on Bryk's and Easton's experiences, working directly with former superintendent Argie Johnson on the restructuring of the Chicago Pubic School central office. Penny Bender Sebring had primary responsibility for conducting the Consortium's surveys of teachers and principals, and was a lead researcher on the study of six actively restructuring schools. Combining survey results with classroom observations, she developed the themes on instructional innovation and drafted Chapter 4. Sharon Rollow drew on the Center for School Improvement's study of 12 elementary schools to create the extensive case descriptions in Chapters 2 and 3. She is the first author of the Prologue and Chapter 2. The theory of micro-school politics presented here draws on her doctoral dissertation research. Easton was a lead researcher on the teacher survey, took primary responsibility for drafting Chapter 3, and also contributed to parts of Chapters 2 and 5 as well. He and Rollow collaborated to develop the empirically grounded typology of organizational change types. The consistent data analytic hand that runs throughout this book belongs to David Kerbow. He carried out the inventive data analyses in Chapters 2 through 5 that allowed us to estimate the prevalence and equity of school political activity and organizational changes, and to explore the causal linkages among these phenomena. He also was a field researcher in our intensive study of actively restructuring schools, and is the first author of Chapter 5. Bryk took responsibility for second drafts of all of the chapters, orchestrating a common voice to our collective enterprise. Finally, Sebring joined him in the final editing and blending of the chapters, the laborious documentation and quality control checks required for a study of this scope, and the numerous publication tasks needed to bring this book to fruition.

We want to express our sincere appreciation to the many colleagues who helped collect data and offered thoughtful advice along the way. In particular, we thank the Steering Committee of the Consortium on Chicago School Research, who guided the earlier studies that led up to this book. We are also indebted to the principals, teachers, and students of the six actively restructuring schools, who allowed us to visit and learn in concrete ways about their inspired and tenacious efforts to reform themselves. The principals (at the time) and schools were: Don C. Anderson, Christian Ebinger School; Carlos M. Azcoitia, John Spry School; Marcella Gillie, Perkins Bass School; Patricia A. Harvey, Helen Hefferan School; Nelda Hobbs, Eugene Field School; and Barbara Martin, Thomas Hoyne School. In addition, the following faculty members assisted us in collecting and analyzing the data: John Attinasi, California State University at Long Beach, Stephen Bloom, National-Louis University, Edgar Epps, University of Chicago; Barbara Farnandis, Chicago State University; Janet Fredericks, Northeastern Illinois University; and Mari Koerner, Roosevelt University. David Kinney was the Project Coordinator.

During the last seven years, our research has benefited greatly from the cooperation of the Chicago Public Schools, and this book simply would not have been possible without it. The Center on Organization and Restructuring of Schools at the University of Wisconsin, which received funding from the U.S. Department of Education, Office of Educational Research and Improvement, supported the development of the case studies on school politics and organizational change. Fred Newmann, the Center's director, has been a superb colleague in support of this research. We also acknowledge several colleagues who helped us in a variety of ways: Benjamin D. Wright, University of Chicago; Albert Bennett, Roosevelt University; Mark Smylie, University of Illinois at Chicago; G. Alfred Hess, Jr., Northwestern University; Larry Friedman, D. William Quinn, and Arie van der Ploeg, from the North Central Regional Educational Laboratory; and Geraldine Oberman, Chicago Public Schools.

Anthony Bryk would like to acknowledge a special debt to David Cohen in the development of this book. Over the years, we have engaged in many conversations about Chicago school reform, school improvement efforts, and educational policy more generally. The ideas we discussed are now so deeply embedded in my own thinking that specific citations and adequate attribution becomes nearly impossible. Suffice it to say that his intellectual footprints run throughout this work.

Our editors, Leon Lynn, Kay Kersch Kirkpatrick, and Rebecca E. Williams, have rescued us from the pitfalls of punctuation and grammar. Sandra Jennings has patiently and accurately produced numerous versions of each chapter. She has done a spectacular job of transforming ragged drafts into this beautiful, desktop published volume.

Finally, we are grateful to our funders, who have been exceedingly steadfast supporters of urban public school reform: The John D. and Catherine T. MacArthur Foundation, the Spencer Foundation, and the Joyce Foundation.

Charting
Chicago School Reform

Prologue

A tragic story unfolded in the pages of the *Chicago Tribune* during May 1988.

> [Chicago Public Schools] are hardly more than daytime warehouses for inferior students, taught by disillusioned and inadequate teachers, presided over by a bloated, leaderless bureaucracy, and constantly undercut by a selfish, single-minded teachers' union.[1]

The series of articles subsequently was compiled into a book titled *Chicago Schools: "Worst in America."* The quote in the title came from a judgment offered by then-U.S. Secretary of Education William Bennett during a brief visit to Chicago. The *Tribune* concurred. The Chicago Public School system was "a disgrace."

Much of the *Tribune* series focused on life at Beacon Elementary School.[2] It also made clear, however, that Beacon was not unlike hundreds of other schools that had fallen victim to the interests of career bureaucrats in the school district's central office, politicians in the city council and state legislature (many of whom sent their own children to private and parochial schools), and a teachers' union that saw its role as protecting the jobs and benefits of its aging membership.

The story told about Beacon was not as simple as the sensational title might have led one to believe. Rather, it was a mixed tale of both heroism and neglect: of a principal who called himself a "lousy" administrator, but who deeply cared about the students and their families; of the inspired efforts of a few teachers who could not compensate for the indifference of their colleagues; and similarly of parents who desperately wanted to do right by their children, but did not know how. In the end, *Chicago Schools: "Worst in America"* painted a picture of despair and hopelessness. It depicted a school community where the best intentions of some were overwhelmed by massive system failure. It was tragic too because the same scenario was being repeated in so many city schools, in Chicago and across the nation.

The *Tribune* series came at a critical time in Chicago's struggle for school reform, and it did much to galvanize public opinion against the status quo. By taking a closer look at Beacon, we gain some insight into the complex nature of daily life in urban schools, and the uphill battle waged for fundamental school change.

A Snapshot of Beacon Elementary School in 1988

Beacon is located in the Uptown neighborhood on Chicago's north lakefront. At the turn of the century, Uptown was as affluent community, as depicted in Theodore Dreiser's novel, *Sister Carrie*. In fact, Beacon was built around that time. Beginning in the 1940s, however, Uptown fell on hard times. Many of the mansions and gracious apartments were converted into rooming houses and single resident occupancies, as Uptown became home to waves of newcomers. At first it was migrants from Appalachia and the South. Then immigrants from Latin America and South East Asia began to arrive. Each group brought a distinctive culture and often a new language into the school. This complicated the work of the principal and teachers, who struggled to connect with children's homes and to make parents feel welcome. It also meant that the school had a transient student population. Many families traveled to and from "home" for extended periods to find work, to visit family members left behind, or to care for sick relatives.

Although Beacon's students are racially and ethnically diverse, they are nevertheless isolated as children of the poor. Gentrification had begun in the mid 1980s, and affluent families had re-appeared in the neighborhood, but their children were either too young for school, or they attended magnet or private schools. These professional families had shown little interest in becoming involved in Beacon. As a result, the school reaped little benefit from the neighborhood's most recent wave of newcomers.

However, gentrification was still having an effect on the school community. As recently as ten years earlier, when there were more blue-collar jobs in the city, Beacon's high mobility rate (approximately 50 percent) was driven by families who first moved into Uptown, then secured decent employment and eventually moved to a better neighborhood. There were always new families to take their place. By 1988, gentrification was reclaiming the community block by block. Mobility was now driven more by real estate speculators who bought up properties, raised the rents, and forced out poor families.

Unfortunately, the neighborhood restoration had not benefitted Beacon's building and grounds. Rather, like most of the older neighborhood schools in Chicago, Beacon appeared worn and run down:

> . . . the brick is sallow, tired looking. Painted window frames have peeled. What passes for a play area around this rectangular, three-story fortress is a forbidding expanse of buckling pavement that spills into a back alley without the benefit of a protective fence. There is no recess. There are no swings. Not even a rusted jungle gym. Just the lonely poles that support three graffiti-scarred backboards stripped of all but one bent basketball rim.[3]

The principal, like his predecessors, put in requests for maintenance and repair, but like so many other things in the system, they languished on waiting lists in the central office. When questioned by *Tribune* reporters, the "bureaucrats at Pershing Road" (the location of Chicago's central office) claimed they were "not to blame—the state legislators are." In a district where most of the buildings are eighty years old or more, additional state funding was needed for capital repairs.

The fiscal crises and budget cuts that had plagued the system for several decades were sorely felt inside the school. "Mac," the principal, and numerous veteran staff recalled when various programs were cut—the year they lost art and music, then their sports and extracurricular programs, and more recently their before- and afterschool activities. The previous year, Beacon's budget for materials and supplies was reduced from $1,500 to $14. Some of the more experienced teachers encouraged new staff to hoard their meager supplies and to journey to Maxwell Street—Chicago's outdoor flea market—when they needed replenishments. In 1988, many classrooms went without textbooks for the first several months of school, or used incomplete sets of outdated, tattered books because orders from the central office were backlogged. While the teachers' lounge still maintained a supply of toilet paper, the children's bathrooms —at least the ones that had flushing toilets—were not so well endowed.

Other neighborhood schools across the city were in much the same straits as Beacon. The only outstanding exceptions were some of the magnet schools that had extra material resources and benefitted from organized parent groups who knew how to raise hell whenever budget cuts threatened them.

Mac had been in the system for thirty-nine years, nineteen of them as principal at Beacon. He was a "survivor," a man who had made his peace with both the teachers he supervised and the administrators who supervised him. With the latter he had struck a bargain; he delivered on-time reports (even if he fabricated the information). In return, they left him alone. His district superintendent, Mr. Baker, was a survivor too. He seemed satisfied because few problems at Beacon ever bubbled up to the sub-district office to demand his intervention. In fact, Mr. Baker described Mac as "brilliant" because of his unorthodox methods for working with students and families. Mr. Baker admired "an old guy like Mac" who still tracked down kids when they were truant.[4] Mr. Baker liked to joke that Mac did not really need a school office, since he spent most of his time in the hallways, out on the streets, and making surprise visits to the cramped and run-down apartments where most of his students lived.

Mac had an implicit treaty with his faculty too. They made few demands on him, and he reciprocated by giving them free rein to run their classrooms as they pleased. Mac did not ask them for lesson plans or homework assignments, he did not call faculty meetings, nor did he especially encourage teachers to enroll in professional development activities. He also expressed little concern about students' academic achievement. While he performed the required annual teacher evaluations, his supervisory style was hands-off. He looked the other way, for example, when Mr. Syncopa, a sixth grade teacher, marched his students up and down three flights of stairs for misbehaving in class. Similarly, Mac believed that Ms. Marconi should handle her fifth graders even when he saw chairs flying and heard children screaming and fighting. "I'll bandage them up when they come out," he laughed. Mrs. Jamece did not even send several sixth grade boys to the principal's office when they refused to quit drawing lewd cartoons on the chalkboard. She knew, as did the rest of the faculty, that Mac would not discipline them. He was more likely to joke around with them, ask them if everything is OK, and send them on their way.

Not surprisingly, in a school where the discipline was lax and supervision nonexistent, little real teaching and learning was going on. Mac did not believe in retaining students. They were promoted from grade to grade in spite of what the *Tribune* writers called, at best, "a passive exposure to learning." In many classes, for example, students sat quietly at their seats coloring and filling in dittoes day after day. One teacher was caught napping by *Tribune* investigators, while another asked his students to quiet down so that he could finish reading a newspaper. (The students did.)

There were a few rays of hope at Beacon, just as there are in every neighborhood school. Ms. Smith, for instance, was a first grade teacher with twenty-four years of experience. Most of her students did not know all of their letters or numbers when she first met them in the fall. By mid-year, however, when the *Tribune* visited her class, they were all reading simple books, handing in homework, and beaming when Ms. Smith said, "Nice work." The students in Ms. Smith's classroom learned to work cooperatively, to say "excuse me" if they inadvertently bumped into each other as they moved between learning centers, and to take care of all of the colorful manipulatives and materials that she bought for them. The children accomplished all of this for one simple reason: They loved Ms. Smith, and learning was what she expected.

There was Ms. Fanizo too. She taught intermediate grade special education students. Many of her students were overage for their grade. Even though Ms. Fanizo had some of the most difficult children in the school, she never had discipline problems in her class. Her students knew that she had a lot to teach them and she, like Mac, connected with their families. It was not unusual to see her in the neighborhood before and after school, helping her students navigate across gang territory and busy city streets. Ms. Fanizo often stopped to talk with parents along the way, not necessarily to tell them something bad about their child—which is what they usually heard from teachers. Instead, she assured them that their child was doing well. She especially made a point to get to know the younger mothers, because she felt that if they came to trust her, she might be able to help them learn some of the basic parenting skills that they so desperately needed.

The *Tribune* also learned about Mr. Iikes, a younger teacher who saw himself as a role model for students. He tried to talk with them realistically about the skills that they would need if they were ever to get out of their neighborhood. He complained that the numerous pull-out programs left little uninterrupted time for instruction with his fourth grade class. The students had much to learn, but he had too little time to teach them.

The reporters observed that the students who were lucky enough to be assigned to Ms. Smith, Ms. Fanizo and Mr. Iikes often came early to school, stayed late, and were largely successful with their schoolwork. The reporters also met former students who continued to visit these teachers for years after they graduated. In some instances the students said that these three teachers were the only adults they felt they could turn to when they needed help with life problems or wanted to share a success story.

The effort of these teachers would be impressive in any school, and seemed especially so at Beacon. Unfortunately, their accomplishments remained isolated, because teachers like these had little to build on or toward. Rather, over time, many teachers of this caliber "burn out." Ms. Fanizo, for example, suddenly went on personal leave in the spring of the *Tribune*'s fact-finding year.

Despite obvious needs, little strategic planning or program development occurred at Beacon. Mac, and a few teachers like Ms. Fanizo, felt that many of the special education students would do better if they were mainstreamed, but they made no effort to accomplish this.[5] Similarly, although Mac knew that there were problems with grouping students homogeneously by ability, this too was a school norm. Remedial classes were always problematic because they tended to collect "troublemakers." Nevertheless, the faculty at Beacon saved these classes for new teachers even though inexperienced teachers are probably least able to deal with a concentration of problem students. A change to heterogeneous grouping would have required Mac—or someone—to reprogram the whole school. Moreover, even if there had been a volunteer from the faculty to do the work, many of the teachers would certainly have complained about the change.

Beacon receives a substantial amount of compensatory funding because it serves many disadvantaged children with low academic achievement. For several years, Beacon had two specially funded positions for reading specialists because it ranked among the 100 Chicago Public Schools with the lowest reading scores. In addition, two large classrooms were equipped with "extra" reading materials. Neither reading specialist, however, liked to work directly with at-risk students. Mac told the reporters that he wished this were not the case, but he was also reluctant to act. These two teachers brought resources into the school, and one of the two was related to a board member which meant she had some clout. As an alternative to teaching classes or tutoring, Mac asked them to order books and organize materials for other teachers in the school.

At base here was a telling story. While it was clear that schools like Beacon desperately needed more fiscal and human resources, in the absence of any real accountability, it was unlikely that additional resources would do much good.

* * * * *

To many inside the school system, the *Tribune* series was regarded as the worst kind of journalism—blatant sensationalism without regard for the people whose lives it exposed. Others, however, praised the paper's editors for having the courage to uncover and publicize the corrupt and selfish practices that hurt those who could least help themselves—the children of the Chicago Public Schools.

In reality, there was truth to both points of view. We know from our research that the story of Beacon was in part overdrawn, and yet, in other respects, it rang sadly true. In 1988 the plight of too many neighborhood schools in Chicago appeared hopeless. The system as a whole was failing the students and parents that it was intended to serve, as well as the teachers and principals whose work it was to support. The story too often told was of many individuals who strove valiantly to do good work. While they may, in fact, literally have saved a few students' lives, ultimately they proved powerless to change their schools and the larger system of which they were a part. Their efforts were overwhelmed by the indifference, incompetence, and in some cases the corruption of that larger system. In the end what became most important about the *Tribune* series was that it got people's attention. The *Tribune* added its voice and force to the fight for better city schools. The snapshot of Beacon helped to fuel the fire that would radically change the governance of the Chicago Public Schools.

1

Framing Our Analysis:

Locating Chicago School Reform Within an Institutional Change Perspective

The past fifteen years have witnessed an unprecedented level of public attention to our educational institutions. A virtual industry of panels, commissions, research reports, and policy analyses has documented numerous problems and proposed a vast array of remedies. Efforts have moved forward to strengthen high school graduation requirements, to enforce stricter codes for student conduct and discipline, and to effect wholesale changes in instruction to deepen students' engagement with subject matter and promote higher order thinking.[1] Other reforms have been directed toward professionalizing teachers by promoting higher standards for certification, by changing the nature of pre-service education, by creating teacher networks, and by empowering teachers with greater decision-making authority at the building level.[2] Still others have emphasized reforming the grade-level organization of schooling, such as ungraded primary schools, and altering the basic social structure of schools to develop smaller, more personal, caring environments.[3]

In scanning this landscape of school reform, one quickly can become overwhelmed by the breadth and diversity of the efforts now underway. Literally every aspect of school organization and classroom practice has been challenged, and often quite radical alternatives have been proposed.

In striving for some larger, more comprehensive understanding of this broadbased discontent with existing arrangements, much attention has focused on the institutional structure of schooling in the United States, the educational problems associated with it, and the most effective approach to their redress.[4] These analyses typically begin with the observation that how a school works (or fails to work) is shaped, in both obvious and subtle ways, by its external environment. In this regard, schools are viewed as "open systems," where the nature of core practices and their overall effectiveness depend on how these external influences operate. When we confront school failure on a massive scale, such as in Chicago and in other large urban centers, it seems highly plausible that the root cause of this failure is not inside each individual school but rather in the external environments that they share. From this perspective, pervasive bad school practices are symptoms of some larger external causes. In particular, how schools are governed is seen as the central problem.

The current governance structures for urban public education emerged late in the nineteenth century. The cornerstone of these arrangements was the public control of schools by democratically elected or politically appointed district school boards. These local boards hired a professional administration, consisting of a superintendent and central office staff, who created bureaucracies to control their rapidly expanding school systems. District operations were further embedded within state governments that have primary, formal authority for public education. The state institutions parallel the district: Each has a school board, a form of superintendent, and a specialized bureaucracy to support its work. In addition, the federal government—although taking a secondary role in some respects—has its own educational bureaucracy, with complex linkages to state-local hierarchy. These structures organize large-scale democratic control of public education. They afford various entry points for political influence and function primarily through a series of professionalized bureaucracies.[5]

The amount of political activity flowing through these structures greatly intensified beginning in the mid-1960s. Many minority and special interest groups, previously disenfranchised, were now "at the table."[6] The issues and concerns raised here were especially profound in large urban centers, given their diverse and extraordinarily needy student populations. The new claims pressed on urban school systems resulted in a complex maze of programs, rules and regulations, and conflicting mandates.[7] Judicial directives on students' rights, school desegregation, and inclusion of handicapped children brought one wave of reforms. Added to this have been pull-out programs for the education of the disadvantaged and separate classes for linguistic minorities. Layered on top are specialized curricular initiatives on such topics as drugs, AIDS, suicide, and sexual abuse. Recently, demands have come for more testing, new core curriculum, and increased school planning and accountability. Clearly, the list of externally imposed initiatives is long and grows each year.

There has been little thought along the way as to how individual schools are supposed to combine all of this to create an effective work environment for adults and students. Instead, each new initiative is typically layered in a disjointed fashion on top of the ones that came immediately before it. Few local participants are fully aware of the totality of a school's operations, the external constraints placed upon them, and the overall impact of these diverse initiatives on the school's sense of purpose and its organizational coherence. This was certainly true at Beacon School, and is a general feature of the larger system of which Beacon is a part. Ironically, this is "not an outcome that any of the major players would want or intend if acting alone. It is truly a product of the system as a whole, an unintended consequence of the way the system works."[8] Most troublesome, critics argue that there is little reason for optimism that the current system can do anything about this, other than to continue to add more of the same.

This line of analysis suggests that fundamental change is needed in school governance arrangements. Absent this, ineffective school performance is likely to continue. While principals, teachers, parents, and interested citizens may work hard to promote better schools, the larger institutional system will continue to frustrate their best efforts.[9] The governance of public education, as currently structured, is fundamentally incompatible with the organizational and instructional changes desired. Unless these arrangements are restructured, wide scale school reform remains unlikely.

A Market-Based System of Schools

Inextricably tied to the growth of special interest groups, each pressing their distinctive cause, has been the expansion of centralized school bureaucracies.[10] Typically, each new program or mandate is accompanied by a new central office department to administer and control its operation. Like the political mobilizing for each new policy initiative, the rules, regulations, and monitoring of these departments focus only on the selected aspects of school operations that each has been charged to redress. The collective effects of all of this specialized program activity, however, are no one's responsibility.

At the school building level, principals now confront a complex web of external control. The number of "downtown bureaucrats" who can block a proposed local action has increased dramatically. In some instances, these bureaucrats wield their power in petty or even despotic ways. Even under better, more cooperative circumstances, this structure greatly complicates local action and demands considerable inventiveness to circumvent. It has contributed to a broadly shared sense among school participants that they cannot effect solutions to the fundamental problems which they confront. Such a normative environment depresses subsequent initiatives and discourages entrepreneurship. Genuine leadership, under these circumstances, requires extraordinary personal commitment. It also often demands courage. The stories are legendary about those who tried to make change and were "savaged by the system." Prior to the passage of PA 85-1418, reform-minded principals in Chicago regularly had to resort to "creative insubordination" lest their efforts be crushed by someone downtown.[11]

Such analyses of the problems of America's schools have played a central role in the growing advocacy for a market-driven system of education. The direct democratic control of school boards and the centralized bureaucracies that institutionalize various political interests are seen as the major obstacles to improvement. Advocates for choice argue that markets should replace direct democracy by school boards as the primary control mechanism. They claim that this approach is more likely to stimulate initiative at the school building level, afford parents a much greater measure of influence over the kind of education received by their children, and eliminate bureaucratic waste. More specifically, these proposals would strip away the accumulated bureaucracies and regulations which market advocates claim have crippled innovation. Much greater authority would be extended to school site leaders to shape their work environs. Relieved of constraints, locally empowered and stimulated by profit incentives, it is argued that more effective schools and more efficient use of public resources would result.[12]

While market proposals vary in their details, they share some common features. They all require a continuing public agency to establish and maintain at least a minimal regulatory apparatus to assure that accurate information is broadly disseminated about educational services and that fair access to these services is afforded. The agency's primary function would be granting vouchers to parents and empowering them to choose among an array of schools which would have to compete with each other. The ability of any public authority to expand its activity beyond this purview would be deliberately constrained. Government would set up the system and then "get out of the way." Schooling would be much more akin to a private commodity which, like any other good or service, involves an exchange in the marketplace. Society would rely primarily on the "invisible hand" of the marketplace to discipline these exchanges, and would only turn to public regulation as a last resort. The seeming simplicity of this control mechanism, especially when contrasted with the political conflict and bureaucratic snarls that often engulf public education, makes this vision very appealing.

Nonetheless, these proposals have drawn many critics. Much of this attention has focused on issues of educational equity.[13] Existing evidence from other public services where markets currently operate, such as health care and post-secondary education, raise questions about how well the poor and minorities fare under these systems.[14] Some legitimation for these concerns can also be found in studies of existing school choice programs.[15] In general, there are reasons to worry that unless regulatory systems are carefully crafted to assure that quality schools are located near where poor people live, and that those people have good information about them, a market system might be even more inequitable than current arrangements.

Proponents of school choice have also been criticized for ignoring the social aims of education. School choice arguments are almost exclusively framed in terms of the individual academic benefits that supposedly will accrue to those exposed to a market system of schooling. However, schools also serve important social and political purposes. Historically they have played a central role in extending not only skills and knowledge, but also those habits of heart necessary for a vital democratic citizenry and convivial free society.[16] From this perspective, the public has a legitimate continued interest in the direct control of America's schools. They are the primary social institutions that shape our future society, and, in this, all citizens have a stake.[17]

Systemic Reform as an Alternative to Markets

Market initiatives and school vouchers are not the only educational reform agenda which develops out of an institutional critique of the current structures of public school governance. Like market critics, advocates for systemic reform also believe that the institutional arrangements surrounding schools significantly impede reform.[18] In fact, advocates for systemic reform voice many of the same complaints, and often use the same phrases to describe the dysfunctional state of affairs created by current educational governance arrangements.[19]

Rather than directly challenging the basic political structure of large-scale democratic control, however, this perspective argues for a systemic change within existing structures. Educational policy needs to be more coherent, this perspective says, and the various components of policy need to reinforce one another. Instead of emphasizing rule accountability for specific processes and services, schools should become outcome accountable. As an alternative to the current maze of conflicting mandates, schooling should be driven by a coherent system of educational goals. Content standards would define the knowledge to which students should be exposed, and would include explicit criteria for judging student performance. New assessments linked to these standards would provide evidence about the adequacy of students' and schools' work. Coordinated with this would be major reforms in pre-service education and a substantial increase in the professional education of existing teachers to support their efforts to achieve academic excellence with all children. Binding together this new common agenda for education would be broadly shared commitments both to the democratic values of individual respect, equality, civic participation, and social responsibility, and to the intellectual dispositions necessary for full participation in a complex modern society, such as active learning, sustained discourse about ideas, and intellectually rigorous examination.

In terms of specific governance changes, systemic reformers seek to increase the authority of both states and local schools while constraining the activities of school districts, including their boards, superintendents and central administration. More specifically, systemic reform seeks to rationalize and legitimize state authority around a coherent system of instructional guidance. The state would establish educational goals that incorporate high academic standards for all students, provide the necessary resources to support those standards, create an accountability system linked to the standards, and coordinate efforts to strengthen pre-service education for teachers and in-service staff development programs. In tandem with these activities, individual schools would have more flexibility and authority to create local work conditions more conducive to the best efforts of teachers and students. Finally, districts would act as intermediaries between the state and individual schools, supporting the instructional guidance initiatives emanating from the state and assuring that resources and programs are equitably distributed so that all children have an opportunity to meet state standards. Concomitant with their new and reduced role, districts would forsake micro-managing local school activity.

More generally, then, systemic reform seeks to restructure and discipline large scale democratic control by focusing attention on the common aims desired for all children, rather than on the narrow and fractious interests that have come to dominate public education debates in recent decades. Along the way, systemic reform also seeks to guide the work of external markets which provide schools with a wide array of services and materials, including textbooks and tests. The activities and services now offered in this marketplace are highly incoherent and often of mediocre quality. A systemic reform agenda should discipline these as well. Under the influence of a reformed external environment, it is argued that individual schools should be more able to develop a shared commitment to this common agenda, and substantial improvements would follow.

To be sure, the principal aim of systemic reform—better academic performance for all—is highly commendable. Nonetheless, this initiative has been criticized because of the relative silence among many of its advocates about how schools might actually change to accomplish this, what resources would be made available to support such development, and the incentives and sanctions needed to encourage serious effort in this new direction. Simply "raising the bar" in the high jump to "world class standards" does little to help an ordinary athlete achieve at a much higher level. Absent strong and sustained support for individual and collective improvement, the more likely consequence would just be increased public frustration about continued failure. Moreover, it is far from clear that anyone really knows how to accomplish the aims of systemic reform in ordinary schools with ordinary teachers on any short time frame.[20]

Even more problematic, systemic initiatives seek to resolve the current incoherence in local practice by reshaping the aims of education through political action at the federal and state government levels. How this distal, and largely professionally dominated, conversation about aims is reconciled with the diversity of interests that have contributed to the current complex state of local affairs is unclear. Moreover, the problems stemming from the extraordinary pluralistic character of large urban school districts remain unexamined. Rather, it is assumed that these rancorous debates can be submerged under a new "one best system of education" with a renewed commitment to universalist values. While the initial successes in developing new math and science standards boded well in this regard, subsequent events around language arts and social studies have generated reason for caution.[21]

Expanded Local Participation as an Antidote to the Current Problems of Democratic Control

Ironically, just as major critiques of large-scale democratic control of schools were taking shape, school reformers in Chicago embraced expanded local democratic participation as a lever for change. Much like the arguments for educational markets and systemic reforms, advocacy for expanded democratic participation took root in an institutional analysis of large urban school systems. Chicago's reformers analyzed the core problem, however, not as democratic governance per se but rather as centralized bureaucracy. They argued that a commitment to democratic control was essential to public education, but that much more of it should be exercised at the school-building level. For this to occur, the influence of the central bureaucracy had to be curtailed substantially.

The reformers at the turn of the century who created the current governance arrangements for public education leaned heavily on the then-popular corporate sector principles of efficiency, expertise, and economies of scale.

Schools were gradually consolidated into large districts where professional administrators sought to formalize control through standardizing operations. These reformers looked to the emerging schools of education to assist in this effort. The education schools developed training programs that organized teachers' work by grade and subject matter, and created assessment instruments that legitimized the sorting and tracking of children. This "one best system" of governance by lay school boards, employing a central office staff, and supported by expertise from universities, won out over other forms of governance that had been prevalent up to that point.[22] In this process, the very definition of public education was shaped. Other alternative arrangements, including religiously sponsored schools and local community control, which had existed earlier in the nineteenth century, were forced out.[23]

The embrace of centralized bureaucracy had especially profound impacts in urban centers. The ties of local school professionals to their communities eventually weakened. Instead, school-based professionals increasingly looked to their central office superiors for guidance. In this process, parents' interests and concerns were subordinated to the expertise of educational professionals. Principles of public participation and local flexibility had been exchanged for established routine, centralized authority, and professional control.[24]

These arrangements have persevered throughout the twentieth century and have been remarkably robust in deflecting any challenge to their legitimacy. Beginning in the mid-1960s, as America sought to redress some of its fundamental educational problems—such as school segregation, exclusion of handicapped children, bilingual education, and education for the disadvantaged—the span of governmental activity increased dramatically. These initiatives, however, often did not produce the desired changes in schools and in teachers' work.[25] In reflecting on such experiences, Chicago reformers concluded that any improvement efforts would likely flounder unless the existing web of centralized control and bureaucratic arrangements was altered. This was understood to be the real source of the massive institutional failure in the Chicago Public Schools.

Thus, in shaping a reform agenda, the Chicago initiative shared some common concerns with market and systemic reform advocates, but also drew upon distinctive local circumstances. Chicago reformers agreed that centralized control by the superintendent, central office, and board of education had to be weakened. Similarly, they concurred that both resources and authority should be devolved to local school communities, predicated on a belief that local communities can more effectively solve local problems.

School-based professionals, however, were also seen as part of the problem. Don Moore, an author of the school reform legislation and director of

Designs for Change, a major school advocacy group in Chicago, argued that "the power of urban school professionals must be curtailed because professional judgment has repeatedly been used as an excuse for practices that are harmful to children."[26] Similarly, in a series of community forums across the city during the mobilization for reform, principals and teachers were sharply criticized by some parents and community members for a perceived lack of concern and effort.[27] If schools were ever to become more responsive to their local communities, and the parents and children that they were intended to serve, a fundamental rebalancing of power away from these professionals and toward parents and community members was necessary.

In response, Chicago took a unique tack. Drawing on a long history of community organizing and a well-established network of community-based organizations, Chicago opted for an unparalleled level of parent and community control. In essence, it chose to shift from centralized democratic control, exercised through a bureaucracy, to expanded local democratic control exercised through school councils. It threw off the "one best system" of education, and banked instead upon principles of citizen participation, community control, and local flexibility. These commitments are captured in the idea of democratic localism.[28]

Finally, unlike other current efforts to restructure large urban school systems, the commitment to democratic localism was seen, by at least some advocates for reform, as part of a larger strategy at urban community building.[29] The loss of local institutions of all kinds—social, economic, and religious—have denuded urban community life and undermined the viability of these communities. Any effort to stem the current destruction and to recreate communities requires a massive commitment to local institution-building. Key in this regard is expanded opportunities for citizen participation and community education about local affairs. With sustained local engagement and some external supports, it is argued that even poor citizens can take control of their circumstances and improve them. From this perspective, Chicago school reform can be viewed as part of a larger movement to renew urban life by revitalizing the public sphere.

Looking Back: Mobilizing for Reform

For years advocacy groups had been reporting on the failings of the Chicago Public Schools.[30] A 1985 study by the Chicago Panel on School Policy, for example, exposed shockingly high dropout rates.[31] Previous school system reports had seriously underestimated the severity of the problem, by counting only those students whose official records explicitly marked them

as dropouts. Many actual dropouts were mislabeled as transfers, preg-
nant, or "enlisted in the military." Using more accurate methods, the
Chicago Panel found that the systemwide dropout rate for the years from
1978 to 1984 was about 43 percent, but the rate was as high as 63 percent
in some racially isolated high schools. Almost one in every two Hispanic
and African-American students in Chicago dropped out of school.

This research also indicated that the school system's retention policy
was an abysmal failure. For those students who had been retained in elementary school, the dropout rates were even more appalling than the
citywide averages. There was no evidence that grade retention had any
positive effects. Rather, retention practices were indicted as a major cause
of students' dropping out.

A report from Designs for Change in 1985 amplified these themes.[32] These
researchers found that nearly half of the children who entered the city's
eighteen most economically disadvantaged high schools dropped out before graduation. And even among those who did manage to graduate, more
than half were reading below the ninth grade level.

Building on their earlier work, the Chicago Panel turned attention in
1987 to the city's elementary schools.[33] They found great differences among
elementary schools regarding the proportion of their graduates who went
on to complete high school. In some elementary schools, 100 percent of the
students eventually graduated. In many more schools, however, fewer than
half ever received a diploma. Clearly, many of the city's elementary schools
were failing to prepare students adequately for high school work.

The case for change also appeared in annual school system statistics
about student achievement. In the fall of 1987, for example, the CPS reported median percentile rankings on reading comprehension from the
Iowa Tests of Basic Skill (ITBS) ranging from a high of the 47th percentile in
the first grade to a low of the 33rd percentile in the fourth grade. Mathematics scores ranged from a high of the 47th percentile in eighth grade to
a low of the 38th percentile for first graders. Moreover, these results were
from a test form that had been in continuous use for almost ten years, and
they were based on norms from 1978 which were among the easiest in
recent memory. While most school systems around the country were reporting above average student outcomes "a la Lake Wobegon," the CPS
failed on this account too. In fact, the full dimensions of the problem would
not become apparent until 1990, when Chicago finally changed forms of
the ITBS and reported results in terms of more recent 1988 norms. With
this shift, CPS rankings in reading and math plummeted even further. Percentile statistics in the low thirties appeared across many grade levels.

Whether the focus was on statistics or media accounts of schools like
Beacon, the indictment was clear. The Chicago Public Schools were "fail-

ing miserably the dual mission of preparing young people to realize the dreams that are their birthright and of providing for the city's future a qualified and productive citizenry."[34]

These reports confirmed a growing sense among the city's elite that major changes were needed. Shortly after his re-election in 1986, Mayor Harold Washington reached out to the business community to ask for their help and support in tackling some of the problems of public education.[35] He invited them to participate in an Education Summit that was first conceived as a limited partnership between the Chicago business community and the public high schools. The intent was to replicate the Boston Compact, which had sought to motivate high school students to stay in school with the promise of a job upon graduation. The plan died, however, when then superintendent of schools, Manford Byrd, refused to consider even first steps without a major commitment of new funds.

The next catalyzing event was the teachers' strike in the fall of 1987. The CPS and the Chicago Teachers Union (CTU) were locked in their age-old battle over wages and work rules. The 1987 strike, the longest in Chicago's history, was also the ninth strike in eighteen years. The press decried both the Board of Education (BOE) and the CTU for their "stranglehold" on the system.[36] Parents were frustrated by the strike as well. They charged that neither the system nor the union seemed interested in the fact that the schools were failing children.

A settlement was eventually reached, and in its aftermath, the mayor's strategy changed. He called for an all-day, open meeting on school reform. The meeting was attended by thousands, and from it Mayor Washington appointed a Parent Community Council (PCC). The Mayor invited the PCC to join the business organizations and the Chicago Public Schools in a new Education Summit. He also asked the Council to sponsor parent and community forums throughout the city. From the testimony at these forums, the summit participants were to draft a proposal for educational reform that the mayor pledged to sponsor.

The reform process that Mayor Washington initiated at this point was a populist one. Ten forums were held at evening hours making it easy for parents and community members to attend. Additional hearings were also scheduled so that school advocacy groups could present their proposals to the Council on weekends. These measures were intended to assure the public that the reform process was accessible to poor and working parents, and that their voices would shape any documents that were eventually drafted.

Much less involved in the Summit activities were professional educators from the central office, the Chicago Teachers Union, and members of the university community. The sentiment of many at both the central office and the teachers' union was, "This too shall pass." While superintendent Manford

Byrd represented the school system, and teachers' union president Jackie Vaughn spoke for the CTU, neither side was especially active in formulating reform proposals. In terms of the colleges and universities, few local professors at that time had much involvement with the district.[37] Not surprisingly, faculty from higher education institutions did not actively seek participation in the Summit. Representation was limited to two university presidents, appointed by the mayor, neither of whom had a particularly strong background in urban elementary and secondary education.[38]

Harold Washington died on the eve of the first forum. His death did not stop the mobilization process. It did, however, create a power vacuum which paved the way for numerous advocacy organizations, community groups, and the business sector to expand their influence. As noted earlier, groups like Designs for Change and the Chicago Panel had been documenting the system's failings for years. Their influence dramatically increased at this time. Similarly, community-based organizations in some neighborhoods became more active. Several of these had been started by Saul Alinsky or his proteges, and they still used the direct, adversarial tactics that were his legacy. When the action moved from the mobilization phase to the spring legislative session downstate, the PCC and numerous advocacy groups and community coalitions were there with competing drafts of legislation.[39]

The formal legislative process spanned two sessions. It was marred by leadership conflict between Democrats and Republicans, extensive use of procedural rules by key lawmakers and the governor, and organized efforts by numerous lobbying groups to influence specific reform provisions. After extensive negotiations behind closed doors in the spring of 1988, the legislature voted along strict party lines and passed a reform bill.

The Democratic enacted reform, however, failed to get the support from Republican governor, James Thompson. He exercised his amendatory veto power to alter the reform package in ways that would increase his influence over Chicago schools. After another round of extended deliberations in the fall legislative session, the governor and the legislature reached agreement on several controversial issues, including provisions for "supernumerary" teachers, as well as the powers and composition of an oversight authority.[40] After much debate and politicking, a compromise bill passed in December 1988. A sharp departure from efforts underway elsewhere, PA 85-1418 shocked some in the reform world and was immediately hailed by others as, "the most radical structural reform of an American urban school system since the mid-19th century."[41]

The reform, however, was not without its critics. Suspicion simmered within the city about the "real motivations" behind the reform. A number of the city's African-American leaders were skeptical.[42] They argued that parents wanted good schools for their children, but they did not wish to run them, nor did they necessarily have the expertise to do so. They feared that this reform was designed to fail in order to achieve some other, still hidden, aims. It seemed hardly coincidental to these critics that radical decentralization swept over the school system just as African-Americans had assumed leadership of the central administration and teachers' union.

Chicago's reform was also criticized in some quarters as anti-professional.[43] This viewpoint was not without some justification since the legislation stripped tenure from principals, granted teachers only two seats (out of 11) on the Local School Council (LSC), and extended only advisory powers to the Professional Personnel Advisory Committee (PPAC). Lending additional credence to this were public remarks by Don Moore, mentioned earlier, about his distrust of Chicago teachers.[44] Moore was not at all sanguine about shifting power from central office bureaucrats to local professionals. Rather, he maintained that real parent and community empowerment must be part of any effort to democratize schools because "evidence and experience in big cities indicates that [when their involvement is limited to advice, their] advice is consistently ignored."[45]

There are some obvious parallels between Chicago school reform and the movement for community control of schools in New York City during the 1960s. In both instances, community activists argued that the system was failing poor and minority children and that a greater voice had to be given to their needs and concerns.[46] In this sense Chicago's reform looked back to New York's for inspiration, but there is also a critical difference: Chicago pushed much further toward a democratic localism than was the case in New York City. The New York sub-district boards are as large as many mid-sized urban districts. In contrast, the fundamental governance unit in Chicago is the individual school. Thus, in Chicago, the distance between the site of political activity and its consequences is radically reduced. Political accountability was intended to be much more personal, immediate, and sharply drawn.

Key Features of the 1988 Reform

Public Act 85-1418 deliberately sought to weaken centralized bureaucratic control and replace it with a complex local school politics. The vertical "problem-solution path," where local school officials looked up into the system for guidance, was rebalanced toward a greater engagement of school professionals with their local communities.[47]

The law attacked the failures of the Chicago school system from two different directions. At the school community level, it encouraged expanded participation among parents, community members, teachers, and the principal by devolving to these local actors significant formal authority and new resources to solve local problems.

The reform legitimized three distinct "sites of power" in each school community.[48] (See Figure 1.1 on pages 24-25.) Parents and community members were empowered through their majority control over the Local School Council (LSC). The faculty gained influence through two seats on the LSC and through a new faculty committee, the Professional Personnel Advisory Committee (PPAC). The formal authority of the principal was also extended substantially. Each site of power gained potential to initiate a serious challenge to the status quo. Similarly, each could block the change initiatives of another.

Complementing this local empowerment were district-wide objectives that encouraged programmatic innovation and set explicit goals for improving student achievement. The Act directed the Board of Education to create a new accountability process and to report annually on the progress of each school. The system was also directed to create its own strategic plan to support local needs. Thus, PA 85-1418 sought to create an overall environment in the CPS that would promote school change.

More specifically, the Act created parent-majority LSCs composed of six elected parents, two elected community members, two appointed teachers and the principal.[49] The chair of the council must be a parent member. Elections occur every two years. Initially, terms were not staggered, but later the law was modified to provide for staggered terms. The LSC has a key power—to hire and fire the school principal. It must also approve the annual school budget and three-year School Improvement Plan (SIP).

The preponderance of parents and community members on Chicago's LSC, and their power to hire and fire the principal, distinguishes Chicago school reform from other parent involvement initiatives where parents typically constitute only a minority faction with an advisory role.[50] Chicago's reform is also quite different from parental involvement provisions that exist in federally funded programs like Head Start and Title VII Bilingual. While parents who participate in these programs may gain new leadership and parenting skills, their influence with regard to policy and decision-making, as well as their ability to challenge professional control, has remained minimal.[51]

In fact, creating structures that afford real opportunities for urban parents and community residents to influence the education of their children has been quite difficult. Even in settings that appear genuinely committed to this aim, it has not generally occurred. For example, Salt Lake City instituted local governing boards in the 1970s, on which parents and professionals were equally represented. Parental influence, however, remained insignificant, regardless of the formal balance of power on these boards.

Typically, parents tended to "go along" with professional initiatives. They neither generated their own ideas nor disagreed on substantive educational issues with the teachers and principals.[52]

Reform activists in Chicago were aware of the limited success of these past attempts to empower local constituencies. They sought to carve out a much larger voice for parents and community.[53] As a consequence, LSC membership was explicitly devised to make parents and community members a legitimate site of power in school affairs.

Chicago's reform also substantially reshaped the principalship. Guidance for this initiative came from several directions. Research advocacy groups drew on findings from the effective schools literature about the importance of principal leadership.[54] Another powerful force was the business community. Business leaders spoke frequently about how principals should be the "chief executive officers" of their schools. At base was an image of good schools with strong leaders who had significant vision, autonomy, resources, and powers.

A call to fundamentally change the principalship also came from parents at the PCC forums. Parents at several of these forums blasted educators for being insensitive to their children's educational, cultural, and emotional needs, and for being in their jobs solely "for the money." They accused school professionals of purposely limiting parents' involvement. Parents often booed when teachers and principals got up to speak at these forums, accusing them of "disrespecting us and our kids. . .of having sick, incompetent minds. . .a fortress mentality. . .freezing us out and limiting us to selling taffy apples."[55] Parents and community members were adamant that school leaders were not attending to their concerns.

If the traditional principalship and the people in these roles were seen as a major source of "the problem," then the authors of Chicago reform saw a reconstituted principalship as essential to a solution. By dramatically reshaping the sanctions and incentives affecting principals' work, the Act sought to get rid of "dead wood" and bring in "new blood" who would stimulate innovation and leverage leadership for change. Because principals were placed on four-year performance contracts subject to LSC review, it was argued that they would be more accountable to local constituencies. Moreover, if the "old guard principals" did not leave by their own volition, then they could be voted out by their LSCs.[56]

Accompanying this emphasis on local accountability was a significant increase in principals' role authority. Principals gained new powers over their budgets, physical plant, and personnel. In contrast to Mac at Beacon School, who was assigned reading specialists by the Board of Education, principals under reform were able to recruit and hire new staff. Similarly, to expedite the removal of incompetent teachers, the remediation process

FIGURE 1.1 Primer on Chicago School Reform

I. ESTABLISHED LOCAL SCHOOL COUNCILS (LSCs)

- Membership:
  6 elected parents
  2 elected community members
  2 teachers
  the principal
  (also 1 elected student member for high school LSCs)
- Key responsibilities:
  Evaluate, hire/fire school principal
  Help principal develop and approve budget and School
  Improvement Plan (SIP)
  Monitor implementation of SIP and develop other local initiatives
- Aim: Parents and community members gain formal authority with
  respect to their neighborhood school.

II. RESHAPED PRINCIPALSHIP

- Removed tenure; four-year performance contracts subject to LSC
  review
- Authority to recruit and hire new teachers
- More discretionary money and more freedom regarding its use
- More control over physical plant and ancillary personnel
- Some effort to shorten process for removal of incompetent teachers
- Aims: Increase principals' authority over building and staff.
  Change basic systems of sanctions and incentives shaping
  principal's work.

III. EXPANDED INFLUENCE FOR TEACHERS

- Voice in selecting/retaining the principal through two votes on LSC
- Advisory role regarding school curriculum, instruction, and budget
  through a Professional Personnel Advisory Committee (PPAC)
- Aim: Increase teachers' role and influence in school
  decision making.

IV. REDIRECTED SCHOOL FISCAL RESOURCES

- A cap on central office administrative expenses
- Implemented a school-based budgeting process
- Required an equitable allocation of funds to individual schools
- Increased discretionary revenues to schools with high percentages of disadvantaged students.
- Aims: Greater revenue equity across the system. New discretionary resources at the school level to foster restructuring.

V. REDUCED LINE AUTHORITY OF THE CENTRAL OFFICE

- Eliminated Board authority to name principals
- Restricted central control over curriculum
- Eliminated line control over regular school operations
- Aim: Assure that authority remains decentralized.

VI. A CENTRAL PULL TOWARD ACADEMIC IMPROVEMENT

- Systemwide goals established for student learning and objectives for school improvement
- Schools required to develop and annually update the three-year SIP
- School system required to report annually on progress
- Escalating levels of sanctions and external intervention by the district in nonimproving schools.
- Aim: Focus local schools' efforts on substantially improving student learning.

was shortened from one year to forty-five days. (Only after an unsuccessful remediation process can an incompetent teacher be removed from the classroom.)[57] Principals also gained a voice in hiring and evaluating new janitorial and food service personnel, and they were given a set of building keys. (Prior to reform, civil service and ancillary staff were accountable to their supervisors only, and principals held keys only at the discretion of the school engineer.)

In this regard, Chicago's reform drew on classic notions about the centrality of leadership at times of major institutional change. As Montesquieu noted several centuries ago, under ordinary circumstances institutions shape leaders. At times of major structural change, however, the reverse is true: Leaders create institutions.[58] Beginning with a rather inchoate set of principles, leaders eventually develop new structures and help to shape new norms that institutionalize the core principles of the reform. If the incentives and sanctions are properly drawn and adequate resources and authority are provided, principals can turn the reform's vision of more locally responsive urban schools into an organizational reality.

The reform's treatment of teachers was more subtle. As noted earlier, there was ample evidence from parent testimony at the citywide forums, and also in the writings of key activists like Moore, that teachers were not to be trusted. Unlike principals, however, teachers were not politically vulnerable. In fact, any reform that was likely to pass the legislature had to be acceptable to union leadership.[59] Thus, the Act took a compromise position with teachers. They were given advisory authority on school curriculum and instructional decisions through the PPAC. Teachers also gained a direct voice in principal selection and retention through their two votes on the LSC.

In comparison to emerging plans elsewhere that promoted greater teacher professionalism,[60] this looked meager. Relative to the anger expressed in some of the forums and to how dramatically the principalship was changed, however, this appears more positive. Moreover, the provision for teachers to have a direct influence over principal selection and retention is actually quite radical, as compared to existing practices in most districts. It significantly recasts the traditional relations of power between principals and their faculties, and bears special note.[61] Thus, while reform of teachers' work was not a major focus of the legislation, the Act did introduce some subtle, but potentially very important changes here too.

Balancing the emphasis on local empowerment were legislative provisions that sought to pull all schools toward educational improvement. These consisted of explicit educational goals for children (e.g., 50 percent of the students in each school were to be at national norms in five years), and an extended set of school objectives on a wide range of topics, including enhanced teacher professionalism, multicultural curriculum, and greater parent involvement. In an attempt to rationalize local school decision making, the Act also mandated elements of strategic planning. Schools were required to develop three-year improvement plans, evaluated and updated annually, to assure progress toward both local and legislatively mandated goals. As part of this process, the school system was also required to report annually on each school's progress toward these goals. Nonimproving schools were subject to a variety of increasingly severe sanctions that could culminate in termination of the principal's contract, removal of the LSC, and placing the school under the receivership of the district's Board of Education.

New resources also became available to support local school improvements. PA 85-1418 changed how state compensatory education funds (state Chapter 1 funds) were to be used. Previously the district had received these monies as general aid; under the new law, they had to be allocated directly to local schools based on the number of disadvantaged students enrolled. As a result, schools with primarily low income populations received substantial increases in discretionary dollars and greater freedom regarding how this money could be spent. In 1993, for example, the per pupil allocation for eligible students under State Chapter 1 was $734. In larger elementary schools with very disadvantaged student populations, the total allocation of this new state aid approached $1 million.[62]

Tying these new resources to the onset of reform offered much needed fuel for local change.[63] Other efforts at restructuring urban schools had reported greater success when new resources were made available to initiate and sustain school improvements. Absent this incremental fiscal support, it is difficult to envision how extensive school restructuring could proceed.

Moving beyond the formal legislative provisions, PA 85-1418 also catalyzed a dramatic expansion of institutional activity directed toward educational improvement. Numerous associations among the city's business and professional leaders began to provide technical and financial assistance to individual schools and to advocate for them.[64] Indeed, since 1988 education has been a sustained focus of activity among many civic groups and community-based organizations (CBOs).[65] The local philanthropic community has committed substantial new funds.[66] Individual faculty members from colleges and universities in the metropolitan area have become more active in Chicago's schools, and several new research, development, and professional education centers have emerged. These activities have generated extensive support for local school efforts and extended conversations throughout the city about school improvement.

Moreover, the content of these conversations is evolving, and these changing understandings are influencing policy. In 1990, attention focused almost exclusively on the formation and training of LSCs. Now, influenced by media accounts and research reports about developments in schools,[67] discussion has shifted to the kinds of additional resources and institutional supports needed to effect substantive changes in classrooms. These are dynamic conversations that have the form and feel of a social movement.[68] Moreover, like a social movement, its character is fluid and its course can only be fully discerned in hindsight. Looking at the reform through a conventional lens of planned social change or strategic planning is clearly inappropriate. The process is still very much unfolding, and its final form has yet to emerge.[69]

The Logic of Our Analysis

The Chicago School Reform Act sought a complete reorganization of the nation's third largest school system. It launched an undertaking of enormous scope that is still very much in the process of developing. This book tells the story of what happened to Chicago's elementary schools during the first four years of this reform. Several main themes characterize our approach to this analysis, each of which is described briefly below.

Variable Nature of School Change

As we look over approximately 500 elementary schools within the Chicago system, we see diverse and varied stories. In many school communities, parents, community leaders, teachers, and principals joined together to take advantage of the resources and the opportunities offered by school reform to initiate broad and deep changes in their schools. In other places, the progress of reform was slower and more uneven. And in still others, there was little sense that schools were moving forward. Although new monetary resources were welcomed, many of the opportunities offered by reform had not been seized. These schools were left behind by reform.

This is not surprising, given the diverse nature of Chicago's neighborhoods and the different resources and circumstances in individual schools as reform began. Moreover, previous experiences with school change caution that it is a multifaceted developmental process which tends to have a very site-specific logic and is likely to proceed at very different rates.[70] Schools with talented faculties, a history of cooperative work, and good relations with their local communities are more likely to take advantage of the additional resources and autonomy provided by a reform like this to move quickly toward instructional improvement efforts. In other schools, however, where base conditions consist of weak faculties marred by distrust, negative community relationships, and serious problems of safety and disorder, the restructuring task is more complex. In these schools, substantial efforts to repair the social fabric of school life must be undertaken if instructional improvement efforts are to have any positive effect. Clearly, because the organizational changes needed in these schools are more extensive, they are likely to require more resources and to take longer.

Democratic Localism as a Lever

Adding to this diversity of circumstances is the fact that the reform deliberately did not provide a blueprint for improvement that each school should follow. Rather than directly mandating specific educational programs and classroom changes, PA 85-1418 focused on reclaiming initiative for parents, community members, teachers, and principals. It formulated a set of policies designed to help each of these participants become an active force for improvement in their local schools. The legislation was premised on the idea that local participants could be a powerful force if they regained a sense of agency with regard to their school.

In short, it was hoped that the new structures and roles established by PA 85-1418 would create a political force in school communities for improvement. It was argued that such a politics could leverage the organizational changes needed to make schools more responsive to the communities, families, and students they serve. This reorienting of the schools' work would sustain the necessary attention for significant changes in classroom instruction and, ultimately in student learning, to accumulate. This basic logic of democratic localism as a lever for school change is summarized in Figure 1.2. Broadly viewed, PA 85-1418 envisioned a process of local school governance promoting fundamental changes in the operation and mission of schools which would culminate in major advances in student engagement and learning. Probing this logic-in-operation and, more specifically, testing the validity of the basic organizing principle of the reform—democratic localism as a lever for revitalizing local public institutions—is the primary purpose of this book.

A Focus on Initiating Organizational Change

When we began this book, Chicago's school reform was still in its early stages. Although the legislation was originally passed in 1988, implementation was deferred until the fall of 1989. Organizing the first Local School Council elections, training councils, and writing by-laws dominated most of the first year.[71] Thus, the 1989-90 school year was taken up almost entirely with initiating the structures and processes of local school governance. Also during that year, half of the schools were required to evaluate their principals and to decide whether to retain the current principal or hire a new one. (The other half of the schools made that decision in the

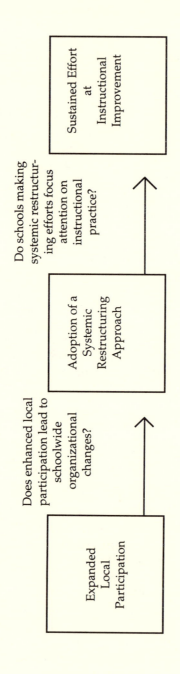

FIGURE 1.2 Logic Behind Chicago School Reform

spring of 1991.) The schools that reviewed their principal in 1990 were ready to begin their school improvement efforts the following fall; many of the other schools, however, had to wait until the spring of 1991 to make a change in principal leadership and initiate improvement activities. In practical terms, then, by 1993 about half of the schools had three years to initiate improvements while others had only two years. Thus, school reform was still a relatively new process for many school communities when we began our analysis in the spring of 1993.

Even so, we were able to pose and answer one very important question. In general, a process of institutional change in schools can be divided into two major components. First is an initiating or catalyst phase where a dysfunctional status quo is seriously challenged. This melds with a second, sustaining phase, where individual roles, rules, and responsibilities are fundamentally reshaped under a reordered authority structure. During this second phase, basic changes may crystallize in the organization of work, in the school's relations to its parents and local environment, and in actual classroom practices. This second phase is still very much in the process of unfolding in Chicago. Only time will tell how much improvement will eventually be institutionalized in restructured operations and a new organizational culture.

As for the first phase, however, the record now appears clear. We argue in this book that PA 85-1418 was successful in catalyzing serious challenges to a dysfunctional status quo in a large number of Chicago school communities. Even though not all schools progressed and some were left behind by reform, nonetheless we judge these initial accomplishments to be quite significant. Against an historical backdrop, which has seen urban schools as impervious to real change,[72] the success of democratic localism in catalyzing initiative at the school-building level deserves both documentation and careful scrutiny. This is a second purpose of our book.

Inadequacy of Short-Term Achievement Trends
for Assessing Institutional Change

The primary, long-term standpoint for judging any form of institutional change—whether it be democratic localism, markets and vouchers, or systemic reform—is very clear. Have substantial improvements in student learning occurred? As a corollary, one might be tempted to argue that student achievement gains should also be the primary evidence for making judgments in the short term. In support of this view is explicit language in PA 85-1418 that established a goal for every Chicago school to reach national norms on standardized assessments in five years and demanded a demonstration of measurable progress toward that goal each year.[73]

As a statement of purpose, as an expression of high aspirations, and as a symbol of serious commitment, we applaud this aspect of PA 85-1418. As a timetable for institutional change in a major urban school system with more than 400,000 students and 25,000 teachers, however, it is simply not realistic. For example, the much simpler and smaller school voucher initiative in Milwaukee, though hailed as successful by its advocates, did not demonstrate achievement gains in its first three years.[74] Similarly, advocates for systemic reform increasingly describe their work as a "generation's effort,"[75] and specifically caution against a project orientation that demands "getting improvements quickly."[76] In short, any institutional reform will likely fail if judged against a standard of large, short-term achievement gains.

As previously noted, the problems of Chicago's schools are deep and expansive. They have accumulated over several decades and require long-term redress. We know from past research that such organizational change can follow a myriad of paths and may not subscribe to the annual improvement model set out in the legislation.[77] Even some of the most successful cases of change in individual urban schools have taken five or more years to culminate in a comprehensive restructuring of school operations. Typically, these schools did not show measurable improvements in student achievement until the later phases. To be sure, substantial changes in organizational operations were occurring two and three years into the process, and there was a logic to these changes, but the "bottom line of student achievement" was one of the last things to move. And it is important to remember that these are the best cases, the ones that are written about and publicly touted. For every success, there are surely many other attempts whose outcomes were less positive.[78]

In fact, a primary emphasis on short-term trends in student achievement could actually be detrimental to the progress of an institutional reform. As schools seriously engage change, uncertainty rises, and controversy is likely to emerge as established routines are discarded in favor of new, untested practices.[79] In this transition, a school may look worse by old standards. In fact, if staff are not adequately prepared for the confusion and conflict associated with organizational change, the restructuring may be abandoned for the security of the old ways. The nature of the information feedback to schools is particularly critical at this stage. Reasonable markers of progress to date, and formative feedback on missteps as well as steps well-taken, can offer constructive guideposts for the next round of action. To continue to reiterate that the ultimate aim has not yet been accomplished, however, can be very debilitating.

Specific Questions

In essence, institutional school reform is like a major corporate restructuring which can take ten years or more to unfold fully. Short-term profitability (in the case of schools, changes in test scores) is not an adequate standpoint from which to judge progress. In fact, short-term profits might plummet as losses are incurred in the process of reshaping the basic mission and operating procedures.

Instead, we need to look more closely during the early phases of such efforts at the political and organizational rearrangements underway to determine whether the envisioned changes are in fact occurring, to identify places where this has and has not taken place (and why this may be so), and to analyze whether the new structures and norms being established are such that the ultimate aims of the reform appear potentially achievable.

More specifically, since the basic premise of Chicago school reform was enhanced parent, community, and professional participation as a lever for school change, we focused on the following questions:

1. **How are the new governance structures actually functioning in Chicago's schools?** Is there any evidence that a local school politics supporting educational improvement has emerged?

2. **How are schools using their newfound autonomy and resources to reorganize their operations and relations?** What types of organizational changes are underway? Are schools pursuing a coherent, thoughtful approach to development, or are improvement efforts fragmented with little attention to quality?

3. **Is there any evidence of sustained attention to improving teaching and strengthening instructional programs?** Are schools adopting instructional innovations that are consistent with recommended "best practices," and advancing these initiatives in ways that are likely to lead to increased student achievement?

As we explored these three questions, we attended to the enormous variety of activity that occurs in a large school system as diverse as Chicago's. Almost everything imaginable was probably happening somewhere in this decentralized system. Thus, we specifically sought to identify: the **major patterns** in local school governance, school reorganization, and instructional improvement developing across the city, **how frequently** these various patterns occurred, and **how equitably** they were distributed among school communities, particularly with regard to race/ethnicity and income level.

In addition, we addressed a fourth and most important question about the validity of the basic logic of the reform:

4. What connections exist between the evolution of local school governance, the types of organizational changes, and instructional improvement efforts? Where expanded local participation has emerged, is there any evidence that it provides an effective lever for organizational change and instructional improvement?

Along the way, we made a couple of critical decisions to limit the scope of our inquiry. First, we decided to focus attention only on elementary schools. On the practical side, we had assembled an extensive array of survey data and field observations for elementary schools; the available information on high schools was much more sparse. Moreover, for a variety of theoretical reasons, including the fact that high schools are larger, more complex organizations and are harder to change, a full assessment of their reform efforts might well be a very different story. Second, we chose to concentrate primarily on those elementary schools whose average achievement levels were substantially below the state average when reform began in 1989.[80] These elementary schools, which made up 86 percent of the system, were the chief targets of the reform legislation. If Chicago's reform was of any merit, these were the places where significant changes had to occur. Unless otherwise noted, all of the statistics presented in this book refer to this lower-performing 86 percent of the city's elementary schools.

Methods and Evidence

While the questions identified above are simple, framing an adequate research plan to investigate them was complex. The diverse and emergent character of Chicago School Reform posed considerable problems. Given the uniqueness of the reform, there were no extant studies of closely related phenomena that could help guide our inquiry. Thus, one key demand on the research design was for an empirically grounded framework, based on experiences in Chicago, to help conceptualize the overall investigation.[81] Fortunately, two independent studies of the implementation of school reform had been carefully documenting the political activity and organizational changes occurring in Chicago elementary schools. Through a synthesis of data from these two multi-site case studies, we were able to build a conceptual framework to organize our work.

Some of our research questions, however, demanded more than just a description of the main types of governance and organizational change that had occurred, as could be accomplished through the case-study synthesis.

Specifically, assessing the overall impact of the reform required enumeration of the frequency of each activity type and how they were distributed across the city. This necessitated major systemwide statistical analyses. The data for these investigations drew on extensive survey information collected by the Consortium on Chicago School Research and extant administrative records from the school system. This allowed us to create a set of indicators of the various activities in each school and provided a basis for addressing the more quantitative questions about school reform.

To understand more fully the actual change processes precipitated by PA 85-1418, we needed some in-depth studies of school communities which had taken advantage of the opportunities provided by reform to move forward. There are many reasons for implementation failure, a number of which were thoroughly documented in the case-study synthesis. To complete our understanding of the operational logic of this reform, however, it was also important to examine how its various features combined effectively with local circumstances to create a productive school renewal process. Since this phenomena was emergent, however, no one could tell at the outset of the reform precisely where this would occur. Thus, retrospective accounts of some of the most successful restructuring school sites became the third major strand in our investigation. Additional details about each research strand are provided below.

Case-Study Synthesis

Our first step in organizing this study was to develop frameworks to identify the distinct types of school politics and organizational change taking place in Chicago. Our main approach to this task involved a synthesis of field reports about activities in Chicago schools. Complementing this was a review of the more general literature on school politics, restructuring and school improvement.[82] The actual development of the frameworks emerged out of a collaboration between two Consortium members: the Center for School Improvement at the University of Chicago (CSI) and the Chicago Panel on School Policy (the Panel). For the first four years of reform, both organizations had been engaged in separate case-study projects involving a total of twenty-two Chicago elementary schools. In both projects, staff had attended a majority of LSC, PPAC, and other school meetings and events since the start of reform. They also had conducted interviews with principals, LSC and PPAC chairs and with many other teachers, parents, and community members.

Included in the longitudinal sample of twenty-two case-study schools were a broad cross-section of the elementary schools. Both studies intentionally selected a sample of schools that varied in terms of such factors as income levels, racial composition, magnet and neighborhood schools, pre-reform achievement levels, and school size. In addition, a number of community factors—including the intensity of local political activity, presence of vital community-based organizations, and the density of neighborhood economic and social institutions—were also considered. The overall aim for both projects was to capture the diversity in the local contextual factors that might significantly influence how democratic localism unfolded in various school communities.[83]

Field workers from these two projects joined together in a consensus process to detail the different forms of local school governance and organizational change which they had observed in the twenty-two schools.[84] They reviewed each case study site in terms of the base conditions at the start of reform; the role of parents and community members, the principal, and the school faculty in local decision making; the actual changes being made; and the emerging capacity of the school to initiate and sustain improvement efforts. Each distinctive pattern, identified in one or more of these schools, eventually became a type classification in the final frameworks. Along the way, we tested our emerging frameworks against the observations of other researchers who had been evaluating the CPS's Creating a New Approach to Learning (CANAL) project, and with staff from the North Central Regional Education Laboratory (NCREL), who had conducted case studies for the School Finance Authority. These individuals offered critiques of our efforts to describe local school governance and organizational change, based on their own independent analyses.

Systemwide Indicators

The core of our systemwide indicators drew on two major surveys conducted by the Consortium during the first four years of reform. In 1991, *Charting Reform: The Teachers' Turn* documented responses from more than 12,500 teachers in 401 of the city's 473 elementary schools. This survey inquired about teachers' attitudes and participation in school reform, about the kinds of change activities they were engaged in, and about the nature of the relationships among teachers, principals, parents, and the local community. The following year, 83 percent of the system's elementary principals responded to many of the same questions in *Charting Reform: The Principals' Perspective.* In addition, we also asked principals about how reform had changed their work, about the strengths and weaknesses in their school faculties, the specific restructuring activities that their schools were engaged in, and the external resources they were drawing on to support their improvement efforts.

We obtained both principal and teacher survey data from 63 percent of the 425 elementary schools whose pre-reform achievement levels were substantially below national norms prior to reform. These 269 schools with complete data constitute the analytic sample for the indicator analyses presented in this book. They do not differ significantly from the other 156 low achieving schools in which we typically have either a principal or teacher survey, but not both.[85] More specifically, the analysis sample is statistically representative of the city's low achieving schools in basic characteristics, including percentage of low-income students, racial composition, percentage of students with limited English-speaking proficiency, and school mobility rates. Thus, we are confident that the statistical reports presented here generalize with high precision to the city as a whole.

Complementing these survey data was a range of information from school system records. This included historical trends, by school, on student achievement, school composition, and student mobility. We also had access to some basic background information on teachers and principals and data about LSC membership and participation. Information about special school programs and discretionary resources, including state and federal funds, were also provided. Taken together, the survey and administrative data afforded a rich base of information for constructing indicators that allowed us to generalize findings from the case-study synthesis schools to the system as a whole, and permitted a rigorous empirical test of our fourth question about the validity of the basic logic of Chicago's school reform.

An In-depth Look at the Experiences of
Actively Restructuring Schools (EARS)

In the spring of 1993 the Consortium undertook original field research in six schools that had taken especially good advantage of the opportunities provided by reform to initiate fundamental change. We sought to identify the common ingredients and processes in these promising school development efforts. In addition, we assumed that any common concerns identified in these "best cases" were likely to be widely shared across the system. Thus, both the progress and problems found in these actively restructuring schools would help us to delimit the state of reform and its longer-term potential.

These schools were identified through a multi-stage process that utilized both systemwide indicator data and reputational accounts. More specifically, we began by reviewing the principal survey reports from June of 1992 about the amount and type of restructuring activities occurring in each school. These analyses identified 103 candidate schools for further consideration. This list was then cross-checked against nomination from twenty different organizations and individuals who had been asked to identify schools where they thought "reform really seemed to be working." Combining the information from these two processes yielded a list of seventy-two potential field sites.

In choosing the final set of six schools, we strove for maximal diversity on several dimensions: racial and ethnic composition, percentage of low income students, size, geographic location in the city, length of principal's tenure, and how long the reported restructuring efforts had been occurring. We sought a representative set of actively restructuring schools, but not necessarily the "six best." In particular, we chose not to visit several schools which had already been subject to extensive media attention in Chicago. Basic descriptive information on the six EARS sites is provided in Table 1.1. Figure 1.3 illustrates the geographic distribution of these schools around the city.

We deliberately assembled a diverse research team to conduct this study. A research coordinator visited all six sites in order to assure that a common field work protocol was followed at each. The research coordinator was accompanied to each school by a different team of two to three other field workers. One of these was a faculty member at a local college or university and the others were graduate assistants from either the University of Chicago or Northwestern University. The composition of these teams was carefully matched to the distinctive characteristics of each particular site, in terms of student population and any special programs that might be operating at that school. Some fifteen different individuals participated in this aspect of the research.

Each member of these three-person teams spent approximately one week visiting their school. Prior to each visit, we assembled an extensive document file on each school, including basic program description information, budgets, and teacher and principal survey reports. During the actual school visits, the site teams conducted interviews with the principal, the chair of the LSC and PPAC, and other key parent and teacher leaders. They also organized focus groups with students and with the LSC and PPAC and observed any meetings that might be occurring during that week. A substantial amount of time was spent observing classrooms in grades one, three, six and eight, with primary focus on reading, mathematics, and social studies instruction. We also examined the major elements in each school's improvement plan and analyzed each school's use of discretionary funds since the inception of reform.

In addition to recording field notes for every observation and interview, each three-person team also produced a brief consensus report that offered their personal observations about the key issues in each school. Upon completion of this data collection, the full EARS research team engaged in a joint review of the notes from all six sites to identify major themes that appeared in common across the six schools. Their analysis offered a basic framing for our continued scrutiny of field notes, and ultimately for the final results presented in Chapter 6.

TABLE 1.1 Characteristics of Actively Restructuring Elementary Schools

School Name	Community	Enrollment	Grades	% African-American	% Hispanic	% Asian	% White	% Limited English Proficiency	% Low Income	Composite IGAP[a] 1989
Bass	Englewood	777	P.K-8	100	0	0	0	0	97	163
Ebinger	Edison Park	305	K-8	7	36	4	53	10	44	212
Field	Rogers Park	1150	P.K-8	43	37	10	10	31	69	210
Hefferan	Austin	652	K-8	100	0	0	0	0	95	169
Hoyne	Calumet	221	K-8	98	2	0	0	1	53	246
Spry	South Lawndale	1357	K-8	3	96	0	1	51	100	174

Source: Chicago Public Schools, 1992.

[a] The Illinois Goals Assessment Program (IGAP) is the state test. At the inception of the tests, the state average was set at 250, with a standard deviation of 100.

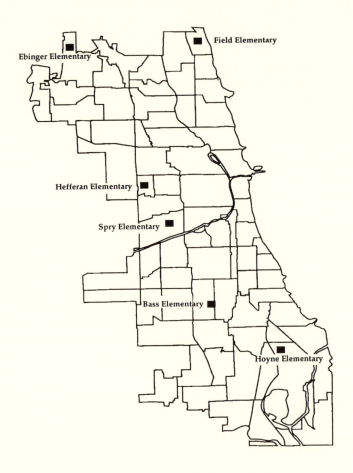

FIGURE 1.3 EARS Fieldwork Sites in Chicago

Organization of the Book

The remainder of this book is organized into six chapters. Chapter 2 addresses our first research question about the nature of the new governance structures in Chicago's school communities. Based on the case-study synthesis, we offer a conceptual framework and a set of short case studies that identify four distinct types of local school politics now operative in Chicago. We then turn to evidence from systemwide indicators to estimate the prevalence of each political type and to examine how each is distributed among different school communities.

Chapter 3 concentrates on the nature of the organizational changes occurring in school communities. As in Chapter 2, we begin with evidence from the case-study synthesis which provided the basis for identifying and describing the major types of activity. Here again, we turn to systemwide indicators to answer questions about the prevalence of these various types and the equity in their distribution.

Chapter 4 focuses on the instructional improvements. This entails examining efforts to bolster the capacity of teachers, as well as examining the introduction of innovative programs and instructional approaches in schools. Systemwide survey data from teachers and principals provide the basis for this analysis. In addition to assessing the prevalence of "best practices" across schools, we also draw on the extensive classroom observations and student focus groups from the field work done in EARS schools. These descriptions offer a textured portrait of classroom life in six key sites of reform.

Drawing on the various statistical indicators developed in Chapters 2 through 4, Chapter 5 formally tests the central policy proposition embedded in Chicago's school reform: that democratic localism is an effective lever for educational improvement. Chapter 6 complements this analysis by providing a more in-depth look at six actively restructuring schools in Chicago. Using evidence primarily from the EARS project, we probe more deeply the mechanisms at work in schools that link expanded local participation to fundamental organizational change and sustained attention to student learning.

Finally, Chapter 7 offers our shared reflections about what we have learned from Chicago's experience that is relevant to catalyzing change in urban school communities. It also sketches out the unfinished business of reform that still lies ahead for Chicago and other major urban districts.

2

Politics as a Lever for Organizational Change

As we began to write this book, Chicago was completing its fourth year of reform. It was clear that unprecedented activity had been initiated in some individual school communities,[1] while others might more appropriately be described as left behind by reform."[2] Taken as a set, these diverse responses to reform afford a natural experiment for examining school politics.

Since local democratic participation was chosen as the principal lever for reform in Chicago, we begin by taking a closer look at what we already know about the nature of school politics. We were concerned as we started our inquiry that the primary analytic frame in educational politics—pluralist bargaining—might prove insufficient to address the full range of activity catalyzed by Chicago's reform. We were observing some profound institutional changes in the way decisions were made at the school level. In expanding our conception, we turned for guidance to recent writings about citizen participation and renewal of democratic institutions. Although these arguments vary somewhat, they all advance a theme that is germane to Chicago school reform: Enhanced democratic activity at the local level can be an effective antidote to unresponsive societal institutions like urban public schools.

Why School Politics Matters

As districts decentralize responsibility, politics at the school level takes on greater importance.[3] The local school becomes a more consequential site of power. Political activity expands as more resources, responsibility, and decision-making authority are devolved to the local level.[4]

The importance of school politics appears especially salient during efforts to restructure schools. Proponents of restructuring—whether initiated by a school's professional staff or by change agents from the outside—have been somewhat naive about the conflicts likely to arise. Schools are being asked to change from hierarchical organizations, with a long history of line control, to more collaborative, democratic entities where broad participation in decision making is valued, and leadership roles are expanded. When changes occur in role, authority, and responsibility, and teachers' relationships with the principal and other colleagues shift, rivalries and jealousies may be unleashed.[5] These political problems can be complicated further, if, as has occurred in Chicago, new authority and leadership roles also emerge for parent and community members.

Restructuring means structural change. Past reforms generally tinkered at the margins of the school.[6] Incremental improvements may have resulted, but core operations remained stable. Now, national attention focuses on the restructuring of our educational system to produce higher levels of attainment for all students. It is argued that the conventional organization of schools is a major source of their failure. To create the new, high performing organizations necessary for better outcomes, fundamental change is required. Thus, just as a devolution of authority seeks to change relations of power within the district and within the school, so too do the incremental reforms of the past give way to a demand for structural change.[7] At the present time, then, reformers challenge the status quo both in governance arrangements and the organizational practice of schools.[8]

Traditional Conceptions of Educational Politics

Most past research on educational politics has been conceptualized through a pluralist lens. Political activity is typically defined as negotiations over the allocation of scarce resources among groups or individuals whose interests are viewed as fixed and static. At base is a conception of individual interests, as articulated in rational choice theory, that sees "individuals as seeking to maximize their utility, rationally choosing the best means to serve their goals."[9] Moreover,

> rational choice theory assumes that individual preferences are given. . . [It] ignore[s] the effects of education, of persuasion. . .and the role of leadership, as if economic man was a biological-psychological miracle, born fully formed, say in his mid-twenties with his preferences "immaculately conceived."[10]

This conception extends directly to explain the behavior of interest groups as well. They are regarded as a unity of like-minded individuals who come together when their interests momentarily align and the situation makes it expedient to do so. Beyond this instrumental aim, however, they remain "unfettered individuals."[11]

Pluralist bargaining within an organization most often takes place in private, one-on-one negotiations. Peterson, for example, noted that much of the real dealmaking on Chicago's Board of Education occurred in closed sessions or even in private conversations that violated the Open Meetings Act. Board meetings then became symbolic events where votes were cast on issues that had already been decided.[12]

These pluralist negotiations may effect incremental change, but the basic structure of political systems—power relations and the representation of interests within them—rarely changes. Neither does how things get done. The institutional basis of work in schools includes a vast array of organizational practices that are generally taken for granted and consequently have proven difficult to challenge; for example, the tracking of students, the "eggcrate structure" of classroom teaching, the separation of subjects and departmentalization of teaching, and so on.[13] Because pluralist politics essentially preserves the status quo with regard to institutional features and political practice, we use the term "maintenance politics" to describe it.

Maintenance Politics at the District Level

Most studies of educational politics in urban districts have focused on the efforts of powerful vested groups to control jobs and contracts.[14] Peterson, for example, analyzed the mayoral appointments to Chicago's Board of Education, and their subsequent decision making, over a multiyear period in the 1960s.[15] Mayor Daley appointed members to the Board of Education in direct relation to their power in city politics. He was aware of the struggle over community control that was occurring at that time in New York City. He wanted to keep Chicago school politics focused on things he could leverage—jobs, contracts, and money—rather than ideological issues like community control. Consequently, Daley added representatives of new interest groups—women, African-Americans, and Hispanics—when it became politically expedient to do so. While these new members may have been female and minority, the mayor took great pains to select individuals whose political views aligned with his. Moreover, as token members they did not have enough votes to challenge the traditional ways of doing things. They had to cooperate with the established interests on the Board in order to have any impact on decision making. In addition, Daley used a mixture of sanctions and rewards, private promises, and public negotiations to both placate and keep interest groups at bay.

Peterson describes Mayor Daley as a consummate machine politician—a term that the author equates with skilled pluralist bargaining.[16] Marginal changes were affected through the Mayor's appointments to the school board and negotiations with members over time, but the basic structure of the system—the organization of work, power relations, and the representation of interests within it—was essentially maintained.[17]

Maintenance Politics at the School Level

The lens of pluralist politics has been used to analyze political activity occurring within the school building as well. Much of this research has focused on relationships between the principal and faculty.[18] Ironically, in many schools, there is little public political activity. Rather, teachers and the principal tacitly understand and accept their respective domains of practice and responsibility, having long ago negotiated treaties about how they will behave toward each other and about the organization of their work.[19] Expectations build up around these treaties, and over time norms develop that maintain a highly routinized and uncontested daily life. There is little need for public discussion, and so faculty and other school meetings become perfunctory. In such places politics seems nonexistent, and organizational practice appears to be intractable.

Most of the real political activity occurs in private, as individual teachers meet with their principal to advance their own interests—be it a plum teaching program, new materials, the best classroom space, the assignment of motivated, well-behaved students to their classrooms, and so on.[20] The primary aim of the principal in these encounters is to use the resources at hand to mediate between the interests of different teachers (or factions of teachers aligned with specific school programs). Through these negotiations, the principal seeks to satisfy everyone and keep the lid on nascent dissent and potential demands for more substantive change.

Any public political activities that occur tend to be orchestrated by principals. Rather than negotiating everything one-on-one, principals sometimes create faculty committees and then send certain issues there for consideration.[21] But these public activities may not be occasions for real debate. Instead, time for discussion is often short, teachers may not be fully informed, and the ensuing conversation is consequently superficial. Such activities create a semblance of representational democracy. Their real value, however, is buffering the principal from criticism about decisions that are made.[22]

Clearly there are times and situations when maintenance politics is constructive, and other times when the same activities might block necessary change. For example, the presence of uncontested standard operating procedures that organize daily life certainly contributes to school efficiency. Similarly, in some instances where consensus may not be necessary or attainable, voting can be a quick and efficient decision-making process. Pluralist bargaining can also be an effective way to allocate resources in situations where they are relatively ample, and so their distribution is not likely to be highly contested. Moreover, placating individuals and factions may be critical to the survival of a polity if the dynamics within it are particularly volatile at a specific time. On such occasions, making side-payments to various parties may temporarily soothe nerves and create an opportunity for people to regroup.[23]

Maintenance politics appears well adapted for "good" schools, where there is little sense that fundamental change is needed. In fact, it can be argued that up to this point the pluralist bargaining frame has been a useful way to conceptualize school micro-politics, because the schools that have been studied generally are perceived by their communities to be good ones.[24] Neither the professional staff, nor students, nor the parents or larger community are sharply critical of their operations. Thus, the changes that are contemplated need not challenge roles, responsibilities, and core operations.

As noted in the Prologue, however, these conditions do not characterize most of Chicago's schools. Advocates of Chicago's reform knew that if politics was to be a lever for change, a different form of political practice was necessary.

Alternative Conceptions

Adversarial Politics

When reform was first passed in Chicago, many worried that the legislation would usher community politics directly into the school building. As bad as Chicago schools were, some feared that this might make them even worse. One potential threat was Alinsky-style organizing.

Saul Alinsky got his start in Chicago's Back of the Yards neighborhood on the southwest side in the 1930s. His brand of community organizing then, and his legacy now, was adversarial by design. Based in working-class neighborhoods, and often organized around the local Catholic Church, Alinsky focused on tangible issues that were of concern to residents and winnable in the short term. Alinsky's strategy was to organize the "have nots" by exacerbating tensions between them and the "haves." He sometimes instigated crises in an effort to motivate the "have-nots" to better define and act in their own interests. In the process, Alinsky personalized the enemy. The immediate aim of political action was to oust the individual who personified the evils of an unfair system. A secondary aim was to organize the "have-nots" into a power bloc that could be mobilized for subsequent actions.

Alinsky-style community based organizations developed in many Chicago neighborhoods, and some survive to this day. Prior to the passage of reform there were several notable instances when these local groups focused on school issues, and succeeded, for example, in targeting and removing callous, ineffectual school principals.[25] However, these short term victories had disastrous consequences in some places. While confrontational politics might succeed in removing a principal, more often than not the teachers identified with their ousted leader, and felt a mixture of resentment and intimidation that a community group could come in and "run their school." Such strategies left long-simmering resentments between professionals and parents, and a latent struggle for power and control.

The difficulty with this form of politics as a lever for organizational change seems obvious. School restructuring is not a quick fix. It demands the sustained attention of principals, teachers, and parents, and community members. Successful collaborative work of this sort depends on many factors, including the development of trust and respect, and the forging of a common commitment to meet the needs of children. None of this seems very likely in a highly adversarial context.

Strong Democratic Politics

These concerns focus our attention on ways to foster a more productive involvement of all local participants in working toward school improvement. It directs our attention to the idea of a "strong democracy," where citizens work together to articulate and advance a locally defined common good. This concept of "strong democracy" rings of classical notions about citizens' participation in the "polis."[26] It is central to the voluntary associations that De Tocqueville saw in frontier America in the 1840s as well.[27] It is also the implicit theory of Chicago school reform.

Four key features comprise strong democratic politics: sustained citizen participation; a greater emphasis on self-government and consensual decision making rather than representative government and voting; public concern as a motivating force rather than private interests; and a legitimation of core values and guiding ideas through public debate.

Participation is thought to be the animating force in a strong democracy. Through personal involvement individuals develop citizenship skills, and thereby become capable of self-government. To achieve this end, it is argued that local communities need to become "schools for democracy . . . free spaces" where individuals can come together to learn to set agendas and chair meetings and perform other necessary, instrumental tasks.[28] In Chicago's legislation the Local School Council was deliberately designed as a new local institution to foster such experiences.

At a more fundamental level, it is argued that when individuals participate in self-governing activities, they develop over time the capacity to be
"deliberating, determining, and deciding. . . [not] impulsive, arbitrary, or
unconsidered."[29] This emphasis on community education toward self governance stands in sharp contrast to conventional ideas embedded in representative democracy, where problems and policy making are often taken out of the
public realm and relegated to experts and lobbyists to solve.[30]

Strong democracy also depends on citizens who maintain concern for
the public. Individuals do not start out with this orientation, however.
Rather, as a result of participation, private interests are transformed into
public concerns. But how does this transformation take place? Through
what activities do private interests become public concerns? And then by
what mechanism can these newly formulated public concerns challenge
organizational arrangements and institutional powers—the status quo?

According to strong democratic theory, the primary activity is talk. When
citizens need to be decisive and take action they must:

> create a public language that will help reformulate private interests in terms
> susceptible to public accommodation; and it aims at understanding individu-
> als not as abstract persons but as citizens, so that commonality and equality
> rather than separateness are the defining traits of human society. [31]

That is, individuals and groups are not born with fixed interests as rational
choice proponents would have us believe. Neither do they enter a coalition
solely on the basis of ascribed characteristics, such as race, age, gender,
and class as is sometimes claimed.[32] Rather, when people engage in political debate, each participant brings into the discussion unique understandings and interpretations of key concepts that have been developed
from their own experiences. These understandings are normative for them,
but may be new to others in the group. In the short term, this transporting
of ideas may exacerbate the differences among people and appear divisive.[33] In the longer term, however, if public discourse is sustained, the
dialogue can become an avenue for resolving conflict. More importantly, it
can promote an enlarged sympathy that serves to coalesce and enrich the
group. In this way public debate becomes the basis for developing coherent and shared understandings that can stimulate coalition building,
motivate unified action, and challenge existing power arrangements
and organizational practice.

In most general terms, ideas matter in a strong democracy, and politics
focus on the meanings of these ideas. Concepts such as liberty, freedom,
equality, rights, and citizen participation have been used in the past by
various groups to question entitlements. Over the course of history this

competition over ideas, imbued as it were with a moral authority, has functioned as a lever for organizing people to challenge the status quo and on some occasions to transform institutional arrangements.[34]

In the context of a strong democratic school community, advancing educational opportunities for children provides the organizing ideas. The authors of Chicago's reform saw expanded parental participation as key in this regard. Uncertain about local school professionals, many of whom they regarded as self-interested,[35] reformers banked on the notion that parents would clearly focus on the children. Given sufficient instrumental authority to complement their nascent moral authority, parents along with other community residents could leverage the political activity necessary to change their school.[36]

Parental concern for their children's welfare has been a mainstay of American education. Their voice has carried weight in conversations about the purpose and operations of schools.[37] Even though largely silenced in many urban contexts, this voice remains strong and persuasive in suburban contexts.[38] Thus Chicago's reform sought to renew parental and community voice by granting these groups majority control of the LSC, and then granting the LSC authority to select a school leader whose values might complement their own. It was argued that principals hired by an LSC would be compelled to engage parents, community, and faculty. This is a dramatic departure from past practice, where principals looked up into the system for direction, approval, and tangible rewards.[39] Further, with their own attention redirected, principals might exert new pressure on their faculties to focus on the needs of the students as well. It was hoped that this heightened local democratic activity would create a sense of urgency among all adults to work together on behalf of children. In this way, democratic discourse and the forging of a common interest could promote structural school change.

Consolidated Principal Power

The rhetoric of strong democracy is engaging in that it captures the hopes and essence of American life.[40] Much of the writing about strong democracy is not, however, empirically based. Moving these ideas into urban schools means confronting some harsh realities. Prior to reform, there was a clear chain of command: Central office bureaucrats told subdistrict superintendents what to do, who in turn told principals what to do, who then told their teachers, who then told their students. By system standards, "good" principals adhered to the command structure and maintained order in their buildings. There wasn't much public dialogue about anything!

"Good" urban principals prior to reform seemed to embrace one of two leadership styles, which, while appearing very different on the surface, led to the same ends. Some were autocrats.[41] They often were sent by the central office to schools that were reputed to be "out of control." The principal's job was to get and maintain order at any cost.[42] The most significant edicts of autocratic principals might be delivered in private—whether they were talking to questioning parents, disagreeable teachers, or an intimidating gang member on the school grounds. In some cases, their rule might mirror the violence that they were sent in to stop; witness a Joe Clark patrolling school hallways with a baseball bat. Other principals might use more subtle tactics of fear and intimidation, such as removing a teacher from a coveted program if she bucked the line, or even transferring a child from one class to another if her parents proved problematic. For the most successful of these principals, such tactics became reputational. Subsequent actions were not always needed; an implied retribution might be sufficient.

Some principals, like Mac from the Beacon School, developed a more paternal (or maternal) leadership style. Mac encouraged his teachers and parents to feel dependent on his continuing protection and guidance. Principals like Mac consolidated and maintained power because they ran their schools like families where the "children" (the faculty and parents) deferred to them. While such family settings might be more comfortable than autocracies, they too prove to be debilitating in the long run. Neither teachers nor parents can ever develop to the point where they can confidently make decisions on their own.[43]

On balance, in many urban neighborhoods, if a strong principal can create peace out of chaos, the majority of the school community will cheer the results—regardless of leadership style. Moreover, in a community where violence is pervasive, and gangs, drugs and weapons are ever-present worries, the strong autocrat or parent figure is preferable to the bedlam and disorder that occurs when there is no legitimate leadership at all.

The success of both types of principals depends on the same factors. They need to develop and sustain a top-down control system that sets expectations for the community and organizes daily life.[44] Principals who can offer some modicum of personal protection to their immediate communities and create a zone of order within their buildings will achieve a loyal following. This, in turn, enables them to consolidate and maintain their personal power, regardless of the passage of any law that encourages a different politics and implies a different leadership style.

In short, consolidated principals' power was the status quo for many Chicago schools when reform was first passed. The nature of this base state raises questions about whether Chicago's legislation, or any other intervention, would be strong enough to disrupt the stable social system described above.

Case Studies of Local School Politics

Blending these theoretical ideas about politics with extended field observations in Chicago elementary school communities helped us to identify
four distinct types of school-based political practice. Some school communities seemed largely untouched by reform. The activity in these schools
closely resembled either the consolidated principals' power or maintenance
politics models discussed above. In contrast, much greater activism
emerged in other school communities. Political practice in these sites also
fell into two different categories—adversarial or strong democratic.

We elaborate below on each of the four types of local school political
activity through short case studies developed from the case-study synthesis of twenty-two Chicago elementary schools. A brief analysis follows each
case. The names of the schools, key individuals, and organizations have
been changed in order to protect confidentiality. In a few instances, the
descriptions are composites of events from two or more schools within the
same type. Some minor details have also been blurred to obscure the identity of the particular events, but all described events are real. Further, these
events are not unusual instances; rather they generally characterize life as
we have observed it in each type of school.

The Howard School: Consolidated Principal Power through Autocratic Control

Five years before reform, Howard was "up for grabs." The principal,
Mrs. Stanley, paid little attention to when teachers arrived at school each
morning nor to when they left. Neither did she confront disruptive parents when they sometimes barged into classrooms to "have a few words"
with their child or with the teacher. Standards of behavior for students
were inconsistently enforced as well. Fighting was commonplace throughout the building, and so was swearing at teachers.

When Mrs. Stanley retired, the central office assigned Mr. Bangor. It was
his first principalship, and he said that his "marching orders were to clean
up Howard. . .it didn't matter how. . .just clean it up." He was scared at
first for his own physical safety as well as for what might happen to his
career if he did not succeed. But in a few years under Mr. Bangor's leadership, Howard changed from "a terrible place where everyone was mad" to
a more amicable environment with civil norms of behavior, standard operating procedures, and established daily routines. Even so, Mr. Bangor felt
that the "place could explode in a second. . .without a moment's notice"
and that he must "monitor everyone and everything constantly so that it
won't spin out of control again." In spite of reform, then, Mr. Bangor's
leadership style remained constant. He was sent in to "get control. . .to do
a job," and that is the job that he continued to do.

Early in reform, Bangor's authority was challenged by a community representative on the LSC. Mrs. Carter said that "he [Mr. Bangor] doesn't deserve a contract because the school isn't any good. . . .Maybe it's nicer than the school down the street, but so what? Our kids aren't getting educated like they should. . . .None of these little children are learning to read!"

When Mr. Bangor heard that Mrs. Carter was organizing against him, he was furious. He lamented the fact that he had been so helpful to the council during the first difficult months of reform. "I did everything for them," he told us. "I stayed late every night to help them. They didn't know how to run a meeting. . . they didn't even know what an agenda was. Some thanks I get!" He regretted his decision to steer clear of the first LSC election as well, saying, "Ms. Smith over at the Green School hand picked her council, but I thought, that's too political. I shouldn't do that. Well, wasn't I the fool!"

Mr. Bangor did not waste much time feeling sorry for himself. He asked his parents for support, and many came to his defense. To reward the most active among them, he reassigned a few of their children to "better" classes. His response to the teachers was more subtle. Mr. Bangor offered the PPAC chair, Mr. Smyth, a new position as "school disciplinarian" shortly after an LSC meeting where he questioned Mr. Bangor's leadership. Once Mr. Smyth became disciplinarian, he stopped attending LSC meetings and also resigned as PPAC chair, claiming that he was now too busy in his new role. In short order, the leadership for any budding teacher opposition had been effectively squashed.

It was also rumored that Mr. Bangor "snooped around" the community a bit to "get some stuff" on Mrs. Carter. No one would say what the "stuff" was, but the two had a few private meetings about that time. While Mrs. Carter did not drop out of the Council, another parent told us: "It was like a cat got her tongue. Someone told that lady to quiet down!"

Mr. Bangor eventually got a contract, and he told us that he "learned a lot from his mistakes." He said that he was "going to really run the school now. . .teachers and parents really want that anyway, and I don't intend to become vulnerable again."

Shortly after his contract was signed, Mr. Bangor went to an out-of-town conference sponsored by a computer company. He came back with a proposal to use a large portion of the school's discretionary money to create a computer lab with a full-time instructor, multiple workstations, and software designed to prepare students for the Iowa Tests of Basic Skills. When several teachers expressed an interest in spending the money differently, Mr. Bangor convinced them that the computers were a good idea. He said that with the lab and a new instructor, every teacher would have an additional preparation period each week. This free time, which was gladly welcomed by the teachers, was sufficient incentive to stifle any alternative initiatives.

Mr. Bangor also became directly involved in subsequent LSC and PPAC elections. He encouraged his allies to run, and he drummed up support for them. He also found school aide positions for two young mothers on the council who previously had raised questions about his contract renewal. They were grateful to Mr. Bangor for the work. He said that they were better off with jobs and "weren't qualified for the council anyway."

*****

Despite the explicit intent of reform to expand parent, community, and teacher participation, some schools have seen little of this. Principals in these sites told us that they were resentful of reform, especially the requirements to share decision making. Even if teachers, parents, and community members actually tried to organize themselves, these principals did not support their efforts and may even have actively worked to undermine them.

Both the LSCs and PPACs in these schools tend to be largely comprised of individuals who do not know each other well, and have little past experience in governance activity. The monthly LSC meetings and bi-annual public meetings that are mandated by legislation may duly take place. Participation and discussion is generally minimal, however, and principals dominate the activity that does occur. Except in crisis situations, no real issues are likely to be considered.[45] Neither the LSC nor the faculty sustains any activity that might effectively challenge the principal's authority. As a result, power remains consolidated in the principalship.

Alexander School: Consolidated Principal Power through Maternal Control

Thirty years ago Alexander School served a thriving community. In contrast, today the community is characterized by female-headed households, an absence of middle class and male role models, a loss of population and community institutions, and a diminution of political activity. Most importantly, this community lacks the extended social networks which traditionally have supported families and children. Without such networks, problems with poverty, drugs, and violence are much more devastating, especially to the "young moms" who struggle often alone to survive and keep their children safe.

In the not-so-distant past, mothers—in this neighborhood and others just like it—were generally older and somewhat more advantaged. Fathers and grandparents were also more active. Today, the main group with potential to become a viable presence is the "young moms," and while the

LSC chair talked about her efforts to "corral" some of them into getting involved, she knew it would not be easy.

One reason is safety. The school does not want to be responsible for people being out after dark, and this forces meetings to be scheduled during the school day. Consequently, those parents who work—some of whom have the most to contribute to the school—can never attend the meetings. A problem for yet another group of parents is embarrassment about their own academic skills and their consequent reluctance to converse with teachers. Finally, in some cases latent hostility keeps parents away. Some young moms have negative memories of their own schooling, and they believe that teachers regard them with disdain. The LSC chair asked and answered her own questions about what "kind of role models these moms are for their kids, when they feel so hateful and hated? It can't be good."

When PA 85-1418 first passed, it looked like the Act might make a difference. Many parents at Alexander were curious about the new law, and there was a flurry of activity. The LSC election was contested, and there was a quorum at the first several meetings. When it came time to evaluate the principal, however, the council was reluctant to engage in any formal review process and preferred to just write Mrs. Green a new contract. There was minimal parent, community, or teacher involvement, minimal discussion, and minimal learning as a result.

By the second year of reform, the initial excitement had dissipated. Monthly LSC meetings were called, but there was rarely a quorum, and never an audience. The council did maintain a core of hard working and well-intentioned women between the ages of 25 and 30. The chair often told us that she was proud that there was no fighting on her council, or in the school, as in some other neighboring schools. Unfortunately, there was little conversation either.

The LSC got moving briefly again late in the spring of the second year, when a systemwide financial crunch threatened the school with closure. Ultimately the school remained open because the Board of Education was pressured by community activists across the city not to close any schools at that time. The experiences around this threat, however, did not unite the Alexander school community. When only fifty parents showed up for a "Save Alexander Rally," the LSC chair felt tired, overwhelmed, and discouraged. Mrs. Green expressed her frustration with the parents too, calling them "the most apathetic bunch" she had ever seen. Once the crisis passed, the principal and the LSC chair called meetings to discuss how the school might distinguish itself enough to avoid future closing lists. The meetings went unattended.

The problems of the LSC were mirrored in the experiences of Alexander's PPAC and the larger faculty, as they too grappled with local school governance. Sixteen candidates competed for the first PPAC election because the faculty, like the broader parent group, was curious. Teachers were confused, however, about the PPAC's identity and purpose. Many thought it was the "Professional Problems Committee" of the union. Others understood that the PPAC was to be advisory on issues of curriculum and instruction, but they were unclear if it was to function independently of the principal. Some members said that they could not discuss pedagogy without the principal; others insisted that they could never develop an independent voice if she joined them.

This issue took up the PPAC's attention for most of the school year, and it was a controversy from which they never recovered. The principal dropped out when she was apprised of the concerns surrounding her participation, and so did the contingent of teachers that wanted her involved. The chair abdicated next, and another teacher volunteered to replace her since, "no one else wanted it." When no candidates came forward for the next PPAC election, the chair had to ask a few of her friends on the faculty to volunteer as a personal favor. The new PPAC met once in the fall but did not meet again for the remainder of the year.

In addition to their inability to organize a PPAC, the faculty showed little interest in their own growth as professionals. Alexander teachers (like a majority of faculties across the city) voted to adopt a closed campus several years earlier. This allowed many Alexander teachers to keep the same short hours (8:30 a.m. to 2:30 p.m.) that their students did.

On balance, some teachers at Alexander, like some of the parents on the LSC, were caring, hard working and deeply concerned about the children. Over the years, these teachers had individually enrolled in countless courses and participated in new programs, but nothing seemed to bring achievement up. Some of these teachers persisted in their efforts, while others became demoralized and one by one gave up. These teachers blamed the students and the young moms for low achievement, and insisted that they "had tried everything." Much of this veteran faculty was "riding out their time" until retirement. Mrs. Green complained that their lack of motivation was a serious obstacle to school improvement.

We note that a majority of the teachers at Alexander attended the Chicago Public Schools. Most were credentialed in Chicago, and have spent their entire careers at Alexander, or a school just like it. These teachers are hard pressed to imagine alternatives. This poses a significant obstacle for Chicago's reform, since the heart of this legislation was the opening up of opportunity, in each local school community, to create alternatives. When we asked the assistant principal, for example, to describe for us "a good school," he said, "Off the top of my head, that's hard for me to say . . . I haven't graduated to that way of thinking yet."

Mrs. Green had a difficult job. She had to do double duty, with parents as well as teachers, to overcome their isolation, hostility, fear, lack of confidence, and lack of skills. Mrs. Green had become the school's "mom." She had been in the school "since forever" (she came to Alexander as a teacher when she was 22) and so "she knew everyone and everything." She had accepted the burden of nurturing a school community. In fact, parents and children often looked to her and the school as a safe haven, which, compared to the neighborhood, it was. Mrs. Green acknowledged that at times she was an "overprotective mother reluctant to let any of her children grow." She also recognized that some of the parents' and teachers' dependence might not be good.

Mrs. Green's maternal style took a personal toll. She often found herself "exhausted" and sometimes "snapped out" in a way that disturbed her and offended the very people she so wanted to succeed. She described with regret:

> I called two teachers in for a conference regarding the performance of their students on the Iowa tests. I remember saying, "I'm ashamed of you. You could have stayed at home, and the students could have stayed at home to get these results. This is ridiculous. You were coming every day, and they were coming every day. For what?" That's terrible, I mean I was so angry to get those scores, that it caught me at a bad moment. I later apologized.

Mrs. Green wanted reform to succeed in her school. She wanted to see her parents and their children create a better life for themselves, and she wanted her faculty to become more professional, not only so the children would learn more, but "so that they would feel good about themselves." She worried about the distance her school community would have to travel to achieve her vision.

*****

The malaise, isolation, and alienation that pervades Alexander's neighborhood is mirrored inside the school. Teachers have few external resources to support their work, and many are no longer motivated to change. Some parents work hard for the school, but their numbers are few. The principal is a tragic-heroine who tries to care for all of them—students, parents, and teachers—but whose maternal leadership ironically stifles initiative and disables others' capacity to grow. At first glance, Alexander appears as a peaceful island amidst a truly disadvantaged community. But that peace is secured at a price: little of significance is ever discussed, and collective activity is hard to organize and sustain. The status quo seems insurmountable.

The Sowell School: Maintenance Politics

Sowell has always been regarded as a good school. It was built thirty years ago to serve the children of a "planned, integrated community." Many of the current faculty requested a transfer to the school when it first opened, and Mrs. Donahue specifically asked for the principalship at Sowell when the previous principal retired a few years prior to reform. Mrs. Donahue and the teachers talk about how lucky they were to be at Sowell, compared to their experiences in other Chicago schools.

For the last several years, enrollment has been dropping at Sowell as rising home prices have placed the neighborhood beyond the reach of many younger families with children. In order to keep its attendance up, the school now enrolls students from a wide area. This change in attendance boundaries has brought in some children from poorer neighborhoods. Their achievement is not as good as that of the neighborhood group, so the professional staff made a decision to place these students in special classes. This arrangement makes it possible for these low income children to have smaller class sizes and to benefit from school aides and some extra materials purchased with categorical funds. Most important, teachers say they are able to slow the pace of instruction to meet the needs of these children, and their parents seem pleased with these arrangements. In fact, they echo the professional staff when they tell you how much they like the school, how much nicer it is than the school in their neighborhood, and how special they, too, feel to be at Sowell.

During the first LSC elections, none of the parents of the poor children ran, nor did any community candidates come from disadvantaged neighborhoods. No one regarded this as a problem, however, because everyone seemed to get along. Council members went to some training, and other than figuring out how to do all that was required of them in the first few months of reform, no big issues caught the council's attention. The PPAC also went through the motions. An election was held, but at the first meeting, when the teachers realized that their role was only an advisory one, one said: "I like the way things are, so why should I take time giving advice about how to change them?"

The principal also thought that reform "took a lot of time, but it was no big deal." When the guidelines came out for developing the first lump-sum budget, she had a meeting with her LSC, and they asked her what the faculty wanted. She did not know, so she called a faculty meeting and presented the budget. She said, "The LSC wants your input. Look over the budget and tell me what you need for your programs next year."

At first the teachers did not say much. Mrs. Weintraub, the LSC teacher representative, suggested that they just revise last year's budget to "reflect inflation, and stuff like that." In contrast, Mrs. Imel, who worked with some of the poor children, said: "Wait. What about buying some new stuff? My friend at the Cortez School works with kids like mine, and her principal used Chapter 1 to buy some computers for her classroom. Can I get some?" Needless to say, several of the teachers thought that computers were a good idea, and within a few moments, everyone wanted one. Mrs. Donahue was then in a difficult position. "I think I can buy some computers for the Chapter 1 children, as Mrs. Imel suggested, but I can't use Chapter 1 to make purchases for the other classrooms," she said. "I can only use that money for the low achieving kids."

The faculty was upset and divided. The teachers who taught the Chapter 1 children left the meeting thinking about what they could do with their new classroom computers. They were already planning the kinds of software to buy. In contrast, their colleagues felt cheated. They were "fussing" together about "all of the perks poor kids got." One even grumbled that she was going to the next council meeting and "let the parents know that the poor kids were going to get computers, while their kids [the LSC members'] weren't!"

Luckily, the principal crafted a plan that she thought would settle the conflict quickly and satisfy both factions. Several of the parents and community representatives on her council worked for large firms downtown, including some of the banks most active in supporting local schools during the early days of reform. She asked her council members if they might be able to get their firms to donate computers, and she used some of her own connections in the corporate world to make similar requests. When it came time for the LSC to approve the school budget, Mrs. Donahue opened the meeting with a special "Appreciation Ceremony" where she recognized several of her LSC members and their employers who had just donated a dozen personal computers and a printer to the school. These were assigned to the classrooms of the more advantaged students. With their discretionary money, the school was able to purchase a similar amount of hardware for the classrooms of the poor children.

*****

In "good" schools like Sowell, most participants are basically complacent because they feel advantaged relative to the rest of the system. The maintenance politics in such places assume a traditional, pluralist mode. The principal is a mediator, and since the passage of reform in Chicago, discretionary money is one of the main things that she negotiates.[46]

Mrs. Donohue's initial strategy was to divide new monies up among teachers and existing programs, rather than to undertake comprehensive new initiatives or to fundamentally restructure existing arrangements. Much to her surprise, this public negotiation proved problematic, as it separated her teachers into interest groups, each with their own programs and projects to fund. She smoothed over the nascent controversy, however, and quickly moved to placate the factions that were developing. By finding extra resources, she restored the peace.

The Sprague School: Adversarial Politics

The school community at Sprague has been fighting since before reform began. Mrs. Rodriguez, the sitting principal in 1989, had long been viewed as ineffective and uninspired. The first LSC vowed to replace her and they were assisted in their efforts by Nuestra Comunidad Unida, a small community-based organization that offered training on the principal evaluation process. Many parents, however, were offended by the influence of Nuestra Comunidad Unida in their school. In reaction, they supported Mrs. Rodriguez.

LSC meetings occurred throughout the spring of 1990 to decide the principalship, and every meeting brought out huge crowds. These meetings came to be called "Council Wars" because they were marked by angry outbursts between council members and the audience.[47] A few meetings were even shut down early by city police when it looked like fights might break out between parents and their representatives. Parents demanded that council members represent them by voting to retain their principal. LSC members shouted back that as elected officials they "had the power" to vote as they pleased.[48]

Several teachers had volunteered to be on the principal evaluation-selection committee, but they eventually quit because they felt that the LSC had already made its decision. They, too, were offended that the council was looking to organizers from Nuestra Comunidad Unida rather than to its own faculty for advice. Although many teachers acknowledged in private that Mrs. Rodriguez was mediocre, they supported her anyway, because they did not want a "bunch of parent puppets" influenced by a community organization taking control of their school. When it was time to vote, only the teacher representatives voted to retain Mrs. Rodriguez. Shortly thereafter, the council offered a contract to Mr. Mendez, an educator from outside the district who was referred to the school by Nuestra Comunidad Unida.

Mr. Mendez made little effort to "heal the wounds" of his troubled school community. He thought that the council's strong support was a sufficient base from which he could run the school, but he was wrong. From the very beginning of his contract, many of his faculty members and parents ignored him. A few teachers told us that they did not respect his credentials, and they did not think that his past experience outside of Chicago was relevant. Others said that it "didn't matter who he was, what he was, or where he came from. . . .We don't like the fact that he got rammed down our throats."

For a time, parents also kept their distance, both from the new principal and the school. Instead, they used their energies to organize for the upcoming LSC elections. They put forward a slate of parents and community members that did not have ties to Nuestra Comunidad Unida or any other community-based organization, and they succeeded in winning a majority of seats on the council. The new LSC then vowed to get rid of Mr. Mendez and replace him with one of their "own." Mr. Mendez was made so miserable that he resigned at the end of two years. Yet the fighting did not really calm down once Mr. Mendez was gone. Although another principal was hired, distrust persisted, and many wondered what would happen as the next round of LSC elections approached.

*****

Schools like Sprague were featured in several newspaper and television reports during the early days of Chicago's reform. Typically, a struggle for power had been simmering in their community for years. With school reform, this struggle enters the school, focusing first on who would be elected to the LSC, then on which community-based organizations (CBO) would train the council, and finally on whom the LSC would select as principal. LSC meetings tended to be the arena where much of the fighting occurred. Although at times there were huge audiences at these meetings and a lot of public debate, this debate often had little substantive content. Argument more often centered on personalities and local institutions, on who is for and who is against whom. The relentless struggle for control consumed everyone's energies and detracted from the school's ability to undertake meaningful improvement efforts. Distrust and antagonism even led to angry outbursts at LSC meetings, starkly exemplifying the conflict that had engulfed the broader school community.

In schools with sustained conflict, power is not consolidated in the principal. Rather, principals tend to be weak politically and ineffective instructionally. With an absence of strong principal leadership, the school community remains factionalized. The LSCs are often divided between members who are aligned with a CBO and those who have no ties to external agencies. Each bloc tends to have a constituency in the broader parent community, and these groups are typically wary of each other.

The principal evaluation process is often a center of controversy in adversarial schools. Typically, the strongest faction on the LSC uses its power to try and replace the principal with one of its own choosing.[49] In many schools it is alleged that this selection is influenced by the CBO. Other parents and community members oppose this involvement of "politicos" in the school; they also oppose the LSC's actions. As a result, they tend to support the sitting principal, even though he or she may not be especially effective.

Teachers also may be factionalized. Some may want to use reform as an opportunity to hire a better principal. They are disappointed, however, to find a process so politicized that there is little room for professional judgment. This faction ends up disenfranchised. They do not especially support the current principal, but they also are unable to get anyone on the LSC to engage with them in a deliberative process to select a new one.

Other teachers tend to be more positive about the sitting administrator. They do not feel that "nonprofessionals" on the LSC should have the right to hire and fire the principal. They also oppose the intrusion of politics into the school. However, their support for the sitting principal may not be an endorsement of his or her leadership style or abilities. Rather, it is a conservative position that seeks to limit the involvement of nonprofessionals in school decision making and thereby maintain the status quo. Some teachers are also motivated by fear about whom the LSC might bring in as a replacement. As one teacher told us: "The devil you know is better than the devil you don't know."

The Thomas School: Strong Democracy

Mr. Sanchez became principal at Thomas two years prior to reform. At his first faculty meeting, he shared a vision of Thomas as "a school for this community . . . a truly bilingual school." He said that prior to reform "it was difficult to really interest anyone in serious change." He "applauded the reform legislation and seized upon it as an opportunity—finally—to make some things happen."

At first, some teachers in the regular program for monolingual English students felt intimidated. No one knew what "truly bilingual" meant, and a few teachers told us that it felt like they were "under the gun . . . to learn Spanish . . . to teach bilingual. . . .It felt like we were going to change to his way of thinking—whatever that was—or look for new jobs."

Over time Mr. Sanchez learned less threatening tactics. He initiated monthly "conversations" with parents and teachers to talk with them about the future of Thomas School. Mr. Sanchez started the first meeting by asking: "What if we had a community school where all of the adults spoke Spanish and English so no child would ever feel left out?" After formally convening these meetings, he would often sit in the back and take notes as the parents and teachers talked about their hopes for the school. Some of the teachers told us that an important consequence of the meetings was that everyone got to "know each other better. . . .Teachers from bilingual and regular talked together—it seems like for the first time—and everyone listened to parents from both programs, too."

Building on this growing base of trust, the parents and principal asked the faculty to take the lead in developing the School Improvement Plan (SIP). They wanted a document that would guide the school's change effort and help them to achieve their vision of a bilingual community school.

Teachers at Thomas had been dissatisfied with their students' academic achievement for some time. Prior to reform, some teachers had done course work to advance their lane placement in the CPS salary schedule, but as a faculty they had not done much together to enhance practice at their school. One teacher commented that "reform changed the game. There was so much more opportunity in the city . . . workshops and activities and things for teachers to take advantage of . . . to get into . . . and now if kids didn't do well it was going to be our fault. We'd get the blame."

At first there were problems. A core of teachers from the regular program had volunteered to draft the SIP. This was essentially the same group that had been enterprising in seeking grants, programs, and professional development activities since reform began. These teachers had attended restructuring seminars at the Chicago Teachers Union, and they were also trained in peer coaching and Teaching Integrated Math and Science (TIMS). Several had also invited university faculty to work with them on their language arts curriculum. As this core group developed the SIP, they began to realize that their involvement was not sufficient. To write a worthy SIP, they needed more teachers to participate; in particular, they needed bilingual teachers to work with them. They reported this to their principal, the LSC, and PPAC, and asked for help.

The bilingual teachers were hesitant at first. They were concerned that if they became involved, bilingual money might get diverted to whole-school initiatives. Heated debates ensued between the two teacher groups. For the most part, Mr. Sanchez did not say much. He gave teachers time to talk through their concerns. He did remind them, at strategic moments, to think about the school's mission statement. He asked: "What does our mission require? Separate funds and faculties, or one school?"

These faculty meetings, which began toward the end of the 1990 school year, were sustained through the winter of 1991. The eventual result was that the planning team expanded, and a mixed group of bilingual and regular teachers drafted the SIP. They wrote into their plan their desire to find "high quality professional development that would help children succeed and unite both halves of the school." The school's budget was also reorganized to reflect these priorities.

Mr. Sanchez, as well as many of the teachers, actively reached out to parents. Mr. Sanchez was convinced that parental involvement would enhance their personal lives and enable them to be better parents. During the first year of reform, he spent many long hours teaching his council about their responsibilities and how they could work more effectively as a group. Several of his teachers shared his vision of parental participation, and they too encouraged parents—including Spanish speaking parents who needed translation assistance—to participate on various committees and to get involved in school activities. They focused their efforts on revising the discipline code, adopting school uniforms, and starting a parent center. When it came to improving the school's academic programs, they were a supportive but deferential group. Although they were interested in learning more about these issues, they mostly listened to teachers and the principal, and went along with their recommendations.

*****

A dissatisfaction with existing arrangements and sustained conversation about improvement—What is wrong with the school? What should our mission be? What must we do to achieve real change?—characterize a school community engaged in strong democratic practice.

Principal initiative often provides the opening route. We observed in our field sites two different patterns of leadership that stimulated strong democracy. In the first, activist principals began working on improvement initiatives prior to the passage of PA 85-1418, but were somewhat stymied in their efforts either by the central office or by a recalcitrant staff. These principals seized upon reform as an opportunity to work independently of Pershing Road (the location of CPS's central office). With the new autonomy afforded by reform, such principals openly encouraged troublesome teachers to leave the school, while at the same time granting greater influence to other teachers in schoolwide affairs.

In the second instance, a principal committed to restructuring was hired by the LSC. The LSC then proceeded to support the principal's efforts to mobilize improvement initiatives across the school. Parents, community members, and teachers were all recruited to participate in these activities.

Parents can also exert leadership in strong democracy schools. When parents are organized politically and are sufficiently knowledgeable about educational issues to hold their own with professionals, they can directly use the power of the LSC to advance changes in a school's mission statement, budget, and SIP. Such councils actualize strong democracy, using LSC meetings as a context for informed and sustained debate. Such practice in turn encourages a broad base of participation and fosters a sustained focus on the needs of children.

Teachers too can lead change. Many have taken advantage of new professional development opportunities available since reform. As they became more knowledgeable about new programs or curricula, they promoted these innovations in their school. Typically, these teachers had to convince their principal to support what they wanted. If the principal objected, teachers might have had to organize with parents and community members on the LSC not to renew that principal's contract when it next came up for review. Either way, teachers were engaging in strong democratic practice as they planned both what changes they wanted and how to organize to get them.

Conflict frequently accompanies strong democratic practice, especially in its early stages. In big urban schools, particularly in ones where there is high student mobility and a diverse parent group, decision-makers may not know each other well and they may feel awkward and act defensively. Some disagreements are just misunderstandings because the basic discussion processes of democratic localism are new. Others represent genuine differences of opinion that surface as each participant learns for the first time about other points of view. If the school successfully addresses some initial problems, however, and if these conversations are sustained over time, a base of shared understandings can grow, positive sentiments and trust among participants arise, and a collective sense of efficacy emerges. The capacity of the school community to tackle problems expands, and the character of discussions about these problems takes on a more supportive tone. Decision making in the school community then functions at a much higher level.

A Look Ahead

Before proceeding further, a brief caveat is in order. The "types" introduced above offer a clarity and simplicity that is valuable for framing analysis. The reality of school politics in any specific community, however, is often more dynamic and complex than a single type can fully reflect. Some schools, for example, showed movement over the first four years of reform from consolidated principals' power to strong democracy. We also witnessed schools moving from adversarial politics—where leadership was weak and much fighting prevailed among parents, community, and faculty—to consolidated principals' power. This occurred when the LSC fired the sitting principal and hired a much stronger person who was able (and also found it necessary) to take control of the school.

In short, to place any school in a single category—even at a given time point—is likely to do some injustice to its local history and circumstances. For the larger descriptive and analytic purposes of this book, however, the political types provide the necessary standpoint for examining developments across the whole system (rather than in any single school). More specifically, they afford a basis for investigating the prevalence of various forms of political activity during the first four years of reform and for ascertaining the kinds of school community contexts where each was more likely to occur.

Prevalence of Different Types of Local School Politics

The case-study synthesis identified four major approaches that Chicago elementary schools have taken to local school governance. We were able to discern within each type the key roles and activities that developed as reform unfolded, and how these roles and activities combined to create a distinctive school politics. We turn our attention now to estimating the prevalence of each type.

To accomplish this, we needed to develop a set of quantitative indicators that would reliably differentiate among the four types. An analysis of the salient features of each type, as illuminated in the case studies, provided the basis for this indicator development task. The resultant measures allow us to identify the type of school politics most likely occurring in each school, to estimate the prevalence of political types across the system, and to examine the equity of their distribution. Ultimately these measures allow us, in Chapter 5, to test the basic logic of Chicago school reform—democratic localism as a lever for organizational change.

Salient Features of Local School Politics

The interplay among the three major sites of power in a school—the principal, the school faculty, and the Local School Council (LSC)—creates a distinctive local school politics. Based on field observations from the case-study synthesis, we identified four salient features that directly distinguish among consolidated principal power, adversarial politics, and strong democracy. (Maintenance politics, by inference, is part of a residual category). Three of these features relate directly to individual sites of power; a fourth concerns the presence of sustained disputes among school constituents.

Facilitative Principal Leadership. Principals in schools with strong democracy display a distinctive leadership style. They support broad participation of both parents and faculty in the decision-making process and spend time promoting this involvement. They encourage a searching for new ideas that might help the school, and are also willing to challenge the status quo to implement them. For example, Mr. Sanchez, principal at the Thomas School, organized monthly meetings among parents and teachers. He constantly encouraged discussion and the exchange of ideas. When the thread of the talk strayed from crucial business, he reminded people of the central school mission. In marked contrast, Mr. Bangor at Howard was more apt to control the situation. Instead of promoting public discussion, he dealt with individuals and issues on a one-to-one basis, involving few people in important decisions. He actively discouraged broader parent and teacher involvement in decision making.

Collective Faculty Activity. For a faculty to exert influence over curricular and other matters, they must have structured opportunities to articulate their views as a group and they must regularly exercise these options. At a minimum, teachers must feel safe to express their views about school operations and how these might be improved. From a more pro-active standpoint, they should exert influence over a broad range of school matters.

Again, Thomas and Howard schools provide contrasting pictures of teacher involvement. Mr. Bangor made major decisions without extensive consultation from the faculty, such as his decision to purchase an expensive computer lab. When some teachers expressed other ideas for the funds available, Mr. Bangor played to their self-interests and persuaded them to just go along. In comparison, Mr. Sanchez encouraged his teachers to meet frequently and to work together on school improvement, in spite of traditional distinctions at Thomas between the bilingual and regular programs.

Active Local School Council. To be a working group, an LSC must meet regularly, have structures for advancing work outside of meetings, and engage participation from the broader school community. Without at least a minimal level of structure and activity, a council cannot function as a viable site of power.

A weak council suited Mr. Bangor's need to control the school quite well. Instead of attempting to strengthen the capacity of the council through training and leadership, as Mr. Sanchez did, Bangor actually diminished its capacity by removing potentially "troublesome" members who might threaten his authority.

Sustained Conflict. Conflict is a necessary part of the school change process. In strong democracies, disagreements can arise about competing visions for the school or about alternative means for addressing common concerns. These differences often can be resolved through extended conversation.

In contrast, some schools engage in *sustained* conflict. The debate here rarely focuses on alternative strategies for improvement, but rather on personalities, group interests, and who will control the school. For example, at Sprague School, members of Nuestra Comunidad Unida were in an extended struggle with other parents and community members not associated with their organization.

The sustained, intense friction accompanying adversarial politics often factionalizes efforts within the faculty and LSC. This, in turn, can undermine a principal's attempts to work toward a politics of inclusion. Because many teachers resented how Mr. Mendez came to be principal at Sprague, for example, they along with parents focused their efforts on replacing him, rather than working together for the good of the school.

For this reason, a fourth feature of local school politics—sustained conflict—seems especially salient. This characteristic directly identifies the presence of adversarial politics in a school community.

Specific Indicators

Using the Consortium's survey data from teachers and principals and various CPS administrative records, we created a cluster of indicators for each of the four salient features of local school governance. Seven or eight individual indicators comprise each cluster. Some of the indicators are single survey items; others are composites of several related survey items. Full details about each specific indicator are presented in the Appendix. We highlight the basic features below.

FIGURE 2.1
Indicators of Facilitative Principal Leadership

Priority use of time
- ❖ Personal professional development
- ❖ Teacher/staff development
- ❖ Working with parent and community groups

Participatory orientation
- ❖ Views conflict as necessary for change
- ❖ Relies on committees to resolve conflict
- ❖ Encourages structured teacher input
- ❖ Supports teachers in taking on administrative tasks

Teachers' roles
- ❖ Principal endorses faculty involvement in school budget planning and hiring professional staff

---

Source: The Principals' Perspective, survey of principals in Chicago Public Schools, 1992.

Facilitative Principal Leadership. This indicator cluster focuses on the principal as a site of power and includes a variety of behaviors and attitudes that are associated with facilitative leadership. (See Figure 2.1.) The first three indicators examine principals' *priority use of time* with regard to their own professional development, teacher staff development, and working with parent and community groups. Making these activities a high priority reflects a principal's inclination to expand the professional knowledge and skills in a school, and to communicate such information broadly.

The next four indicators measure the *participatory orientation* of a principal, which also strongly influences the type of politics that will develop in a school. In order for school change to occur, a principal must be willing to let conflict about educational issues surface. For this potential contest of ideas to be productive, the conflict must receive some form of public hearing, for example, through teacher committees and other structures for interaction and input. Whether a principal includes teachers in the administration of the school is another key indicator of openness to change.

The final indicator of facilitative principal leadership deals with the principals' views about *teachers' roles* in two key areas: school budgets and hiring personnel. Principals who encourage teacher participation in these two activities clearly demonstrate a willingness to share power over critical decisions.

A principal with many positive responses on these eight indicators appears willing to risk conflict, is open to change, and seeks to expand participation in school affairs. The case studies tell us that such leadership behaviors and attitudes are associated with strong democracy.

Collective Faculty Activity. Seven indicators tap several key aspects of teachers' professional involvement and collective activity. (See Figure 2.2.) First is a sense of *teacher voice.* Free, open communication is a basic prerequisite to democratic life. If teachers fear retaliation for expressing their concerns, meaningful collective faculty activity seems unlikely. Moving beyond a freedom to speak, do teachers actually exercise significant influence in the school? More specifically, is there *teacher influence* over staff development, school curriculum, planning the overall school budget, and hiring new professional staff?

Also important is whether the school has structures in place to promote teachers' *collective activity.* Do teachers spend time working together on school committees, including the Professional Personnel Advisory Committee (PPAC)? Although the mere presence of these committees is not a sufficient indication of a strongly engaged faculty, some forum for collective activity is a necessary condition for formal teacher input. In addition, we included an indicator of teacher collegial activity around coordination of work.

FIGURE 2.2
Indicators of Collective Faculty Activity

Teacher voice
  ❖ Teachers feel safe to express opinions.

Teacher influence
  ❖ Teachers' influence over a range of school decisions.

Collective activity
  ❖ Teachers participate frequently on LSC or PPAC.
  ❖ Teachers work frequently on school committees.
  ❖ Principal reports that teachers coordinate their work.

Teachers share decision making
  ❖ Teachers are involved in implementing the SIP.
  ❖ Principal says that the PPAC plays an important role
      in developing new programs and ideas.

Source: *The Principals' Perspective,* survey of principals in Chicago Public
Schools, 1992; *The Teachers' Turn,* survey of elementary school teachers, 1991.

The final indicators in this cluster focus on the extent to which *teachers share decision making.* Are teachers familiar with the School Improvement Plan (SIP)? Did they participate in its development and implementation? Does the PPAC help develop programs and ideas?

In schools with positive reports on these seven indicators, the faculty is active in local school governance. It represents an influential site of power in local school affairs. Such collective action is consistent with the profile of strong democracy described above.

Active Local School Council. We know from the case-study synthesis that some LSCs were significant sites of power. These councils engaged in extended discussions about the school and made important decisions to support improvements. Because the Consortium had not directly surveyed LSC members when this research was undertaken, our information on LSC functioning is not as extensive as for the other two sites of power. As a result, we were unable to measure the full range of activity occurring within councils. We were able, however, to identify whether an LSC was a functional, working group.

Our specific indicators include: the frequency of LSC meetings; the presence of LSC subcommittees; the number of guests at meetings; turnover of parent/community membership; the percentage of parents who voted in the

---

FIGURE 2.3
Indicators of Active Local School Council

❖ At least one LSC meeting per month

❖ At least one subcommittee

❖ An average of three or more guests per meeting

❖ Four or more stable parent/community members on the LSC
   since the second election

❖ More than 5 percent of parents voting in the second election

❖ More parent/community candidates in the second election than positions available

❖ Principal does not "strongly agree" with the statement: "I am
   able to get the LSC to do what I want."   .

Source: The Principals' Perspective, survey of principals in Chicago Public
Schools, 1992; CPS records of LSC elections.

second LSC election in October 1991; and the number of candidates who ran
in the same election. Principal reports about their ability to control the LSC
was another key sign. (See Figure 2.3.) As a set, these indicators point to non-
functional LSCs. For example, LSCs that met less than once a month and had
no standing subcommittees to conduct work outside of council meetings were
unlikely to be influencing policies at the school.

Even LSCs with acceptable reports on this set of indicators, however,
may not be strong policy-making groups. Some LSCs met regularly and
had the necessary organizational structure to conduct business, yet from
field observations, we know they just "went through the motions." Without more specific information about the actual deliberations occurring
within the LSC, we cannot make these more refined judgments. Nevertheless, this indicator cluster does help to identify schools where LSC activity
does not meet at least a minimal level of activity.[50] This information is
especially useful when identifying schools with consolidated principal
power, in which the absence of a functioning LSC is an important criterion.

Sustained School Conflict. Eight survey indicators capture the extent
and duration of conflict within a school community. (See Figure 2.4.) These
indicators draw from both the principal and teacher surveys, which were
administered one year apart. Thus, the survey reports establish both that

---

FIGURE 2.4
Indicators of Sustained School Conflict

Principal agrees that:
     ❖ LSC is dominated by conflict
     ❖ LSC is uncooperative
     ❖ Relations with the community are not good
     ❖ The school is not a happy family

Teachers agree that:
     ❖ There is more conflict in the school since reform
     ❖ LSC is uncooperative
     ❖ Relations with the community are not good
     ❖ The school is not a happy family

Source: The Principals' Perspective, survey of principals in Chicago Public Schools, 1992; *The Teachers' Turn*, survey of elementary school teachers, 1991.

school conflict was evident from the perspective of two sites of power in the school and that this conflict extended over a two-year period. This indicator cluster identifies adversarial relationships within the school, the LSC, and between the school and its local community.

Examining the Validity of the School Politics Indicators

Before attempting to estimate the prevalence of the political types across elementary schools, we first assessed the validity of the indicators developed above. If the indicators are valid, they should distinguish among the schools analyzed in the case-study synthesis. For example, strong democracy schools (as identified on the basis of field observations) should offer very different indicator reports from schools with consolidated principal power.

Our analysis involved a two-stage process. We began by comparing the distribution of each specific indicator across the case-study schools. (Each school had been categorized according to political type based solely on the field observations.) Next, we examined the validity of the four indicator clusters as composite measures of each salient feature. For example, schools identified through the case-study synthesis as strong democracies should demonstrate a greater tendency toward facilitative principal leadership than the consolidated principal power schools.

To increase the power of our validity analysis, we expanded the case-study sample of schools beyond the twenty-two schools directly observed by the Center for School Improvement (CSI) and the Chicago Panel on School Policy. These additional schools participated in a federally funded school improvement project (Project CANAL) which was formally evaluated by the Chicago Public Schools. Key informants from the CPS evaluation staff, who had an in-depth, long-term knowledge of these schools, were asked to classify them based on their data and field observations. In total, field study reports from forty-two schools were used for the validity assessment of the school politics indicators.

Validity of the Individual Indicators

The two most prevalent categories of school politics in the expanded case-study sample were consolidated principal power and strong democracy. The sample sizes here (twelve and twenty-one respectively) were sufficient to use statistical procedures to examine whether individual indicators differentiated between these two political types. To assess the discriminating power of the individual indicators, we computed separate box plots on each indicator that had a continuous scale. The distributions for strong democracy and consolidated principal power schools were then compared. For indicators that had a categorical scale, the percentage of positive responses were contrasted for each group of schools.

Facilitative Principal Leadership. Consistent with the field reports, we found significant differences between the consolidated principal power and strong democracy case-study schools on all eight indicators of facilitative principal leadership. A consistently lower proportion of the principals in consolidated power schools demonstrated an openness toward broader participation. In addition, they tended to devote less time to professional development and school community communications. Although individual principals in strong democracy schools did not necessarily display all of these characteristics, as a group they responded much more positively to the indicator set.

Figure 2.5 displays box plots for the five continuous indicators of facilitative principal leadership for case-study schools classified as either consolidated principal power or strong democracy. (The results for the remaining three categorical indicators are shown in Table 2.1.) The vertical "box and whiskers" on the left in each display show the distribution of responses from principals in schools with consolidated power. The "box and whiskers" on the right side show how principals in schools with a strong democratic politics responded. The horizontal line inside each box indicates the median response. For example, on the "working with parents and community groups" indicator, the median principal in consolidated power schools spent one hour per week in this activity. In strong democracy schools, the typical principal reported spending two hours per week. The

Priority Use of Time

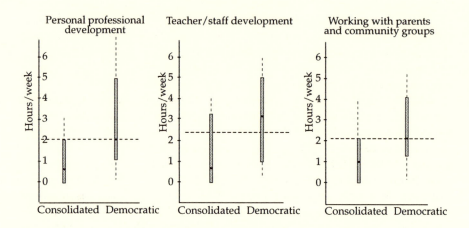

Participatory Orientation

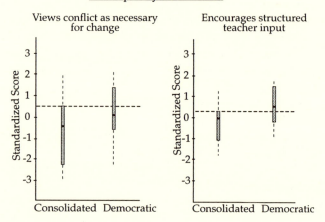

FIGURE 2.5 Incidence of Facilitative Principal Leadership Indicators
in the Case-Study Schools

vertical line at the top of each box marks off responses made by the top quarter in that group. Similarly, the vertical line at the bottom of the box marks off the bottom quarter. The box itself represents the distribution of responses by the middle 50 percent with each group. For the "working with parents and community groups" indicator, the top quarter of principals with consolidated power responded two or more hours; in contrast, the top quartile of principals in strong democracy schools responded four or more hours. In terms of the bottom quarter, principals with consolidated power indicated that they spent no time on this activity compared to about one hour per week for principals in strong democracy schools.

Table 2.1 displays results for three indicators based on single principal survey items. Each of these indicators strongly differentiates between the two political types. For example, in the strong democracy case-study schools, 74 percent of principals supported a formal role for teachers in budgeting and hiring professional personnel. The corresponding figure in consolidated principal power schools was only 25 percent.

Collective Faculty Activity. Strong democracy schools also consistently reported more collective activity among teachers than consolidated principal power schools. Note in Figure 2.6, for example, that teachers in strong

TABLE 2.1 Additional Principal Leadership Indicators by Politics Type

	Percent of Case-Study Schools	
	Consolidated Principal Power	Strong Democracy
Principal agrees with: "I rely on committees to make decisions about conflictual matters."	17	37
Principal disagrees with: "Teachers should teach and leave the school administration to me."	45	89
Principal agrees that faculty should play a formal role in "spending the school budget" and "hiring personnel."	25	74

Source: The Principals' Perspective, survey of principals in Chicago Public Schools, 1992.

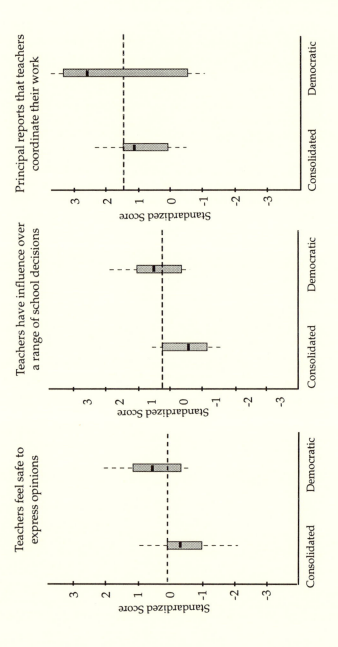

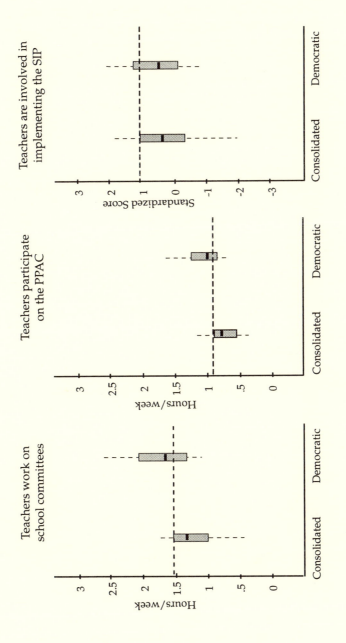

FIGURE 2.6 Incidence of Collective Faculty Activity Indicators in the Case-Study Schools

democracy schools indicated significantly greater voice in school decision making than teachers in schools with consolidated principal power. For example, teachers in the top quarter of schools with consolidated principal power feel about as safe in expressing their opinions as teachers in the median strong democracy school. Teachers in strong democracy schools also reported spending much more time working on school committees. The teachers in the median strong democracy school reported spending more time than teachers in the top quarter of the consolidated principal power schools. In fact, the reports for teachers in the bottom quarter of strong democracy schools on time spent on school committees resembles responses from the typical (i.e. median) consolidated principal power school. An additional indicator of collective faculty activity, not shown in Figure 2.6, was a single principal survey item, "The PPAC plays an important role in developing new programs and ideas." More than half (53 percent) of the principals in the strong democracy case-study schools agreed with this question, whereas only about a third (36 percent) of principals in the consolidated principal power schools did so.

Active Local School Council. While the majority of the case-study schools meet the individual criteria for an active council, displayed in Table 2.2, consolidated principal power schools tended to report somewhat less

TABLE 2.2 Indicators of Active Local School Councils

	Percent of Case-Study Schools	
	Consolidated Principal Power	Strong Democracy
At least 1 LSC meeting per month	67	100
At least 1 subcommitte	83	79
3 or more guests per meeting	82	89
4 or more stable parent/community members	82	86
More than 5% voting in 2nd election	70	86
At least 8 parent/community candidates for 2nd election	75	95
Principal disagrees with statement, "I am able to get the LSC to do what I want."	42	89

Source: The Principals' Perspective, survey of principals in Chicago Public Schools, 1992; administrative records, the Chicago Public Schools.

activity than the strong democracy schools. All of the strong democracy schools reported at least one LSC meeting per month, whereas only 67 percent of the consolidated principal power schools had monthly meetings. Small differences favoring strong democracy schools also emerged on indicators of the number of guests per meeting, stable parent/community representation, and percentage voting in the second LSC election. The biggest differences appeared on the principals' response to the statement, "I am able to get the LSC to do what I want." Whereas 89 percent of the principals in strong democracy schools disagreed, only 42 percent of principals in consolidated power schools did so. Principals who fail to disagree with this statement suggest that their councils have only very limited involvement in school decision making. Such LSCs basically "rubber stamp" principal initiatives. This, coupled with the other indicators, points to an ineffectual LSC.

Sustained Conflict. Only two of the case-study schools were classified as having adversarial politics. In both instances, at least four of the eight specific indicators from principals and teachers reflected the presence of school conflict. None of the other case-study schools had more than two indicators of conflict out of the entire set of eight. Moreover, in adversarial schools, both principals and teachers agreed that the LSC was dominated by conflict. No such agreement occurred in any of the other 40 schools. Thus, even though the number of schools available to validate this indicator cluster was small, the difference in response patterns was so large that we feel confident about its validity.

Examining the Validity of the Overall Indicator System

Composite Indicators. Each specific indicator within the four indicator clusters provides information about the type of politics occurring in a school. No single indicator alone can capture the complexities of school politics, but together they provide a detailed sketch of a school. By combining the various indicators of facilitative principal leadership, collective faculty activity, and an active Local School Council into three composite measures (indicator cluster scores), we have extensive evidence about each of the three sites of power at the school. When joined with the fourth indicator cluster—on the presence or absence of sustained conflict—we have a robust basis for characterizing how interactions among the three sites of power shape a distinctive local school politics. For example, in a strong democracy school, we are more likely to find a combination of facilitative principal leadership, collective faculty activity, an active LSC, and the absence of sustained conflict. In contrast, in a school with consolidated principal power, principal leadership will tend to be non-facilitative and the level of activism among faculty and the LSC will be weak. Sustained conflict will also be absent here.

To test these expectations, we developed a uniform method for scoring each individual indicator. We created a "cut point" for each that delimits whether a particular characteristic is declared "present" or "absent" (or in the language of diagnostic assessments, "positive" or "negative") in a school. This procedure is straightforward for the categorical indicators. Schools which meet the criteria for an individual indicator are scored "positive." For the continuous indicators displayed in the box plots, the procedure was slightly more complex. We marked a school as "positive" on an indicator when it scored above the 75th percentile for schools in the consolidated principal power group. (These cut points are denoted in Figure 2.5 and Figure 2.6 by the dashed lines.) If a school scored above the cutoff value, we interpreted this as a signal that the school was probably not dominated by the principal (although there was some chance that it could be). By inference, such a school is more likely to be pursuing strong democracy.

The composite score for each cluster is a simple count of the number of individual indicators within a particular cluster that were scored positive

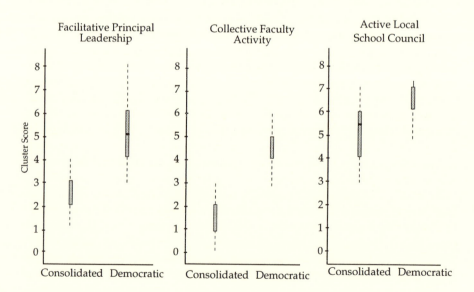

FIGURE 2.7 Indicator Cluster Scores for the Case-Study Schools

for a school. Each cluster score measures the degree to which a particular feature (e.g., facilitative principal leadership) characterizes a school.

Figure 2.7 compares the box plots on the three composite cluster scores for consolidated principal power and strong democracy case-study schools. Political activity across each of the three sites of power is clearly different in these two groups of schools. There are many more indicators of facilitative principal leadership, collective faculty activity, and active LSCs in the strong democracy schools. The most pronounced differences appear for collective faculty activity, where there is virtually no overlap in the two distributions. The consolidated principal power schools have between zero and three indicators of collective faculty activity, whereas the strong democracy schools have between three and six. The median number of indicators present in the consolidated principal power schools is two; the median in the strong democracy schools is five.

Less dramatic but still significant differences between types appear on the facilitative principal leadership and active LSC clusters. For facilitative principal leadership, the bottom quarter of the consolidated principal power schools have only one or two of the eight indicators present, and the top quarter have only three or four. In contrast, the bottom quarter of strong democracy schools have three or four indicators and the top quarter have six or more. In regard to active LSCs, the bottom quarter of the consolidated principal power schools show positive evidence on three or four of the indicators, and the top quarter show positively six or seven times. In strong democracy schools, the bottom quarter show evidence of an active council on five or six indicators and the top quarter show positive evidence on all seven indicators.

Comparison with the Case-Study Classifications. As a final test of how well the indicator system reproduces the case-study classifications, we employed a discriminant analysis. This analysis creates a discriminant function which helps us estimate how able we are to identify the political type of a school, based on its cluster scores. If the cluster scores are sufficiently discriminating, the analysis should accurately place each school in the same political type as was independently assigned to the school by the field staff who studied that site.

In fact, a discriminant function based on the three cluster scores for facilitative principal leadership, collective faculty activity, and an active LSC correctly classified 96 percent of the schools that were originally identified by field reports as either consolidated power or strong democracy.[51] (See Table 2.3.) Clearly, the three indicator clusters provide an excellent basis for distinguishing between consolidated principal power and strong democracy schools.[52]

TABLE 2.3 Case-Study Schools[a] Classified into Political Types by
Field Workers Compared to Discriminant Analysis Results

	Classified by Field Workers	
	Consolidated Principal Power	Strong Democracy
Classified by Discriminant Analysis		
Consolidated Principal Power	10	1
Strong Democracy	0	12

[a]This analysis is based on the 23 elementary schools that participated in both the principal and teacher surveys.

Source: The Teachers' Turn, survey of elementary school teachers, 1991; *The Principals' Perspective,* survey of principals in Chicago Public Schools, 1992; case studies of 42 elementary schools; administrative records, Chicago Public Schools.

Using the Discriminant Analysis to Classify Other Schools

In addition to validating the indicator system, the discriminant analysis also provides us with a statistical tool for characterizing the type of school politics occurring in other schools in the system. The "discriminant function" generated in the validation analyses can be applied to data from other elementary schools in order to place them in the most appropriate political type.

More specifically, the discriminant analysis allows us to estimate the probability that a school falls in a particular category given its score on the three composite measures.[53] If we want to be very certain that a school is, say, strong democracy, we can require that the probability be very high. Alternatively, we can relax the criterion somewhat to include other schools that have a slightly lower, although still high, probability of being strong democracies. By varying these threshold probabilities, we are able to establish reasonable boundaries for the percentage of elementary schools that were either consolidated principal power or a strong democracy. Specifically, we chose a 0.90 probability to establish a lower bound estimate for the percentage of schools in a type; we chose a 0.75 probability for creating an upper bound for the prevalence in a category.

As noted earlier, schools with adversarial politics were identified solely on the basis of the reports about sustained conflict. Procedurally, this subset of schools was identified first and removed from the analysis. Discriminant scores were computed for the remainder of the schools and then used to identify those that were clearly strong democracy or consolidated power. A residual category, those not clearly categorized as sustained conflict, consolidated principal power, or strong democracy, still remained. Included here were schools with maintenance politics and other mixed forms of politics. Since we had only a small number of maintenance politics schools in the case studies (six out of forty-two), we were not able to develop a direct statistical estimate for the incidence of this type of political activity. The operative distinctions characterizing maintenance politics are subtle, and the available indicator data did not permit an adequate separation of such schools from other schools with some features of both consolidated principal power and strong democracy. The percentage of schools classified as showing "mixed forms" of politics, reported in the next section, might safely be interpreted as an upper bound on the prevalence of maintenance politics in Chicago elementary schools.

Prevalence of Different Types of Local School Politics

We estimate an upper bound for the number of schools with sustained adversarial politics at 9 percent. (See Table 2.4.) In these schools, both teachers and principals endorsed at least one negative indicator

TABLE 2.4 Prevalence of School Politics Types

	Percent of Elementary Schools	
	Lower Estimate	Upper Estimate
Adversarial Politics	4	9
Consolidated Principal Power	37	44
Strong Democracy	28	34
Mixed Characteristics	13	26

Sources: The Teachers' Turn, survey of elementary school teachers, 1991; *The Principals' Perspective,* survey of principals in Chicago Public Schools, 1992; case studies of 42 elementary schools in Chicago; administrative records of the Chicago Public Schools.

about extensive conflict. The number of schools where principals and teachers each reported two or more indicators of conflict provides a lower bound estimate of adversarial politics at 4 percent. Thus, we infer that adversarial politics occurred in between 4 and 9 percent of Chicago elementary schools during the first four years of reform.

As noted earlier, the results of the discriminant analysis provide the basis for estimating the prevalence of consolidated principal power and strong democracy. In general, consolidated power schools did not display broad participation in decision making. In these places principals were typically not oriented toward facilitative leadership, teachers were not collectively organized, and LSCs were more likely to be inactive. We estimated that between 37 and 44 percent of the elementary schools had these characteristics. (As mentioned earlier, the lower bound is based on a 0.90 probability of correct classification; the upper bound is based on a 0.75 correct classification probability.)

In contrast, strong democracy schools were more likely to have a principal who engendered discussion about key educational issues, teachers who were collectively engaged in the planning process, and a Local School Council that met regularly and drew in other participants. We estimate that this form of politics was present in between 28 and 34 percent of Chicago elementary schools.

Finally, between 13 and 26 percent of the schools remained in a "mixed" category. Included in this group are the maintenance politics schools described in the case studies. Theoretically, we expect the incidence of maintenance politics to be relatively low since all of the schools included in this analysis had test scores significantly below national norms in 1989. The need for improvement was obvious to most school participants, and broad participation in maintaining the status quo was unlikely. In addition, this category also likely includes schools that are in transition (or perhaps just unstable) between consolidated principal power and strong democracy. For example, a small number of schools reported that their principal was not inclined toward democratic participation, but their faculty was highly engaged and influential in decision making. Somewhat more prevalent was a pattern where the principal appeared oriented toward strong democracy, but faculty activity was relatively weak. Such relationships among these two sites of power are not unexpected. Strong democracy can take time to develop, and all participants in the process may not move at the same pace.

Distribution of Types of Local School Politics across the City

Recall that significant concerns were raised during the mobilizing for Chicago's school reform about how well it would work in the different types of school communities across the city. In particular, some African-American leaders worried that many schools in their neighborhoods might not be able to effectively use the opportunities created by the reform to make improvements. More generally, it is reasonable to expect in any decentralization initiative that individual units will vary substantially in how they exercise their newly acquired authority. Thus, examining the distribution of political practices across the city is an important concern.

From the standpoint of equity, we examined the relative prevalence of the four types of school politics across school communities of varying economic status and racial and ethnic composition. In addition, we explored the possible effects of school size. Earlier Consortium studies had indicated that local control appeared to be working better in small schools, and it seemed important to continue to examine this finding.[54]

In most general terms, each of the four categories of school politics can be found in schools with virtually any composition of students. One can walk into most any neighborhood in Chicago and find a school where principals are actively promoting expanded participation, and teachers, parents, and the local community are actively involved. (See Figure 2.8.) Nevertheless, some types of politics are somewhat more prevalent under certain circumstances.

Low-Income Composition. Chicago elementary schools educate mostly poor children. Sixty percent of the low-performing schools (that is, where test scores are clearly below national norms) have more than 90 percent low-income students; in only 9 percent of the low performing schools are fewer than half the students from low-income families. Figure 2.9 shows the prevalence of each political type in schools with differing percentages of low-income students.

In relatively advantaged schools (schools with less than 50 percent low-income students), adversarial politics occurred two times less often than the rate for the system as a whole.[55] This politics was most likely to occur in schools with mid-range school poverty (between 50 and 90 percent low-income students). It was under represented in the most impoverished schools (more than 90 percent low-income students).

Strong democracy was somewhat more likely in the relatively advantaged schools, occurring about 1.2 times more often than in the system as a whole. Given the higher level of human and social resources in these school communities when reform began, these results are not surprising.

It is important to note that the presence of consolidated principal power appears unrelated to the income composition of the school. This type of school politics appears equally likely whether one is looking at the most advantaged schools or the most disadvantaged schools.

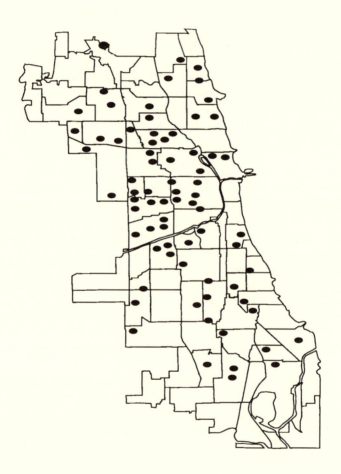

FIGURE 2.8 Strong Democracy Schools

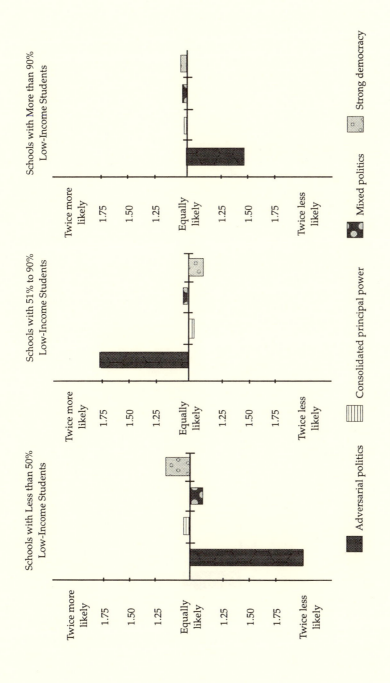

FIGURE 2.9 School Politics by Percentage of Low-Income Students

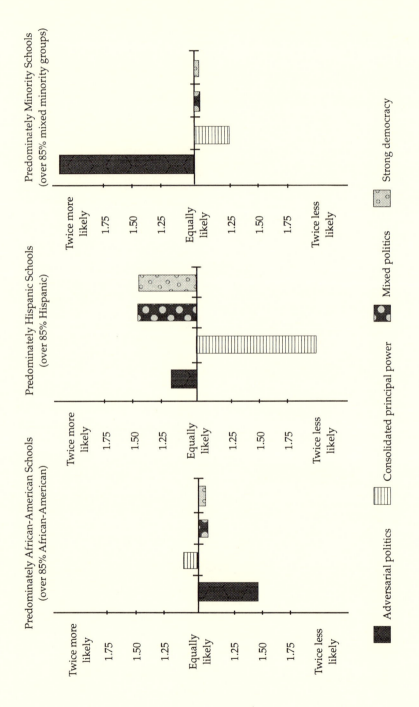

Predominately Minority Schools
(over 85% mixed minority groups)

Predominately Hispanic Schools
(over 85% Hispanic)

Predominately African-American Schools
(over 85% African-American)

Adversarial politics   Consolidated principal power   Mixed politics   Strong democracy

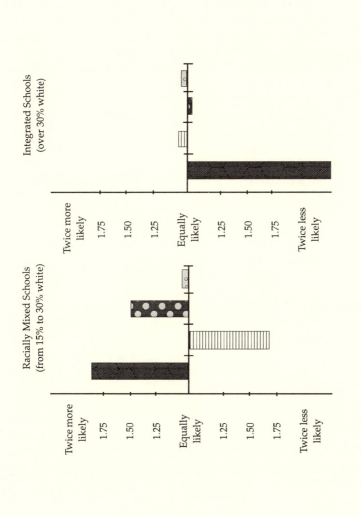

FIGURE 2.10 School Politics by School Racial Composition

Racial Composition. Schools that were either predominately minority or racially mixed (i.e. schools with fewer than 30 percent white students and no single racial or ethnic group comprising more than 85 percent) experienced adversarial politics at considerably higher rates than all other racial and ethnic categories. (See Figure 2.10 on pages 88 and 89.) Both of these types of schools typically have students from many different backgrounds, and the diversity of interests represented here offer more seeds for conflict. In contrast, both predominately African-American and integrated schools display less adversarial politics than the school system as a whole. In both of these two categories, there is a clear leadership elite, African-American or white respectively, and basic issues about organizational control, at least along racial and ethnic lines, are less likely to emerge.[56]

Interestingly, Hispanic schools demonstrate a marked tendency toward strong democracy. In fact, 42 percent of the predominately Hispanic schools are classified in this political type. Correspondingly, these schools are approximately twice less likely to have consolidated principal power. This particularly favorable pattern in racially isolated Hispanic schools runs counter to early media accounts of school conflict in Chicago that featured some highly contested decisions about school principals in a few Hispanic neighborhoods. Possible explanations for this relationship are explored in later chapters.

School Size. Theoretically, Chicago's decentralized school reform should work better in smaller schools. In such places, it is easier to maintain personal interactions and informal exchange among participants. Where such positive social interactions occur, patterns of trust build up, and the school benefits from a form of social capital.[57] This is fertile ground for the growth of democratic localism.[58]

Indeed, adversarial politics is considerably less likely in schools with fewer than 350 students. (See Figure 2.11). Mixed politics and strong democracy also occur somewhat more often in small schools. Thus, we have some supportive evidence that smaller school size lessens the likelihood of sustained conflict and can facilitate the formation of strong democracy. The emergence of the latter, however, is by no means assured. At best, small size is a facilitative factor. The actual pattern of relationships that emerges in any school depends largely on the leadership of the principal, faculty, and LSC. For example, a controlling principal can be just as autocratic in a small school as in a large one, perhaps even more so.

*****

Prior to school reform in Chicago, there had been little or no tradition of local influence over school affairs. In creating Local School Councils with unprecedented powers, the authors of the legislation sought to expand local democratic activity, so that parents and communities along with local school professionals would have a greater voice in the operation of their school. Although only about a third of the elementary schools demonstrated strong democratic practice during the first four years of reform, we judge this to be a significant development given the long institutional history of hierarchical domination and autocratic control. Moreover, the equity in the distribution of these results across types of school communities makes this even more noteworthy. From this standpoint, it seems clear that one of the major objectives of the legislation—mobilizing broader local participation in school affairs (as a lever for change)—was actually advanced in many school communities. Next, we turn attention to the specific kinds of school change that this expanded local participation actually fostered.

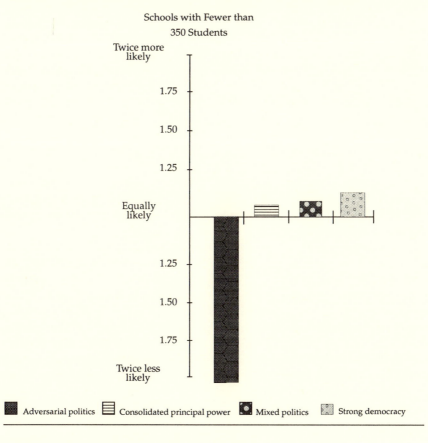

FIGURE 2.11 School Politics in Small Schools

3

Catalyzing Basic Organizational Change at the Building Level

We have seen that PA 85-1418 activated extensive participation by parents, community members, and staff in the local affairs of many Chicago school communities. Strong forms of democratic activity emerged, in some schools, in virtually every neighborhood of the city. By creating a new forum for a broad base of community activity and civic education, these developments are of considerable value in their own right.[1]

In examining PA 85-1418 as a vehicle for educational improvement, however, we must explicitly consider the criticisms that have been raised about other recent efforts to decentralize school governance, as these concerns bear directly on the merits of Chicago's reform. In brief, previous attempts to implement school-based management have frequently been described as different people, and sometimes more people, making the same old decisions. It is argued that these efforts to change who controls and influences school policy have largely remained disconnected from any serious consideration of whether and how such structural changes might be expected to lead to improvements in the conditions of teaching and learning.[2] Earlier attempts in the 1970s and 1980s to give local school professionals more control over school-site operations, for example, did not consistently affect curriculum, teaching, or student learning.[3]

The framers of Chicago's school reform legislation acknowledged these issues and worried about how best to address them. The explicitly stated purpose of PA 85-1418—to create more effective educational institutions—was clear. To effect such changes, however, reformers argued that a revitalized democratic localism was needed. For example, Fred Hess, director of the Chicago Panel on School Policy, wrote:

The act was never intended to solve student achievement problems itself. .
. .The philosophy was to create the opportunity for local actors to solve the
different problems encountered in different locales within the city. Thus,
the act is not intended to solve the problems by itself but to create the opportunity for the problems to be solved. The long term questions are, did
the opportunity get adequately created and did people take advantage of
the opportunity to make changes radical enough to improve the learning
opportunities for students?[4]

Similarly, Don Moore, director of Designs for Change, argued that governance change is not an educational solution but rather a critical first step
toward such a solution:

Properly crafted changes in governance can create potent incentives for
improving the quality of educational services to students in big city school
systems . . . and have a major impact in improving educational services to
students at risk and improving student performance.[5]

In short, the architects of Chicago's reform believed that, given expanded
authority and fiscal resources, local participants would eventually change
their schools in fundamental ways. This chapter probes more deeply the
nature of the organizational changes that actually occurred during the first
four years of Chicago's school reform.

In order to appreciate the approaches pursued toward improvement in
Chicago, it is important to have a fuller understanding of the context for
these new initiatives. Local participants' past experiences in their communities, and with their schools, provide an important grounding for their
ideas about appropriate improvements. This local analysis, however, also
interacts with larger policy conversations about the problems of truly disadvantaged urban communities and the need to promote systemic school
change. An active Chicago media, coupled with a wide range of workshops and training opportunities associated with reform, promoted broad
discussion of these professional analyses.[6] In the interaction of this local
history and professional discourse, participants framed their understandings of their own conditions and possible routes to improve them.

The Problems of Urban Communities and Their Schools

During the last two decades, profound economic and social changes have
swept over the nation's major cities. Many urban neighborhoods have been
ravaged by a loss of basic institutions—businesses, churches, banks, health
and social service agencies, and community organizations. Little of what
we normally envision as communal life exists in some of the poorest communities.[7] Today, concerns for personal safety are paramount. Residential

mobility is high as families seek better housing and a safer place for their children. This insecurity and transience weakens the social ties necessary to bind neighborhoods together. Mistrust characterizes many social encounters among residents and between residents and their public institutions. The relationships among extended families and neighbors, who know and care about each others' children, is a valuable social support for families. In many urban school communities, however, this social capital is now limited.[8] To counteract this loss, it is argued that schools must take on increased responsibility to strengthen the social ties among parents and the school itself.[9]

Problems of urban life weigh heavily on parents and children who know about failure firsthand and have come to expect it "as the way things are around here." The life circumstances for children are particularly devastating.[10] Early on, they learn about peers who drop out of school. They see friends who persist to graduation but cannot get jobs. They see cousins and brothers who do not live long enough to drive a car or vote in an election.

Not surprisingly, many minority and low-income parents transmit conflicting signals to their children about education and learning. Although these parents may speak about the importance of going to school and getting an education, much of their behavior actually contradicts this.[11] Overwhelmed at times by feelings of exclusion and low self-esteem, parents can convey a sense of hopelessness to their children.

Such concerns carry over into the interactions of parents and teachers and their perceptions of one another. An atmosphere of distrust and suspicion permeates many of these encounters. Teachers see parents' goals and values as impediments to students' academic accomplishments. As one teacher at Beacon School told the Tribune reporters: "Give me the parents of these children. Let me show them how to parent and we wouldn't have the problems we have."[12] Parents, in turn, believe that teachers are antagonistic toward them and fail to understand the difficult conditions that shape their children's lives. This misalignment of perspectives and values between home and school seriously undermines the work of urban schools.[13]

Conflicts between local school professionals and parents were highly visible during the initial mobilization for school reform. Although a "bloated central office" was generally seen as the major impediment to meaningful school change, as noted earlier, many teachers and principals also came in for sharp criticism at the community forums organized by Mayor Harold Washington.

Such analyses direct attention to reshaping the basic relationships between schools and parents. Urban children need a more consistent home and school social environment that promotes their personal well-being and creates a supportive context for learning. Unless this happens, the academic efforts of schools will be frustrated. This perspective implies that urban school improvement requires fundamental changes in both their organizational form and moral order.[14]

These analyses also have important implications for the work of teachers. It has been frequently noted that teaching has a weak technical core. While research has generated many useful concepts and ideas to inform teaching, the craft of teaching remains more akin to art than science.[15] The spontaneous, situational character of classroom decision making makes regular demands on teachers' ingenuity and judgment. In the absence of a definitive knowledge base to justify action,[16] teachers depend in large part on the endorsement of colleagues and support from parents to warrant their efforts.[17] This social support also helps to sustain a high level of commitment to teaching.[18] Unfortunately, many urban school professionals work in a context where the legitimacy of the central office has been undermined, and the local community is suspicious and sometimes even overtly hostile. Absent strong professional and communal support, teachers remain largely isolated, with a weak authority base for action. In such situations, serious efforts by local professionals to change their schools will remain infrequent. In contrast, when there is strong community support, coupled with pressure to improve, effective school change efforts are more likely to result.[19]

In this regard, the heightened local political activity described in the previous chapter offers a unique potential for urban school improvement. Chicago school reform created both a rationale and a context where parents, communities and local professionals might work on reforming their relationships with each other. If successful, this could lead to a major change in both the work conditions for teachers and the learning environments for students. Chicago's reform thus responds to an important dimension of the problems of urban schools that is not directly addressed in most other current reform proposals.

More generally, at base in the Chicago reform is an expansive vision for the school as a community institution. Here too PA 85-1418 is unique in its emphasis among contemporary efforts to improve urban schools. The spirit of PA 85-1418 encourages a fundamental rethinking of how schools might work in truly disadvantaged neighborhoods. It challenges them to join with other neighborhood institutions to take a more constructive role in redressing the damages wrought by the larger economic and social forces at work in urban centers.[20]

The Problems of Urban Teachers and Their Schools

The 1970s and 1980s brought many new curricula and specialized programs into public schools. External regulations sought to delimit their autonomy and make them "rule accountable."[21] Accompanying these new programs and regulations was increased specialization, and an expanded bureau-cracy that made schools more complex organizations. Teachers often had little knowledge of the full range of programs in their buildings, nor did they have many opportunities to interact with their new colleagues. More-over, while many of these externally imposed interventions failed to pro-duce their intended consequences, they often made the work of teachers more difficult.[22]

Not surprisingly, many teachers grew cynical and withdrew behind their closed classroom doors. They defined an increasingly narrow range of re-sponsibilities for themselves and maintained a skeptical view of those out-side. Given this history, it is not surprising that some teachers initially viewed the Chicago School Reform Act with a jaundiced eye. The bright ideas of earlier reforms had come and gone. They thought: "This too will pass."

Such negative perspectives represent an important context for local school improvement efforts. Past research on school change has demon-strated that the "deep history" of a school can have a powerful influence on subsequent efforts to reform it.[23] The failure of prior change efforts fos-ters widespread pessimism about whether it is possible for "things to be fundamentally different."

Moreover, this perception that things will not change represents a shared history of many Chicago schools. Beginning in the late 1970s, the central of-fice of the Chicago Public Schools, like other urban school bureaucracies, sought to control more directly the practices of local schools. These efforts, however, were often poorly conceived and implemented. An attempt in Chicago, for example, to introduce a mastery learning curriculum in reading misfired badly. So did a uniform policy on grade retention. These failures contributed to a broadening crisis of legitimation for central office initiatives more generally.

The 1970s and 1980s also brought very dramatic changes in the eco-nomic and social conditions of many urban neighborhoods.[24] The current teacher workforce, which is now relatively senior, experienced most of these changes first-hand.[25] Having lived through this, many teachers now retell a "golden age story." "Back in the old days," the story goes, when the com-munity was different and when students came to school ready to learn, teaching was simpler and more effective. If we also take into account the dilapidated physical conditions of schools like Beacon and the scarceness of basic instructional materials, we begin to better comprehend the social reality of urban teachers.

Thus, engaging teachers in reform and convincing them that their work conditions and their schools could be different is an important beginning step in any schoolwide restructuring effort. The democratic localism of PA 85-1418 was as novel to Chicago's teachers as it was to parents and community members, and they too had reasons to be distrustful. The anti-professional rhetoric that accompanied reform in Chicago made teachers defensive and raised doubts about whether they would actively engage the processes set out in PA 85-1418.[26] Expanded parent participation might ameliorate some problems of order and discipline around the school and even help to keep students in school. Strengthening ties between the school and its local community might generate supplemental resources to support teachers' work. But questions about how to improve what teachers did with students in classrooms still needed to be addressed. If student learning was to improve, faculty had to participate actively in reform, along with parents and community members.

A Call to Change Teaching and the Work Conditions of Teachers

Urban school reform poses fundamentally different problems now than those confronted by similar efforts just two decades ago. A post-industrial economy makes greater demands on our education system and attaches greater economic rewards than ever to individual educational attainment. Where only a few years earlier we would have triumphed a higher level of standardized test scores and lower high school dropout rates, these aims have now been replaced with national goals of "world class attainment standards for all."[27] This represents a daunting task for a school system like Chicago's that has not been able to achieve even a broad base of basic skills. It calls for nothing less than a fundamental revolution in classroom teaching, and a restructuring of schools in order to sustain such teaching.[28]

It has been noted that the formal mechanisms for coordinating and controlling teachers' work in schools are rather weak.[29] As was the case at Beacon, treaties are struck between school administrators and teachers which afford teachers considerable autonomy in their classrooms (assuming they maintain some minimal standards of order). In exchange, teachers generally defer to their principal extensive discretion to "run the building." As reformers sought to make schools more effective, however, this organizational control system had to come under intensive scrutiny.

One well established approach to improving organizational efficiency draws on scientific management theory. Its major proponent, Frederick Taylor, attempted at the turn of the century to rationalize work production in America's then burgeoning industrial revolution.[30] Central to this approach is a standardized work technology with narrowly defined jobs and a close supervision of workers to maintain their attention to their routinized tasks. As an incentive, workers are compensated according to their productivity, but they are in essence exchangeable parts who are expected to follow rules and not take risks.

Applying these ideas to schools demands that educators develop clear, measurable objectives. Classroom teaching should be routinized around scientifically established practices and closely monitored with standard observational protocols.[31] Another critical component is frequent charting of student progress through standardized tests. In most general terms, this overall strategy involves standardizing the system of classroom inputs, teacher behavior, coupled with vigorous monitoring of student output. The idea is that by constraining teachers' methods and content decisions, a more standardized quality of instruction will occur. The early research on effective schools embraced these ideas, and they continue to have some forceful advocates among urban educators.[32]

Few school districts have fully implemented this mechanistic control strategy.[33] As a result, we have only limited knowledge about its educational effectiveness. A number of general lessons about this approach have emerged, however, from research in the corporate sector, where scientific management theory has been vigorously pursued for more than fifty years. It is clear that mechanistic control systems tend to limit workers' commitment, with collective bargaining agreements delimiting the extent of those commitments.[34] Unit productivity depends in large measure on the loyalty of workers to their superiors and the effectiveness of these superiors in cultivating such loyalty. Most important, the effectiveness of the overall system is predicated on work situations that are dominated by a well-defined technology. In contrast, this control mechanism tends to break down in work settings where flexibility is needed, such as when workers must decide how to respond to ever-changing, unpredictable conditions.

These latter observations are particularly relevant in the context of the new directions for teaching and learning that are now broadly advocated for America's schools. Although our analyses of instructional change is the primary focus of Chapter 4, we note at this point that a mechanistic control strategy appears theoretically incompatible with the currently espoused aims of "teaching for understanding" and "authentic achievement." Advocates for such instructional reforms conceptualize teaching not as a technical production process where efficiency optimization is the prime value (as would be the case under scientific management theory), but rather as a complex form of human and social activity that is more akin to a professional practice. From this perspective, quality in teaching has a dynamic and situational character that depends upon teachers' deep knowledge of subject matter, attention to student cognition, and a sensitivity to local context. It is argued that, if we are to develop and sustain a broad base of such practices, a fundamental shift in the nature of the school as a workplace is needed.[35]

More specifically, the coercion and fiscal incentives that guide human behavior in a "control-oriented system" will not produce the levels of individual and collective commitment needed.[36] Instead, to attain better schools, the work of school professionals must be made more intrinsically attractive. Organizational control must rely more heavily on shared moral sentiments and normative commitments embodied in a conception of "teachers as professionals" rather than of "workers loyal to their superiors."[37] Unless this happens, the desired innovations in teaching will be only sporadically implemented, and the institutions themselves will not change. At base here is the proposition that, unless the whole system is switched over, the existing structures of influence and authority operating within schools and the established organizational practices, norms, and mores will defeat any serious reform effort.

Recent writings on teacher development highlight some specific features of school context that are important in this regard.[38] It is difficult for teachers to become more reflective, for example, when no time is provided in the work day for such activity. Similarly, it is difficult for teachers to learn from one another when, for most of the day, they are isolated from their colleagues, and have little opportunity to interact with professional educators outside their school community. Likewise, it is difficult for them to sustain innovation and classroom experimentation in schools where risk taking is not supported.

In a related vein, past efforts at in-service training for teachers have focused exclusively on a transfer of specific knowledge, skill, and materials. These practices ignore important lessons from research on teacher development, which emphasize how much teachers draw on what they learn informally on a day-to-day basis to carry out their craft.[39] If we are to encourage more sustained learning among school faculties, then the basic organization of schools must change to promote this. The proper model for the school as a workplace is not that of the factory, but rather the professional community.[40]

In sum, a wide range of arguments and strands of research all point in the same direction. Changing the structure and culture of teaching at the school building level, away from a "control-oriented" system and toward a "commitment oriented" approach, is viewed as a key to improvement.[41]

Leadership for Change

These arguments about the need for fundamental change in the school workplace turn us toward a related concern—how are local schools to effect such organizational changes? As noted in Chapter 2, the transition from hierarchical domination to an effective democratic localism places demands on leadership at the school building level. Similar leadership demands emerge as we focus on the reshaping of the school toward a learning organization with shared professional commitments for student development. Although this leadership can arise from any of the three sites of local power, the principalship is again particularly advantaged.[42]

The deference that teachers have historically granted to principals can now be used by principals, if they are so inclined, to facilitate this organizational transition. Given their highly visible role, principals have unusual opportunities to create the symbols, to articulate the values and to shape the images that can come to define how the school sees itself. Moreover, when their public statements resound with important ideals about professionalism and a shared responsibility to children and to the local community, this conversation can catalyze a sense of outrage about the status quo and create a powerful force for individual change.

In addition to this source of moral authority, principals also maintain considerable instrumental authority. Moreover, as noted earlier, this authority has expanded in significant ways under reform. The greater influence that principals now hold over the school's discretionary budget and the hiring of new personnel represent two powerful new instruments for restructuring organizational life.

In short, principals can use their positional authority, both moral and instrumental, to promote change toward a commitment-oriented learning organization (or what we hereafter we refer to as a "school-based professional community.")[43] The school principal, more than any other single person at the school-building level, has the power to catalyze a change initiative.[44] We also note that the reverse is true: The principal maintains sufficient authority to undermine the collective efforts of others in this regard. Toward what ends and under what conditions principals exercise leadership thus become important considerations.

Developing a Capacity for Self-Guidance in Local Schools

The increased local autonomy that accompanies decentralization brings new responsibilities to each school. In the past, the basic systems of instructional guidance (i.e., curriculum, staff development, and assessment) and the closely allied functions of strategic analysis (budgeting, planning, and evaluation) were all centralized "downtown." Schools were simply told what to do. Now, schools must envision their own futures and marshal all of these elements in charting their own way. The availability of expertise and resources to guide these developments within schools, however, is uncertain. Pre-service programs for both teachers and administrators, for example, have been very limited in these areas, and there has been little in the past work experiences of most local school professionals to prepare them for these new tasks.

A concern about strategic action in local decision making is even more significant in Chicago, where substantial authority is now vested in parents and community members, many of whom have had limited education. Moreover, the ideology of democratic localism, which encourages local participants to take control of their schools, can bring with it an aversion to outside expertise. Interestingly, the new literature on enhanced democratic participation, discussed in the previous chapter, is largely silent on the question of how local political practice might engage effectively with outside expertise.[45] This issue is especially important because recent research on "success stories" of school restructuring document a central role of ongoing professional development for faculty supported by sustained ties to external organizations and expertise. Surely, some schools will restructure successfully on their own; others are likely to need sustained outside assistance. Set against this backdrop, one might reasonably wonder about the effectiveness of school improvement efforts under Chicago's democratic localism.

At the most basic level we worried whether schools would engage outside ideas at all. The rhetoric of democratic localism can easily turn into a parochialism of "We know what is best for our children," which denies legitimacy to all outside knowledge and expertise. It was precisely these concerns about parochialism that contributed to the emergence of urban school bureaucracies at the turn of the century.[46]

More generally, how local schools can best approach improvement efforts remains a controversial topic. Studies of externally developed innovations emphasize the importance of local implementation considerations, as opposed to formal planning, in determining the success of these innovations.[47] Some analysts have gone so far as to triumph the intrinsic nonrationality of schools. From this perspective, planning is described as a myth designed to obscure the fact that most decision making is really more akin to randomly reaching into a garbage can for some artifact. Most of the time, according to this perspective, schools just "muddle through."[48]

The sharpness of these critiques, however, must be counterposed against the detailed requirements set out in a traditional planning model. This approach may dictate that a year or more be spent on establishing measurable short-term and long- term goals. During this period, an extensive search is also made of alternative ways to reach these goals, and a detailed implementation plan established. Included as part of the latter is a regular evaluation program that analyzes progress against the established goals.

Such formalized planning strategies tend not to work very well in social systems whose operations depend largely on personalities and the nature of social relations among participants. "Optimized decision making" is especially difficult in schools which typically confront multiple, often conflicting aims and work within a relatively uncertain technology. In addition, since schools are quite open to their external environments, and these externalities can and frequently do intrude, planning often requires spontaneous redirection to accommodate newly surfaced concerns.

These caveats notwithstanding, however, it would be a mistake to underestimate the value of strategic action. Especially at times of major structural change, as is implied in the very term restructuring, traditional routines (including the way decisions are made) are all subject to question. Recent case studies of successfully restructured schools offer evidence of a more important role for planning than was found in earlier analyses. The life cycle and rhythms of this planning, however, had an evolutionary character and did not follow the textbook descriptions outlined above.[49] To be sure, there was a discernible vision and a direction that emphasized successful, even if small, first increments.[50] There was clear intentionality in both the evaluation of current efforts and planning next steps. But serendipity, local particularism of person and place, and sometimes just good or bad fortune also came into play and had to be taken into account in charting the future.[51] Nonetheless, evaluation and analysis were regularly engaged throughout this evolutionary process.

Case Studies of Organizational Change Efforts

We have used these ideas about the nature of urban schools and past attempts to restructure them to analyze the various improvement activities occurring in Chicago. The extensive field observations in the case-study synthesis of twenty-two schools detail individual stories that are unique in some important respects. In each site, local personalities engaged concerns specific to that school community. Moreover, a distinctive local history shaped how these problems were defined and the responses that were eventually embraced.

As we compare across the case-study synthesis schools, however, we can also discern some common patterns in their developments. Although these patterns, or what we will refer to again as "types," do not fully describe all of the nuances and intricacies of each case, they do identify important themes common to subsets of schools. Moreover, this identification of types offers us a very useful framework for summarizing the developments across the entire Chicago Public Schools system, and for examining more detailed questions about how various types of organizational changes were distributed among school communities by race, ethnicity, and income composition.

Each of the cases presented below represents a distinct type of organizational activity. A new principal at Hynes School inherited a legacy of inattention to basic operations. He confronted a very troubled social environment that required immediate address. At Rhodes School, some new programs were added, but the overall approach to improvement remained unfocused. Although the initiatives were more extensive and looked better at Travis School, core organizational problems remained unaddressed. In sharp contrast, the Bella School took good advantage of the opportunities created by reform to initiate fundamental changes in school operations. The developments at Bella represent the best of what some Chicago schools were able to accomplish during the first four years of reform.

The Hynes School: A Focus on Environmental Order [52]

Hynes School is located in a poor, racially isolated community on the west side. Boarded-up abandoned buildings, covered with graffiti, surround the school, and gang activity, drug traffic, prostitution, and violence are rampant. "Hardly a day goes by without gunfire somewhere in this neighborhood," one teacher told us.

The pre-reform principal at Hynes, Mrs. Evans, was well intentioned, but overwhelmed by the deteriorating conditions of the neighborhood and her school. She was dismayed too by the needs of her students and families. She "felt defeated from the start. . . .It would take miracle workers to help these kids—much less teach them—and all I've got is not enough books, a crumbling building, and a faculty that's tired." Mrs. Evans had been in the system for a long time, but she had never been known as especially pro-active. Her reputation made her perhaps a bit defensive, but she justified it by saying: "It doesn't make sense to spin your wheels if you know you can't win."

Hynes's faculty felt powerless too. In the past, when the neighborhood, students, and families were different, many of the teachers had been successful. Now they were "burnt out" and resentful of everyone—the media, parents, reformers, administrators—who had no respect for them, yet wanted them to be the "social workers, cops, moms, and preachers to a bunch of poor, angry, sad, scared kids." One teacher complained that "some moms don't do their job." At the same time however, she sympathized with others because they are "all alone . . . and struggling against what must feel like insurmountable odds to keep their kids safe, clean, fed, keep a roof over their heads. Never mind helping them do well in school."

In response to all of this, the professional staff developed a "fortress mentality." At the beginning of the each school year, teachers vied for the rooms that had working locks, and those so fortunate could lock the troublemakers out. When the school day started, all of the exterior doors were locked as well, so that gang members could not get in and out of the build-ing. Mrs. Evans encouraged teachers to get out of the neighborhood as soon as the students left at 2:30 p.m., to check their cars before they got in them, lock up, and get on the expressway before rush hour started. Even though the staff knew that many of their children were going to empty apartments, after-school activities were not even contemplated. In the winter months, the school did not want the responsibility for anyone out after dark. The fall and spring seasons were even worse, because good weather and extended daylight meant the gangs would be active on the streets. The building shut down each day with the closing bell.

Mrs. Evans' contract came up for review by her Local School Council during the first year of reform. She was not a bad principal, according to most of her faculty, even though one teacher told us "it was demoralizing to hear her say all of the time how tired she felt." She also had said that she was not particularly impressed with "reform." She complained about the increased paperwork and meetings that reform demanded. She said that the whole process "sapped her energy" and took time away from "doing the job the way I've always done it, the way it's supposed to be done." She also told us privately that:

> any law that put parents in charge is crazy. . . .There's only one woman with a high school diploma on my LSC, and the two who are trying to get their G.E.D are in parenting classes trying to learn some basics there too. Do you think they're really qualified to tell me what to do?

Mrs. Evans avoided her contract review by announcing to her LSC and faculty that she was going to retire at the end of the year.

Shortly after her declaration, Mrs. Evans quit attending LSC meetings. Then she went on sick leave, and while few regarded her actions as ma-levolent, she left the school effectively without a leader for several months. This made the process of recruiting and selecting a new principal even more difficult, because most LSC members were already feeling intimi-dated about the task. One parent told us that she:

> went to some trainings about it, and learned a lot . . . but that doesn't mean I want this responsibility. I didn't even graduate high school, and now I'm supposed to decide on the principal? What fool put that in the law? Looks like if we make the wrong choice, we get the blame.

The council went ahead with their task in spite of their fears, but they hesitated to make a final selection. Instead, as the legislation provides, the LSC rank ordered the three people they had interviewed, and submitted the list to Mr. Greenbaum, their subdistrict superintendent. He selected

Mr. Washington, an assistant principal and football coach at a nearby high school. He said Mr. Washington would be good because he "was a good role model for the kids . . . especially the boys. He knows the neighborhood, and that's what you need around here."

Mr. Washington came in with a burst of energy and enthusiasm, behavior that stunned his new school. He told us that he scheduled a faculty meeting his first day on the job, and even before his first monthly LSC meeting, he had met with most of the members individually. He made a point too of being in the lunchroom and on the playground almost every day as well, talking with students and learning their names. He told us these early conversations were "important . . . a strategy . . . a way to make myself known, get to know people . . . get the pulse of the place." He also admitted that he was shocked that "a few teachers didn't even come to that first meeting to meet me. . . .Imagine being so disinterested that you don't even want to check out the new boss?"

Mr. Washington was surprised too that teachers had so little to say when he would ask them informally what their goals were for the school. Similarly, most parents seemed unable to talk about aims and aspirations for their own kids, beyond a few cliches and platitudes. He said he'd never been in such a "depressed place" before.

> I try to talk with the students all the time about who they are and what they want. . . .Some of the older boys told me that they wanted new basketball hoops so that they could be 'like Mike' [Michael Jordan]. Others seem so discouraged . . . so resigned to their sorry lives that they don't even speak up.

Mr. Washington told us that he "didn't give up. I'm not the kind of guy who can just show up to work every day and get a paycheck." But he did revise his plans.

After spending a few weeks at Hynes, Mr. Washington said:

> . . . I guess I woke up. . . .It's not like I gave up on my dreams. . . .I just realized that change was going to be a whole lot harder than I realized . . . than those reformers ever dreamed. And it's not like I'm so gullible. . . .I was coaching at a school down the street . . . not in some suburb that's out of touch with the urban condition. I didn't give up though. I just thought, "Whoa, this may take a hundred years."

Although Washington knew that he could not "fix" all the problems that plagued this school, he was convinced that he could at least do some things that would make it a safer place. He said:

I had to make a hard choice. I could spend a year or two trying to get people involved, and I really do believe in that, or I could try to do some things myself at first, and hope that I was successful and that people would begin to come around. Nothing good was ever going to happen here if parents were afraid to walk into the building, kids were scared, and teachers were hiding behind locked doors. It didn't take a rocket scientist to know that safety was where we needed to start.

Departing from the fortress mentality of his predecessor, Mr. Washington chose not to isolate the school from its community. He wanted to unlock the doors, and create an environment where "everyone knew everyone" and where adults looked after kids. Mr. Washington had a considerable amount of state Chapter I money to spend during the second year of reform (in excess of $300,000). So he asked the LSC for approval to use some of these funds to hire a security officer. The council thought it was a good idea, and so Mr. Washington recruited Bob, a retired police officer who lived nearby and had nieces and nephews enrolled in the school. Mr. Washington suggested that Bob begin by getting to know some of the young mothers and offering to help them set up parent patrols to ensure the children's safety between home and school. The principal went on some of these first walks, and his participation seemed to encourage everyone.

Once the patrols were well underway, Mr. Washington started on his next course of action. In an empty classroom he set up a parents' center with a phone, books, and a coffee pot. He encouraged parents to stop by as often as they could, and he asked his teachers to drop in and have a cup of coffee with the parents whenever they had a free moment, or to stop in if they needed someone to help them in their classrooms. Both the parents and teachers were reluctant to use the room at first, but eventually, a few of the moms decided to "check it out," and so did some teachers. Over time the room became a popular meeting spot, but there was always a danger, one mother told us,

> that you might stop in for a cup of coffee and end up spending the day in somebody's classroom, or making dittoes for one of the teachers, or helping out on a field trip, or whatever was needed at the time.

Nonetheless, there was a growing core of mothers—their protestations to the contrary—who seemed pleased to be of service to the school and pleased to be asked. They became a regular presence in the building.

After two years of school reform, Hynes had a long way to go before it might achieve the goals of the legislation. But for the first time in a long time, many in the school community thought that it was on the right path.

* * * * *

One year after Mr. Washington became principal, the Hynes School was reclaiming its environment and creating a school for the community. This early focus on improving order is not surprising. Problems of safety and order in urban schools represent very basic concerns. Unless these are resolved quickly, the school cannot focus its attention on matters of children's learning.

In his efforts to jump start change, Mr. Washington used his positional authority to initiate some new directions for the school and to build teacher, parental, and community support around this. The sight of the parent patrol winding its way through the neighborhood twice a day signaled a new responsiveness in the school to past concerns and an expanded presence in the community. Similarly, the new parent center indicated that parents were welcome in the school, and their energies and skills were valued. More opportunities were being created for local school professionals to engage constructively parents and community members around school improvement.

The Rhodes School: Peripheral Academic Changes

Thirty years ago the Rhodes school community had a wealth of small but thriving businesses, as well as family-owned clubs and restaurants. There were several churches, parish schools, skating and bowling emporiums, and a single screen movie theater.

Today, empty storefronts are all that is left of the old commercial strip, and residents must take a bus several miles to get to the nearest mini-mall to do their shopping. Enrollment at Rhodes has been declining, as many families have left the area looking for a safer neighborhood with better housing.

When school reform first came to Rhodes, the building and grounds had been neglected for years. There was gang graffiti on the walls, the grass was overgrown, and the last vestiges of the basketball court and playground were a set of broken swings, a broken backboard, and broken glass scattered about. Inside, Rhodes was tired-looking, even though the janitors worked hard to keep it clean. Children's artwork did decorate most of the first floor walls, and this covered up some of the cracks in the plaster and chipping paint. There were also bright bulletin boards and display cases everywhere announcing Black History Month, best attendance awards, and the honor roll. The professional staff at Rhodes told us that "reform or not, we try to be proud of our school." As one teacher said:

> For the most part, teachers work hard even though conditions are lousy. We're always out of everything. But we do the best we can and that's OK

because most of the children try hard and they're well behaved. Scores are too low, but with a community like this, I don't know what more we can do.

Rhodes received approximately $180,000 in new state Chapter 1 discretionary funds during the first year of school reform. This was their first installment, and, like most schools across the city, while they were excited about the money, they were a little bit disbelieving that it was really theirs to spend. Because purchasing had been centralized "for forever" in the CPS, they were also totally unaware of what things cost.

In January, Mrs. Meyers, the principal, was informed by central office that the first school improvement plan (SIP) and lump sum budget were due in the spring. She had never worked on plans like these before, and she knew that no one on her LSC or faculty had either. She put the SIP as the first item on the agenda of the February LSC meeting, but her council was anxious to discuss the budget first. One teacher representative remarked, and only partly in jest, "Let's make sure we do the budget first and spend the money quick, before the Board of Education decides to take it away. We can work on the SIP later."

Mrs. Meyers suggested, with the council's unanimous approval, that the first thing they do was "spruce the place up"—use the money to repair plaster and paint and to buy playground equipment. Mrs. Meyers and the LSC were disappointed to find out that they still had to go through the central office for the plaster and paint, and also that there was a waiting list. Nevertheless, Mrs. Meyers used some of the school's discretionary money to buy new playground equipment, and she also had the basketball court fixed up. These expenditures actually left most of the discretionary budget untouched, and so the council asked if it wouldn't be good to use the new funds to bolster the school's academic programs. They asked their principal if the faculty had a wish list, and so Mrs. Meyers called a faculty meeting to discuss the budget and school improvement plan, and to solicit faculty input. The teacher representatives volunteered to put up flyers in the teachers' lounge a week before the meeting stating: "The LSC wants YOU!" The meeting was also announced on the public address system several times the day before and on the morning of the meeting.

Faculty meetings were a bit out of the ordinary, because Mrs. Meyers, like many Chicago principals, rarely called them unless there was some edict from Pershing Road to announce. Consequently, she was pleasantly surprised when most of the faculty showed up at 8:30 a.m. for the meeting. (One teacher told us that she "was curious to find out what the LSC might want with ME!")

Unfortunately, like the LSC, they had never engaged in school planning or purchasing, and so they did not have a strategy for developing a realistic SIP, nor did they have any sense of the cost of new programs, materials, equipment, and personnel. The teachers were pleased that the LSC was asking for their advice, because they had heard from friends at other schools that some LSCs were not too interested in a dialogue with staff. Needless to say, they did not really know how to respond. A first grade teacher said it sounded great to "get the chance to improve their academic programs." She said that she wanted "a new Xerox machine, so that we can finally get rid of the ditto masters and join the twentieth century. Let's get a Xerox for every floor and enough paper to last the year." A fifth grade teacher later told us:

> . . . it was a shame . . . that first faculty meeting about the SIP and budget. Mrs. Meyers suggested that we start out by sharing our 'visions' like some of the reform training manuals suggested. But that got nowhere, really, and everyone started acting cynical. It doesn't make sense to take a bunch of teachers that have been stuck in one little place for so long—that haven't been to a professional conference, even a workshop outside of the district— and tell them to imagine a better future . . . even give them money to pay for it! We know how to keep doing what we're doing. I guess we haven't been motivated to do much else.

In short, when the faculty's first brainstorming session faltered, Mrs. Meyers intervened. She did not have any specific proposals either, but as she listened to her teachers talk, she remembered a principals' workshop that she had attended the previous summer in one of the western suburbs. She told her faculty that the group met:

> at a prestigious, suburban elementary school. . . .You wouldn't believe the equipment they had . . . a science lab with microscopes and stocked with chemicals—even in an elementary school—and an audio-visual center in the library that was out of this world! If that's what's good enough for their kids, shouldn't we buy it for our children too?

Mrs. Saunders, an upper grade teacher, asked where they would put all of the equipment if they bought it. Mr. Meyers reminded her that:

> space isn't a problem. We've had declining enrollment, and we've got at least one empty classroom on every floor. We could have a science lab, library, media center. You name it. We've got the room and we've got the money. All we have to do is write it into our SIP!

So Mrs. Meyers reported back to the LSC at the next monthly meeting, and these items were written into the SIP before they were even costed out for the budget. A parent on the council, Mrs. Carter, then asked if there was enough money for the LSC to have a wish list too. She remarked that when her children were little they liked Head Start because of all of the art supplies that they had. She said that she had liked Head Start too, because she got to come in and work with her children. Mrs. Carter asked if they might not add art classes, at least for the younger children, and a parent project to attract some of the young moms to volunteer in the building. Mrs. Carter went on to say that she was tired of being the "only mom" who was ever in the building, and she lamented that she was "not so young."

Mrs. Meyers said that they should have art for all of the students, and so the council decided that they wanted an art teacher and maybe a music teacher too. Mrs. Meyers said that she knew of some schools in the neighborhood that were sharing half-time teachers for art and music. She offered to write the positions into the budget and work on recruiting the teachers over the summer. She asked if she should set up an art studio and music room. She explained to the parents that the faculty might like this arrangement because it would enable them to stay in their classrooms and catch up on their paper work whenever the students went to art or music. The LSC thought that this arrangement made a lot of sense. The principal then asked Mrs. Carter if she wanted to follow up on the idea for a parent project. She indicated that she would do that too.

The LSC was not sure what to do next until Mrs. Meyers remembered a conference that all of the principals in the sub-district had been invited to a few months before. It was sponsored by one of the big educational computer companies in the city, and a salesman, Mr. Morris, had been seated at her luncheon table. He had asked each of the principals to fill out an informational sheet that detailed how many classes at each grade level they had in their buildings, and how many students and teachers they had. By the end of the meeting, Mr. Morris left each of them with a purchase order that he had already filled in. It covered all of the hardware and software that Rhodes would need and listed several drill and skill programs that were geared to improving student achievement on the ITBS. All that the principal needed to do was sign the order and mail it in, dedicate a classroom to become a computer lab, and recruit an instructor.

Mrs. Meyers dug the purchase order out of her desk and showed it to her council at the next meeting. When Mrs. Carter asked if the teachers would need any computer training, Mrs. Meyers said no, as it would be the instructor's responsibility to work with the students in the lab. The council authorized her to write an instructor's position into the budget, and to look for a computer teacher over the summer as well. The council talked briefly about how much all of their new initiatives would cost. Mrs. Carter asked if they shouldn't hold off on their purchase order until their new teacher was on board. But Mrs. Meyers reminded them that they had

$180,000 in new state Chapter 1 money, in addition to several other discretionary sources, and thus postponing purchases was unnecessary and perhaps unwise. For one thing, they had to get their budget in. In addition, she told the council that the salesman had warned her that the quoted prices might not last forever. Persuaded by these arguments, the council decided to buy the equipment right away and lock it up in one of the empty classrooms.

With all of these new plans, purchases, and initiatives, Mrs. Meyers was certain that she was ready to put her SIP and budget to paper. She told her council that she would develop the two documents for their approval at the next LSC meeting.

* * * * *

At the start of reform, Rhodes, like the Hynes school, mirrored the conditions of its community. It too was a tired place, and the faculty was a veteran one, that "knew how to do what it had been doing," but had little ability to imagine alternatives. Neither was there capacity to plan strategically for the future when opportunity and resources became available.

Mrs. Meyers and her faculty and parents had been isolated in a disadvantaged community for a long time. With no source of sustained, expert guidance from the outside, they were ill-equipped to think strategically about their students' needs, or write a realistic budget. Most importantly, absent a coherent vision of school development, their initiatives were scattershot. Some, like the computer system, were bought virtually sight unseen, while others, like the media center, were imported from affluent suburbs. None of Rhodes' initiatives were tailored to the specific needs of their students, nor did they develop from a deep knowledge of what it takes to improve urban schools.

Rhodes, like Hynes, presents an interesting although different dilemma for Chicago school reform. It is a vivid illustration that, even in school communities where most people get along and are well-intentioned, the reform may not lead to fundamental changes. The substantive conversations about the school and its needs to improve remain superficial. There is little internal capacity for strategic analysis and budgeting, and no external guidance that might help the school construct thoughtful alternatives and move with deliberation toward a better future.

The Travis School: "A Christmas Tree"

At 9:10 on a sunny winter morning, the Travis School is bustling with activity. A camera crew from a local television station is outside the front office packing up their equipment. One of the newscasters has just completed a series of impromptu interviews with a few teachers and children.

He heads toward the front door but then pauses. The long corridor in front of the office has caught his eye. He directs his crew to take out their cameras again and take a few shots of the various lists, plaques, commendations, pictures, and letters on the wall.

The first section is a long list—twenty-two programs—titled "New Initiatives At Travis." The list starts at the top of the cinder block wall and ends where the wall meets the floor. It is organized by discipline. For example, under the sub-heading Literacy the list includes "Reading Recovery," "Whole Language," "SRA Direct Instruction," "Classroom Libraries" and "Drop Everything And Read (DEAR)!" The heading for Math includes "Professor B," "The Algebra Project," "Family Math" and a new textbook series. The Social Services list inventories seven additional programs. And that is only a partial count. On the next section of the wall, there is another panel that enumerates the school's partnerships. There are pictures and letters of commendation on yet another one.

As he leaves, the newscaster shakes his head. He says to no one in particular: "What a school!" We catch up with him in the parking lot, and he tells us that: "Travis is my favorite school to cover in the city." He says that he and his crew:

> try to get to Travis when we get assigned to cover the CPS . . . because there's so much happening. The teachers are a good group. Well, they should be. Their principal gets them every new program and piece of equipment I've ever heard of. Did you see those programs and all of those awards? They've got about every reading program that's been invented! Did you see the new furniture that the principal hustled up for the faculty lounge? It's beautiful! Every bit as good as the suburbs, and they're sitting right here in the middle of the projects!

He goes on to explain that he graduated from the CPS

> a long time ago . . . and I've done pretty well . . . and I like to do stories that show how hard people in some schools are trying . . . stories that make the system—or at least this school—look good.

At first glance, Travis is indeed a showcase school. This is the impression that the newscaster carries with him. Curiously, however, just as Travis shows up on many people's mental lists of exemplary schools, it appears on more problematic lists as well. Despite all of its new programs and advantaged teaching conditions, Travis remains among the lowest 100 schools in the district in reading and math achievement.

The principal, Mrs. Fletcher, and her teachers take these negative rankings very seriously, and they are frustrated. The teachers are always attending workshops for their various new programs. "Everything that comes down the pike," one of them tells us. Her colleague chimes in:

> Some Saturday mornings I can't remember which workshop I'm supposed to go to. I know it's a bad weekend when I'm supposed to be at two at once, or when what they tell us to do in "Whole Language" one week, is the opposite of what the facilitator is suggesting in "Direct Instruction" a week later. Now that's an interesting problem! So to implement all of this stuff, I just try one thing one day and something from another workshop the next.

Mrs. Fletcher is energetic, thoughtful, and smart. She reads a lot, goes to conferences, and seems to know everyone in town—educators, administrators at the central office, politicians, reformers. She has been tireless in her efforts as the school's ambassador, using her own considerable political skills and personal connections to pull resources and people into her building. She has used her discretionary resources to buy as many new programs as she can. Her entrepreneurial activity did not start with reform but certainly intensified as the corporate and philanthropic communities became more interested in helping schools. Mrs. Fletcher says:

> My teachers are doing their absolute best. They're trying terribly hard, most of them. There's so much out there to do. And I keep finding more, and asking them to do more! Sometimes I feel like we're juggling too many balls in the air, and either we're going to drop the balls, or we're going to be so tired, and pulled in so many directions, we're the ones who are going to drop!

Mrs. Fletcher and the faculty have been serious about their efforts to engage parents too. The LSC almost always has a quorum, because Mrs. Fletcher and her School Community Representative make sure that all of the members receive reminder calls (or notes home with their children if they do not have phones). On occasion they have been known to arrange rides and babysitting too.

At the principal's suggestion, the LSC has started several committees that engage even more parents, and these groups do a lot for the school. The principal and many on her faculty have worked hard to make parents feel welcome in these various committees and other activities of the school. They set up a parent room where there's a "bottomless pot" of hot coffee every morning, books, magazines, and a phone, and they just started a "welcome wagon." They recently received a grant to begin a training program for room parents and classroom volunteers, and they are looking for new grants to start a G.E.D. and a parent education program in the building.

Mrs. Fletcher knows that in theory these bridges to parents and the community are supposed to improve her school. She is frustrated, however, because nothing they do—parent involvement, social services, and new programs—seem to bring up student achievement. Mrs. Fletcher is concerned that some of her teachers and her core group of parents may become demoralized. "It's ironic, isn't it?" Mrs. Fletcher asks us in a quiet, reflective moment. "We're working harder than ever, we're running all over the city, we're winning all of these awards, we're moving in a hundred different directions, we're buying everything and starting everything, but I feel like we're falling further behind. So what's the answer? What's the missing link?"

* * * * *

Travis served children who live in a high-rise, public housing project. The professional staff knew firsthand about the challenges that their young students face, and, for the most part, they were empathetic. Seeing that many of their children had so little, they tried to get them everything that they could: a plethora of programs, beautiful trade books and materials, fully-stocked labs, computers, the works. The principal was relentless in her pursuit of the most highly regarded programs and masterful at raising money. Moreover, individual teachers from Travis were at virtually every professional conference in the city and beyond. All of the activity and "stuff" in the school impressed the TV reporter, much like a Christmas tree laden with ornaments dazzles a child. Yet all that they tried did not add up to what they wanted for most students—improved academic outcomes. The individual effort of many different teachers and the principal had not come together to produce a collective focus on strengthening the core of the school. Their many diverse efforts remained fragmented and uncoordinated. It was as if the branches of the tree sagged from the weight of all the ornaments, while the trunk was withering and the roots were dry.

Travis presents yet another and different dilemma for Chicago reform. It contrasts with Hynes, which was debilitated by its own lethargy. It is dissimilar from Rhodes, as well, which suffered from what we might call a "crisis of imagination." We see at Travis an energetic staff carving out its own autonomy prior to reform and using the legislation as an opportunity to garner additional resources to do even more. For all of their independence and initiative, however, they seem unable to focus their plans for academic improvement. It is a problematic image. The professional staff is running itself into the ground, and the school seems likely to collapse under the burden of multiple and conflicting projects and initiatives.

The Bella School: Emergent Restructuring

On his first day of eighth grade Maurice wrote in his journal:

> If I want to go to a good high school, I need to listen to my teachers, and stop playing so much so that I can get my work done. . . .It is time for me to stop relying on my parents so much, and show them that I can do it on my own.

Maurice's classmates echoed his statement in their journals. "Last year I worked harder than before," wrote Dijan. "This year I need to keep it up." Yolanda used the occasion to remind herself that in eighth grade, as in seventh, she had to remember to:

> take pride in my work . . . start it when it is assigned . . . do not wait until the last minute . . . ask questions when I need to . . . help other students if I can . . . and try to always do my best.

These upper grade children are participating in a program designed to help them engage in personal writing and to take responsibility for their own learning. The new program is the most recent development started when Mrs. Greeley took over as principal, a year prior to reform. Previously, she had been a first grade teacher at Kerlinger. She told us that when she did her teacher preparation out east eighteen years ago, she read "a lot of the early literacy and process writing stuff . . . [Donald] Graves, [Lucy] Calkins and others, and tried to adapt their ideas to an inner city classroom." She said that her students always loved the extended writing activities that found their way into virtually everything that she did. She had some difficulty with her principal and some of her parents at Kerlinger, though. Every year they complained that she let her young students "get away with" inventive spelling, when they should have been learning to "spell right."

When the Chicago Area Writing Project (CAWP) initiated its work in city schools, Mrs. Greeley made sure that she and several of her colleagues went to some of the first trainings. CAWP, a teacher-led initiative modeled after the Bay Area Writing Project, is designed to encourage student writing and to improve the teaching of writing in elementary schools. Mrs. Greeley enjoyed the initial workshop series so much that she trained to become a teacher leader, just as she was finishing work on her administrative certificate. Shortly thereafter, when a principalship came open at Bella, and Mrs. Greeley got the position, she "felt like she was on a mission." She was going to become one of the system's first "writing principals." When we asked her what that meant, she said that she:

didn't want to waste her time and energy fighting with "the administrator" about the value of inventive spelling and whether young children should have access to trade books and encouragement to write. She wanted to "BE the administrator," and use the principalship like a "bully pulpit" for writing . . .

Mrs. Greeley convinced a colleague from Kerlinger, Mrs. Abel, to seek administrative transfer and come with her. When the two first arrived at Bella, they were viewed with suspicion. Mrs. Abel, who used to team teach with Mrs. Greeley at Kerlinger, said:

No one knew what to make of us. This strange "writing principal" and her trusty side-kick, Abel. It looked like we were out to take over the school. And we were. But eventually they realized that we weren't evil. We were the opposite. Cheerleaders for writing . . . for high standards . . . for best practice. . . .What could be evil about that?

Mrs. Greeley said that, even though they started the writing initiative prior to reform, when the legislation finally passed, it:

was a huge help. It gave me new authority to push my ideas. . . .It certainly helped on the personnel side, because with reform when I had an opening on my faculty, I didn't have to wait and see what dregs the Board sent. Instead, I could beat the bushes—which means call my friends at CAWP— and recruit a good writing person to fill the position. The new money couldn't have come at a better time either. My students are all low income, and achievement here was low. I was lucky too because my school—the building and grounds—weren't in such bad shape, like some of the schools are. So with all the new money that we had, I could pay my teachers to attend trainings. . . .I told them that they'd be paid for their time only if they attended every session. It was blackmail, maybe, or a bribe . . . but so what if it helped ensure good and consistent attendance? I asked Mrs. Abel to run workshops for the teachers back at school sometimes, too, and I paid stipends for these as well. I had discretionary money and I was willing to spend all of it on my teachers if it meant that I was getting them together as a group, to learn some good practice.

Mrs. Greeley said that transforming Bella into a writing school did not happen overnight. In fact, four years into reform, and with five years in the principalship, she said it was still an "uphill fight." She explained that when the writing work began, some teachers were enthusiastic right away, others had a "wait and see" attitude, while a third group seemed—by the way they looked at her—"to dare me to ask them to change." But she pushed forward with her ideas, and, over time and with sustained, focused professional development, her core group expanded. A few of the most recalcitrant teachers "were encouraged to leave."

During her third year at the school, Mrs. Greeley asked Mrs. Abel to take over the leadership of the writing initiative. In essence, Greeley used discretionary funds to create a new position for Mrs. Abel, as instructional supervisor in writing. Her faculty affectionately referred to her as "coach." Abel mentored teachers in their classrooms, encouraged peer observation, facilitated faculty conversations about teaching and learning, and worked with each teacher regarding assessment of students' progress. She said that "at first it was hard" to convince some of the teachers that, even though she was a long time friend and colleague of the principal, she was coming into their rooms "to help them . . . not evaluate or spy." She reported that over time and with some pain, the teachers made progress. They were "not just learning how to teach writing better, but as a professional community that's slowly coming together to talk and learn." She compared the traditional norms of the faculty to that of a group of students which is accustomed to being told to be quiet, orderly and "do your own work." Tell either group to become a "community of learners," and at first, they think its some kind of trick. "But now five years into it, and they're starting to trust us," Mrs. Abel remarked:

> Most important, they're starting to trust each other. They're beginning to value all of the different meeting times that we've scheduled for them to talk about instruction, and they're using that time to zero in on students' work—how to analyze it and promote further progress. One benchmark of their development is the fact that they can talk together about the problems that they're having, and rely on each other's expertise to solve them. I'm not saying there aren't still some bumps in the road, but we've come a long way from the faculty that handed out dittoes and told children to be quiet!

Mrs. Greeley explained that she did not lose interest in the writing initiative when she turned it over to Mrs. Abel. Rather, she was trying to expand instructional leadership in the school, which in turn would allow her to attend more to other needed initiatives. Specifically, she knew that she had to strengthen ties to parents and the local community. She was especially interested in two programs. The first paired students with grandparents and other adults who lived in a nearby senior citizen's home. They were invited to the school to read with children and help them with their homework, and some of the older students were encouraged to make regular visits to the center to visit some of the residents who were homebound. Mrs. Greeley was also interested in helping parents extend the literacy practices that the teachers were emphasizing in school with more supportive activities at home. She offered a stipend to a few teachers who might research these programs and work with the school community representative to get an initiative of this type started.

The principal told us that it was also time to start laying the groundwork for new practice in science and math, but she:

> wasn't going to rush anything. . . .Teachers—just like everybody else—get overwhelmed when things come at them too fast. They feel like they've lost control, and then everything gets confused and disorganized. But if we can pace the professional development right—just like we try to do for the children—then we can ensure that the learning is deep and meaningful and that it will last. . . .Remember those discussions in your teacher education classes about 'depth versus coverage?' I'll vote for depth, every time!

* * * * *

Bella, like the other case-study schools depicted here, serves poor students who are at risk for failure. But that may be where most of the similarities end.

This school seems furthest along the road to a systemic restructuring that will lead to improved academic outcomes for students. Bella got a head start on the process because its physical plant was in good shape, and safety and security were not overwhelming concerns here, as they were in schools like Hynes and Rhodes. Bella's progress can also be attributed to the fact that a new principal, Mrs. Greeley, had a vision for the school and was quite strategic in pushing it forward. Moreover, she had ties to external sources of expertise, and deliberately recruited Mrs. Abel to help with this. The two embarked on an ambitious program of teacher development that brought expert knowledge into the school. Expectations for students' work were raised, and so were the standards for teachers. And teachers and students were no longer left to "sink or swim" in isolation in their classrooms. Rather, there were strong incentives for teachers to work collegially, time was created for them to meet together to reflect upon their practice, and a new moral order fomented a sense of responsibility in teachers to hold themselves accountable for students' learning.

The first priority was improving literacy. The more profound, long-term aim, of course, was to extend teachers' learning into all of the core academic areas. Greeley and Abel knew, however, that if they wanted meaningful change in teaching and learning that they could not hurry the process. Thus, their plan for academic improvement was a slow and evolving one that had to start with a frank appraisal of teachers' practice, and was based on a major infusion of teachers' professional development. Yet it was not by accident that it was developing in a way that was focused, comprehensive, and coordinated. The professional community that was forming around this plan, if sustained, promised to strengthen the academic core of the school.

At the same time, Mrs. Greeley also sought to work with parents, and bring them into partnership with the school. Toward this aim, she attempted to re-create Bella as a community institution that could be sensitive and responsive to the needs of students, families, and the larger community. The work to create viable school-community ties was not as far along as the literacy initiative four years after the start of reform. The vision, nevertheless, was encompassing of a responsible and self-guiding institution that, over time, might anchor and nurture its community.

Types of School Organizational Change

Each of the four cases detailed above identifies a distinctive pattern of organizational change. These patterns vary in both their substantive emphasis and depth of activity. We now turn to a more detailed elaboration of the distinctive features of each type.

Environmental Order

At the start of reform, many schools felt that they had to take greater control of their physical and social environments before they could attend to improving their educational programs. These schools faced severe difficulties associated with poverty, the lack of viable community and school-district resources, and unsafe neighborhoods. They typically attempted to build alliances with alienated parents and community members and to recruit them into the very schools where previously they had felt unwelcome or unwanted.

The condition of schools like Hynes at the start of reform required that basic human needs be met before anything else—including the mandates and goals of reform—could be addressed. Thus, the adults in each of these school communities made a commitment to making their school a safe, child-centered, and caring place—perhaps the only such environment their students and families might know. Principals like Washington banked on the hope that if the school could become a safer and more welcoming environment, with more opportunities for constructive social interaction, then parents might develop a stronger connection to the school and its mission.

The social problems in the surrounding neighborhoods, including family disorder, crime, lack of security, and the social isolation of parent and community members, also necessitated the immediate attention of the full school community. In many schools, ensuring the physical welfare of children, school personnel, and visitors, and the safety of their possessions, was (and still is) a problem of immense proportions. In response, Washington hired security personnel, formed parent patrols, and built networks with the local police and other community groups. While improvement may have occurred at Hynes, security concerns in dangerous neighborhoods remain ever-present.[53]

Another similarity that Hynes shared with many other schools is that it was housed in an old and decrepit building. Thus, improving the physical environment constituted another set of challenges. Inside some schools, leaky roofs, uneven heating, cracked windows, peeling paint, and inadequate plumbing constantly distracted students and staff from academic endeavors. Other schools were so overcrowded that cafeterias and gyms had to be used for classrooms. Although schools spent some of their discretionary monies to alleviate these problems, major changes to the building or grounds required capital improvement funds from the Board of Education. A school community has to make a long-term, concerted effort to attain such funds. Even today, many school communities continue to struggle to provide a decent physical environment.

Some schools—like Alexander and Howard which were described in the previous chapter, and Beacon, which was depicted in the Prologue—also needed to rebuild the basic social order inside their buildings. Over many years, a laissez-faire attitude had become established in these schools. Under reform, local school leaders (often a new principal working with a few key teachers and parents) decided that they wanted the school to operate differently and to relate in new ways to the surrounding community. They established rules to define appropriate and inappropriate behaviors for both students and adults. They enforced "standard operating procedures" for conducting school business, and they clarified the chains of command and the distribution of responsibilities and authority. Just as students had to learn to follow the school's new standards of discipline, teachers and parents had to learn to operate in ways that promoted the desired school climate and order. Undergirding this new social order was the cooperation of the interested parties who set the rules and saw to their enforcement.

In addition to redressing organizational problems, schools also initiated new programs to improve student attendance, promote a more positive affective environment, and enhance motivation for students to learn. Some school communities, for example, sought to augment the social functions of their schools by adopting uniforms, giving attendance incentives, or using discretionary money to offer extended-day sports, music programs and other activities.

Early in reform, improvements in environmental order were the primary focus for many schools in the system. Had we sought to classify Chicago elementary schools in terms of their improvement activities during the first or second year of reform, the vast majority surely would have been in this category. By the end of the first four years, most were engaged in at least some academic initiatives as well. While concern about order and safety remains prominent in many schools, virtually all schools moved into one of the other categories described below. The increasing amount of discretionary funds available as reform progressed played a significant role in this.

Peripheral Academic Changes

Schools of this type were often still working on basic improvements to their physical and social environments, such as increasing school security or student attendance. Significant attention, however, also focused on adding new academic programs. Principals like Meyers at Rhodes used new discretionary funds provided by state Chapter 1 to hire staff and to purchase materials and equipment that they believed would make their schools more like those in affluent communities. The most common of these new supplemental programs were computer labs, science labs, and art and music programs. These schools may have also intensified their remedial efforts with before-school, after-school, and summer school programs. In some cases these were good choices, but in other cases not. For the most part, these "add-ons" did not affect the core instruction provided to most students, nor did they affect the daily work lives of most teachers.

Although these new additions may increase student opportunities, they do little to promote a more coherent educational program. In some cases, they may even exacerbate already existing programmatic fragmentation. In fact, unclear direction in school improvement efforts is a common feature of this type of school. While the principal, faculty and LSC at Rhodes put considerable effort into itemizing school needs, they had little strategic sense of the changes that were needed, and consequently attended little to prioritize activities and sequence them. Rather, Rhodes procured new programs, personnel, and resources in an almost haphazard fashion. Their choices sometimes had more to do with the sophistication of the marketing initiative for the program than with any calculated assessment of what the school really needed. This was certainly the case for the decision to buy computers that resulted from the salesman providing each principal at the luncheon with a completed purchase order.

Moreover, adding new programs tends to deflect attention away from the school's more fundamental academic shortcomings. No effort was made, for example, at Rhodes to integrate the new art and music programs and computer lab with the students' regular classroom instruction. Add-on programs such as these are popular in part because they create a sense of improvement without requiring classroom teachers to modify their routines. They also generate a sense of pride and success because they are readily implemented—space is allocated, equipment and materials are purchased, and one or two new teachers are hired. Responsibility for these new initiatives, then, rests entirely on the shoulders of the new teachers, who tend to act independently of the other staff. Unlike schools attempting systemic change, groups of teachers in schools like Rhodes seldom plan and make improvements together. Thus, teachers' contributions remain fragmented and limited.

"Christmas Tree" Schools

Some schools in Chicago have become well-known showcases because of the myriad of programs that they boast for students, and sometimes for parents as well. The programs range widely in content, purpose, and methods, and they may include a variety of curricular, instructional, social, and technological approaches.

The difference between "Christmas tree" schools, like Travis, and peripheral academic change schools, like Rhodes, is a matter of degree. At Travis, there were many new programs—not just a few—and a great deal of activity and hoopla surrounded them. Some of these new initiatives may have some real strength and integrity. But, because they do not cohere as a group and may even conflict, their impact is minimal at best, and potentially negative.

This is certainly the case at Travis, where professional development in two philosophically opposed reading approaches—whole language and direct instruction—were offered on alternate Saturdays. This competition created problems for the faculty, who could not remember which workshop they were assigned to, nor did they know where they should really focus their attention. Imagine the disruption it creates for students as their schedule gets complicated to accommodate all of these programs. In general, the addition of new programs on top of old ones, without careful evaluation of fit and appropriateness, can result in a disjointed and fragmented set of daily experiences for students. This confusion is compounded year by year as students might go from a phonics-based, direct instruction approach in first grade, to a teacher who embraces whole language instruction in the second grade. Such lack of coordination seems surely counterproductive in terms of student learning.

Another characteristic of these schools was the aggressiveness and entrepreneurship with which the principal sought out new programs. In contrast to Meyers at Rhodes, who was content with the discretionary funds that reform allocated to schools, principals like Fletcher actively pursued additional resources through grants, donations, and in-kind contributions. These principals (and/or their staff) spent a great deal of time writing proposals and developing contacts that would lead to even more programs for the school. Such extraordinary effort is commendable, but it does extract a price. Much of this attention is responsive to new external opportunities, and this leaves less energy for following through on existing activities. Moreover, being a school's ambassador necessitates that the principal spends a lot of time away from the building. This further diminishes the time and energy that is left to focus on local needs.

The pace of life is frenetic in Christmas tree schools. It follows a seemingly endless cycle of soliciting funds, starting new initiatives, and then being distracted by the need to solicit more funds for even newer programs, because the first funding, and the programs it supports, are due to disappear. It is not surprising then that so few of these programs receive the necessary time, attention and commitment to be well implemented. Consequently, few survive beyond their initial funding.

Emergent Restructuring

Undertaking systemic change is a radical departure from the unfocused approach to school improvement illustrated at Rhodes and Travis Schools. At Bella, Mrs. Greeley pushed the faculty to examine their educational program critically and holistically. She asked her staff to question sacred cows (e.g., their own instructional practices) and commit themselves to long-term change efforts. Improving teaching and learning in every classroom became a central concern once Greeley and her colleague came to Bella. Involving parents and members of the community in the literacy program provided further support for the professionals' efforts, and generated a feeling that parents and professionals were embarking on a common mission. The fact that the Bella school community was relatively safe and the building in good shape was an advantage over many other CPS schools. At Bella they could focus on pedagogy right from the start.

In emergent restructuring schools like Bella, concerns about quality arise throughout the school. The quality of teaching practice becomes a primary focus, with principals like Mrs. Greeley and teacher leaders like Mrs. Abel taking an active role. Some reach out to local universities or groups like CAWP for needed staff development. They may move to strengthen overall staff capacities by carefully recruiting good new teachers and encouraging some weaker teachers to leave. In general, the principal of an emergent restructuring school works to cultivate higher quality in teachers, instruction, and programs.

Under the guidance of a teacher leader or principal, school faculties engage together in extended staff development programs. Teachers continue to plan together and collaborate, adapting what they learn to their own classrooms. Some even form support groups or use peer coaching to promote the new practices. Although most teachers did not participate in such collective activities at the start of reform at Bella School, a large and growing number of teachers eventually got involved.

The school community in places like Bella began to form structures to sustain educational improvement. For example, principals recognized teacher leaders' commitment by establishing new roles for them and/or by compensating them financially. They also developed formal committee structures, where teachers evaluated use of resources, such as funding for staff development or the restructuring of teachers' time. Complementing this professional activity, the school also reached out to parents and the local community. Sustained attention focused on strengthening the relationships among all the adults who must work together to improve learning opportunities for children. This is the essential social foundation for broad-based school improvement.

We note that conflicts among teachers may actually increase as these new leaders challenge their colleagues to re-examine established practices. Gradually, however, and with sustained external support, more teachers begin to agree about the direction change should take, which also leads to more comprehensive, coherent improvement. Members of these school communities adopt a school specific view of "what we need to improve." They begin to consider and select innovations that are appropriate for their schools, rather than just buying readily available, popular, or add-on programs. In this way, the schools build toward a shared vision of school improvement and comprehensive change. At these schools, planning and changing go hand in hand.

Recap and Look Ahead

The four school improvement types described above are functionally related to one another. As noted earlier, most schools began reform with a focus on environmental order. Given the troubled nature of many Chicago neighborhoods and the past history of parents' and teachers' interactions with local schools, this is not surprising. This initial emphasis also appears to reflect a more fundamental feature of organizational decentralization. When local units are given some authority to act with regard to their own affairs, they frequently begin by realigning the character of daily life in the organization. Participants feel a strong need to create a new social order that is more sensible to them. This might mean changing basic work routines, articulating new standards of behavior, and certainly addressing concerns about safety. Responding to the basic personal and social needs of participants is an important first step in taking control of the work environment and assuming responsibility for the organization's effectiveness. Without such efforts, participants may remain deeply troubled by the organizational life, and their personal commitment, as a result, may be limited.

Maintaining environmental order is an enduring concern, but all of the case-study synthesis schools eventually shifted priority toward academic improvements. The major distinction among these initiatives is between schools pursuing unfocused academic initiatives (peripheral changes and Christmas Tree schools), and those pursuing systemic approaches to school restructuring (emergent restructuring). The distinction among schools with unfocused initiatives is one of degree and duration. Christmas tree schools were pursuing more add-on programs, and often better ones, than were schools undertaking peripheral academic changes. But neither group was striving for the deeper organizational changes that are the aims of the emergent restructuring schools.

Like the political types developed in Chapter 2, the organizational change types should also be interpreted carefully. Some schools show characteristics of more than one type, and over time schools may not only develop (i.e. move toward systemic restructuring), but can also regress. Moreover, organizational changes interact with the political activity occurring in a school. The sudden loss, for example, of a dynamic principal, who is leading change in his or her building, can derail an emergent restructuring initiative. Similarly, the election of a new LSC can promote radical changes that undermine previous developments. Nevertheless, for the larger descriptive and analytic purposes of this book, these types are informative in describing the organizational activity in schools.

Prevalence of Organizational Change Types

The case-study synthesis documented that a variety of approaches to organizational change were being pursued in Chicago elementary schools. The focus and quality of these efforts varied considerably. Schools differed in how they engaged their parents and the local community, in the scope of the connections that they forged to outside expertise, and in the ways in which this outside assistance was integrated into school life. These cases also documented changes in the character of the basic working relationships among the professional staff, in the depth of teachers' commitments to changing their classroom practices, and in the breadth of participation and seriousness of attention to the school improvement planning and implementation processes.

We identified as part of our analysis one particularly promising form of organizational change, which we labeled emergent restructuring. Schools in this group were taking a systemic approach to school improvement. They focused on strengthening connections with parents and the local community. At the same time, there was also sustained attention to restructuring faculty work and renorming the professional culture toward a learning organization, where professionals share a commitment to student development. There was a shared sense that the status quo had to change and concerted efforts to advance a more coherent vision of their school.

Paralleling the school governance analysis presented in Chapter 2, we now turn our attention to estimating the prevalence of the different types of organizational change occurring within the school system. In particular, we focus attention on distinguishing schools where systemic restructuring appears to be emerging from those that are pursuing more unfocused initiatives.[54] Using the extensive data from the Consortium's surveys of teachers and principals, we developed five indicator clusters that differentiate these two broad improvement approaches. Taken together, these indicator clusters provide the basis for estimating the prevalence of the two different approaches to organizational change and for examining how they are distributed across schools.

Salient Features of Organizational Change

A number of characteristics distinguish the emergent restructuring occurring at schools like Bella from the more incremental, unfocused approaches observed at Rhodes and even Travis. Integrating the field observations from the case-study synthesis with the findings from past research on urban school change reviewed in the opening of this chapter, we identified five salient features that distinguish schools pursuing systemic change from those engaged in more marginal approaches.[55]

Engagement of Parents and Community Resources. Schools pursuing a systemic agenda have a "client orientation."[56] They maintain a sustained focus on strengthening the involvement of parents with the school and their children's schooling. They also actively seek to strengthen the ties with the local community and especially those resources that bear on the caring of children. As these personal interactions expand and become institutionalized in the life of the school, the quality of the relationships between local professionals and their community changes. Greater trust and mutual engagement begins to characterize these encounters. In contrast, schools with unfocused initiatives may set more distinct boundaries between themselves and their neighborhoods. Extant problems in these relationships may not be directly addressed. The broader community resources that could assist improvement efforts in the school are not tapped. These schools remain more isolated from their students' parents and their communities.

Access to New Ideas. For a school to restructure and renorm, a process of organizational learning must occur.[57] New ideas must enter the school about core matters such as curriculum, instruction, and school organization. This introduction of proposed innovations often comes through personal connections of school staff to local colleges, universities, or other educational enterprises. It may be a natural consequence as new faculty are hired and bring with them new ideas to the school. In most general terms, the restructuring school is open to its external environment, actively seeking out and trying new ideas about how it might work differently. In contrast, schools with unfocused initiatives are more passive in this regard. They are less likely to actively seek out new information and more likely to just draw on whatever happens to cross their paths. Faculties in these schools remain more isolated and tend to repeat traditional practices.[58]

Professional Community. In addition to new ideas entering a school, mechanisms must exist by which these ideas are discussed and eventually become collectively held. In schools making systemic changes, structures are established which create opportunities for such interactions to occur. As teachers develop a broader say in school decision making, they may also begin to experiment with new roles, including working collaboratively. This restructuring of teachers' work signifies a broadening professional community where teachers feel more comfortable exchanging ideas, and where a collective sense of responsibility for student development is likely to emerge. These characteristics of systemic restructuring contrast with conventional school practice where teachers work more autonomously, and there may be little meaningful professional exchange among co-workers. In the absence of a sense of colleagueship, innovative practices remain isolated in individual classrooms, and true collegial activities such as peer evaluation or coaching are limited.[59]

Internalizing Responsibility for Change. There was a key difference between the professional staffs at Bella and Rhodes schools; at Bella, there was a publicly expressed sense among the professional faculty that "business as usual" could not continue.[60] When staff internalize responsibility for students' failure to learn, they are more likely to focus attention on the need to change their own practices and to sustain efforts toward this end. Alternatively, as noted in the introduction to this chapter, teachers can also reconcile chronic student failure through a "golden age myth" that explains current problems in terms of the changes in the community, families, or the students themselves. In these situations, where teachers externalize responsibility for students' failure, they are less likely to feel a sense of urgency about initiating change. Beginning and sustaining the difficult and uncertain work of school restructuring is much harder under such circumstances.

Strategic Educational Planning. Schools undertaking systemic change place a strong emphasis on the improvement planning process. While principals may take a lead role in developing these improvement efforts, there is broad participation across the school community in discussing these ideas and adapting them to local needs. As teachers devote time and energy to identifying possible improvements, they also develop an investment in their success. This contrasts with schools, such as Rhodes and Travis, where principals are still making most of these decisions on their own. The choices among possible improvement efforts appear more happenstance in these schools, and the rationales used resemble the descriptions of "garbage can decision making models" noted earlier. There is often little attention to integrating these new activities with existing operations. More likely, they are one more new innovation layered on top of current practices.

Specific Indicators

As in Chapter 2, we created a cluster of indicators for each of the five key features of organizational change identified above. Each indicator cluster consists of between three to five specific indicators. Many of these specific indicators, in turn, are composites of multiple survey items. The Appendix presents details about the construction of each individual indicator and the five composite clusters. Basic descriptions of each are summarized below.

Engagement of Parents and Community Resources. This cluster consists of four specific indicators that tap the density of communication between the school and local community, the presence of both formal and informal mechanisms to promote this communication, and the quality of the relationships that occur. (See Figure 3.1.) The first measure indicates the presence of extensive communication among LSC, community members, and teachers. Schools with a high value on this indicator are places where frequent interactions are occurring between professional staff, parents, and the local community. Much attention focuses on improving the quality of communication around the interests of the students. The second specific indicator, extensive ties to the neighborhood, measures the extent of formal connections and internal structures in a school to access community resources. Included here may be a wide range of resources such as social services, adult education programs, and recreational activities. Within the school, this indicator assesses the presence of formal programs for the coordination of social services to support children and their families. The third indicator, increased parent communication, is based on teacher reports that informal communication with parents and opportunities for parents to participate in the life of the school

FIGURE 3.1
Indicators of School Organizational Change

Engagement of parents and community resources
- ❖ Extensive communication among LSC, community members, and teachers
- ❖ Extensive ties to the neighborhood
- ❖ Increased parent communication
- ❖ A sense of trust

Access to new ideas
- ❖ Regular contacts with external educational organizations
- ❖ Teachers' participation in professional development
- ❖ Hiring new faculty

Professional community
- ❖ Principal endorses participatory management
- ❖ Restructured and extended teacher roles
- ❖ Collegiality among the faculty
- ❖ High teacher commitment
- ❖ A shared sense of school mission among faculty

Internalizing responsibility for change
- ❖ Teachers report that students are capable of learning
- ❖ Teachers refuse to explain student failure in terms of bad attitudes and habits
- ❖ Reform has affected classroom practices
- ❖ Instructional practices will change due to SIP

Strategic educational planning
- ❖ Broad participation in SIP development
- ❖ Much attention to effective implementation of the SIP
- ❖ Increased faculty time commitment

Source: The Principals' Perspective, survey of principals in Chicago Public Schools, 1992; *The Teachers' Turn*, 1991, survey of elementary school teachers.

have increased since reform. The fourth and final indicator in this cluster focuses on teachers' reports about the sense of trust conveyed by parents about teachers' judgments on school matters. Schools that are high on this indicator appear to have established positive, mutual relationships with their parent communities, in which there is frequent interaction and discussion.

Access to New Ideas. A learning organization must have extensive ties to external sources of knowledge and expertise. Three specific indicators focus on this aspect of organizational change. The first indicator, regular contacts with external educational organizations, focuses on institutional ties. It assesses the frequency of school contacts with universities, educational advocacy groups, professional educational organizations, and other external sources of professional knowledge. The second indicator focuses on individual staff activity. A high level of teacher participation in professional development means that many teachers in the school voluntarily participate in workshops and subject matter networks and take graduate courses. The third, hiring new faculty, measures yet another mechanism by which new ideas enter a school—through new staff. This indicator is based on the percentage of the faculty who have been hired since reform.

Professional Community. [61] Five indicators measure the emergence of professional community at a school. The first indicator, principal endorses participatory management, marks the degree of leadership support for teacher involvement in shared decision making. The next indicator focuses on internal structural change toward teacher engagement. A school with a high value on restructured and extended teacher roles indicates that the faculty are now involved in collaborative activities such as peer mentoring and curriculum planning. The last three indicators in this cluster highlight the extent of professional renorming among the faculty. Collegiality among the faculty means that teachers feel supported and encouraged by their colleagues and work cooperatively with each other. In schools with high teacher commitment, principals report that most of the faculty display a strong sense of responsibility for student learning. This commitment extends to a willingness to try new approaches to instruction and engage in a continual learning process. Finally, in a true professional community, faculty share a sense of school mission. In such a context, teachers are much more likely to agree with each other about the basic purposes of the school.

Internalizing Responsibility for Change. The four indicators that comprise this cluster are all based on responses from the teacher survey. The first two assess teachers' attitudes about student learning and their responsibility for improving it. A high value on teachers' reporting that students are capable of learning implies that most teachers in the school believe that students can master the material which they are trying to teach. In a closely related vein, the indicator, teachers refuse to explain student failure in terms of bad attitudes and habits, identifies a school faculty that rejects this rationalization for poor achievement. The last two indicators in this cluster focus on teachers' classroom behavior. Reform has affected classroom practices identifies schools where many teachers report that they have already made changes in instruction since reform began. Instructional practices will change due to the SIP reveals teachers' expectations about the future. A high value on this indicator means that the faculty envisions that more instructional change lies ahead.

Strategic Educational Planning. Three indicators measure the breadth of commitment to developing and implementing educational improvements at a school. Schoolwide participation in SIP development measures the extent to which different school constituencies were involved in forming the local School Improvement Plan. Attention to effective implementation of the SIP is based on staff reports of the relevance of the SIP to school activity. A high value here means that teachers believe that the SIP actually describes what is happening at their school and that this document is frequently referenced to guide local efforts. Finally, increased faculty time commitment indicates that a broad base of faculty are willing to spend more time on endeavors to press this agenda forward, including communicating with parents and individualized work with students, as well as additional time working with other teachers and the principal.

Examining the Validity of the Organizational Change Indicators

Prior to using these indicator clusters to assess the prevalence of systemic organizational change, we first scrutinize their validity. We begin by considering each specific indicator. Then we examine the overall validity of the five cluster scores. Our analysis follows the same basic procedures used in Chapter 2. We compare both the specific indicators and the cluster scores against independent ratings of the thirty-six schools on which extensive field observations were recorded. Included here is information from twenty-two case-study synthesis schools and a supplemental sample of fourteen schools that were extensively observed by others. If the individual organizational change indicators are valid, they should differentiate between the emergent restructuring schools, identified on the basis of field observations, and those pursuing less focused approaches. In addition, the school type designations, assigned by the indicator system, should closely resemble those made independently by the field researchers.

Validity of the Individual Indicators

Field researchers classified fifteen of the thirty-six schools as pursuing unfocused initiatives and twenty-one as emergent restructuring. To examine the discriminating power of the individual indicators, we computed separate box plots on each indicator for these two groups of schools. Figure 3.2 on pages 135-137 displays the box plots for the unfocused schools on the left and the systemic restructuring schools on the right. As in Chapter 2, the top of the "box" again marks the 75th percentile for that group, and the bottom marks the 25th percentile. The dashed horizontal line within the box is the median score. The "whiskers" extending up and down from the box indicate how the more extreme scores trail off. The scale on the left hand side of each plot has been "standardized" for most indicators in order to make the displays for the different indicators comparable to each other.[63] In the access to new ideas cluster, the indicators were left in their natural metric of counts and percentages.

It is important to recall that the distribution for any individual indicator may overlap for the two groups of schools. Each indicator is fallible and at best marks a tendency toward systemic restructuring (and away from an unfocused approach). Not every school with a systemic approach to organizational change will necessarily receive a high score on every indicator. Similarly, schools with unfocused approaches will not always get low scores. The basic distributions, however, should be consistent. That is, we expect the group of schools identified as emergent restructuring by the field researchers to have a higher distribution of scores than the group of schools identified as unfocused.

Engagement of Parents and Community Resources. As expected, the schools identified as emergent restructuring by field observers tend to score higher on each of the four indicators included in this cluster. (See Figure 3.2.) In the case of increased parent communication, for example, there is very little overlap in indicator scores for the two groups. The 75th percentile for unfocused schools falls among the bottom quartile for the systemic restructuring schools. Clearly, the two groups of case-study schools are markedly different in this respect.

On balance, the differences between the two school groups are not always as dramatic. There is more overlap, for example, on the indicator of extensive ties to community. Even here, however, the 25th percentile of the systemic restructuring schools is higher than the median in the unfocused group. Although the observed differences are not as large, nonetheless, the basic direction of the relationship is highly consistent. Both formal programs and informal mechanisms for improving community ties are much more likely to be reported in systemic restructuring schools.

In general, the pattern of results across the four indicators supports our contention that the survey data capture important aspects of what the field researchers observed.

Access to New Ideas. As expected, the schools with systemic approaches to restructuring report more contact with external educational groups, more personnel changes and more professional development. The box plot distributions for systemic schools are consistently higher than for the unfocused schools on all of the individual indicators in this cluster. These differences are particularly large for hiring new faculty and for contacts with external educational organizations. In the average unfocused school, only 15 percent of the teachers had been hired since reform, whereas in the systemic schools about 20 percent had been hired since reform with a large proportion reporting more than 30 percent. Similarly, the typical unfocused school reported about one contact per month with an outside educational agency. The typical systemic school, in contrast, reported three per month. In the most active systemic schools (i.e. the top quartile) there is at least weekly contact. These schools appear to have established sustained relationships with external sources of knowledge and expertise.

Professional Community. The case-study schools with a systemic approach to school restructuring have consistently higher score distributions on the five indicators of professional community than do the unfocused schools. In systemic schools, we are much more likely to find that the principal endorses participatory management, and that this leadership orientation is manifest throughout the whole school. In such circumstances, for example, principals indicate much higher levels of teacher commitment: The boxes for the two groups do not even overlap! Principals also reported much more movement toward restructured teachers' roles. Here too, the boxes for the distributions in the unfocused and systemic case study schools do not overlap. This means that the weakest systemic schools (i.e. lowest quartile within this group) resemble the most positive of the unfocused schools (i.e. the upper quartile for this group). In general, the systemic and unfocused schools have very different data patterns on the indicators of professional community. The survey data clearly discriminate between these two groups on this organizational feature.

Internalizing Responsibility for Change. Schools with systemic approaches to restructuring also differ from schools with unfocused approaches in the extent to which teachers have internalized a sense of responsibility for student learning and are changing their classroom practices to promote this improvement. Here too some of these differences are quite large. For example, on the behavioral indicator where teachers report that teaching practices will change due to the SIP, the bottom quarter of systemic restructuring schools are comparable to the typical unfocused schools. Similar large attitudinal differences appear on teachers' beliefs that students are capable of learning. Although the differences are somewhat smaller for the remaining two indicators, the

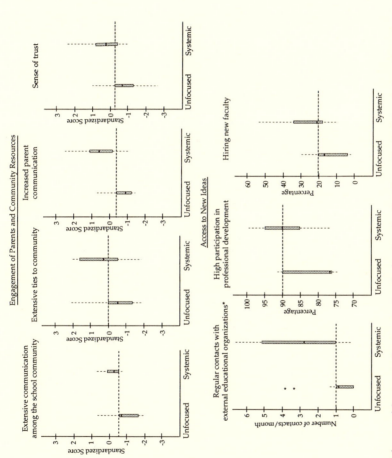

FIGURE 3.2 Incidence of Systemic Restructuring Indicators in the Case-Study Schools (continues)
*The asterisks denote two outlying cases among unfocused schools. These two sites had much higher reports about external contacts than all other schools in this group.

136

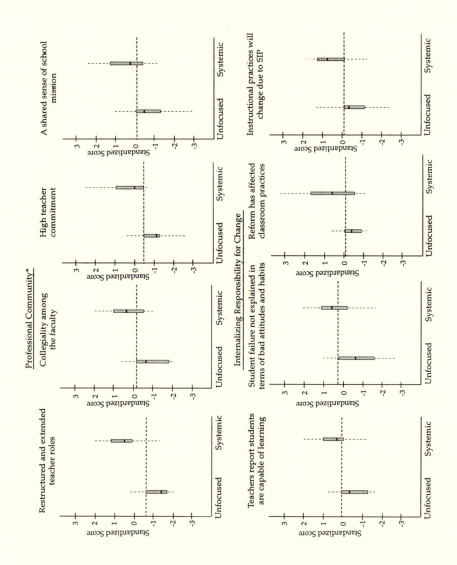

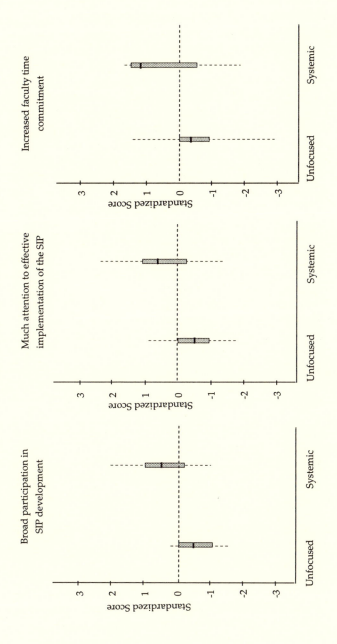

FIGURE 3.2 Incidence of Systemic Restructuring Indicators in the Case-Study Schools

*The indicator, "Principal feels participatory management will remain" is a categorical variable based on a single item from the principal survey. For unfocused schools, 60 percent agree; for systemic schools, 88 percent.

overall pattern is similar. In general, the teacher survey reports demark a very different pattern of attitudes and behavior toward instructional change in the case-study schools which field workers identified as engaged in systemic restructuring.

Strategic Educational Planning. The final cluster contains three indicators of involvement, commitment, and participation in planning. The case-study synthesis found higher levels of these activities in the systemic restructuring schools than in schools with unfocused approaches to organizational change. The survey indicators corroborate this finding. For example, the reports from the typical systemic restructuring school on broad participation in SIP development are comparable to or exceed those found in the very best of the unfocused schools. In schools with active restructuring efforts, the LSC and PPAC are more likely to be involved in the development of improvement plans, and the resulting plans are much less likely to be viewed as primarily the principal's initiative. Along with this, teachers in systemic restructuring schools report that attention is much more likely to focus on effective implementation of the SIP, and there is increased faculty time commitment to these efforts.

Validity of the Overall Indicator System

Composite Indicators. As noted earlier, a school with a systemic approach to organizational change will not necessarily show "positive" on all of our individual indicators. Nor will an unfocused school come up "negative" on every aspect of its change activities. Each of the nineteen individual indicators provides a piece of information suggesting whether a school has an unfocused or a systemic approach to organizational change. A single indicator alone cannot say much about the complexities of change and school improvement. By aggregating across a series of indicators within each cluster, however, and then eventually across the five clusters, we uncover the general signal conveyed by these data.

As in Chapter 2, a uniform method for scoring the information in the nineteen different indicators was developed. "Cut points" for each individual indicator signify whether a characteristic is present or absent in a school. Since all except one of the indicators is continuous, we used the box plots previously displayed in Figure 3.2 to help us in this regard. More specifically, we mark a school as "positive" on an indicator when it scores above the 75th percentile for the unfocused schools. (Cut points are denoted in Figure 3.2 by the dashed lines.) This method insures that a school scoring positive on an indicator is unlikely to be engaged in an unfocused organizational approach. Consequently, by inference, it is much more likely that the school is undertaking a systemic approach.

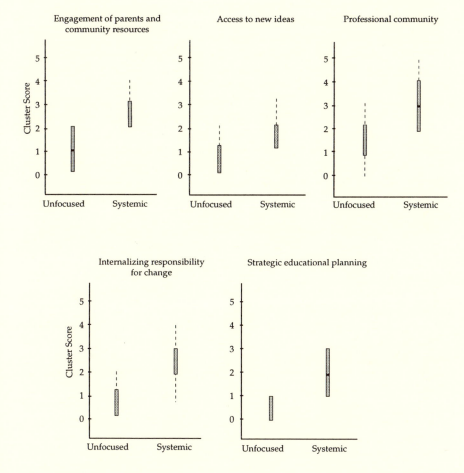

FIGURE 3.3 Indicator Cluster Scores for the Case-Study Schools

The composite score for each of the five salient features of school restructuring is, as in the previous chapter, a simple count of the number of individual indicators within a particular cluster that were scored positive for a school. Thus, the values of the composite scores imply the extent to which a school can be characterized as having each of the salient features. The differences between case study schools pursuing an unfocused approach and schools adopting a systemic organizational change approach are displayed in Figure 3.3.

The box plots reveal significant differences across each indicator cluster. The distributions between unfocused and systemic schools, in fact, do not overlap extensively for any cluster. For example, in the cluster on engagement of parents and community resources, none of the unfocused schools have a score over two. In contrast, the lowest score for a systemic school is two. One quarter of these schools scored the maximum possible value of four for this cluster. This scenario holds true for the other four clusters as well. Systemic schools show evidence of internalizing responsibility for change, an openness to new ideas, and an emerging professional community among the faculty. In addition, these schools are more likely to be engaged in strategic educational planning.

Comparison with the Case-Study Classifications. As a final test of the validity of the indicator clusters, we examined whether the five composite indicators allow us to correctly classify the type of organizational change occurring in the case-study schools. If the classifications made on the basis of the statistical data closely reproduce the independent judgments made by field observers, we would have a great deal of confidence that the indicator system is providing valid information about the organizational changes occurring across the Chicago Public Schools.

Again, as in Chapter 2, we deployed a discriminant analysis to test this classification validity. Using the five cluster indicators to distinguish unfocused change from emergent restructuring, we were able to correctly identify 91 percent of the schools. Out of the twenty-two case study schools with complete indicator data, the discriminant analysis only misclassified two cases. (See Table 3.1.) These results represent a very high standard of reliability in the classification of schools based on these measures.

Prevalence Estimates

The discriminant analysis, which was used to validate the overall system of organizational change indicators, also provides a function of the five composite indicator measures (based on the relationships that exist in the case-study sample), that can be used to classify any other school for which we have indicator data. Specifically, the discriminant function allows us to compute the probability that a school is either unfocused or

TABLE 3.1 Case-Study Schools Classified into Organizational
Change Types by Field Workers Compared to Discriminant Analysis Results[a]

	Classified by Field Workers	
	Unfocused Improvement Approach	Systemic Restructuring Approach
Classified by Discriminant Analysis		
Unfocused Improvement Approach	8	1
Systemic Restructuring Approach	1	12

[a] This analysis is based on the 22 elementary schools that participated
in both the principal and teacher surveys.
   Source: The Teachers Turn, survey of elementary schools teachers,
1991; *The Principals' Perspective,* survey of principals in Chicago Public
Schools, 1992; case studies of 36 elementary schools; administrative
records, Chicago Public Schools.

emergent restructuring.[63] Following the same procedures developed in
Chapter 2, we use these predicted probabilities to develop range estimates
for the prevalence of the two major approaches to school improvement.
Again, we chose a .90 probability to establish a lower bound estimate for
the percentage of schools in a type, and a probability of .75 for creating an
upper bound estimate. Combining the results from these two alternatives
provides a reasonable range of the percentage of schools in each category.
The "true" percentage is likely to be somewhere between the upper bound
and lower bound estimates. Schools with mixed results (i.e., high on some
of the salient features and low on others) were placed into a third category
of "showing signs of both approaches." Again, an estimated range is provided.
   It is important to remember that this analysis focuses only on the 86
percent of the Chicago elementary schools that were significantly below national norms prior to reform. Consequently, the percentages
reported below refer to schools that were in greatest need of making
substantial changes.
   Applying the discriminant function to all of our indicator data, we
estimate that between 31 and 39 percent of all CPS elementary schools

TABLE 3.2 Prevalence of Organizational Change Types

	Percent of Elementary Schools	
	Lower Estimate	Upper Estimate
Unfocused Improvement Approach	31	39
Some Features of Both Approaches	20	35
Systemic Restructuring Approach	35	41

Sources: *The Teachers' Turn,* survey of elementary school teachers, 1991; *The Principals' Perspective,* survey of principals in Chicago Public Schools, 1992; case studies of 42 elementary schools in Chicago; administrative records of the Chicago Public Schools.

followed an unfocused school improvement approach during the first four years of reform. (See Table 3.2.) In comparison, between 35 and 41 percent of elementary schools showed characteristics of systemic improvement efforts. The remaining schools, between 20 and 35 percent, showed some features of both approaches. This is not at all surprising considering the realities of change and improvement. Schools may begin to move toward systemic change and perhaps suffer a setback. Or a sub-group of teachers may work together, but their efforts do not broadly affect the whole school. In general, a systemic approach to school improvement requires time, commitment, and energy from both teachers and principals—even during its emergent stages.

Distribution of Organizational Change Types Across the City

Both unfocused and systemic restructuring initiatives can be found in a diverse array of schools, without much regard for where they are located or the types of students they enrolled. The map in Figure 3.4 demonstrates that systemic organizational changes are widely distributed around the city. In general, the opportunities provided by PA 85-1418 for school restructuring have been quite equitably distributed among schools within the system. A few differences across schools are worth noting, however.

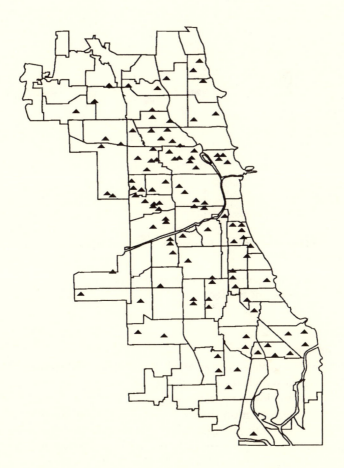

FIGURE 3.4 Schools with a Systemic Restructuring Approach

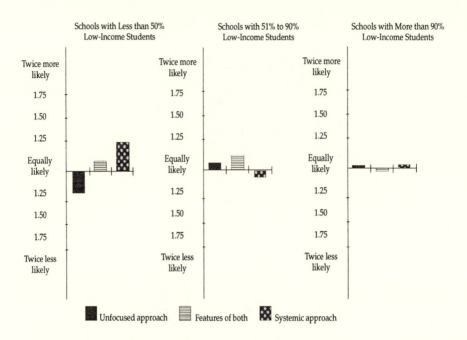

FIGURE 3.5 School Organizational Change by Percentage of
           Low-Income Students

Low-Income Composition

As in the school governance analysis, these relationships are not strong, though the trends which do emerge are not surprising. (See Figure 3.5.) The schools with the lowest percentages of low-income students (less than 50 percent) are slightly more likely to be pursuing a systemic approach and less likely to fall into the unfocused category. Although the additional community and parental resources in these schools do appear to provide some support for the systemic approach, they certainly do not assure such an outcome. As for the most impoverished schools (with greater than 90 percent low-income students), the three categories of organizational change are about equally likely.

Racial Composition

As with low-income composition, the association between a school's racial and ethnic composition and its organizational approach is not strong. (See Figure 3.6.) Hispanic schools are less likely to fall into the "features of both" category and slightly more likely to be pursuing a

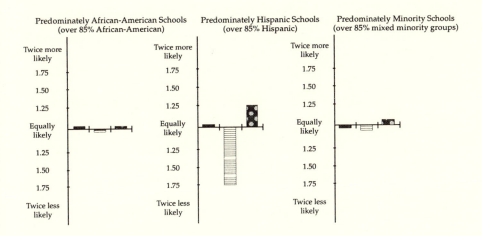

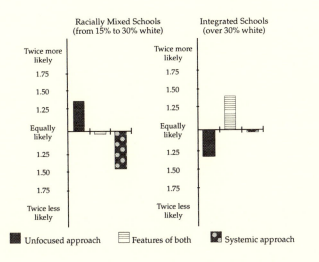

FIGURE 3.6 School Organizational Change by School Racial Composition

systemic approach. Again, we find some evidence of a favorable set of reform outcomes in predominately Hispanic schools. In contrast, racially mixed schools are more likely to be unfocused and not pursuing a systemic organizational approach. Since these schools are also more likely to have adversarial politics, as seen in Chapter 2, we have further evidence that schools with a diverse racial composition have a somewhat less favorable set of reform outcomes.

School Size

Small elementary schools (those with fewer than 350 students) are 1.50 times more likely to be pursuing a systemic approach to improvement than all other schools (see Figure 3.7.) They are also 1.20 times less likely to pursue an unfocused approach and more than two times less likely to fall into the mixed category. Thus, we have some evidence that smaller schools size can facilitate positive organizational change. As previously noted in the discussion of school politics, a smaller school size tends to facilitate personal interactions and informal communications. Both enhanced collegiality among teachers and broader engagement with par-

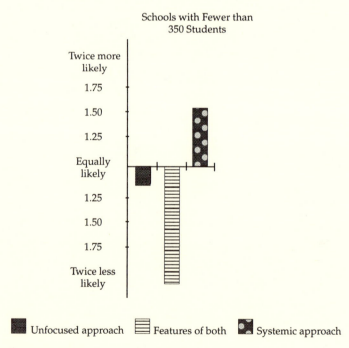

FIGURE 3.7 School Organizational Change in Small Schools

ents are easier to attain. Since these are two major facets of systemic school restructuring, the patterns of results is not surprising. We caution, however, that small size only acts as a facilitating factor in this regard. That is, when adults seriously want to promote better working relationships with each other, they are more likely to be successful in a smaller social network. On the other hand, a small school can be just as negative a social environment as a large school, when adults do not share a sense of purpose and commitment to each other.

* * * * *

The architects of the 1988 reform legislation banked on the ability of local actors to promote fundamental changes in their schools. The evidence in this chapter suggests that, during the first four years, many elementary schools across the city worked on such changes. Of highest priority were issues of environmental order, and most schools seized the opportunity to improve safety and the condition of their buildings. Most elementary schools also moved beyond this to initiate some deeper organizational changes. In some cases, their efforts were haphazard: adding a computer lab, an art program, or teaching a new language, for example, without addressing improvements in the core academic program. But in about 40 percent of the schools, there was evidence of a more systemic approach to school improvement. In these schools, there was a serious and inclusive schoolwide planning process; new ideas flowed into the school; the faculty was beginning to form as a professional community; and relationships were repaired and strengthened between the professionals in the school and parents and the local community. Considering the stubbornness of social problems in American cities and the disappointing history of attempts to reform urban schools, this is heartening news. It points to a relatively large group of schools that were, in fact, beginning to live out the reform in ways that were consistent with the legislation.

4

Instructional Change

The previous two chapters have documented that the first four years of Chicago's school reform catalyzed a remarkable level of new activity in many school communities. A dysfunctional status quo was challenged, and a broadly shared commitment to restructure core operations emerged in its place. An expanded base of teachers, parents, and community members became involved in local school affairs. Their efforts were in turn supported by an inclusive and facilitative school leadership.

While these developments are impressive, they are nonetheless of limited value, unless they eventually connect to improved instruction and enhanced student learning. The Bella School in Chapter 3 offers specific testimony that this was happening in at least some places during the first phase of Chicago school reform. This chapter turns attention to the critical question, "Is there any evidence that the local school governance and organizational change stimulated by PA 85-1418 effected a transformation of instruction on a broad scale?"

What Students Should Know and Be Able to Do

Just as Chicago launched its reform, the national debate about the aims of education was beginning to shift. During the late 1970s, considerable attention focused on effective schools programs. These efforts emphasized principal leadership, clear goals, high expectations for students, an orderly environment, frequent monitoring of student progress, and parental involvement. Although this movement embraced the mantra of high expectations for all students, it largely defined these expectations in terms of improved levels of basic skills.[1]

Accompanying this were media accounts that regularly highlighted disappointing results in annual reports of student test scores. Concerns mounted, particularly in cities, regarding the high proportion of students who were dropping out of school before graduation. These concerns were further buttressed by international comparisons showing that the academic attainment of American students lagged even behind children in some developing countries.[2]

By the latter part of the 1980s, however, the content of these conversations about student achievement had shifted dramatically. Reformers were now speaking about preparing a work force for the twenty-first century, where use of advanced knowledge and more complex intellectual activity would be commonplace.[3] The implications for our public school systems were extraordinary. Reformers now proclaimed as a universal aim the kind of education which just a few years earlier had been deemed necessary only for our social elite. This truly marked a historic moment, a major turning point, in American education.[4]

The current movement seeks to engage all students in more challenging intellectual activity. Educators want students not only to acquire information, but to be able to use it and manipulate it in complex thinking and problem solving.[5] Such expanded academic aims for children in turn have major pedagogic consequences. Teaching as telling, knowledge as the accumulation of facts and discrete skills, and learning as recall give way to a more activist vision of student learning.[6] Many observers have documented that students spend most of their time in traditional classrooms learning bits of superficial information about a broad set of topics, but they rarely have an opportunity to delve deeply into a particular subject. Such practices foster mechanistic routines where students are passive receptors and invest little interest or engagement in learning.[7] In contrast, it is now argued that there should be less emphasis on topic coverage and much more time devoted to immersion in subject matter. Indeed, a hallmark of this reform philosophy is that "less is more."[8]

In large part, this concern for challenging intellectual work for all students is rooted in the distinctive context of an emerging post-industrial economy. In the past, it was sufficient for most students to attend school for a few years to learn to read and speak standard English and acquire basic computation skills. The economy simply did not demand more cognitive skills from most workers. A higher level of education was not necessary to obtain jobs that afforded a comfortable middle-class lifestyle.[9] These conditions, however, have changed dramatically in the past two decades. High school graduation is no longer a ticket to success. In fact, male high school graduates' real income has declined substantially since 1973. As our economy has shifted from manufacturing to service industries and high technology enterprises, well-paying jobs now demand more accomplished, educated workers than they have in the past.[10]

Much as the advent of the industrial revolution brought massive changes to public education, the emergence of a post-industrial economy now places new demands on schools. Employers increasingly lament that many of their new employees cannot master technical knowledge, solve problems, and work independently to carry out non-routine tasks. It is argued that, in order to prepare students better for the present and future workplace, schools must demand higher standards of performance from all.

These major societal changes have also provoked a re-examination of long standing concerns about how best to advance educational equity. Arguments for more rigorous academic standards have typically been viewed with considerable skepticism by equity critics. Serious concerns were raised, for example, during the mid-1980s about increased high school course standards. It was feared that such standards would further disadvantage poor and minority students by making it harder for them to complete school successfully. Research on the actual effects of increasing these standards, however, found no evidence of this. In fact, some recent studies have documented that disadvantaged students actually benefit from more demanding academic course work.[11] It is argued now that real equity can only be achieved *through* excellence.[12] Only if schools better prepare all students for participation in an increasingly complex, technological society will at-risk students be able to hold a place in the American mainstream.[13]

Complementing these economic arguments are recurring political and social concerns about preparing students for meaningful participation in a democratic society. Schools must teach intellectual skills and social habits that build citizens' capacity to communicate openly with one another, respectfully resolve differences, and engage in collective action on the pressing problems that affect our common lives.[14] As the nature of public affairs has become more complex and diverse, this too has "raised the bar" for public education. At base here is an argument, which dates back to the founding fathers, of the strong and direct link between education and democracy.[15] People are not natural-born citizens; rather they need to be educated to assume this role. From this perspective, much more attention needs to be given to fostering civic literacy—to developing the basic skills and dispositions needed by all citizens to engage in critical thinking about public problems and to maintain civil public debate about how these problems might best be resolved in a pluralist society. The very survival of our society, in fact, depends on the ability of our schools to advance this social practice.[16]

From this perspective, current concerns about developing students' capacities to think critically and to construct knowledge are not new. They have been at the center of the progressive education movement for almost a century. Dewey, for example, argued strongly that students' interests provide clues to their "dawning capacities," and meaningful educational activity builds on these interests. Organizing instruction in this way helps to develop and shape students' own powers. "Education must be conceived as a continuing reconstruction of experience..."[17]

Likewise the Woods Hole Conference, which was convened after the launching of Sputnik, gave a strong boost to inquiry. Scholars who attended the conference shunned the emphasis on rote learning which characterized most school classrooms and called instead for learning activities that inspire students to make use of their own intuition, to follow their hunches, and to modify their understandings on the basis of experience. Learning through discovery would lead students to a deeper understanding of what they studied, as well as an appreciation of the interconnectedness of knowledge.[18]

Although past embraces of progressive ideals have cycled back and forth, the current movement does not appear to be just another swing of this pendulum.[19] Given the arguments raised above about fundamental shifts in the nature of our economy, a major transformation of our educational system seems inevitable. Specifically, without a broad commitment to more rigorous intellectual work for all students, both economic success and societal welfare are at great risk.

For these reasons, we concluded that an analysis of the educational impact of PA 85-1418 had to consider whether it was promoting the kinds of deep educational changes that are increasingly demanded of our school systems. Unless urban school reforms prepare poor and disadvantaged students to compete on an equal footing in a post-industrial economy, rather than being relegated in mass to low-paying service sector jobs, these reforms will be judged a failure.

On balance, it is important to acknowledge that some educators have expressed concern about the efficacy of progressive teaching practices for poor and minority students. Since such students comprise the overwhelming majority in school systems such as Chicago, these argument have particular salience. These educators point out that poor and minority students often come to school with a weaker background in basic skills than middle-class students do. African-American students, for example, may have fluency in particular language forms but lack skills in the generally accepted, standard forms of communication. Hence, these critics caution that too much emphasis on progressive teaching practices may detract from mastery of the core skills on which more advanced education in turn depends. In this regard, these critics specifically point out that past attempts at progressive reform in urban schools have not especially helped disadvantaged children.[20]

It is important to recognize that the issue is not, as it is often framed, one of basic skills versus more complex cognitive activity. Obviously, students need to develop both capacities. From a pedagogic perspective, this means that teachers need to work with students on intellectually engaging tasks while at the same time helping them develop written and oral communication and other basic skills. As Lisa Delpit has argued, "[if] minority people are to effect the change which will allow them to truly progress, we must insist on skills *within the context of* critical and creative thinking."[21] Consequently, the challenge for urban schools is to adopt an agenda for instructional improvement that affords challenging intellectual work for all students while at the same time assuring that basic skill acquisition occurs.

Although the rationale for challenging academic work for all students seems clear, how to achieve this on a broad scale in ordinary urban schools is much less so. Past experiences indicate that such developments will not happen quickly and that accomplishing this will demand profound changes in most classrooms—in who teaches there, what they do, and how their work is supported. Thus, in evaluating the initiating phase of Chicago school reform, we sought to examine whether the basic infrastructure was being transformed in ways that would promote deep instructional improvements over the longer term. We already considered in Chapter 3 the professional work conditions for teachers. Here, we focus on two other critical facets of the technical core of instruction. First, schooling is a human resource-intensive enterprise. Its effectiveness is directly linked to the quality of its teacher. Thus, we examine efforts to improve teacher capacity.[22] Second, the productivity of a school faculty depends on the merits of the instructional ideas and materials with which they work. In this regard, we enquire whether what are now generally regarded as the most promising instructional innovations were finding their way into Chicago schools.

Strengthening the Human Resources of Schools

Massive attention to human resource development is required in urban schools, both to strengthen basic skills instruction and to promote more challenging academic work for all students. Teachers will have to unlearn comfortable beliefs and practices, acquire a much deeper understanding of subject matter content, alter their views of how student learning best occurs, and ultimately modify their classroom practices to foster more active participation by students.[23]

Achieving these kinds of changes in teaching will not come easily. Historically, educational improvements, such as the curriculum reforms of the 1950s and programs for disadvantaged children like Title I and Head Start, did not provide the necessary support so that teachers could effectively implement them.[24] Even under reasonably good conditions (which most urban schools do not enjoy) the evidence is sobering regarding the time, effort, and support that are needed to truly develop "teaching for understanding."[25]

Three basic mechanisms are available for improving the knowledge, skills, and competence of teachers. First, a faculty can be re-shaped through recruitment of new, more capable members. Under Chicago's school reform, principals gained considerable authority to hire teachers. Whereas before they had to fill vacancies with whomever the central office sent, as Mac did at Beacon, principals now can recruit teachers of their own choice without regard to seniority considerations. In the hands of a savvy school leader, this can be a powerful device for building a stronger faculty.

Second, sustained professional development activities over time can alter the basic knowledge, skills, and dispositions of teachers and promote movement toward a school-based professional community, as discussed in Chapter 3. Through professional education activities, teachers gain access to new ideas and have opportunities to work with colleagues, both inside and outside of school, on cooperative endeavors to improve instruction.

Third, non-performing teachers can be removed. This can be accomplished through informal means, such as counseling out those teachers who are resistant to change or whose approaches are not in sync with the emerging vision for the school. Sometimes this is simply a matter of a principal being more visible in hallways and classrooms, making his or her concerns known. At other times, principals may need to become more deliberate: for example, giving a problematic teacher an undesirable assignment or an inferior room. In very concrete ways such as this, a principal can convey a message that "perhaps you would be happier somewhere else."

Principals may also initiate the formal process for teacher removal. Streamlined somewhat under PA 85-1418, these procedures call for a remediation period of forty-five days (down from 180) before a teacher can be dismissed for incompetence. During this time, a teacher receives extensive mentoring and support to try to improve his or her teaching performance. The teacher is allowed to stay only if adequate improvement occurs. Carrying these procedures through is a time consuming process that requires a great deal of documentation and often ends unsuccessfully. For these reasons, principals generally turn to this only as a last resort.

We now consider how these three basic mechanisms for faculty improvement were utilized by Chicago schools during the first phase of reform. For this purpose, we return to some of the data previously considered in Chapter 3 pertaining to schools' access to new ideas. We then explore in more depth the patterns of human resource development under reform and some of the issues affecting this. We also examine the equity with which these developments occurred across different kinds of school communities.

Recruiting New Teachers

Most principals reported that PA 85-1418 brought significant change in this area. Almost 70 percent agreed that school reform brought them much more autonomy in selecting teachers than they had in the past. Of all the changes engendered by reform, principals gave the most positive ratings to this one.[26]

Moreover, this increased local discretion over faculty hiring was accompanied by a considerable upturn in faculty openings. Table 4.1 reveals that, during the first two years of reform, 29 percent of the principals hired enough new teachers to make up 11-20 percent of their faculty. Another 29 percent hired 21-30 percent of their faculty, and more than 35 percent hired more than 30 percent of their faculty. Although we do not know all of the reasons for these extensive faculty changes,[27] it is clear that principals were

TABLE 4.1 Proportion of Faculty Hired Between 1989-1991

Percent of Faculty Hired Between 1989-1991	Percent of Elementary Schools
1 - 10	5
11 - 20	29
21 - 20	29
31 - 40	22
41+	15

Source: The Teachers' Turn, 1991, survey of elementary school teachers in Chicago Public Schools.

able to recruit significant numbers of new teachers of their own choosing. In some instances, as elaborated in Chapter 6, this led to dramatically re-shaping an entire school faculty.

Staff Development

Like teachers in many urban school systems, most Chicago teachers are veterans. Table 4.2 shows years of experience of Chicago teachers in 1991. More than half the teachers had sixteen or more years of experience, while only 12 percent were at the beginning of their career, with four years or less experience.

In our 1991 survey, we asked teachers how long they planned to remain in teaching. Table 4.3 shows these results, organized by age group. While older teachers indicate they would remain active for fewer years, the majority of teachers in each age category planned to work for six or more years. Among the 31-40 group, more than half planned to continue for sixteen or more years. Teachers in their 40s and 50s also intended to remain in teaching for many years, with more than half of each group estimating six to fifteen years.

TABLE 4.2 Length of Experience of Chicago Teachers

Years Teaching	Percent
1 or less	4
2 to 4	8
5 to 11	17
11 to 15	16
16 or more	56

Source: The Teachers' Turn, 1991, survey of elementary school teachers in Chicago Public Schools.

TABLE 4.3 Plans to Remain in Teaching for Predominant Age Groups

	Percent of Chicago Teachers	Percent Planning to Remain in Teaching		
		2-5 Years	6-15 Years	16+ Years
Age Group				
31 - 40	24	13	30	54
41 - 50	41	8	54	36
51 - 60	21	35	55	6

Source: The Teachers' Turn, 1991, survey of elementary school teachers in Chicago Public Schools.

In short, the Chicago teaching force is primarily a middle-aged to older group of individuals with considerable experience, most of whom plan to continue working for many more years. Considering these circumstances, the professional development of existing staff must be a primary mechanism for strengthening teachers' knowledge and skills. Improved pre-service education, while critical for new teachers, will affect only a small, albeit growing, percentage of the work force during the next several years.

For these reasons, it seemed important to take a closer look at the actual nature of staff development in Chicago schools. We know that most teachers are involved at least minimally each year in some kind of staff development. For instance, in the 1991 teacher survey, 87 percent of the teachers reported that they had participated in at least one professional development activity during the previous year. Specifically, 62 percent attended workshops or courses sponsored by the Chicago Public Schools; 55 percent participated in workshops or courses sponsored by professional organizations; and 44 percent took courses at colleges and universities. (The percentages exceed 100 because some teachers took advantage of more than one program.) Similarly, in the 1992 principal survey, two-thirds of the principals stated that they had active professional development programs in their schools and that teachers were involved in planning these programs. (See Figure 4.1.)

Nonetheless, our data also suggest that these professional education experiences remain too infrequent or peripheral to have a broad impact on student learning. For example, only 15 percent of the principals thought that adequate time was devoted to staff development, and only 10 percent felt they had enough time for teacher evaluation. Evidence from the case-study synthesis corroborated these results. In one of the schools, for example, not a single member of the faculty had taken a course at a local college or university during the previous ten years. Staff development at the school consisted solely of the two in-service days mandated by the district each year.[28]

A school's ties to outside groups afford another avenue for access to new information and ideas. In Chicago, such organizations include universities, professional organizations, a federally funded educational laboratory, the state board of education, a federally funded math and science center, and many others. These organizations bring expertise, materials, professional development opportunities, research results, and instructional resources that can strengthen classroom teaching.

To determine the extent to which schools were developing such institutional relationships, we asked principals to name organizations with which their school had regular, ongoing contact. These organizations were then

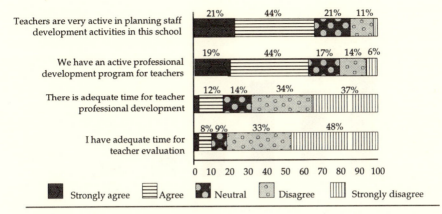

FIGURE 4.1 Staff Development Efforts

Source: The Principal's Perspective, survey of principals in Chicago Public Schools, 1992.

categorized according to whether they were educational, recreational, law enforcement, religious, cultural, etc. Their responses are summarized in Figure 4.2. It is significant that one-third of the principals did not list any educational organizations, and another 23 percent said their school had fairly infrequent contact—as little as once a month—with such groups. At the other end of the spectrum, 9 percent of the schools had almost daily contact or more with some external educational group.

Removing Non-Performing Teachers

Although the reform law contained a provision designed to streamline the process of dismissing non-performing teachers, principal survey results indicate that the 1988 reform largely failed on this account. As of 1992, almost three-quarters of Chicago principals remained dissatisfied with these procedures. Even under the new law, removing teachers continued to be quite difficult.

On balance, it is important to recognize that principals generally did not want to remove large numbers of teachers. For example, the principal survey indicated that 60 percent of the principals wanted to remove 10 percent or less of their faculty; only 9 percent reported they wanted to see 20 percent or more of the faculty leave. Moreover, evidence from the experiences of actively restructuring schools, detailed in Chapter 6, suggests that at least some principals were quite effective in using more informal means to encourage teachers to leave. A principal's visibility around the school,

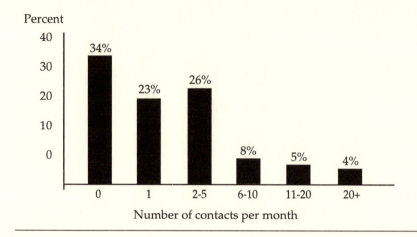

FIGURE 4.2 Contacts with External Educational Organizations

Source: The Principal's Perspective, survey of principals in Chicago Public Schools, 1992.

the formation of schoolwide planning committees, the school improvement planning process, and the emerging vision of the school made it all too obvious to some teachers that they could no longer continue working as usual. Unfortunately, we do not have precise systemwide statistics on the incidence of such "counseling out" of teachers.

Equity Considerations

A major concern throughout this book has been how reform efforts differentially affected the many different types of elementary school communities in Chicago. We have seen in previous chapters that expanded local participation and constructive organizational changes took place across a broad cross-section of communities and student populations. Now we examine the relative prevalence of human resource development across the city. A parallel analysis on the adoption of instructional innovations follows in the next section.

To examine the equity of human resource development, we created three indicators based on the data discussed above. (See Figure 4.3.) The first indicator, *hiring new faculty*, is the proportion of the school's faculty hired since reform. The data are taken from teachers' responses to the 1991 survey regarding the number of years they had worked at the school. Teachers who indicated they had spent two or fewer years at the school were counted as new hires. The second indicator, *active staff development*, is based

---

FIGURE 4.3
Indicators of Human Resource Development

Hiring new faculty
❖ The proportion of the faculty that were
hired between 1989 and 1992

Active staff development
❖ Principal says teachers are very active in planning
staff development
❖ Principal says the school has an active professional
development
❖ Principal says there is adequate time for teacher
professional development

Regular contacts with external
educational organizations
❖ Schools have 3 or more contacts a month with an external
educational organization

Source: The Teachers' Turn, 1991, survey of elementary schools teachers in
Chicago Public Schools; *The Principals' Perspective,* survey of principals in
Chicago Public Schools, 1992.

on principals' responses to the following questions about their school:
"teachers are very active in planning staff development;" "the school has
an active professional development program;" and "there is adequate time
for teacher professional development." In the analyses that follow, a school
is classified as having *active staff development* if the principal agreed with
all these statements. *Regular contacts with external educational organizations*
is the third indicator. It is measured by the frequency of contacts schools
have with such organizations. Three or more contacts a month with an
external educational organization is considered regular contact.

Figure 4.4 compares schools serving students with varying levels of family income on these three indicators. In general, *hiring new faculty* and *regular contacts with external educational organizations* are equitably distributed among schools with different income compositions. Staff development opportunities, in contrast, were somewhat more likely in schools with fewer low-income students by a factor of 1.5. Schools with between 50 and 90 percent low income students were least likely to engage in staff development, and schools with the highest proportion of low-income students were about average.

Shifting attention to the racial composition of schools, the only distinct pattern to emerge was for *active staff development*. (See Figure 4.5.) African-American schools were more likely to have *active staff development*, and predominately minority, racially mixed, and integrated schools were less likely to have it. Racial composition of the schools appeared to make little difference in *hiring new faculty*. *External educational contacts* were slightly more prevalent in predominately minority and racially mixed schools.

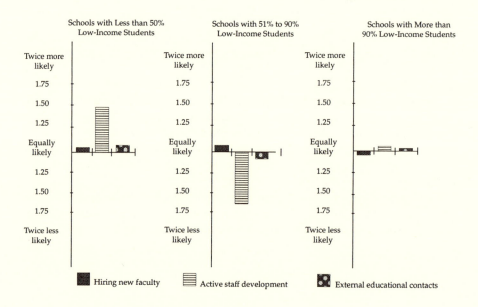

FIGURE 4.4 Human Resource Development Opportunities by
Percentage of Low-Income Students

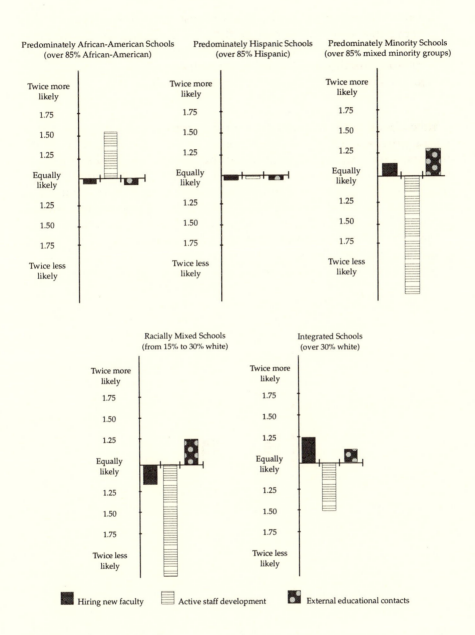

FIGURE 4.5 Human Resource Development Opportunities by
Racial Composition

We also compared the prevalence of these indicators across schools of varying size and found no large differences. *Hiring new faculty* and *contacts with external educational organizations* were somewhat more likely among small schools, and *active staff development* somewhat less likely. (See Figure 4.6.)

* * * * *

Taken in total, four years into reform, some progress had been made in strengthening the human resources in schools. On the positive side, principals were actively using the authority granted under reform to hire teachers of their own choosing. This resulted in substantial changes in many schools. Most principals also indicated that their schools had active staff development programs, but it appears that neither enough time nor resources were set aside for this at this point. Similarly, although principals were able to remove some teachers primarily through informal means, dealing with non-performing teachers continued to be a serious problem. When viewed relative to practices before reform,

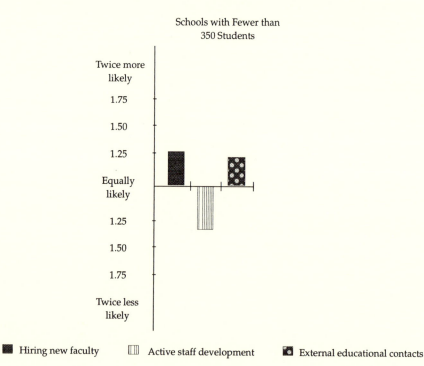

FIGURE 4.6 Human Resource Development Opportunities in Small Schools

as depicted in the Prologue at Beacon School, these developments represent a significant accomplishment. Relative to the heightened academic aspirations articulated at the beginning of this chapter, however, they appear more mixed. Clearly, much more needed to be done.

Adopting Instructional Innovations

In examining the evidence for changes in teaching, we also directed attention to materials and techniques which teachers were using, and, more generally, to the ideas about instruction that were guiding them. Was there any evidence that large numbers of Chicago teachers were departing from past practices that placed primary emphasis on a rote learning of basic skills, and were they beginning to provide opportunities for all students to engage in more challenging intellectual activity? These are perhaps the most critical questions to ask about the first phase of reform. Bringing new teachers into a school is unlikely to alter the nature of the learning opportunities afforded children if these teachers continue to teach in the same old ways. Given the traditional and parochial character of the Chicago school system noted in the Prologue, there was some reason to worry whether any new educational practices would take root. Moreover, since there was little direct provision in PA 85-1418 to advance such initiatives, developments would have to spontaneously arise from the decision-making process in individual school communities as they planned their own improvement efforts and allocated their discretionary resources. At the most basic level, we considered the question, "Would schools focus attention on major instructional improvements?"

Introduction of "Best Practices"

A series of questions in the principals' survey asked about the adoption of a variety of new instructional practices in schools. Included here were hands-on math, hands-on science, cooperative learning, writing across the curriculum, and literature-based reading. Interest in these activities grew in the late 1980s just as Chicago's reform was beginning.[29] The extent to which teachers were incorporating these practices in their classrooms provides evidence about the openness of school faculties to new ideas. Table 4.4 displays the results.

In general, principals reported considerable exposure of students to these practices. In about two-thirds of the schools, principals indicated that at least half the students were engaged in these activities. The only exception was cooperative learning, which was a bit less prevalent, with only 52 percent of the principals reporting the involvement of half or more of their students.

TABLE 4.4 Prevalence of "Best" Practices

	Percent of Principals reporting that half or more of the students were involved[a]
Hands-on Math	68
Hands-on-Science	63
Cooperative Learning	52
Writing Across the Curriculum	69
Literature-Based Reading	70

[a]Principals were asked whether "almost all," "about half," or "less than half" of the students in their school were exposed to these practices. This table combines responses for "almost all" and "about half."

Source: The Principal's Perspective, survey of principals in Chicago Public Schools, 1992.

An Emphasis on Authentic Instruction

Each of the practices considered above constitutes a major reorientation of school curriculum. Each seeks to change the opportunities afforded students to engage in more challenging intellectual work. Each creates tasks that require students to analyze and manipulate ideas and combine them in order to explain events, justify a conclusion, or offer an interpretation.[30] As a group, they encourage students to delve more deeply into a particular topic or discipline, and to engage in extended conversations with peers and their teachers about the central ideas under study. They also promote a social climate that emphasizes mutual respect in the classroom, and where students help each other and work cooperatively together on shared tasks. All of this stands in marked contrast to more traditional instruction, which emphasizes coverage of a wide range of topics where students receive pre-packaged bits of knowledge, but where little opportunity is provided for sustained, active student inquiry.

We also included in our principal surveys a number of questions that sought to examine the nature of teachers' pedagogic practices and whether strategies aimed at more authentic instruction were making their way into classrooms. Table 4.5 summarizes these results.

TABLE 4.5 Restructuring Classroom Teaching

Classroom Activity	Percent of Schools
Students use computer technology extensively	77
Use of small group work in classrooms	71
Academic disciplines integrated in the curriculum	61
Learning tasks aim for depth rather than broad exposure	58
Students have access to and serve as peer tutors	61
Assessment that emphasizes student production rather than reproduction of knowledge	55
Learning emphasizes "multiple intelligences,"	51
Students involved in planning, conduct, and evaluation of their work	16

Source: The Principals' Perspective, survey of principals in Chicago Public Schools, 1992.

Four years into school reform, small group work was reported as a regular practice in almost three-quarters of the city's elementary schools. Extensive use of computer technology was also commonplace. About half the principals reported attention to integrating academic disciplines in the curriculum, learning tasks that aim for depth rather than broad coverage, peer tutoring, instructional activities that are sensitive to "multiple intelligences" and multiple cultures, and assessment methods that stimulate student production of knowledge rather than reproduction. The only practice which principals said was not widespread was the involvement of students in planning and evaluating their work.

These responses suggest that teaching practices designed to promote authentic learning for students were emerging across a wide spectrum of schools. On balance, it is important to keep in mind that these results are based on principal reports.[31] Absent direct classroom observations, it is difficult to know how intensively any new instructional development was actually being pursued in a school, or how well the envisioned changes were being implemented. Nonetheless, these reports do show, at a minimum, that instructional innovations were at least making their way into many Chicago schools. While an individual report about a particular practice might be misleading, these data in aggregate provide a useful indicator of the extent to which school communities addressed issues of instructional innovation during the first four years of reform.

Even though PA 85-1418 contained no direct provisions mandating specific instructional improvements, and there was little leadership from the central office pushing in this direction,[32] considerable local attention did focus here.

Equity Considerations

To gauge the prevalence of instructional innovations in different kinds of schools, we created two indicators based on the data discussed above. (See Figure 4.7.) *Adoption of best practices* is based on the principal's reports of the exposure of students to the instructional practices discussed earlier. Broad adoption is defined as exposure of half or more of the students in a school to four of the five best practices: hands-on math, hands-on science, writing across the curriculum, cooperative learning, and literature-based reading instruction.[33]

The next indicator reflects an *emphasis on authentic instruction*. A strong emphasis is defined as adoption of all the practices shown in Table 4.5 (page 167), except the involvement of students in planning their work. In such schools, principals reported that there was deep engagement of students in subject matter, students are active participants in the learning process, and assessment methods emphasize student production rather than reproduction of knowledge.

FIGURE 4.7
Indicators of Instructional Innovations

Adoption of best practices

❖   Half or more of the students are exposed to 4 of the 5 best
    practices: hands-on math, hands-on science, writing across the
    curriculum, cooperativelearning, and literature-based
    reading instruction

Emphasis on authentic instruction
❖   Principals report that there is deep engagement of students in
    subject matter, students are active participants in the learning
    process, and assessment methods emphasize student production
    rather than reproduction of knowledge

Source: The Principals' Perspective, survey of principals in Chicago Public Schools, 1992.

Figure 4.8 compares schools serving students with varying levels of family income on these two indicators. In general, the *adoption of best practices* was equitably distributed among schools with different income compositions. An *emphasis on authentic instruction* was a little less likely to occur in more advantaged schools (i.e., with less than 50 percent low income students).

Turning to the racial and ethnic composition of schools, predominately African-American, Hispanic, predominately minority, and integrated schools show very similar patterns on these two indicators (see Figure 4.9). Racially mixed schools, however, were less likely than other types of schools to indicate *adoption of best practices* and an *emphasis on authentic instruction*. Earlier we reported that racially mixed schools, as well as predominately minority schools, were also less likely to offer opportunities for staff development.

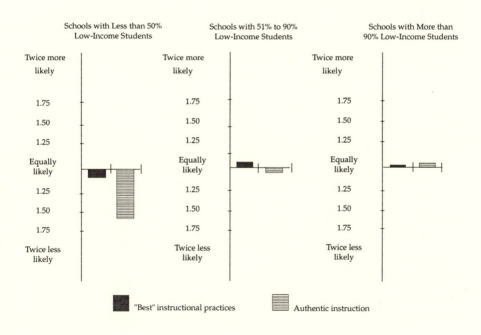

FIGURE 4.8 Adoption of Instructional Innovations by Percentage of
Low-Income Students

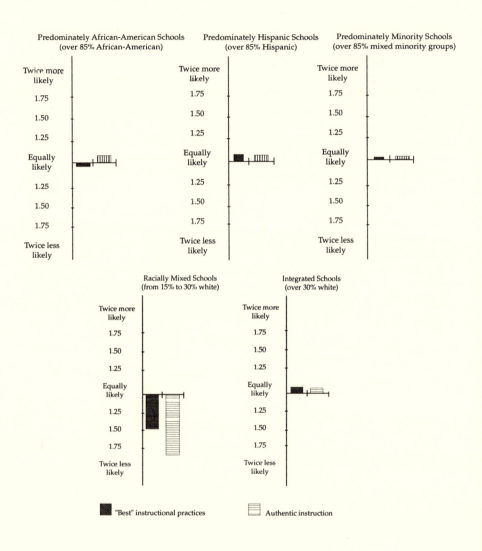

FIGURE 4.9 Adoption of Instructional Innovations by School
        Racial Composition

It is worth noting that in Chapter 2 we reported that racially mixed and predominately minority schools were more likely to experience adversarial politics. We also learned in Chapter 3 that an unfocused approach to change was more commonplace in racially mixed schools. Thus, the reports on staff development and the adoption of instructional innovations are consistent with the previous equity findings. Taken together, we have a considerable body of evidence, all pointing in the same direction. Racial and ethnic heterogeneity in the membership of a school community can impede productive work on improvement efforts. Each division along a racial or ethnic line affords an occasion for misunderstandings to arise that can promote conflict, which, in turn, may undermine the collective efforts necessary to sustain school change, including improved teaching practice. To be sure, some racially mixed communities in Chicago have successfully managed these concerns. Others, however, have not.

We also compared the prevalence of these indicators across schools of varying size. Authentic instructional practices were a little less likely to occur in small schools, but differences were minimal. Figure 4.10 displays the results.

In sum, although we found some differences, the overall pattern reflects considerable equity in the distribution of instructional innovations. Productive changes were occurring in schools located throughout the city, including those in some of the most disadvantaged neighborhoods.

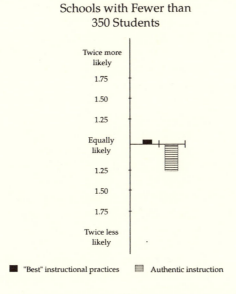

FIGURE 4.10 Adoption of Instructional Innovations in Small Schools

Observations of Classroom Instruction

The indicator analyses helped us to assess the prevalence of efforts to strengthen the teaching force and introduce instructional innovations across different kinds of Chicago elementary schools. They do not, however, offer much descriptive detail about actual classroom life. For this purpose, we turn to the third strand in our overall research plan, the in-depth examination of the experiences of six actively restructuring schools (EARS).[34]

A key aim of the EARS study was to explore efforts to improve instruction among schools that were aggressively taking advantage of the opportunities provided by reform to initiate local change. Although these six schools were not necessarily the "best cases" in the entire CPS, each school had developed a reputation for innovation during the first four years of reform. By all extant accounts, reform was working in these places. Thus, an examination of these schools helped us to ascertain the state of classroom practice four years into reform, the kinds of progress that could be made under reasonably good circumstances, and the impediments to improvement that still remained. In the latter regard, it was safe to assume that any common problems encountered across these six sites were likely to be characteristic of many other schools in the system.

Specifically, we examined the nature of classroom instruction in each of the six schools, how each site was approaching staff development and teaching improvement, and the concerns and frustrations that were confronted along the way. We observed language arts and mathematics classes in grades one and three and mathematics and social studies in grades six and eight. We also interviewed the principals and Local School Council chairs, and a broad cross-section of teachers, students, and other school staff. In terms of the classroom observations, we looked for explicit evidence of teaching practices designed to promote more challenging intellectual work for students.

In general, observers encountered students actively involved in learning in about three quarters of the fifty classrooms visited in the six schools. These classrooms were comfortable places where teachers had established open and supportive relationships with their students. For the most part, teachers treated students with a great deal of respect, understanding, and appreciation. We frequently saw teachers listening closely to students, praising their good work, and urging them to do their best.

Classroom activities were often quite spirited. For example, in a first-grade mathematics lesson, we observed a teacher introducing the concepts of ones and tens. She held up bundles of ten sticks and single sticks and had the students practice counting by tens and ones. Students had ample opportunities to manipulate the sticks, and they waved them about eagerly as they sought to provide answers to the teacher's questions. By the end of the lesson, every student had participated. Another first-grade class was just as enthusiastic about identifying geometric shapes, which they had cut out of construction paper, pointing out the distinctive features of each and matching the various shapes to their definitions.

Not surprisingly, given the wide variation in grades and subject matters observed, we found substantial differences in the kinds of classroom activities occurring. Some activities were specifically designed to be responsive to students' specific linguistic background and culture; others sought to expand beyond this to advance a multicultural perspective. Hands-on activity frequently occurred in all of the EARS schools, and many teachers organized students into cooperative learning groups at least some of the time. In this regard, our classroom observations validated the principal survey reports of best practices (described above) that were used to form the indicators for the prevalence and equity analyses.

By far, the most common activity was teacher-directed, didactic instruction occasionally mixed with more innovative methods. Teachers had established routines that introduced students to new subject matter in an orderly manner. Classroom management was generally not a problem. In most instances, the teacher had only to remind a few students of the task or the rules for behavior, and such reminders consumed only a small portion of classroom time. Generally, in EARS classrooms there was a healthy mix of structure, rules, social support, and acceptance.

To provide more context for these generalizations, we offer below brief narratives from four classes we visited. They run the gamut from innovative instruction aimed at challenging students to think for themselves, to more traditional teacher-dominated practice, to a classroom characterized by disorder and disrespect.

Connections to Students' Lives: Mrs. Stephenson's Reading Lesson
Mrs. Stephenson's classroom was a vibrant and animated place.[35] All of the walls and bulletin boards were filled with colorful posters of news events, festivals, African-American leaders, the Mexican flag, and pictures of George Washington and Abraham Lincoln. Lots of trade books, as well as dictionaries and other formal instructional materials, lined the shelves on either side of the room. Students sat in five rows of five facing Mrs. Stephenson's desk at the front of the room. The class we observed was a "walking reading group." This meant that students from three third-grade classrooms who were reading at about the same level came together each day for their lesson.

Judy Stephenson had been teaching at this school for twenty years. She liked the school because she felt free to be creative and felt very supported in her work with the children. People "trust me to do what I do best," she reported. Stephenson was acutely aware of students' cultural backgrounds, and she was concerned that the small group of Hispanic students in this school had opportunities to affirm their cultural heritage just as the majority group of African-American students did. She found it fulfilling to be a part of the fabric of these children's lives. She loved her job and said she would not want to work anyplace else.

Mrs. Stephenson began the lesson by posing a series of questions about a story the children had just read, "Angel Child—Dragon Child." The main character was a Vietnamese girl named Ut who immigrated to the United States with her grandmother. At first, Mrs. Stephenson asked factual questions, which the students answered quickly. When they were unsure, she encouraged them to read back over the story to find the appropriate reference. She also asked them to look up unfamiliar words in a dictionary. New concepts such as *will, bankruptcy,* and *inheritance* were written on the board, and students copied them into their notebooks.

It soon became clear to the students, however, that Mrs. Stephenson wanted much more from them than just brief factual answers. She probed, "What is a will and why does one need one?" When one little boy gave an explanation, Mrs. Stephenson asked, "How did you learn this?" "My grandfather died and left a will," he replied. Mrs. Stephenson offered an affirming comment in return, "Peter is only in third grade, and he already knows about wills." As they moved through the discussion, the students continued to offer examples of how something in their own personal or family background related to the story.

Mrs. Stephenson also wanted students to reflect on the key themes of the story. She prodded, "How do children feel when they first come to this school?" Should we laugh at people who dress differently, or speak a different language than we do, or have very little money?" Finally, she asked, "Why do you think the author chose this title for the story?" One student offered an interpretation: "She was an angel child when she cried and a dragon child when she was brave." Another found evidence of the title in the text: "'I stood and bowed like an angel child,'" he said. During this discussion more than fifteen of the twenty-five students took turns answering questions, often relating their answers to some personal experience. Throughout the fast-paced lesson, Mrs. Stephenson sustained a vigorous classroom conversation about the core themes of the story while at the same time checking students' comprehension of the basic story facts and reinforcing new vocabulary and concepts.

* * * * *

Mrs. Stephenson's class was one of the better ones we visited. Even thirty-five minutes into the lesson, no student had broken attention for longer than a few minutes, and that was usually to talk to a neighbor about a home situation similar to the one under discussion. The overwhelming majority maintained attention and participated actively for the whole period. Efforts to engage significant student thinking were evident throughout the lesson. Mrs. Stephenson encouraged students to reflect on the meaning of the story and the motives and feelings of its major characters. Substantive conversation dominated the classroom as students discussed with the teacher, and each other, the situations in the story and how these related to their own personal experiences. At the same time, there was also clear attention to skill development: in this instance, new vocabulary words and use of the dictionary. Social support for learning was also manifest in the give-and-take of discussion. The core content of this lesson, in fact, focused on students' social development—the importance of tolerance and building an empathetic understanding of others who are different from ourselves. Simultaneously, students worked at building their language skills, developing an appreciation of multiple cultures, and recognizing the connections between the written word and experiences in their own lives. Throughout the class, the teacher modeled how learning takes place—through critical reading, research, listening, and informed discussion.

A Mixed Attempt at Authentic Instruction: Mrs. Turnbull's Third Grade Reading Lesson

Unlike the traditional arrangements of desks in Mrs. Stephenson's room, Mrs. Turnbull's classroom was specifically organized for student interaction. All of the desks, including hers, faced each other in a large circle near the middle of the room. An open area at the front of the class was set aside for large-group work. It was here that the entire class gathered to read and discuss a new book, "Sam, Bangs, and Moonshine."

The previous day, students had learned about the author. They read that she was a mischievous child, much like Sam, the main character of the book. In the story, Sam was portrayed as an imaginative young girl who often invented new tales for her young and gullible friend, Thomas. She spun stories about her mother being a mermaid and about a magic carpet in her room that turned into a chariot pulled by dragons. Her favorite "story," though, was about her pet kangaroo that always seemed to have just "stepped out" whenever Thomas came to visit. Sam sent Thomas on many adventures looking for her kangaroo—to the old lighthouse, to the windmill, and finally to an isolated beach.

This lesson began with enthusiastic volunteers from the class raising their hands for an opportunity to read aloud to the whole group. Several children took turns reading, and, as the story unfolded, Mrs. Turnbull interjected questions. Some were factual, intended to establish the plot; but she also asked about the author's purpose for writing, and probed about characters' personalities and the motives for their actions. Although the questions were relevant and thoughtful, the students had difficulty sustaining meaningful discussion. For example, Ms. Turnbull asked why Sam "invented stories." One student suggested that she was seeking attention. Another offered the opinion that she was simply lying about events. There was some agreement from other students: "Yeah, she's just lying." There was not a deliberate effort by the teacher, however, to help students sort through competing explanations, either in terms of the facts of the story or what might have been the author's intentions. While students were actively conversing, their discussion did not often move to the level of analysis or evaluation.

Mrs. Turnbull shifted the discussion to ask students to compare the characters in "Sam, Bangs, and Moonshine" with other characters that they had read about in previous stories. One student suggested that Sam was like the "boy who cried wolf." Several other suggestions of links to past readings ensued, one after another. However, again, students did not explore their suggestions in any depth. Follow-up questions such as: "How were these comparable?" or "Can you explain that more fully?" were not often used by Mrs. Turnbull. The students' nominations of characters became just a list of names.

At several points during this large group session, Mrs. Turnbull interrupted the flow of reading to ask particular students to be quiet or to pay closer attention. Several were directed to leave the large group and return to their seats. Ultimately, these disruptions detracted from the focus of the lesson. In the teacher's words, this class can "get a little crazy sometimes."

Mrs. Turnbull had only begun teaching at the school two years earlier. Her previous experience had been in a Chicago Catholic school that used a direct instruction approach. "It was very structured in my classroom then, because the principal wanted it that way," she said. "The kids had to be quiet. It was very boring for both the students and me! The students may have been learning but they were bored to tears." Her expectations for student learning had not changed since she came to the Chicago Public Schools. Mrs. Turnbull clearly expected her students to work very hard, and she conveyed these expectations to their parents as well. In this school, though, she was free to experiment with other instructional approaches. In fact, she was encouraged by her principal and other colleagues to do so.

Like Mrs. Stephenson, Mrs. Turnbull sought to integrate the teaching of basic skills within the web of a larger lesson specifically designed to engage students actively. During the reading lesson, for example, she stopped at several points to focus attention on new vocabulary words. When the students suggested simply that Thomas was "nice," Mrs. Turnbull directed one of them to look up the word in a thesaurus and to write synonyms on the board. Later the class returned to the words the student had found (*pleasant, agreeable, good, fine*). A few students briefly elaborated on how Thomas had exhibited each of these qualities.

The lesson also attempted to incorporate small-group work. After the whole class had read the first half of the story, they divided into groups of two or three. Their instructions were to write an ending to the story based on the first half that they had just read. The time allocated for this activity, however, was quite short—only fifteen minutes. Several groups began working immediately, with a few students taking the leadership role to write down suggestions. Mrs. Turnbull provided encouraging comments to them: "No one else will come up with an ending like that." Other groups, however, seemed confused about how to proceed and what was expected of them. They never really burrowed into the activity in the short time allowed. In fact, even the most diligent of groups had only minimal notes by the end of class. Again, the quality and depth of the students' learning experience was somewhat compromised, in this case, by the lack of sufficient time.

* * * * *

Clearly, the intention of the lesson was to identify general themes in the story and to engage students in a substantive conversation that would elicit complex cognitive activity. The intentions and results, however, did not fully coincide in this instance. Despite attempting to actively engage students, the intellectual quality of students' work was limited. Usually one student answered a question, and there was not follow up or further probing of answers . Little time was left at the end of the lesson for synthesizing information and drawing conclusions, and too much time was taken up with minor disciplinary problems. In fact, the shifts in activities may have created some of the classroom management problems.

In general, Mrs. Turnbull was unable to press students beyond simple "question and answer" activities to engage the deeper meaning embedded in the story. Even when she led with a probing question, students' responses were brief and did not draw out connections to the story. While Mrs. Turnbull had serious intellectual objectives for the lesson, her attempts to advance these were often frustrating. As she acknowledged in our interview about this particular class, "it is often a process of trial and error."

A student-centered learning approach places considerable demands on the teacher as a facilitator of students' learning. Mrs. Turnbull arranged her classroom in supportive ways and attempted to use appropriate instructional techniques (e.g. classroom discussion and small group work), but she had difficulty eliciting and maintaining the quality of learning that these arrangements were supposed to advance. In form, this class resembled much of what we saw in Mrs. Stephenson's room. The classroom actually had a better physical layout for student-centered work. However, interruptions to discipline students, an inability to extend and deepen discussion, and a time constraint inconsistent with the objectives of the lesson all conspired to undermine active and authentic learning. Students marched through the lesson in a sometimes mechanical fashion that ultimately limited their opportunity to think, to criticize, and to evaluate their own ideas.

Sound Basic Instruction: Mrs. Lopez's Math Class

The student desks in Mrs. Yolanda Lopez's sixth grade math class were arranged in the shape of a U, with one row of chairs inside another. The teacher's desk was located behind the students' desks in one corner of the room, and there was a television in the opposite corner. Maps, flowers, and a Mexican flag hung on the wall. On one side there was a display of igneous rocks and a single computer. On the other side, large windows faced out to the street.

Mrs. Lopez was in her second year at this school after having taught for fifteen years in another Chicago elementary school. Although she had not completed all the course work for a certificate in bilingual education, the principal had recruited Mrs. Lopez to fill an urgent need in this area. At the time of our visit, she was taking the last two courses she needed for certification.

Mrs. Lopez had joined a faculty that she described as open, caring, and friendly. She was grateful for the ample materials and equipment at the school, and she relished the free flow of ideas and energy among the adults. She claimed that when she has an idea for a new lesson or project, she could just go next door to the resource teacher and get help. She noted that it was not uncommon for teachers to observe in each others' classes. This was dramatically different from her previous school, where she said "you could drop dead in the middle of the floor, and they'd go, 'hummm.' "

To begin the lesson, Mrs. Lopez drew a rectangle on the chalkboard and reviewed the steps for finding the perimeter. Going back and forth between Spanish and English, she engaged her students in questions and answers about the proper procedure. Several students participated, and one eventually gave the correct response.

Mrs. Lopez went on to explain how to find the area of the rectangle. She then wrote another problem on the chalkboard, and the students solved it readily. After writing a third problem on the board, she instructed students to work on their own or with one or two partners. Without any disruption, students moved around to find their partners and they began to talk with one another in low voices. Sometimes a student would go over to another group to ask a question or explain something.

As the students worked in small groups on these problems, Mrs. Lopez called four students over to her desk. She reviewed some basic geometry principles, and then helped them set up the problem. After these students returned to their desks, Mrs. Lopez circulated around the room to answer individual questions. She offered positive feedback to those students who were on the right track: "I see you're using your notes. Good! That's fine. Excellent!" In the space of a few minutes, she checked with every group. When she paused at the desk of one of the four students she had helped earlier, she said, "Very good, Cristina. I am so happy that now you understand it. That's exactly the right way to do it."

Mrs. Lopez continued to place problems on the board for students to solve. The students worked quietly by themselves or in pairs. At one point, when the students became noisy, Mrs. Lopez quieted them with a "shushhh." Towards the end of the period, she brought the class back together and reviewed the algorithms for finding the perimeter and areas of rectangles. Then she wrote a final problem on the board and asked the class several questions. The students waved their hands anxiously, hoping to be called upon.

In our interview with Mrs. Lopez after the class, she explained that this group of students had not had a regular teacher for two years. It had been just one substitute after another. She said the students were really ready to learn now, "they are like little sponges. They absorb pretty much what's presented to them."

* * * * *

The students in Mrs. Lopez's class were asked to employ standard algorithms to solve problems. There was little attention to getting students to think about the underlying concepts or to connect their computations to real problems that they might confront at home or in their neighborhood. On the other hand, Mrs. Lopez was enthusiastic in her work with students and they clearly responded to her energy and the sense of caring she conveyed. Most of the students stayed actively engaged in the learning task, and their class work clearly demonstrated their knowledge of geometry and measurement concepts. In addition, Mrs. Lopez recognized the opportunities offered by the school to learn new methods that might push her children toward more challenging work and she was interested in doing so. It is also important to note that these students had been without a regular teacher for two years. At this point, not only did they have a regular teacher, but she was also bilingual. For this class, instruction was getting better.

A Demeaning Experience: Mrs. Gregory's Third Grade Math Class

The majority of the classrooms we observed were like Mrs. Lopez's. These were orderly environments with children productively engaged in learning. Although there were occasional forays into instruction designed to engage students more deeply in thinking and conversing about ideas, for the most part classroom activity remained fairly routine.

In about a quarter of the classrooms visited, however, teaching and learning activities were clearly problematic. The lessons involved minimal academic content delivered in a disorganized fashion. Instruction was uninspired, monotonous, and dreary. There was little energy or spark from the teachers, and if students attended to the lesson, it seemed to be more out of a sense of duty rather than interest. In several instances, we observed teachers dealing harshly with students, publicly rebuking them for the smallest infraction. Mrs. Gregory's class was one of the latter.

The children were seated in five rows with five desks in each row; Mrs. Gregory's desk was front and center. The room was cluttered and messy with materials stacked haphazardly on tables and desks near the windows. The bulletin boards were covered with posters about reading, safety, and presidents' birthdays. Their faded colors suggested that they had been there for some time. They seemed unrelated to anything currently going on in the classroom.

As the lesson began, students were talking, shouting, and making fun of each other. Mrs. Gregory boomed out instructions. If the door had been open, she would have been heard all the way down the hall. She told the students to take out their mathematics textbook, and she picked up the teacher's guide. She then directed a student to hand out ten plastic tokens to each child.

Mrs. Gregory ordered the students to make five groups of two. On the board she wrote 2+2+2+2+2=10. She asked why the problem is not written like this and instead is written as 2x5=10. Not waiting for an answer, she said that it is too much work to do it this way, and that is why multiplication is used. She told the students to repeat the rule. They chanted, "multiplication is repeated addition, multiplication is repeated addition...."

The next step was to have the students combine the tokens into two groups of five. But as the students started grouping the tokens, Mrs. Gregory apparently forgot the directions she had just given them. She yelled that she wanted five groups of two and admonished the students for not paying attention. When a few children tried to protest, Mrs. Gregory maintained her position. The children looked confused, and most did nothing. Others started playing with the tokens. When two boys tried balancing them on their elbow, Mrs. Gregory shouted at them to stop. Then she ordered them to stand in the corner. For the rest of the lesson, she read questions aloud from the teachers' guide that went unanswered. No more than half the students seemed to be paying attention.

To maintain control, Mrs. Gregory relied on humiliation and fear. At one point, she told the students that "they were pitiful" and that they "behaved like kindergartners." On another occasion she shouted out to two students, "Look at me! You will just have to leave, and I'm going to call your mother!" The children made no effort to leave, and so she shoved them into their seats. Throughout the entire period, she shouted at students to "shut up" and "pay attention."

*****

Although Mrs. Gregory had intended this to be a hands-on lesson with math manipulables, the tokens were not really used much at all. There was no overall framework or direction for the class activity. The students appeared confused most of the time, and it seems doubtful that any mathematics learning actually took place. Mrs. Gregory was clearly frustrated in her plans and appeared personally exasperated much of the time. As a result, she dealt harshly with students. To us their infractions appeared small in comparison to her explosions. Mrs. Gregory's behavior set a tone for the classroom that certainly seemed intimidating to the observers, and presumably was to the students as well.

Perspectives on Instructional Change in
Actively Restructuring Schools

We close this chapter with contrasting perspectives about what these six schools accomplished under the first phase of Chicago's reform. The appraisals offered by teachers and students give abundant testimony to how much these schools were affected in a relatively short time period. We heard many accounts about what these schools were like before reform and how things had changed. Our independent observations, key informant interviews, and document reviews generally corroborated these reports. Taken together, the teacher and student views offer an important counterbalance to the "outsider perspective" that we brought as researchers. In comparison to school life prior to reform, much had changed. Relative to the high aspirations that we now hold for schools, however, much more still needed to be done.

Teachers' Views

Teachers expressed considerable optimism regarding instructional change,[36] a growing sense of shared purpose with colleagues, and a high degree of personal satisfaction. In teachers' own words:

> I am seeing a lot of changes being made. I think they are good. I feel in some cases like someone who has just started teaching for the first time. I am really excited; I am, about the changes. I truly believe that they are for the best.

> To educate the child and to improve the quality of life for the child. . . . I believe the teachers here really believe this now. They share it and they put it into action.

> I think the faculty does [have a shared vision]. They know that the purpose is to get these children prepared for real life situations. I think that's what everybody feels. . . .We believe that all children can learn, no matter what the background is. And I've always thought that I don't care where the child comes from. There are days when a child's needs aren't being met at home; it might have some effect on what they are doing. But basically all children can learn. I think we all think that way.

> I think that sometimes it's trying, trying at times, very challenging, very intriguing, motivating. . . .But most of all I think it's very rewarding. I think that it's a very positive atmosphere.

> Being at this school and teaching here everyday, it's hectic, it's sometimes horrible, it's often times wonderful. I've met some of my best friends here. I've had children of children here already. . . .I like teaching here because I am able to be creative.

> The most rewarding thing I have ever done in my life [teaching here under reform]. . . .It is just a fantastic joy and an honor.

On balance, a few teachers in each school felt that reform had not really affected either their school or their teaching, while other argued that the rudiments of change were already in place in the school prior to reform. Still others indicated that they were doing the same things that they had always done and that they saw no increase in communication and cooperation among the staff. Nonetheless, while we are cognizant of these discrepant voices, the overwhelming majority of teachers in these school communities appeared energized by recent developments. Although not all of the teachers we interviewed could articulate the specific connections, it seemed clear to the research staff that the expanded participation, at the heart of Chicago's reform, had catalyzed many of these changes.

Students' Views

Students' perspectives about their schools, teachers, and reform were strongly shaped by the context of the particular communities in which they lived and the ways in which the outside world affected their lives.[37] First and foremost, concerns about safety and personal well-being dominated students' comments. Many specifically contrasted their concern for safety outside of school with the nature of their life inside. They were especially vocal about the dangerous streets they crossed on their way to and from school. Several students mentioned violent crime and drug dealing in their neighborhoods. They said that they did not go outside after school or in the summertime because it was too dangerous:

> There's a lot of stuff happening, so we can't feel safe in the neighborhood. People fighting and people shooting. Gangs everywhere . . . outside they sell drugs and all that stuff . . . but it's sure safe up in the school.

> There's a lot of gangbangers around my house. There aren't problems around school. Around my house it's like every day you hear on the news that this person got shot by this place. Most of the places are close to my house.

Given this context of daily life, students were especially appreciative of teachers who "really listen" to their troubling stories and anxieties about growing up. Some students noted that their teachers encouraged them to write daily journals about their experiences both inside and outside of school. Other teachers offered personal support and saw that troubled children got help from other staff:

> [Our teachers] try to keep us safe. When we have some personal question, you can ask that to them; they know how to explain the thing.

> [Our teacher] can help you with something, like if you have problems and you talk to him about it, and he gives you good advice about it.

> [Our teacher is] a very nice and kind person. She's always here for us . . . She will listen.

When we specifically turned the conversation toward academic achievement, the vast majority of students reported their teachers pressed them to work hard, praised them for good efforts, gently reprimanded them when such efforts were not forthcoming, and were willing to give extra help so they could succeed:

[The teacher is] always helping us and everything so we can do better in school. . . .My teacher and my family tell me that I have to do well, so I can get a good education, to go to college and then have work, good work.

I try every day because she's always encouraging us. We have all kinds of class slogans, like we never say "I can't." We always say "I can." And she says that no one is dumb. . . .My teacher will actually come and tutor and maybe have a conversation with you, [if] she knows you're not working hard.

My teacher tries to get us one-on-one at least two times a day. She has after-school conferences. She has tutoring after school or in the morning. If you have a problem, she says just write her a note and put it on her desk. She will get it.

If you have a problem, [the math teacher] will show you how to do it, and he is one who takes the time to show you really how to do it and really teaches and makes it possible for you to learn how to do it.

On a few occasions students even offered some insight about the high standards that were expected of them. For example, in one focus group, a student reported, and classmates concurred:

My teacher makes it better for me to understand what's going on, because when she gives an explanation, it takes me one step further in my lesson . . . she gives us a chance to say something. She makes it easy because we don't always go to the textbooks and do worksheets. We always talk about it. We do a lot of writing and discussing in this class. We answer hard questions that make you think . . . She asks like, if there's something that a boy did in the story that was bad, and she'd say, 'Do you think it's bad what he did?' And then you've gotta answer why. She says it is important, you've got to support your answers.

Taken in total, such testimony stands in stark contrast to life at Beacon Elementary School prior to reform, as recounted in the Prologue. More generally, it differs from the comments about schools and teachers that frequently arose at the parent-community forums which led up to the passage of the reform legislation. (See Chapter 2.) The adults in each of these six school communities were coalescing around the care and education of children, and the children had noticed.

An Outside Researcher Perspective

We argued at the beginning of this chapter that urban school reform must be judged against more challenging standards for teaching and learning than ever before. Urban schools must not only teach basic skills more effectively, they must also move beyond this to engage all students in serious intellectual activity. Productive adult work in a post-industrial, technological economy, and responsible participation in a diverse and complex democratic society, require students to reason deliberately, to be resourceful, to solve problems, and to engage in reflective and civil communication with others.

We observed distinct progress in many Chicago elementary schools. Principals gained more autonomy in selecting their staffs, and the majority of schools took advantage of this to hire new teachers more attuned to each school's emerging mission. Principals also reported considerable attention focused on instructional innovations designed to immerse students more deeply in subject matter and to promote students' thinking about ideas. Our direct observations in actively restructuring schools, however, suggest that these efforts to promote more challenging intellectual work were still in their early stages. While many teachers were experimenting with new approaches, we found little evidence that these new practices had been sufficiently honed to have a significant impact on student learning. In this regard, our direct classroom observations forced us to moderate somewhat our interpretation of the relatively positive reports about instructional innovations in the principals' and teachers' surveys. Our view of the survey reports is that they signal a growing awareness of the need for new teaching strategies, a beginning effort to incorporate them in classroom life, and a conviction that these practices must expand. Four years into reform, this demarked the extent of progress on instructional improvement in actively restructuring schools.

In fairness, we emphasize that we did observe many positive instances of teaching and learning in these six schools. Classroom's like Mrs. Lopez's were much more commonplace than Mrs. Gregory's or even Mrs. Turnbull's. The vast majority of teachers provided a nurturing atmosphere; they urged their students to try hard and do well; they provided feedback and found numerous ways to reward good performance; and they were successful in keeping their students engaged in learning.

From the vantage point of the more stringent pedagogical standards outlined at the beginning of the chapter, the evidence presented here may seem discouraging. Despite greater flexibility in hiring and more local control over instructional programs and staff development, movement toward more challenging intellectual work was at best only beginning to emerge, even in actively restructuring schools. We must remember, however, the context in which these schools operated. Many students in the EARS study reported that their schools now provided a "safe haven" from a neighborhood where gang activity and drug dealing were common. Sustained, cooperative efforts between local school professionals, parents, and community members that had been catalyzed by reform had pushed out into the community to address these larger problems. Moreover, while instruction clearly fell short of the challenging standards that we brought to our classroom observations, it had by most local accounts also improved during the previous several years. If nothing else, there were fewer Mrs. Gregorys. Both students and teachers testified to improvements which they valued. In sum, it is truly a story of a glass both half full and half empty.

In closing, we note that Chicago's reform initially evoked widespread teacher skepticism. Many viewed it as anti-professional (and not without cause). Four years later, however, it was clear that many new opportunities had opened up, and teachers were quite enthusiastic about the possibilities.[38] The evidence presented in this chapter indicates that many schools were moving forward recruiting new faculty, expanding opportunities for staff development, and beginning to embrace a commitment to improve instruction and to demand more intellectually challenging work for students. Principals, teachers, and students saw real progress. They also recognized that they still had a long way to go.[39]

5

Testing the Basic Logic of the Chicago School Reform Act

The previous chapters have provided a framework for understanding the diverse political, organizational, and instructional activities engendered by Chicago school reform. Changes in local school governance created a complex set of political relations within schools. Some obstructed improvements; others facilitated them. Efforts toward organizational change were also quite disparate. In some schools, activity was haphazard, with little sense that these schools were moving forward. In others a nascent restructuring of the school began to affect the overall quality of the institution. Finally, schools reported instructional emphases that ranged from traditional practices, where students were passive recipients of knowledge, to the introduction of more challenging intellectual activities which sought to engage students more deeply in subject matter and to encourage them to take more active responsibility for their own learning. Although we observed great variability among the city's schools, overall reform has precipitated a major upsurge of constructive activity in each of these areas.

This chapter returns to the posited connections among the three key areas of activity as set out in Chapter 1. We now formally test the basic premise of PA 85-1418: that democratic localism is an effective lever for educational improvement. As noted earlier, two interrelated questions are embedded here. First, does enhanced local participation support systemic organizational change? In analytic terms, we are asking if the nature of a school's local politics is substantively linked to its approach to organizational change. Second, do schools making systemic restructuring efforts focus attention on new instructional practices that can significantly enhance student learning? In other words, is systemic organizational change associated with efforts to improve a school's human resources and introduce "best practices" into classroom instruction?

School Change as Consequence or Correlate of School Reform?

Before examining these propositions in detail, we need to consider a prior question. The discussion, to this point, has implied that the activities in Chicago elementary schools, documented in Chapters 2 through 4, resulted from the passage of PA 851418. However, it is also possible that many of these efforts began prior to reform, and proceeded forward independent of the legislation. Surely, at least some of the key activities—such as collaboration among teachers, supportive connections with the community, or introduction of new instructional practices—were present in some schools prior to PA 85-1418. The crucial issue here is whether there is evidence that reform catalyzed any of these initiatives.

The case-study synthesis documented many examples of new and different political activity resulting directly from reform. In schools such as Thomas and Bella, a focus on instructional improvement accompanied systemic organizational change, and in both of these school sites the field evidence is very clear that these changes were directly linked to school reform. Similarly, the experiences of the six actively restructuring schools discussed in the next chapter documented powerful effects of PA 85-1418. Nonetheless, the question remains: Are we looking at a few unique cases or something more broadly characteristic of the system as a whole?

Prevalence and Timing of Various Restructuring Activities

To address these concerns, we turn to data from the Consortium's principal survey, where we asked specifically about particular aspects of school reform. This survey contained a series of questions designed to assess the scope and timing of restructuring activities in three areas: teachers' work, school-community ties, and authentic classroom practices.[1] These data provide insight into the types of innovations occurring in schools and when they were initiated.[2] As such, they bear directly on the question of what can and cannot be attributed to school reform.

Reorganizing Teachers' Work. Restructuring the school as a workplace— to encourage meaningful collegial interaction and to extend teachers' roles— is a complex undertaking. Figure 5.1 (page 192) displays principal reports about the frequency of adoption of several activities in this domain, both prior to and since reform.

Principals indicated that the two most prevalent innovations—making program decisions based on student performance, and enhanced coordination between teachers and other service professionals—occurred in more than 40 percent of schools prior to reform and have been introduced in about another quarter of the schools since the passage of the legislation. Both of these practices were, according to principals, commonplace in Chicago schools by 1992. Neither of these, however, constitutes a major change in teachers' work. That is, each can be accommodated relatively easily within conventional school practice.

In contrast, workplace practices that required extensive changes in teachers' basic roles and scope of responsibilities were less prevalent overall and more likely to have been initiated post reform. For example, principals in fewer than a fifth of the schools reported that teachers were developing new curriculum and working collaboratively together pre-reform. Over a quarter of the principals indicated, however, that such activities were initiated "since reform." Similarly, the percentage of schools where staff were involved in differentiated roles (mentoring, advising, direction and supervision) doubled approximately over the first four years of reform. These data suggest that enhancing teacher professionalism was indeed a significant change focus during the early years of reform.

School-Community Ties. We also examined school efforts to expand relationships with individual parents and community members, and more generally with community agencies and educational institutions. Figure 5.2 (page 193) displays the frequency of such activity. The principals overwhelmingly reported that formal parent and community volunteer programs were active in their schools (50 percent) prior to reform and had increased since reform by 33 percent. The prevalence of formal mechanisms to coordinate with community agencies almost doubled, reaching 63 percent during the first four years of reform. Programs involving parents in students' academic lives were somewhat less prominent (27 percent prior to reform and another 31 percent initiated since reform). Arrangements with an institution of higher learning for professional development were slightly less common: About half of the schools had such an arrangement at the time of the survey. However, more than half of these relationships had begun since reform, another sign of how reform opened a parochial system to new ideas in ways that were previously uncommon.

The final item, external mentoring programs, was a scarce resource that schools had to diligently seek out. Not surprisingly, this was the least prevalent activity, with only 21 percent of the schools reporting such a program. The majority of these initiatives also began following the introduction of school reform. Again we note that the more innovative activities, which

	Percent of Schools			
	Initiated prior to reform	Initiated since reform	Under consideration	Not a priority
1 School makes program decisions based on student performance.	41	28	23	8
2 Teachers work closely with parents and human service professionals.	41	22	33	4
Staff helps to design staff development based on local needs assessment.	30	35	31	4
3 Staff participates in collegial planning and curricluar development.	19	26	41	14
Teachers encouraged to experiment, develop new programs, curriculum.	16	28	42	14
Staff functions in extended roles with students: e.g., mentoring, advising.	25	19	37	19
4 Differentiated roles for teachers: curriculum direction, supervision of peers	17	18	42	23

← More prevalent initiatives (rows 1–2)

Less prevalent initiatives → (rows 3–4)

FIGURE 5.1 Reorganizing Teachers' Work

Source: *The Principals' Perspective,* survey of principals in the Chicago Public Schools, 1992.

	Percent of Schools			
	Initiated prior to reform	Initiated since reform	Under consideration	Not a priority
School has formal parent and community volunteer program.	50	33	15	2
School has formal mechanisms for coordinating with community agencies.	33	30	30	7
School has a program for parent involvement in students' academic life.	27	31	36	6
School has arrangements with a university for professional development.	21	30	35	14
School offers adult education programs for the community.	18	18	27	37
School participates in an external mentoring program.	7	14	39	40

← More prevalent initiatives

Less prevalent initiatives →

FIGURE 5.2 School-Community Ties
Source: *The Principals' Perspective,* survey of principals in the Chicago Public Schools, 1992.

often require deeper organizational changes, became proportionately more frequent after the advent of reform.

Authentic Classroom Practices. As reported in Chapter 4, principals were asked about a range of new instructional practices that might be appearing in their schools. We focus here on the extent of the introduction of these practices since reform. (See Figure 5.3.)

Extensive use of classroom computers was the most frequently adopted innovation. Principals reported that they were used in 75 percent of the schools, with 36 percent initiated before reform and 39 percent since reform. (Many of the case-study synthesis schools allocated their discretionary resources, during the first four years of reform, to purchase this equipment.) Small-group work was also reported as a regular practice in three-quarters of the city's schools, with one-half beginning the practice prior to reform and one-fifth since reform.

Several items in this inventory also asked about specific teaching practices associated with "authentic instruction." Features such as deep engagement of students in subject matter, making students active participants in the learning process, and assessment that emphasizes student production of knowledge became more prevalent. Principals in about one-third of the schools reported initiating these activities prior to reform, and about another one-quarter indicated their schools had moved in this direction since reform. In general, these data suggest significant increases in instructional innovation since reform, especially of more "authentic" practices.

Summing up: Restructuring Efforts Prior to and Since Reform. In order to develop a more concise summary of these principal reports about school change efforts, we categorized the degree of innovations adopted in teachers' work, community ties, and classroom teaching for each school, both prior to reform and three years afterward. To do this, each of the three sets of practices was separately scaled using a procedure called Rasch analysis.[3] A key advantage of this technique is that the individual practices are hierarchically ordered on an interval scale from less prevalent to more prevalent. Moreover, a "fit statistic" is computed for each measure that identifies how well each principal's responses fit this hierarchical scale. When the items do form regularly ordered hierarchies, as in the three cases described here, we can use the "Rasch measure" to summarize each school's degree of innovation.

Specifically, we identified four levels of innovation adoption through the Rasch analysis. Schools classified as "minimal" were likely to have the practices in category 1 (see Figures 5.1, 5.2, and 5.3), but less likely to have those in categories 2 through 4. Schools classified as "limited" were likely to have implemented the practices of categories 1 and 2,

	Percent of Schools			
	Initiated prior to reform	Initiated since reform	Under consideration	Not a priority
1 Students extensively use computer technology.	36	39	24	1
Use of small-group work in classrooms.	51	24	23	2
2 Academic disciplines integrated in the curriculum.	38	26	32	4
Learning tasks aim for depth rather than broad exposure.	36	22	41	1
Students have access to, and serve as, peer tutors.	29	25	35	11
Emphasis on student production, rather than reproduction, of knowledge.	34	22	41	3
3 Learning emphasizes "multiple intelligences" and multiple cultures.	29	22	40	9
4 Students involved in the planning, conduct, and evaluation of their work.	9	5	46	40

← More prevalent initiatives

Less prevalent initiatives →

FIGURE 5.3 Authentic Classroom Practices
Source: *The Principals' Perspective*, survey of principals in the Chicago Public Schools, 1992.

but not 3 and 4. The "moderate" schools were likely to have also implemented the practices associated with category 3, but not those in category 4. Finally, schools classified as "extensive" were doing all of them. Table 5.1 displays the resulting distribution of schools.

In terms of reorganizing teachers' work, the percentage of schools reporting extensive or moderate restructuring of teachers' work more than doubled, from 14 to 34 percent during the first four years of reform. Conversely, the proportion of schools reporting limited or minimal restructuring decreased after reform from 86 to 66 percent. These latter schools limited their efforts primarily to the more conventional practices, such as developing relationships with human service professionals and enhancing teacher participation in selecting in-service topics. Even here, we still see a general pattern of organizational change since reform.

As for school-community ties, some of the most dramatic shifts since reform were reported in this area. Four years into reform, 64 percent of the principals reported moderate to extensive activity—more than twice as much as prior to reform. In addition, fewer than one-fifth of the schools remained in the minimal category. Given the nature of the Chicago reform,

TABLE 5.1 School Efforts at Restructuring: Pre- and Post-Reform

	Percent of Schools					
Degree of Change	Teachers' Work		School-Community Ties		Authentic Classroom Practice	
	Pre	Post	Pre	Post	Pre	Post
Extensive	8	18	14	40	16	36
Moderate	6	16	13	24	8	17
Limited	20	35	16	20	20	24
Minimal	66	31	57	16	56	23

Source: The Principals' Perspective, survey of principals in the Chicago Public Schools, 1992.

these results are not surprising. PA 85-1418 deliberately sought to reconnect local school professionals to the parents and communities they were supposed to serve. Reform sought to encourage schools to look into their communities for resources and solutions to local problems. In this regard, the principals' survey reports confirmed the case-study observations: Reform had a major impact on school-community ties.

In terms of classroom practices, fewer than one-fourth of the schools reported extensive or moderate restructuring of classroom teaching prior to reform. The overwhelming majority restricted their classroom improvement efforts to introducing computers and small-group work. Accompanying the early implementation of reform was a substantial increase in attention to instructional improvement. Four years into reform, 53 percent of the schools indicated moderate to extensive activity in this area. Only 23 percent continued to report minimal change efforts. Taken in total, these data document a significant surge in instructional change after the passage of reform.

*   *   *   *   *

In sum, principals reported extensive changes in the organization of teachers' work, school ties with the community, and use of authentic classroom practices. As expected, some of these efforts were initiated in schools prior to 1989. It is also clear, however, that much new activity emerged with reform. The expansiveness of the change efforts and the fact that they touched so many schools, documents a broad base of new organizational activity across the system. It seems highly unlikely that this widespread activism would have occurred in the absence of reform. The absolute size of the increase, more than doubling in just three years, tends to argue against this. So does the fact that the largest percentage increase occurred for school community ties—the most direct and immediate aim of the reform.

A First Look at Testing the "Logic of Reform"

We now turn to formally testing the key propositions embedded in Chicago's school reform. Our first approach involves descriptive comparisons across the types of school governance, organizational change, and instructional innovations introduced in Chapters 2 through 4, respectively. With this background, we then employ a path analysis as a final test of whether expanded democratic participation in Chicago leveraged systemic organizational changes that focused attention on instructional improvement.

School Politics and Organizational Change

Based on results from the case-study synthesis, we anticipated three salient connections between the nature of school governance and organizational change.[4] First, we posited that adversarial politics would inhibit systemic school restructuring and lead to an unfocused approach to organizational change. This connection is based on the observation that sustained conflict within a school over basic issues of control tends to dominate the activity of all involved. This diminishes the opportunities for the cooperative efforts necessary to carry out meaningful school improvements.

Second, the case-study synthesis also provided several examples where consolidated principal power inhibited systemic improvements and led to unfocused changes. In the most extreme cases, principals blocked efforts to significantly alter the status quo. In other schools, with more reform-minded principals who "ran the show," teachers and parents tended to remain largely uninvolved in school reform and unengaged in collective discussion about change. While principals can play a key role in catalyzing local initiative, ultimately more professionals and parents must be drawn in and remain involved if broad-based institutional change is to occur. In these case-study sites, at least, this did not happen.

Finally, we found in the case-study synthesis that in schools where strong democratic practices emerged, there was greater likelihood of systemic restructuring. This connection—the key premise of PA 85-1418—suggests that a political practice which engages a broad base of people, who have a stake in the local school and who sustain discussion about educational issues, can create valuable human and social resources to support meaningful school change.

Using the type classifications for school governance and organizational change identified in Chapters 2 and 3, we now examine the linkage between a school's political practice and its organizational change efforts. Figure 5.4 displays these results.[5] Of the schools with adversarial politics, 70 percent reported unfocused approaches to school improvement. Only 9 percent of these schools reported systemic initiatives. Given the extent of conflict present in these schools during the first phase of reform, these results are not surprising. It is difficult to imagine how systemic efforts could emerge under such circumstances.

The results in Figure 5.4 also support the second hypothesized connection. Among the schools with consolidated principal power, 43 percent had an unfocused organizational approach. Another 31 percent of the schools reported some features of both unfocused and systemic activity, and the remaining 26 percent of the consolidated principal power schools indicated systemic restructuring efforts.

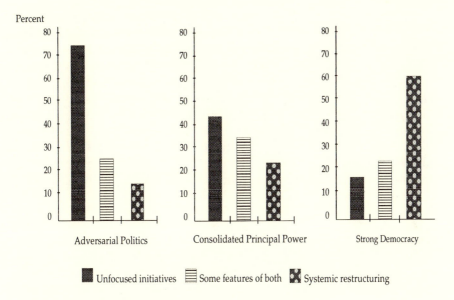

FIGURE 5.4 Local School Governance and Approaches to
Organizational Change

The reported prevalence of systemic efforts here is actually somewhat greater than we had expected based on the case-study synthesis. Two possibilities seem likely to account for these findings. First, in every indicator system, there is some measurement error that causes misclassification. Less-than-candid responses on the school surveys tend to inflate reports about the extent of desirable activities, such as how well-developed the reform efforts may be. This results in a more favorable organizational change classification than a school might deserve.

Second, some of these schools are probably making a transition toward a strong democracy focused on emergent restructuring, and, as a result, the data reports are uneven. For schools that are at an early stage in the transformation from a hierarchical, control-oriented system to a commitment-oriented learning organization, principals may well use their considerable role authority to pull their institution toward more broad-based initiatives. (See, for example, our description of Mrs. Greeley's initial activities upon arriving at Bella school, and more generally, our discussion on principal leadership in Chapter 6.) It is important to remember that school change is a process that occurs over time. The survey data only captured a snapshot of the process at a particular moment.[6]

Finally, we turn to the key premise of Chicago reform: that increased participation will promote systemic restructuring. The data in Figure 5.4 provide strong support for this idea. By far the greatest number of the schools with strong democratic politics, about 60 percent, report systemic restructuring efforts. An additional 24 percent show at least some features of systemic restructuring. In contrast, only 17 percent of the strong democracies indicate unfocused school improvements. These results provide our first broad-based evidence supporting the logic of Chicago school reform—enhanced democratic participation can be an effective lever for systemic organizational change. We note that the corollary is also true. Our evidence indicates that if school politics do not engender broad-based participation, fundamental changes in organizational roles and responsibilities are much less likely.

Organizational Change and Instructional Innovation

In our case-study synthesis, we found a connection between organizational change and instructional innovation. In schools like Bella with a systemic restructuring agenda, we observed more attention to altering the instructional core; that is, how students and teachers interact with respect to subject matter. Unfocused schools, in contrast, did not concentrate as much on changing basic classroom practices. Without a strategic process, and with little sense of collegiality and professionalism within the faculty, the new resources provided by PA 85-1418 were devoted toward add-on programs that tended to exacerbate the already fragmented quality of school life. These new programs were not well coordinated or incorporated into the central operations of the school. Moreover, with no organizational basis to push for instructional improvement, any impetus for change typically originated from isolated programs or individual teachers.

In contrast, schools with systemic restructuring agendas developed their practices through a more collective process. A nascent professional community facilitated the incorporation of new information from external groups. In this context, progressive teaching practices were more likely to be introduced and to germinate.

Figure 5.5 contrasts principals' reports about the introduction of authentic teaching practices in schools pursuing unfocused and systemic organizational initiatives. The results reported here are based on the Rasch measure of the authentic classroom practices used in Chapter 4 and discussed earlier in this chapter (see Figure 5.3). Included are activities such as deep engagement of students in subject matter, making students active participants in the learning process, and assessments that emphasize student production of knowledge. An extensive use of these teaching strategies implies that a school has made a major commitment toward more "authentic" instructional experiences for children.

As expected, marked differences were found for the two organizational change approaches. Sixty-four percent of the systemic schools reported a moderate or extensive emphasis on introducing authentic classroom practices. In contrast, only 42 percent of the schools in the unfocused group reported such an emphasis on authentic instruction.

Similar differences were also found in the principal reports about the introduction of new curricular approaches labeled as "best instructional practices" in Chapter 4. More than one-fourth of the systemic schools reported that almost all students participated in cooperative learning groups. (See Figure 5.6.) For unfocused schools, the comparable figure was only 10 percent. In fact, 59 percent of the unfocused schools reported that less than half of their students experienced cooperative learning. ("Less than half" was the lowest response category available to principals on the questionnaire).

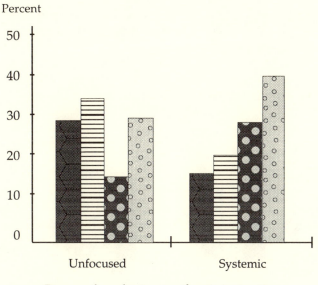

FIGURE 5.5 Organizational Change and Authentic Classroom Practices

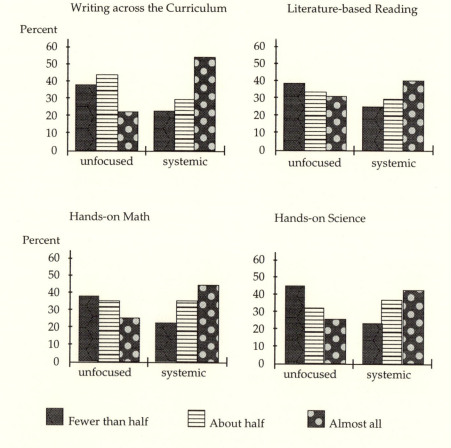

FIGURE 5.6 Organizational Change and Adoption of
"Best" Instructional Practices

The differences between the systemic and unfocused schools were also quite stark for efforts to promote more student writing across the curriculum as well as literature-based reading. Fifty-one percent of the systemic schools emphasized writing across the curriculum for all students; the corresponding percentage in unfocused schools was only 19 percent. Similarly, 40 percent of the schools with an emergent restructuring agenda introduced literature-based reading for students compared to only 30 percent of the unfocused schools.

Unfocused and systemic schools also differed on the introduction of new teaching strategies that relied on the use of manipulative materials and classroom experiments in mathematics and science. Forty-four percent of the systemic schools reported "hands-on math" for all their students, while only 26 percent of the unfocused schools did so. Systemic schools were also more likely to use "hands-on science" instruction. Only 23 percent of these schools reported that fewer than half of their students were involved in such activities. In contrast, 45 percent of the unfocused schools reported such limited use.[7]

In general, these analyses offer affirming evidence of the second hypothesized link in Chicago reform: The adoption of a systemic restructuring approach is strongly associated with initiation of instructional change. When schools are engaged in systemic restructuring, the urgency for change felt by teachers is fueled by new ideas about how school practice could and should function. Within a budding professional community among the faculty, an increasingly public forum exists for examining these new ideas, raising questions about them and eventually diffusing them across the school. This social intellectual activity is complemented by a strategic management focus that allocates the necessary resources to support needed changes and follows through to ensure that quality implementation occurs. Finally, parents and community not only provide supplemental resources, they also offer social support to professionals' improvement efforts. At its best, this lends a moral authority to the actions of local school professionals to improve the learning opportunities afforded "our children."

A More Rigorous Test

On balance, it might still be argued that perhaps some factors other than school reform may account for these observed patterns. As noted earlier in the chapter, for example, some schools were making improvement prior to reform. Could this account for the results presented above? In particular, schools that began the restructuring process before reform, or introduced instructional innovations prior to reform, may have been in a better position to take advantage of the additional autonomy and resources connected to the legislation. It could be argued that the prior initiative of some schools had more influence on subsequent developments than the reform itself. Specifically, to evaluate adequately the contributions of strong democracy to systemic restructuring, and the contribution of both of these in turn to innovative instruction, it is essential that we take into account the level of prereform activity in the schools.

Another potential explanation for observed differences is that some schools served more advantaged student groups, and this accounted for the relative progress of these schools. We have already explored this topic in some detail in Chapters 2, 3, and 4, where we considered separately each of the key components of Chicago's reform. Although we found that school background factors, such as racial composition or the percentage of low-income students, had some impact, they were not powerful predictors of strong democratic practices or systemic organizational change. Nonetheless, before we conclude that the Chicago School Reform Act actually catalyzed broad-based change efforts, it is important to take a closer look at all of these factors simultaneously in a single analysis.

A Path Analysis Model

For this purpose, we turn to a statistical technique called path analysis. This procedure allows us to separate out the effects of background characteristics and prereform restructuring activity from the key relations of interest in this study. The path analysis thus provides a more rigorous test of the linkages posited in the logic of reform. The aim of a path analysis is to identify the direction and magnitude of "paths," both direct and indirect, by which one factor is related to another, such as the connection between strong democratic practices and systemic restructuring. Importantly, path analysis allows us to take into account the fact that any relationship of interest sits within a network of many other relationships. For example, the emergence of a systemic restructuring approach is influenced both by the extent to which the school has adopted strong democratic practices and by other basic characteristics of the school, such as racial composition or school size. Path analysis permits us to assess the unique contribution of each factor, while simultaneously taking into account the other relationships that are also present in the data. Figure 5.7 displays the model used in our analysis.

Each numbered arrow in the figure represents the direct effect of a particular school attribute or some key aspect of Chicago's reform. Arrow 1, for example, depicts the relationship between basic school characteristics, such as a school's student mobility rate and the percentage of low income students, and the adoption of strong democracy in the school. In parallel

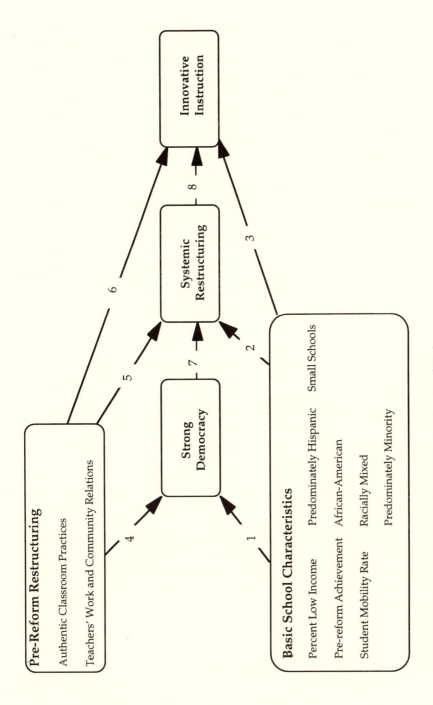

FIGURE 5.7 Analytic Model to Probe the Logic of Reform

fashion, arrows 2 and 3 represent the influence of these school character-istics on systemic restructuring and instructional innovation, respectively.

In parallel, a school's level of restructuring prior to reform may directly influence the extent that the school progresses in developing productive political relationships among the principal, teacher, and parent commu-nity. This potential effect is represented in arrow 4. The nature of the pre-reform activity may also be a factor in the approach that the school takes to organizational change under reform. For example, a school that had estab-lished more collaborative work among teachers prior to reform should have more social resources to draw upon to pursue systemic restructuring un-der reform. Arrow 5 depicts this expected relationship. Similarly the de-gree of instructional innovation since reform is likely to build on the extent of such activities prior to reform. Arrow 6 portrays this relationship.

Our primary interest in the model, however, is with arrows seven and eight, which link strong democracy, systemic restructuring, and instruc-tional innovation. It is here that we represent the key logic of Chicago school reform—strong democracy facilitates systemic restructuring, which in turn promotes the introduction of innovative instructional practices. Notice that we have not posited a direct relationship between strong democracy and instructional improvement. Instead, we argue that this relationship is indi-rect, mediated through the effect of school politics on organizational change. (The path analysis also allows us to test the validity of this proposition.)

The key point is that the impact of basic school characteristics and pre-reform restructuring levels are taken into account in the model. Thus, not only are we able to judge the strength of their separate influences, we are also able to control for any confluence they may have with the relation-ships of primary interest.

Measure Construction

Three concepts are of central concern in the model—strong democratic practice, systemic organizational change, and instructional innovation. In order to formally test the path model, we needed to create measures for each of these key concepts. We return to the discriminant analysis, intro-duced in Chapters 2 and 3, to measure the likelihood of strong democratic practice and systemic organizational change in a school community. Recall that we used the composite indicators of principal, faculty, and Local School Council activity from the case-study synthesis schools to develop a gen-eral discriminant function that we then applied to all schools for which we had indicator data. More specifically, using a school's information about principal leadership, collective faculty activity, and LSC activity, the dis-criminant function estimates the probability that a school has strong demo-cratic governance. We now use this probability as the basis of our measure for the likelihood that a school has adopted a strong democratic approach to governance.[8]

Similarly, we used the discriminant analysis from Chapter 3 to develop our measure of systemic restructuring.[9] From this discriminant function and a school's data on the five salient characteristics of organizational change (engagement of parents and community resources, access to new ideas, professional community, internalizing of responsibility for change, and strategic educational planning), we computed the probability or likelihood that a school has embraced systemic organizational restructuring. This probability provides a basis for the measure of the second key concept.

Third, we constructed a composite measure of the extent of instructional innovation in the school. This scale joins the two indicator developed in Chapter 4 of authentic classroom instruction and adoption of "best instructional practices." The result is a composite measure of the degree to which a school has introduced instructional practices that engage students as active participants. Since these were the main ideas being advocated in Chicago for instructional improvement during the early 1990s, high values on this measure indicated extensive school efforts at instructional innovation during this period.

For the school's level of restructuring prior to reform, we constructed two measures. The first is a composite variable that combines information about the amount of restructuring of teachers' work and of school-community ties before the passage of PA 85-1418.[10] As the opening essay of Chapter 3 suggested, urban schools face particularly difficult circumstances in developing trusting ties to their parent community. In addition, professionals within urban schools typically work in isolation from one another. Assessing the nature of these social relations among teachers and between teachers and parents prior to reform allows us to take into account a school's social resources for change as reform began.

In addition to evaluating the quality of the school's social relations prior to reform, we also formed a measure of the amount of instructional innovation prior to reform. These early initiatives provide a potential base on which subsequent improvement efforts might build. Specifically, we use the measure of authentic classroom practices prior to reform, introduced earlier in this chapter, for this purpose.[11]

The model also includes several school characteristics that we wish to take into account. Many of these have already been introduced in previous chapters.[12] They include the percentage of low-income students enrolled at the school, the student mobility rate,[13] the school's racial composition, school size, and average pre-reform achievement. As in previous instances, the racial composition of schools was classified into mutually exclusive categories: predominately Hispanic, predominately

African-American, predominately minority, racially mixed, and integrated.[14] Small schools, with fewer than 350 students, were also identified for specific consideration.[15] Finally, pre-reform achievement level was measured for each school using the 1989 math and reading scores on the Illinois Goals Assessment Program (IGAP). A composite measure was created for each school by taking an average of the third-, sixth-, and eighth-grade scores in both subjects.

Results of the Path Analysis

Figure 5.8 presents the results. All of the variables discussed above are included in the model; however, only those with significant associations are actually joined by arrows or "paths." The numbers associated with each arrow are "standardized regression coefficients," and reflect the relative importance or magnitude of influence for each path.[16] We also note that, like analyses in previous chapters, the base for our examination is the 269 elementary schools whose test scores in 1989 were below national norms.

First, we consider the associations between basic school characteristics and the three key concepts of Chicago reform—strong democracy, systemic restructuring, and innovative instruction. As expected from the equity analysis in Chapter 2, the prevalence of strong democratic politics is equitably distributed among the various types of elementary schools in the city. As the lack of significant paths indicate, basic background characteristics are only weakly predictive of a strong democratic politics. In general these results reinforce the findings from Chapter 2, where we found that strong democratic activity had emerged in almost every neighborhood of the city.[17]

The only significant exception is in predominately Hispanic schools where strong democratic practices are more prevalent than average. The case-study synthesis offers a possible explanation for this relationship. In several of the case-study sites, which were Hispanic schools, an extensive array of productive ties existed among community-based organizations, churches, and other religious groups. The presence of these social resources in the school community appeared to contribute to the emergence of strong democratic governance. A base of positive social relations acted to strengthen participation in these schools and provided a supportive context for discussion of educational issues.

Next, we examine the direct influence of basic school characteristics on the adoption of a systemic restructuring approach. As we saw in Chapter 3, schools pursuing this approach were also quite diverse in their characteristics. These results are confirmed here as well. The extent of systemic restructuring is significantly related to only one basic characteristic: school size. Small schools (with fewer than 350 students) were more likely to have

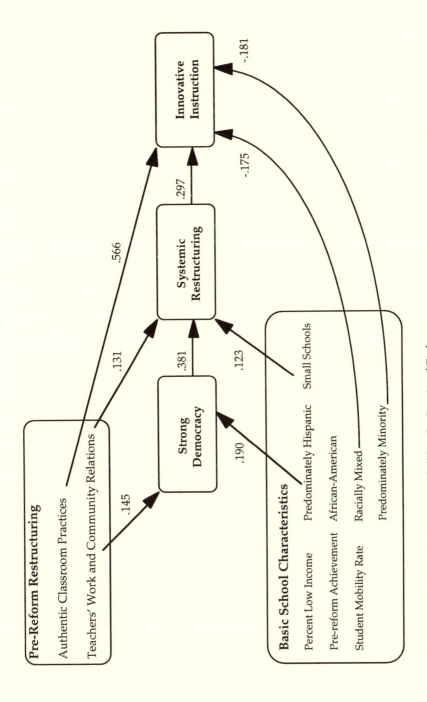

FIGURE 5.8 Path Analysis Model for the Logic of Reform

a coherent approach to school improvement. While school size does not have a direct effect on the nature of local school politics, it does appear to facilitate systemic organizational change. In general, smaller school size facilitates more informal social interactions among teachers, the principal, and other staff. In such a situation, it is much easier for a professional community to emerge that is committed to deep organizational changes. Here too, these statistical results are highly consistent with observations from the case-study synthesis.

The direct impact of basic school characteristics on instructional innovation, contains two significant "arrows." Both racially mixed and predominately minority schools tend to have fewer new instructional initiatives. As we saw earlier in Chapters 2 through 4, the internal diversity within these schools make them more problematic contexts for reform and restructuring. While these compositional factors were not significantly related to the likelihood of strong democracy and systemic change in the path model, they are directly linked to instructional innovation. In general, our case-study synthesis suggests that the diversity of culture and language found in these schools creates organizational environments where even basic issues of social control can become challenging. Thus, the findings documented here, that these school communities engage in less instructional improvement, is not surprising.

We now turn our attention to the influence of pre-reform restructuring activity. As expected, we find strong positive effects for schools' initiatives taken prior to the formal implementation of the reform legislation. Elementary schools that had developed more dense ties with their parent community, as well as more cooperative working conditions among their teachers prior to reform, were more likely to pursue strong democratic practices under reform. Positive social relations at a school provide a foundation for the continued discussion of educational issues and for the facilitative leadership that is characteristic of strong democracy. Schools with previously established values and norms of inclusion are thus advantaged as they pursue a more collective and open approach to school decision making. This does not imply, however, that schools that had not begun this process prior to reform were unable to establish strong democratic practices. Rather, they were just somewhat disadvantaged as they began.

This pattern is also evident as we focus on the impact of pre-reform activity on the nature of organizational change in an elementary school under reform. Positive social relationships in the school prior to reform contribute significantly to a systemic approach toward school improvement. In particular, the expanding roles for teachers, and the development of a more professional community that are key characteristics of emergent systemic restructuring, are supported by the pre-existing level of social capital in the school community. Thus, schools that had stronger social relations prior to reform were able to move further in their efforts toward focused organizational change under reform.

The final relationship of note, between an elementary school's prereform activity and instructional innovation, reveals a very strong association. Not surprisingly, schools that had begun to adopt more authentic classroom practices prior to reform expanded these practices after reform. Consequently, four years into reform, "best" instructional practices were more broadly employed throughout these schools than in those that had only begun the adoption process after 1988. In general, introduction of new classroom approaches requires time to diffuse throughout a school. Again, this does not imply that schools that did not address these aspects of instruction prior to the reform made insignificant changes. It only means that the level of implementation in those schools was not likely to be as extensive as in those that began at a more advanced starting point.

Of most importance, even after adjusting for these differences in school characteristics and pre-reform activism, the results in Figure 5.8 firmly support the primacy of the central connection between school politics, organizational change, and instructional improvement. The statistical link between strong democracy and systemic restructuring is especially strong. A constructive school politics plays a central role in the school's adoption of a more focused approach toward organizational change. More specifically, strong democracy creates an environment in which all participants are able to voice their concerns. Subsequently decisions are more likely to have a collective character which supports systemic change.

Similarly, the path analysis results indicate a strong influence of a systemic restructuring approach on adoption of innovative practices in the classroom. Elementary schools which approached organizational change in a systemic fashion—through altered roles, relationships, and broad strategic planning—were much more likely to have introduced classroom practices that make students active participants in the learning process. Even after controlling for pre-reform restructuring activities, systemic organizational change continues to be quite influential on the degree to which a school pursues instructional innovation. These results indicate that, even in schools with a disadvantaged starting point, positive organizational efforts created vital links to new classroom practices.

The nature of a school's political activity also played a role in the instructional improvement process; although, as the path analysis indicates, these effects work indirectly through the impact on organizational change. No direct linkage was found between strong democracy and instructional improvement.[18] To be clear, strong democratic politics is an important resource for school change. The actual impact on instruction, however, depends more directly on the development of a systemic restructuring that includes such key features as strategic planning, professional community, and strong school-community ties. Absent such organizational developments, strong democratic practice does not by itself stimulate greater instructional innovation.

Interestingly, the level of student achievement prior to reform did not have a direct effect on democratic practices, systemic restructuring, or the introduction of instructional innovation under reform. Although there is a significant correlation between pre-reform achievement and instructional innovation, this relation works through the amount of restructuring occurring in schools prior to reform. That is, prior to reform, authentic classroom practices were more likely to be found in higher achieving schools.[19] After the reform, however, school improvement efforts were more equitably distributed. Significant reform activities occurred in all levels of schools—both very low achieving and relatively higher achieving.[20]

* * * * *

In summary, the path analysis supports the general logic posited in Chicago's school reform. These results add further credibility to basic descriptive evidence presented in the earlier sections of this chapter and to the case-study synthesis in chapters 2 through 4. Expanded local participation can be a very productive lever for systemic organizational changes that focus attention on instructional improvement.

The actual nature of these linkages, however, is quite complex. The fact that a systemic restructuring approach to school improvement is associated with the adoption of instructional innovations serves, at least, a dual role. First, a systemic change initiative leads schools away from simply adding peripheral programs. It encourage attention to the organizational core, which naturally leads to focus on instruction.

Second, it also creates an environment in which more fundamental changes in teaching practice can take deep root. As noted in Chapter 4, innovative practices take time and require substantial support to be implemented properly. These practices require significant new learning by teachers; they demand change not only in what is taught but also in how it is taught. In addition, they entail altering classroom management to fashion new roles and relationships among students as well as between teachers and students. As teachers move to transform their classrooms, initially they often experience frustration and failure. Support from colleagues, parents, and outside assistance groups is critical in sustaining teachers through this uncertainty. The emergent community among local school professionals, coupled with more positive school-community ties, can be a major resource in this regard.

In closing this chapter, we note that the descriptive and path analyses presented here have a strong linear, sequential quality to them. We do not wish to imply, however, that schools necessarily progress in this direct fashion from politics to restructuring to instructional change. Real change certainly has a more complex and subtle dynamic than is possible to capture with the kinds of analytical tools used in this chapter. These processes will often intertwine as school participants may simultaneously adopt and revise new instructional approaches and ways of working together. This point is supported by the strong association between a school's previous levels of restructuring and its ability to push further on a coherent improvement strategy. Moreover, these developments are intricately tied to the peculiarities of each school context; not only its prior work on restructuring, but also its longer term social history.

Statistical analyses of the sort presented here help us to address questions such as whether inclusive leadership is linked to professional community-building within the faculty or whether more collective planning promotes progressive instructional practices. Although they can be very useful in establishing the validity of these hypothesized relationships, elaborating the specific mechanisms by which these elements actually link together is a more detailed task. To address this purpose, we turn in the next chapter to our field observations from six actively restructuring schools. These accounts provide a basis for a deeper understanding of the actual mechanisms that interconnect the broad propositions of Chicago reform at the school level.

6

A Closer Look at Actively Restructuring Schools

We have found that many Chicago schools took advantage of the opportunities afforded by reform to initiate fundamental changes. Every aspect of school life, ranging from the nature of the school's relationship with parents and community to the quality of classroom practice, was reconsidered. Moreover, these efforts to strengthen school operations and introduce instructional innovation were much more common in school communities with a strong local democratic practice.

To better understand the role of democratic localism in these changes, we took a closer look during the spring of 1993 at six Chicago elementary schools which seemed to be taking good advantage of the opportunities provided by reform. The experiences of these actively restructuring schools (EARS) provide insight into the key ingredients and processes of a successful school development effort under Chicago's reform legislation. In addition, it is safe to assume that any common concerns found in these schools are likely to be widespread across the system. Thus, both the progress and problems identified at Bass, Ebinger, Field, Hefferan, Hoyne, and Spry schools[1] help to delimit the current state of Chicago's reform. (Chapter 1 provides a description of the EARS sites and our field research methodology.)

Spry School: Reform Begins?

On March 9, 1990 a headline in the *The New York Times* read, "Democracy Divides Chicago Schools." The story began:[2]

> The hallways were empty and the classrooms filled at Chicago's Spry Elementary School Wednesday morning. But outside a room where a parent-led council talked in closed session about hiring a new principal, nearly 100 angry parents crowded in front of the double doors.

> They shook their fists, clapped in unison and yelled, "Out! Out! Out! Out!" It was a double demand—that the council members come out and address them and while they were at it, that they resign their posts. As the shouting swelled, Tomas Revollo, a Board of Education official overseeing Chicago's school decentralization, strained above a din he was helpless to stop and said, "This is democracy."

The *Times* described a school "torn down the middle, with teachers distracted from teaching and the students, some as young as 5 years old, forced to choose sides in a bitter debate" because the principal, Ben Natzke, had just been dismissed by the Local School Council. Many teachers were not speaking to one another. Charges of racial prejudice surfaced as this predominately Hispanic council had ousted a non-Hispanic principal saying only that it "wanted a change."[3] The in-fighting turned violent outside the school, with reports of fist fights among parents, slashed tires, and smashed car windows.

With a foreboding tone, the account continued:

> Teachers supporting Mr. Natzke say they fear what the council and a new principal might do. "If they succeed in removing the principal," said T. J. Wilborn, a seventh-grade teacher, "next year it will be the school engineer, the lunch room jobs, then the teachers."

> Mr. Natzke, for his part, is predicting disaster. "They're going to hold the school hostage for the next two years," he said. " We're going to lose two years in teaching these kids."

> The Chicago Principals' Association is vowing to fight the ouster with appeals to the Federal Equal Employment Opportunity Commission. "When you see highly qualified, very successful and experienced principals bounced out of their jobs, there can't be a principal in this city who feels comfortable right now," said Bruce Berndt, the group's president.

The article concluded with a haunting question, "Is this the essence of reform?"

To be sure, the early events at Spry did not look like any conventional definition of planned change. Not surprisingly, many discounted the possibility of any positive changes accruing from this seeming chaos. Yet, somehow, just three years later, Spry school would emerge as an exemplar of constructive initiative under this reform.

This chapter probes the common themes at work at Spry and five other actively restructuring Chicago schools. Although these schools varied in many ways, all productively used the opportunities provided by reform. In each case, a strong democratic practice emerged that supported sustained efforts at systemic restructuring.

The analyses presented in the last chapter indicated a strong statistical association between expanded participation and fundamental organizational change. The descriptive detail provided in this chapter offers insights into how strong local democratic activity actually supports systemic restructuring. Based on an analysis of the common themes found in these six actively restructuring schools, we conclude that three key mechanisms—a recasting of the principal's role, expanding social support for change, and opening the flow of ideas—interact here. These three mechanisms were central to the change process in each school, and we believe they are key to reform more generally.

Common Themes in the Unfolding of Reform

The experiences at Spry during the first four years of reform, as well as at the other five actively restructuring schools that we studied, were complex and varied. Each was rich in the particularities of its own school community—its issues and concerns, its personalities and distinctive resources. Change was neither smooth nor well-charted. Although the story at Spry was more controversial than most, school change was often a matter of "two steps forward, one step back." As Don Anderson, the principal at Ebinger, remarked about his efforts to bring a Total Quality Management strategy to his school: "Just when you think you have got it perfect, some new thing comes in that throws everything off." Likewise, Nelda Hobbs at Field, who worked on reorganizing this large elementary school into several schools-within-schools, commented:

> "For some people it's working well; others are still floundering. . . .There is certainly enthusiasm, interest, frustration; all sides of it are here. There are some days when the kids are so bananas that you think nothing has helped, and then other days everything seems to be connected. It is something you just have to fine tune as you go along."

Fully telling the stories of the unfolding of reform in these six schools could easily fill another book. Our intent here—to examine the interconnections between the political life of a school community and its organizational change efforts—is more limited. Any general insights about these interconnections are most likely to be found in the common themes, rather than the particularities, that characterize these school development efforts. On balance, in choosing to skim over many of the precise details that constitute school change, we do not wish to imply that such change is straightforward and simple. In fact, our data do not indicate that to be the case.

An Active and Supportive Local School Council

The passage of PA 85-1418 was widely heralded as a radical plan of parent and community empowerment over local schools. Some critics, like those interviewed by *The New York Times,* worried about the likely chaos and confusion that would ensue as uneducated parents, many of whom had been victimized by this very system, would now take control. They feared what might happen when parents and community members started telling the professionals what to do.[4]

For the most part, these concerns proved unfounded. As the results presented earlier in Chapter 2 document, most LSCs did not become the adversarial local community boards of education that some had envisioned. To the contrary, principals, teachers, and LSC and PPAC chairs generally reported that the LSC was a positive addition to their school community.[5]

For many this was a surprise. This sentiment was well captured by a teacher we interviewed at Hefferan:

> I am so impressed with this LSC . . . because I had heard all the rumors about "these parents." "These parents" don't know anything. They don't have any educational background. They can't . . . not here. This is one of the most impressive LSCs that I have seen in the city.

Even though Hefferan is a very disadvantaged school in a very poor neighborhood, this teacher went on to note that there was some expertise in the parents and local community which the first LSC was able to draw upon:

> Experience and expertise is definitely here. One LSC member is a vice president of a local corporation, another is a manager for Rush Presbyterian-St. Luke's Hospital, and another works in the criminal court system. So you see people with a strong business and educational background within the Local School Council. . . .What I also like about the LSC is that their total attention is on what is best for the children. They don't have a lot of hidden agendas to promote themselves or maybe get a job for a relative. Instead it is what is best for the children at Hefferan.

Selecting a School Leader. The single most important responsibility exercised by an LSC was its evaluation of the school principal and decision to award (or not award) a four-year performance contract. In each of the six EARS schools, the LSC endorsed a person committed to the students and parents in their particular community. At one school, Bass, this meant retaining a principal who had already initiated significant improvement efforts prior to reform. In a second, Ebinger, it meant holding onto a relatively new principal who had started a lot very quickly. At Hoyne, the principalship was vacant, and the LSC set out with deliberateness to fill this position. At Field, Hefferan, and Spry, the LSC went through a process that eventually denied a contract to the original principal and chose a new person instead. In 1990, Field, like Spry, was among the most conflictual school communities in the city. Our observations, three years later, offer testimony to how new leadership can help to move a school beyond adversarial politics and catalyze major organizational change in a very short period of time.

Although we do not know all of the details of these principal selection processes, since they occurred two or three years prior to our inquiry, we can distinguish some general features.[6] Of perhaps most significance, at least some council members in each EARS school had expertise to bring to this critical task. In the more advantaged schools, such as Hoyne and Ebinger, parents and community members on the LSC brought considerable professional expertise from their own work. In some of the more disadvantaged schools, the teacher representatives played a particularly important role. At both Spry and Field, for example, the faculty members on the LSC helped to organize council opposition to the pre-reform principal.[7] They joined with parents and community members who were also actively seeking advice from a variety of sources (including citywide advocacy groups, community-based organizations, staff from the Chicago Board of Education, and local colleges and universities). Some of these parent and community members brought relevant experiences with community organizing and political campaigning to the process. Thus, in contrast to schools with consolidated principal power, there was a broad base of human resources in these councils.

Even so, the task of evaluating principals appeared daunting and frightening. No one had ever done this before, and there was not much official guidance on how councils should go about the process. As one teacher representative on an LSC stated:

> When I became a council member, I had never been in another school. So it was difficult to compare how things were here. . . .When reform started, we became exposed to other people in other schools [through a program at Roosevelt University] and began to learn about these wonderful things and exciting innovations and couldn't understand why we weren't doing that.

The level of enthusiasm and motivation that we saw in our instructors [who were CPS principals]; we just knew something wasn't right here. I felt our students deserved the best we could possibly give them. . . .In January and February of '90 there was a lot of fear, and the terrible thing about fear is that it stretches the truth and people were afraid of change. . . .I think a lot of people couldn't believe that parents and teachers could possibly know what to do.

In spite of these fears, these LSCs were able to work through the process. Although the final decision was not always unanimous, the councils were able to move on. For example, at Spry one former LSC member noted:

We had certain members who wanted to keep the principal. That was OK. We weren't alienating them. We respected their opinions and we just tried to figure out how we're going through this journey together. In the end, even the members that had voted to keep him after a couple of months realized that we had made the right decision.

Thus, even in the cases where the decision-making process was conflictual, councils were able to maintain a focus on "making the school a better place for kids."[8] This stands in sharp contrast to LSCs, such as Sprague discussed in Chapter 2, where sustained adversarial politics played out among local community interests and individual personalities. Although participants argued vehemently at times, a base of social support for school change was maintained in EARS schools.

The LSC-Principal Dynamic. Once a principal was selected (or retained, as at Bass and Ebinger), the LSCs saw their primary role as supporting their new leaders. They entrusted these principals to help them realize their collective aspirations for their schools. These principals, in turn, enjoyed a mandate to promote change. Good, close working relations characterized this dynamic.[9] EARS principals were quite active at their council meetings, often sharing power with LSC chairs.[10] Frequent informal communication, especially between the principal and LSC chair, was the norm outside of meetings.

Strong LSC support for school staff to promote change is evident throughout our field interviews. Nelda Hobbs put it this way:

Many things that have gone on [in the past here] with good intention have been misinterpreted by people in the community. But now the LSC trusts me, and they come and we talk. They understand what we are trying to do. So now they have become my "soldiers." Instead of me having to dispel rumors, they go and dispel them, and that makes a big difference. . . .We have a great working relationship . . . we work as a family.

And a Field LSC member agreed:

> There isn't a week that goes by that [the principal] doesn't grab me in the hallway and tell me, "This problematic event has occurred. What am I going to do?" We just say, "You do what you have to do! And we will approve whatever you need!" The LSC has backed her entirely. We believe in what she is doing.

We heard similar comments at other schools. For example, an LSC member at Bass said:

> See, my job [as LSC member] stops at Mrs. Gillie's [the principal]. I say, "Mrs. Gillie, what do you think we are doing wrong? What do you think we are doing right? What do you think we need to help the children with? What can we do? What do the teachers say about this? This is the kind of thing that we [the LSC] talk about. We will talk to the kids, and they know we are involved. The teachers know that they are not out there by themselves . . . We hope there aren't many fences [between people]. We want to get close to each other, the kind of closeness that ensures integrity within our school environment.

Likewise at Hoyne, an LSC member commented:

> Our efforts here are certainly to bring more parents into the process . . . extending the school home relationship and linking them because teachers can only do so much. Once that child leaves the classroom and goes home, teachers have no control. . . . Our role is certainly one of support here. As you know, the principal is always the point person in terms of where ideas are coming from. When these proposals are brought to the table, we always look at them carefully and give them serious thought. . . . The point is to keep the morale of teachers high. When they have to worry, those feelings can be reflected in the classroom and ultimately in the student. So we always want to keep our teaching staff happy.

Much of the responsibility for the functioning of the LSC devolved to the principal, who saw this as a new part of his or her job. While these principals valued the strengthened ties to parents and community and appreciated the personal support of council members, working with an LSC was a major new undertaking for which they had received no formal preparation prior to the onset of reform. Among other things, this meant a major increase in principals' work load.[11] The initiating activities—getting a council organized, developing by-laws, making sure they understood their basic responsibilities and functioned effectively as a group—were especially daunting. In reminiscing about the early days of reform, Nelda Hobbs said:

It is another layer of responsibility. . . .This whole legislation is a bit complicated for the average person who is really trying to do it by the law. I just know what I have—a commitment to kids, and I know where I am trying to go with the kids, and I figure that if I am doing that I'm not going to break the law, knowingly. I don't think you can expect anyone to do all of that stuff on their own.

In general, LSCs have neither a budget nor a staff. As a result, most councils remain dependent on their principals for support and guidance. Since EARS principals saw their councils as valuable new local resources providing service to their schools, keeping councils vital was an important added dimension to their work.

Focus of LSC Initiatives. LSCs in the EARS sites took active roles in efforts to improve parent and community involvement in the schools, to encourage parents to support children's learning at home, to enhance and maintain the physical plants, and to improve order and safety both inside and outside of schools. For example, at Bass school, an LSC member talked about her work in the community:

I work out in the community a lot. We try to make ourselves available for those parents that view the school as the power structure and unapproachable. So as we walk down the street, we have become the persons who are approachable. They can talk to us. . . .There are a lot of ways that we can get the message across that this is a place where you need to be.

Similarly, a parent LSC member at Spry told us:

We have a safety committee. We work with the police department. The police send different people here [to Spry school] to work with us on different problems in the community and then they come back the next month to report on what they did on those problems. . . .[We tell them], "they are selling drugs in this house" and the police come back to tell us what they have done about it. And we work with the Boys and Girls Club. The Club donated the property; so we put up the playground for the school next door, and we work with St. Ludmilla's [the nearby Catholic Church].

Such institutional collaboration at the community level is an important consequence of Chicago's reform that can make a significant difference in the quality of students' lives. For example, a parent at Spry told us:

[Gang members] really scared the children because they used to just go around doing things to people. But my son has not been bothered anymore. I consider this school a real safe haven, because they don't put up with this stuff now. If something happens, they take care of it, even if it is on a holiday or weekend. A child's coat was stolen out on the playground on a weekend. [Someone at the school] recognized the boy and they called the police and they got the boy's coat back.

Similarly at Hefferan, an LSC member spoke about how they provided security for the children:

We [the LSC members and other parents] are here in the morning. We watch the people coming in. We watch the children being dismissed in the afternoon. What is so important is that our [adult] male population is a part of this. The don't stand up with their hands crossed upon their chest. They are out talking to children, directing them, offering them suggestions, what did you do and so forth, so that they can model while they monitor the building. I think this is the essence of what should happen in education. . . .They are out here and they don't have badges on or anything. They are just with the children, walking the playground, looking to see.

In general, LSCs have heightened the attention of school staff and other community professionals to local needs. On some occasions, such as the collaboration between Spry and the neighborhood Boys Club to create a playground, LSCs have found creative and efficient solutions to local needs. With both fiscal resources and authority to act, the LSC solved this problem on their own. Putting this in perspective, it is hard to imagine how the Chicago Board of Education could have worked out such a cost-effective resolution.

In fact, LSCs can lead to a real expansion of resources for children. As an LSC member at Hefferan commented, for example :

[We are] really looking at identifying people who can help us to obtain resources beyond what comes through government money and the Board of Ed. So if we want to do something special for children, we still have opportunities to do that because we will write proposals, we will seek outside resources, we will go and speak on behalf of what is going on here. Anytime, anyplace.

Professional Initiative for Instructional Improvement. Shifting our focus to specific school activities aimed at instructional improvement, we found, not surprisingly, that it was the principal and teacher leaders who created these initiatives rather than the LSC. The comments of the Hoyne LSC members, offered earlier, certainly reflected this. Similarly, an LSC member at Ebinger noted: "The development here has been largely principal-driven as opposed to being LSC driven." It is noteworthy that these comments came from the two most advantaged schools in the EARS sample.

The reliance on the judgments of local professionals is even stronger in the more disadvantaged sites. For example, an LSC member at Hefferan commented:

> We have confidence in our educational leader. I don't think any of us at any time have questioned Pat Harvey's [the principal] decisions. We understood very early on that our first goal is to support our educational leader. . . .We look to our principal to make those decisions and to keep us informed about what is going on. We trust her judgment. . . .All of the teachers are respected, and the school staff too. That includes the people who work in the lunch-room and the engineers. We try to make everyone feel important. Everybody contributes to the education of children.

To be sure, there were many conversations in the LSC about the need for instructional improvement. And these were real discussions; the LSC was not just a puppet being controlled by the principal or teacher leaders. Rather, professional staff actively discussed with parents and community members their concerns in these areas, and really worked at building a common understanding about the school's needs. For example, the principal at Ebinger linked each LSC member with a particular class for a whole day in order to give them a better sense of the teachers' work:

> They started out on the playground, brought the children into class, did the lunch count, did attendance, and started class. They were in each class for 40 minutes. The council was learning about what teachers had to go through. That it is not just 'open up a book and discuss world events.' It is dealing with wet pants and scraped knees. A child's not here, and somebody is cry-ing, and it's a lot of other things besides learning. They [LSC members] are less apt to just say now "Well we need the best books, and we need this or that program." They are more likely now to pay attention to what is in place here and what we are trying to do.

In short, while the direction for instructional improvements typically started with the professional staff, considerable effort focused on keeping parents and community members involved.

Our Analysis. The councils in EARS schools were vital institutions. They each played a central role in catalyzing the organizational change efforts underway at their school. They selected principals to lead them, and then they supported these individuals as they challenged the status quo and began moving their schools forward. The LSCs were an important context for ongoing discussions about the improvement of the school community. They helped out wherever they could, but they certainly did not "tell the professionals what to do." With only three school staff members out of eleven on each LSC, this result was especially noteworthy.

In most general terms, an effective partnership emerged within these actively restructuring schools among local professionals, parents, and the community. At base here is a subtle blending of individual respect and mutual trust. This key social dynamic, which is a significant problem in many urban schools, had been transformed into a resource with positive impacts on students and teachers alike. With parents backing the efforts of the school staff, a more consistent and supportive learning environment resulted for students. Similarly, with professionals taking an interest in the needs and concerns of parents, they were more likely to receive support back. This in turn helps teachers feel (and be) more efficacious in their work. In the context of the longstanding, widespread distrust and hostility between parents and local professionals prior to reform in Chicago, this was a remarkable turn of events.

Principal Leadership

Through both their words and actions, EARS principals endorsed a commitment to fundamental change. As noted in Chapter 3, principals could maintain good standing prior to reform if they kept the lid on affairs in their own buildings and followed major directives from the central office. This vertical orientation—looking up into the central administration for direction and approval—gave way to a more horizontal focus. Principals in these six schools were actively engaged with the ideas, concerns, and initiatives of parents, teachers, students, and other members of their school communities. These principals had a local mandate to improve student learning. Responding to this mandate became a primary standpoint against which they judged their own work.

We heard innumerable comments from teachers and staff about the strong commitments enlivened by their school leaders in this regard. At Bass, for example, a teacher remarked:

> [Mrs. Gillie] has laid a foundation for us to be great teachers. I see that in our future we are going to keep this vision going. I am going to try. I think this is the epitome of a teaching professional. She demands excellence and she won't accept less.

A staff member at Ebinger commented:

> This school is very well run . . . it is more like a family than a workplace. It all starts with the principal. He lets everybody know that they are special. He cares about you. He extends himself; he interacts with the children as much as he can.

And at Spry, a teacher stated:

> We have got an excellent principal now. This fellow is first-rate, and it makes everybody feel that the primary thing of importance is not making the school look good for downtown [the central office], but making this a place of learning for students. And that is of paramount importance.

The enthusiasm, optimism, and passion for improvement displayed by these principals inspired a collective effort to revitalize the schools' missions and operations. The teacher at Spry went on to summarize this well:

> I see our new principal as such a positive thing through reform. I know that there is much more, but I think the leader of a school really sets the tempo, the feeling of what is going on. Someone who is energetic and makes you feel positive and optimistic about what might happen at your school really changes how you feel about teaching. I think if that didn't happen and we kept our old principal, we would be just sitting here going, "This is a bunch of baloney," because nothing would be happening.

Similarly, the comments offered by students in focus group conversations affirmed this sense of change:

> I like what my principal and assistant principal are doing. Everyone is working together, like the counselors and teachers. Everyone is working together to make this place better.

> We have a nice principal. She has good ideas. . . .The last principal we had, it was different. He didn't change anything about the school. Since [the new principal] has been here, things have begun to improve. We have more understanding teachers and more programs.

> This [new] principal is better, much better. There are no gang problems here no more. Nobody fights with other people. They don't bring guns, no knives. [The new principal] is trying to get us to relate to each other, make friendships with everybody, not only people from our own country. And the teachers are making it a good school. It is getting better and better and better here.

In short, we found in the EARS schools a broad base of opinion that these schools were changing and that the principals were playing key roles in these developments. Such responses encouraged us to take a closer look at what these individuals had done to effect this.

Reaching Out into the Community. Being a "good principal", for these six school leaders, meant engaging the local neighborhoods. When Don Anderson came to Ebinger in 1989, for example, the school was losing enrollment. Although Ebinger is located in a stable middle-class neighborhood, it had not had a particularly good reputation in recent years. Many of the students who attended kindergarten at Ebinger transferred out at first grade. Through a series of "Principal Talks" around the community, Anderson sought to change local perceptions about the school. He wanted people to know about Ebinger's recent accomplishments and its plans for the future. He also listened to their concerns and assured community residents that their issues would become an important part of his agenda. When we visited the school in 1993, enrollment was rising and student mobility was down. These two demographic indicators corroborate our field observations—people were taking notice of the significant changes occurring in the school.

All six principals embraced the idea that their schools had a communal responsibility to fulfill. Involvement with the community around the care and welfare of children was just part of the job. Nelda Hobbs, for example, described a recent effort to close down a local drug house:

> All of last year I worked this alley behind the school building here. Drug dealers hung out in that building, and a lot of our kids live there. They would take the kids' bookbags and money. . . .I found a local detective to work with me. So we got two people to let us use their lofts so that we could observe, and in two days we got four of them. . . .My "principaling" has to go beyond these four walls. I walk or drive my attendance area almost every day. There is so much out there that adversely affects our kids. . . .It is really a community network now. If you appeal to them [various other community institutions], they will help in any way they can.

Similarly, Carlos Azcoitia helped to focus public attention on a nearby liquor store that appeared to be marketing its products toward Spry youth. The area around the school had also been a haven for gangs. Azcoitia worked with parents and community members to make the neighborhood safer for children. He told us:

> The key lies in helping people see that they are in power to do something. The school can be an organizer. . . .We are in the process of identifying leading families in the eight blocks surrounding the school. We are going to train them in issues of health, safety, and education with an objective that they will go into the homes of their neighbors and come up with strategies if, for example, gang graffiti is proliferating in a certain place, or there is a family where the children are going uncared for.

More generally, these principals promoted efforts to make the school a central institution of community life. The schools extended their hours of operations and the facilities were opened up to a wide array of activities. These developments were especially marked in Field and Spry schools, both of which serve immigrant neighborhoods. Being a vital community school in such a context meant educating not only the children, but also their parents and new community residents.

At base here was a recognition of the need for reciprocity between the school and its community. These principals saw their schools as important community resources. In their view, helping to reweave a fabric of institutional cooperation within the community was an important part of making a school a responsive institution.

Garnering Resources from the City. Moving beyond the local neighborhood, EARS principals also actively cultivated connections across the metropolitan area to expand the resource base—both dollars and ideas—to improve their school operations. For example, Marcie Gillie at Bass and Don Anderson at Ebinger brought a Total Quality Management philosophy into their schools and drew on resources from the Kellogg School of Business at Northwestern University to support this. Pat Harvey established strong ties to several local corporations: Rush Presbyterian-St. Luke's Medical Center and Turner Construction, for example, contributed to the equipping of a state-of-the-art science laboratory at Hefferan. Nelda Hobbs, with assistance from the Center for School Improvement at the University of Chicago, moved to restructure her large elementary school into several schools-within-a-school. Similarly, both Barbara Martin at Hoyne and Carlos Azcoitia at Spry developed a number of external connections to support professional development and improve instruction in core areas, such as writing and science.

In this regard, these principals shared an entrepreneurial spirit. Rather than waiting for new programs and materials to be sent down from the central office, they actively cultivated external institutional ties that might help them achieve their objectives. In contrast to the "Christmas tree schools" described in Chapter 3, however, there was a selectiveness to this activity, a commitment to quality in the choices made, and a focus on following through for a successful implementation. Thus, it was not just a matter of getting more resources. Rather, these resources had to work in the context of what principals felt they needed to improve their schools.

An Evangelizing Spirit and a Common Good Rhetoric. EARS principals used the myriad of personal interactions that comprised their daily work to spread the word about their hopes for the school, what it could and should become. They constantly reminded people of what education should be about—the kinds of intellectual and social experiences that are good for kids, the kinds of adults who make a good faculty, the ways that teachers should relate to students and their parents, and, most generally, the kind of community institutions their schools should be. They invited conversation about each of these ideas. They articulated a strong stance and were willing to engage in conflict, if necessary, to move their schools forward.

In this regard, EARS principals constantly had to make judgments about what was needed to advance school improvement and what the impediments were. While these principals were genuinely committed to an inclusive process, they were also unwavering in their core beliefs. Not all people and not all ideas could be supported. Barbara Martin at Hoyne talked about it this way:

> Everything comes through the filter of what is best for the children. Unless you talk to me at that level, we are really not talking the same language. Now teachers come in to complain about something. I say, "How does this affect your instructional program?" [Teacher response:] "Huh, I didn't come in here to talk about instruction." And they look at me like, "Is this woman completely lost? Doesn't she know that I am not talking about kids?" But the point is that is what we should be talking about. That is the real issue. . . .I have found one thing in the principalship. You have to know what your goal is. You have to live it day in and day out, and you have to think about it constantly. It is not something you put on the wall. You have to know, "This is what I am here for. This is going to guide me."

This strong sense of the principal's resolve was clearly understood throughout these school communities. A teacher at Bass, for example, commented about Marcie Gillie that:

> She expects the best from the children. Everyone is worth saving. Everyone can learn. We don't give in to hopelessness and negative attitudes, and that permeates the staff, and the children and the parents.

At base here, in the way these principals spoke about their schools and their work, is a very powerful rhetoric: "Everything we do must be for the children." This rhetoric afforded a persuasive basis for public argument. It also offered a critical standpoint against which competing proposals could be evaluated.

In anchoring a local discourse around what is "good for children," a basis for common-interest politics was advanced in these school communities. Where so much of the political life of schools typically focuses around teachers jockeying for preferred assignments and access to marginal resources, and parental requests for special treatment for their children,[12] the principals introduced a strong countervailing influence. The power of this conversation about children's welfare played out vividly at Spry, for example, in the turnaround following the highly contentious decision to remove Ben Natzke, the pre-reform principal. One of the teachers whom we interviewed talked about how Azcoitia's commitment to advancing learning for all children influenced people:

> Carlos is openly concerned with the children and excludes politics and his own personal interests. That I think won the doubters over. . . .He has an open door. It is constantly opening and closing with parents coming through it voicing their concerns.

To be sure, both individual and group interests persisted in these schools. Arguments seeking to advance these interests, however, had to contend increasingly in public with this common-interest discourse that emphasized the good for children. As an LSC member at Bass pointed out, for example:

> There is no hidden agenda. Whatever is going on is posted for any and all to see. You know where everything is, and all the resources are being used for the greater good of all. There is no one pet project that gets boosted, or someone that is much more important than what is done for the greater good.

The principled stance taken by these leaders enabled a very positive dynamic between them and their school communities. By relying on arguments about the "good for children" to advance specific initiatives, these principals seized the high ground. As parents, community members, and school staff learned that their principals were serious about a commitment to children, these principals gained a moral authority to complement the instrumental authority granted under PA 85-1418. That is, not only did these principals have direct role authority, they also developed over time a substantial base of personal influence that accrued from the social consent of other local participants. Moreover, as these school leaders used their power to challenge a dysfunctional status quo and advance improvement initiatives in the interests of children, they were able to extend their base of social support within the school community. This, in turn, further expanded their moral authority.[13]

A Distinct Local Vision. In the past, a highly centralized system enforced a uniformity across schools that denuded most schools of any special character. In contrast, EARS principals were going to some length to mark their schools as distinctive places. Developing new school symbols was a key strategy used by principals in this regard. Some marketed school T-shirts, jackets, or uniforms. Others championed a school logo, bought new school-specific stationery, or had business cards printed for the staff. Although these initiatives appeared small, they signified a great deal in their school communities.[14] School members were increasingly becoming a part of an important local organization with its own identity.

Each principal spoke with intensity and fervor in a language that was both local and possessive about how "**this** school can be good for **our** kids and **our** families." It is perhaps too grand to call this a mission and too fluid to call it a plan, but each principal, nonetheless, conveyed a clear intentionality that guided his or her work. This combination of values and a distinctive local language might best be described as a "vision-in-outline" for the school community.

At Hefferan, for example, Pat Harvey was committed to nurturing and caring for children in the two square blocks surrounding the school, to shaping their will to learn and educating them all. At Spry, Carlos Azcoitia envisioned the school as a central institution of a strengthened community life that expanded civic participation and reclaimed the public spaces of the neighborhood from drugs, gangs, and violence. Within this enabled community, all children would learn. Don Anderson at Ebinger advocated a constant focus on quality in everything the school did and in involving everyone in the process. For Nelda Hobbs, engaging the whole school community around a schools-within-a-school structure was the key to improving educational opportunities for children.

As these various visions-in-outline came to be understood and embraced by students, parents, and teachers, local participants became more engaged in the schools and committed to their improvement. For example, a parent at Field school commented about their school-within-a-school initiative:

> Well, it's exciting. It's new. It makes this school seem like we are really moving forward. We are going forward with something that we haven't heard other schools are doing. They [the teachers] are very energetic and very zealous about what they are working on, and it is good to see that spirit. It is really good to see the spirit of the students too. It is like something has been lifted off of them.

Again, in the context of the limited engagement and weak sense of agency among local participants prior to reform, these changes represented important initial steps in a larger developmental progression. These schools were becoming responsive, self-guided local institutions.

"The Quick Hits." Even stirring rhetoric quickly appears hollow if not accompanied by complementary action. Thus, another key feature of these schools was that each principal attacked and made rapid progress on some highly visible problems. At Spry, for example, the initial focus was on alleviating overcrowding by finding some supplemental space in the

community for extra classrooms. At Hefferan, the public areas were cleaned up, and restoring order and safety were emphasized. At Bass, it was as simple as getting some basic classroom supplies for teachers who had grown accustomed to being told, "There is no money."

The specific actions taken in each school varied depending on local needs, the amount of discretionary resources available, and the supplemental assistance that could be garnered. Nonetheless, some common consequences accrued. Local participants began to see an array of positive results associated with current school leadership and with reform more generally. These early initiatives offered very concrete signs of change in each school community. A clear message was being delivered: Parents, community members, and teachers working together with the principal could effect a material difference in children's experiences. There was an emerging awareness that the school could be different, and local participants could make it happen.

Our Analysis. As noted in Chapter 3, many parents and teachers had been alienated from the Chicago Public Schools in the past. They had little reason to believe that they could make a difference or that anyone would really care if they tried. In contrast, each EARS principal was engaged in a sustained, conscious effort to promote local agency—to convince students, parents and teachers that together they could make the school a better place. The expanded parent and community programs, mentioned earlier, were a key part of this. Initiatives on professional development and professional community, discussed in the next section, represent another important strand. The quick solutions to at least some key school problems were a catalyst in this regard, as were the new symbols that marked school membership. Tying this all together was the public persona of the six EARS principals. Each constantly exhorted their school community to: "Look at what we have already accomplished. We can do more."

We also note the numerous important interconnections between the new role carved out by these principals and the basic aims of the reform. In their openness to people and ideas, these principals signaled their support for an inclusive school politics. This is a key initial step in the transformation of a school from principal domination to a more broadly participatory institution. Similarly, as we shift attention to the schools' improvement efforts, we notice how the initial successes in EARS schools bred increased trust and expanded the social resources for further school improvement. Principals' actions were clearly key in this regard. They used the instrumental and moral authority acquired under reform to catalyze change in their buildings. A major lesson thus emerges from the Chicago reform—transforming the principal's role can be a powerful lever for change.

Strengthening Professional Competence, Commitment, and Community

Complementing the focus on renewing local agency and expanding local participation in school affairs were efforts to strengthen the technical core, where students interact with teachers around subject matter. Ultimately, significant changes were needed here too if major improvements in student learning were to occur. Key in this regard was the capability of individual teachers, and their commitment to work productively together as a professional community.

EARS principals set a high priority on strengthening their schools' human resources. Prior to reform, faculty were usually assigned to schools by the central office, and most principals had relatively little influence over these decisions. The Chicago School Reform Act granted principals the right to select new teachers as vacancies arose, an option that EARS' principals aggressively pursued.[15] In addition, much of the discretionary money provided under reform was used to create new staff positions. These new slots made it possible to further recast the composition of the faculty. Some staff were also encouraged to leave, providing even more opportunities to bring new blood into the organization. Further supporting these efforts for faculty renewal was a commitment to intensive staff development.

Hiring New Faculty. EARS principals spoke at some length about the attention they gave to the hiring process. They searched for good people to recruit, checked references and past teaching experience, and described carefully crafted interview protocols. Most importantly, principals suggested to us that they were not just hiring a grade-level teacher or a subject-matter specialist; rather, they were building a faculty team compatible with the vision of the school community that they sought to promote. Teachers had to be good at what they were supposed to teach. They also had to care genuinely about the community and its children, be able to act as positive role models, and have broader interests that might engage students beyond the classroom.

Barbara Martin, for example, talked about her interviews with prospective teachers in this way:

> They sit here and hear what I expect, what I am asking for, looking for, and I do not ask them to make a decision immediately. [I say to them] You need to go home and think about what you are looking for in a job. I am talking about extending yourself beyond the normal school day, to go beyond the instructional program. I have told you my philosophy about children and their right to a quality education. Our school is 52 percent poor, but I find no correlation between intellect and poverty. Poor children are not dumb children. So the point is we need to talk about this. And, this is an African-American school. We need to talk about this too. I need you to think [about the fact] that I expect each one of these children to have the best that you

can offer, and I am not just saying it. I intend to see that it is done. So you need to go home and think about what I am saying.

EARS principals aggressively used personnel selection to reshape faculties around the vision-in-outline for their school communities. For example, Don Anderson, in discussing his efforts to engage a Total Quality Management orientation at Ebinger, said:

> We have been very lucky in attracting and selecting the right people, and it's worked very well. Before reform you could not do that. You were just given a teacher, and you did your best with what you were allowed to do. Now, you can really establish a tremendous staff.

Similarly, Carlos Azcoitia deliberately sought out teachers who could speak both Spanish and English for assignment to both bilingual and monolingual classrooms. He reasoned that even if the children spoke English, their parents might not. Bilingual communication was an important consideration if Spry's staff was going to strengthen its ties with the local community and build trust.

Many of these new teachers became agents for change in their schools. With the support and encouragement of their principals, they brought new ideas into the organization and a willingness to question extant practices. A veteran teacher at Field School noted, for example:

> I will be brave enough to say—this is my own idea—that new teachers come a lot more ready [to try new things] than the teachers that have been here for years. Many times, you know, teachers are used to doing things in one way and they don't want to try new things. These new teachers challenge us, but in spite of that, we are doing things together and it's very healthy.

Similarly, another teacher at Spry noted:

> They bring new ideas, and mostly what I love, they bring motivation. We need to be sparked. We are ready, but I think we need those people to motivate us, to say to us, hey, did you see this, or I went to this in-service and I learned this. . . .So there is energy. I think this is very important when you have been teaching for awhile; it is like you become a dinosaur—here forever. It is exciting to see. It motivates me and it keeps me on my toes. . . .Also, personality-wise, they are very willing to work together and are open to do more things like team teaching. Instead of someone who has been here for awhile and has their room and things like how they want it, they [new teachers] are more open to trying alternatives, which is what we should all be doing.

Increased Attention to Staff Development. Prior to reform, few teachers were encouraged to seek out professional development.[16] In contrast, EARS schools actively supported such behavior. Discretionary resources were made available to cover workshop fees; classroom coverage was arranged if needed. Upon return to school, teachers were encouraged to talk to their colleagues about what they learned and how it might help them.

Advocates for systemic reform emphasize the need to engage whole segments of a school faculty in professional development (e.g., all primary teachers involved in literacy instruction or all upper-grade mathematics teachers). Current best practices for professional development involve intensive programs that are sustained for a year or longer, with provisions for in-school support and follow-up assistance as teachers attempt to introduce new content and methods into their classrooms. [17] In this regard, it is argued that individual workshops, in which only a few teachers from a school participate for an hour or two or perhaps a full day, are not a particularly effective approach. Deep schoolwide changes in instruction require a more substantial intervention.

We observed some examples of this in EARS schools. The middle-grade teachers at Spry, for example, were involved as a group in a sustained staff development effort on writing across the curriculum through participation in the Illinois Writing Project. Similarly, at Ebinger, the upper-grade teachers were in one of the first groups to be trained by the Teachers' Academy for Math and Science at the Illinois Institute of Technology. This program seeks to help teachers integrate mathematics and science instruction in their classrooms.

Programs such as these hold out new standards for instruction in schools and can dramatically expand teachers' perspectives about the nature of their practice and what it means to be a professional. As part of the initiative at Ebinger, for example, twice every two weeks during the course of a year, classroom substitute teachers were provided so that the faculty could leave the building for a full day of professional education activities. According to Don Anderson, this intensive training had a profound effect on his faculty:

> So now they are used to this [type of training] and see the need to train further. It gave us a higher level of experience and knowledge in this particular area but it also created a higher level of professionalism [with regard to teacher development]. Longer term, this will expand out into all other areas of education throughout the building.

On balance, intensive facultywide efforts such as these were more the exception than the norm, even in these six schools. Much of the staff development still involved short-term workshops attended by one or two teachers or a small group. Nonetheless, the increase in even these more modest forms of activity served an important purpose during the early mobilization for restructuring in these schools.[18] It afforded a conduit for introducing new ideas into the school. Moreover, as teachers increasingly selected external professional development (rather than just attending the compulsory in-service days previously organized by the central office), faculty norms were evolving toward independently seeking information and continuous improvement. As Don Anderson articulated, such activity readied his school faculty for the more sustained and extensive staff development that was clearly needed.

Counseling Out Weak Staff. As noted earlier, although individual initiative was generally encouraged, not every idea nor every person was supported by EARS principals. This critical perspective is seen most clearly as we turn attention toward the third strand of human resource development—removing weak staff.

EARS sites experienced a substantial change in faculty membership during the first four years of reform. (See Table 6.1.) In five of the six schools, over 40 percent of the 1993 faculty were not there in 1989. In the most extreme case, Hoyne, 80 percent of the faculty were new. As principals took control of their respective schools under reform, they conveyed an openness to people and a real interest in sharing authority for the school and its improvement. They were, however, resolute about the standards of quality they expected. Those who fell short and were either unwilling or unable to improve were encouraged to leave.

This encouragement took several forms. EARS principals were highly visible in their schools and classrooms. Teachers quickly learned that the former privacy accompanying a closed classroom door would no longer be the norm. Uneasy with this new scrutiny, some teachers decided they would be happier in another school and requested a transfer. At Hoyne, for example, a teacher told us:

> You work with one principal for twenty years or so and this principal says, "Do your own thing. I won't bother you. You don't bother me." So, you just went to your classroom and did whatever you did. Then comes this change in the administrator. This one [i.e. Barbara Martin] wants to see your lesson plans. She want to see you put up bulletin boards, change your classroom and what not. . . .The change was like jumping from cold to hot. So they couldn't deal with it and left. They complained. But I did not have a problem with that because, where I came from, that was just what you were expected to do. After being here for twenty years and nobody ever collected your lesson plans, I know that had to be difficult for them.

We also heard of numerous other strategies, such as changing a teacher to a less desirable assignment, to signal a principal's dissatisfaction with poor practice. In short, though a variety of means, the message was quickly conveyed to such teachers that "you might be happier elsewhere."

When counseling failed, principals turned to the formal process for faculty termination. Unanimously, EARS principals complained that this procedure was cumbersome and time consuming, and that they did not receive the support that they needed from the central office.[19] All had their own "horror stories" to tell. Nelda Hobbs, for example, at Field recounted:

> I had one [bad teacher], and he couldn't do anything. I went through the whole E-3 process [the formal proceeding for dismissing an incompetent teacher], but before it was over the Board transferred him to another school. They gave me a lady from the McCutcheon School and sent him over there. Well the lady came here, she became ill, and went on sick leave. They told me I could not hire anybody else until her position was declared vacant. Finally I get to hire someone I wanted, but his security check didn't get processed, so I had to wait. In the interim, they send back that guy whom I originally had, and who didn't work out at McCutcheon. Well he shows up here one morning and says, "I'm reporting for work." That is when I called Channel 5. You know, whenever you call the newspaper or the media, you get results. I hate to do it because it is bad publicity for the schools, but it is one way to get rid

TABLE 6.1 Restructuring of School Faculties

School	Faculty size in 1989	Faculty size in 1993	Number from 1989 still on the faculty in 1993	Number of new members	Percent of 1993 faculty who were in the school in 1989
Bass	36	49	27	22	55
Ebinger	22	26	14	12	54
Field	57	65	37	28	57
Hefferan	54	69	41	28	59
Hoyne	12	15	3	12	20
Spry	87	99	69	30	70

Source: Based on data provided by the Chicago Teachers Union.

of a bad employee. When they [central office] heard that I called the media, they sent him to Senn High School instead. . . .He is a real Mickey Mouse. He used to jump my first and second graders, hold them up in the air by the collar. Finally they learned to start biting him, just to get away. . . .

As in this case, the E-3 process often never goes to completion. In this instance the central office intervened once the media were alerted. In other situations, principals' signaling of resolve to pursue this process was sufficient to prompt the teachers in question to request a transfer to another school. Regardless of the precise details, as weak teachers were pushed out, others were put on notice that the principal was serious about moving the school forward.

Thus, initiating the E-3 process, although onerous and personally difficult, had a significant organizational effect. Beyond just moving out a particular incompetent teacher, it also sometimes encouraged other weak teachers to request transfers. It "lit a fire" under still others who wanted to stay but who also recognized that the status quo had changed. Moreover, the new faculty who were recruited to fill the resultant staff vacancies were much more likely to embrace the emerging school vision. Thus, not only had a bad teacher (or two or three) been replaced by better ones, but there were broader social consequences for the faculty as a whole. The teacher leaders who had embraced reform began to enjoy more support among their colleagues, and peer pressure for improvement emerged. A genuine collective responsibility for change grew among EARS faculty. For example, Nelda Hobbs commented about the development of schools-within-a-school at Field:

Initially, many of the teachers thought that just being on the committee [to develop the initiative] was good enough. And then people started saying we have to do this and that . . . and then it got contagious. There was nowhere to hide. They pretty much forced people. You know, not in a real serious negative way, but there was a lot of positive energy.

In this process, the principal's problem with incompetent teachers became collectivized as well. Nelda Hobbs discussed another problematic teacher at Field who had been arrested for knocking a child's tooth out, but was eventually reassigned to the school by the central office. Hobbs spoke of how the other faculty, in effect, shunned him. She commented that, with the commitment to schools-within-a-school, "They police their own ranks. Nobody wanted him as part of their school."

Teachers' Shared Decision Making. The efforts described above to enhance the human resources in EARS sites were complemented by considerable attention to reshaping the basic work conditions of teachers. A key development in this regard was giving teachers a much larger say in how their school operated. This embrace of shared decision making was rooted in a keen political sense that better decisions occurred when everyone was involved. More specifically, there was a recognition that change is difficult to achieve without a significant buy-in from the affected parties.

Each school created internal faculty committees to support shared decision making. Specific responsibilities were devolved to these committees, and a clear message was sent by the principal and LSC that teachers' participation was valued. Three of the schools (Bass, Hefferan, and Spry) had been involved in a Chicago Public Schools-supported effort to promote more school-based decision making, called Project CANAL. These schools were trained to use a schoolwide core planning team and several design teams, each of which focused on a specific problem area. The core planning teams coordinated the work of the various design teams, and sought to promote better communication throughout the school community and to assure a direct connection to the School Improvement Plan.[20]

In non-CANAL schools, the specific committee structures differed but the same purposes were addressed. For example, at Hoyne, a small school with fifteen regular teachers, the faculty worked as a "committee of the whole." Similarly at Field, much decision making was pushed down into the separate schools-within-a-school faculties. These smaller groups, of approximately ten to fifteen teachers each, were responsible for most of the instructional development and planning for their respective units. In all six schools, most of the faculty participated in some manner.

Interestingly, the Professional Personnel Advisory Committee, established by PA 85-1418, was not the primary vehicle through which teachers voiced their views in any of these schools.[21] Instead, each faculty evolved its own governance forms specific to its circumstances. Although some committees worked better than others, these structures generally provided extensive opportunities for faculty participation in school-based decision making.

Again, much of the onus for initiating this organizational change fell to the principal. As noted in Chapter 2, many Chicago principals traditionally ran their schools in a rather autocratic fashion. Not surprising, faculty were distrustful and suspicious as reform began. To move schools forward, principals had to send strong messages that professional collaboration was to replace principal domination. At Hefferan, for example, Pat Harvey talked with the faculty about this specific issue shortly after becoming principal: "One of the first things I told them is that we were going to have shared decision making, and we had to build trust if we were ever going to have improved learning here."

Developing Professional Community. The conventional organization of schools provides few occasions for teachers to talk together about how they can improve student learning.[22] The fact that teachers spend most of the day working in isolation in separate classrooms is a major impediment in this regard. It is not surprising that norms of privatization, where teachers are averse to public examination of their classroom practice, are salient in such a work place.[23]

In response, EARS schools modified teacher schedules so that faculty would have time to meet, and rooms were made available for them to congregate and talk. At Hefferan, for example, Fridays were scheduled for special programs, freeing regular classroom teachers for work on curriculum, instruction, and professional development. At Hoyne and Field, discretionary resources were used to pay the building engineer to extend the school hours and to pay teachers' stipends for meeting after school and on weekend retreats.

Beyond just creating more time, principals strongly encouraged teacher collaboration. Barbara Martin, for example, directly attacked the norms of privatization that restrained teachers from really assisting each other. She maintained a very public presence in classrooms and encouraged others to do the same. Four years into reform, she said, a very different set of professional norms had evolved at Hoyne school:

> The teachers invite each other into their classrooms a lot now. [They say] "This is what I am doing," and people now feel very comfortable exposing their weaknesses. We have no problem with this anymore.

Nelda Hobbs offered similar observations about the new norms that had emerged in two of the schools-within-a-school at Field:

> They go in and teach each other's classes and see how each other works. One of the first things they learned was that each person had somewhat different expertise and could be a real resource for each other. If they felt comfortable with something they had observed, they were going to go back and try it in their classrooms.

Teachers also commented about these new professional relationships. For example, a teacher at Field talked about sitting in another teacher's classroom:

> Just the fact that I am sitting in her classroom has been very helpful to me. She can teach more math in fifteen minutes than I can in a whole week of work. I have some exposure [to the new math standards], but nothing like what she has had. She is a great resource and she wants to help me.

Changes such as these can transform school faculties from congeries of certified staff into genuine professional communities. Arguably, this is one of the hardest features of a school to reform. It is embedded in the deep history of "how things are done" in schools and is codified in prevailing work rules. Moreover, both the school schedule and the physical layout of the building, with separate classrooms and no common work areas for teachers, strongly reinforce this. Thus, the movement toward professional community in each of the EARS schools required a coordinated attack on an interrelated set of structural and normative constraints.

Expanding Teacher Responsibility. The ultimate aim for an expanded teachers' role in school decision making reaches beyond just increasing the number of people involved "in making the same old decisions." Such participation should also foster greater leadership development among teachers and more collective responsibility for the welfare of the school community and learning by all of its children. We heard numerous comments to this effect in EARS schools. A teacher at Ebinger, for example, noted:

Here are these teachers, myself included. We are here at 7:50 a.m. I don't have to be here until 8:30 a.m. This is the only school I've been in, and I have been in nine, where the faculty takes it upon themselves to just do what has to be done.

Similarly, a teacher at Hoyne stated:

Everyone is striving to be better. No one is just sitting back. Every time we do something, we evaluate it, and see if maybe next year we can do it better.

And, at Bass, a teacher remarked:

It forces me to rethink things. I thought I was a very good teacher. You haven't seen anything yet. I'm not as good as I intend to be; but I'm getting better. [Working here] forces me to look harder, look deeper, change, try this. Well it didn't quite work out, try to change it again. That is what I have to do— seek, ask, try, try it again, just don't get stuck in a routine. Don't be stagnant, be open.

Several teachers spoke in very personal ways about how their capacity for leadership had developed since reform began. A teacher at Spry, for example, expressed this quite well:

I saw myself as a real follower. I have always been a person who said, "Let me do what I have to do in my classroom. That is what I do best, and that is what I am happiest doing. Just leave me out of this other stuff [i.e., school committees and other collective activity with adults]." I feel that reform has grabbed me and put me in new positions than in the past, I did not think I was capable of, but I'm finding that I am. Several years ago, I would have said, "Oh I can't do that. I am not a leader. I don't want to be in charge of anything." But now I know I am capable, I can.

Teachers also spoke directly about a growing sense of obligation for the school and its students. For example, a teacher at Ebinger described how teachers have assumed responsibility to share with their colleagues what they have learned at outside workshops:

The teachers [when they come back] will just call a meeting on their own, just to get together to share these ideas. *No one is directing this.* We have learned something that may be helpful, and we should share it.

Similarly, a teacher at Hoyne commented on how they now share responsibility both for the character of student life in the school as well as their classroom learning:

We saw a weakness [student behavior in the lunchroom] and we attacked it as a team. I'll pop in the lunchroom and look around and see if my group is doing well. You see a lot of teachers doing this now. So we have teamwork, and we are communicating with each other. We are now doing the same thing academically, looking at the learning standards we hold and trying to push kids beyond them.

In general, teachers in all six EARS schools were quite aware that new professional norms were emerging in their schools under reform.[24] They indicated that they now had good relationships with other faculty members and that their schools provided "a cooperative environment", "camaraderie", and "a family-type atmosphere." In the past, teachers had "worked to rules" which, while embodying some minimum performance standards, also delimited responsibility beyond those requirements. The expanded teacher leadership and collective responsibility observed in these schools represents a marked contrast to the pre-reform status quo.[25]

Our Analysis. Profound organizational shifts were advanced in EARS schools. The new opportunities for collegial interaction helped teachers to better understand their colleagues and appreciate them as hardworking, dedicated, committed, and caring. In a very personal sense, they knew each other better and were growing to trust each other.[26] Reform also created numerous opportunities for new leadership to emerge. This development of human potential was helping these schools to become more effective, self-guided local educational institutions.

Thus, four years into reform, EARS schools had an expanded professional leadership to attack more complex problems, stronger social support within the faculty for this development, and a heightened commitment among teachers to address these issues. Taken together, a productive mix of human and social resources had developed in these schools. Leadership for change, which began with the principal, became more broadly manifest among others in the school community. The expanding trust within the professional community became a resource for future collective action. Finally, the heightened agency among individual participants fueled affective engagement and motivated further action.

In terms of the dynamics of these developments, a few key benchmarks merit note. As reform began, there was a group of faculty in place in each school who were ready to embrace change. Their numbers expanded as new faculty members were recruited who shared the emerging vision for the school. As new organizational beliefs became part of daily routines, each school began to develop a "new history"—much more hopeful in affect and professional in content. To cultivate these changes, EARS principals used the expanded authority associated with their new role under reform to increase professional participation and empower others. That is, they constructively used the power granted them to catalyze change in their school communities and ultimately to democratize them.

On balance, it is important to emphasize that the development of a professional community is an evolutionary process. Schools proceed at different rates, and progress can be very uneven—sometimes spurts are followed by backward regression. As we compare the six schools, Bass appeared furthest along in this process. It had stable and talented leadership prior to reform, and its staff benefited significantly from the school-based decision-making training offered by Project CANAL. Hoyne had an almost entirely new faculty recruited since reform. As a group, they appeared to be forming along lines similar to Bass. Ebinger and Spry were also moving in this direction, but the professional community did not encompass the full faculty, and substantial pockets of resistance were still obvious. At Field, professional community was emerging in two of the schools-within-a-school, while the others remained more problematic. Hefferan was least far along in this regard.

External Connections to Support School Development

Restructuring is a difficult task for a school to take on by itself. Diverse resources and expertise are required to catalyze and sustain the change process. Although the central office provided very little organized assistance during the first four years of reform,[27] EARS schools drew upon an extensive array of outside connections—including individual faculty at local colleges and universities, programs supported by area foundations, the business community, and other institutions—to guide and support their organizational development. As noted earlier, Hefferan relied on Turner Construction Company and Rush-Presbyterian St. Luke's Hospital to contribute equipment, money, and volunteers in order to bring a state-of-the-art science center into the school. The Total Quality Management philosophy at Ebinger was supported by a connection to the Kellogg School of Management at Northwestern University. The Center for School Improvement at the University of Chicago provided extensive organizational development support for the schools-within-a-school restructuring at Field. Similarly, Project CANAL was an important organizational resource for the efforts at Bass, Spry, and Hefferan.

In addition, most of the EARS principals pursued external professional support for their own work. Several took advantage of summer leadership programs offered by the University of Chicago, the University of Illinois at Chicago, and the North Central Regional Educational Laboratory. Most participated in one or more organized networks of CPS principals around the city. All also formed their own personal connections to administrators in the school system, other principal colleagues, and local faculty, who provided both professional advice and personal support. Similarly, teachers in EARS schools established numerous connections with various staff development and instructional improvement efforts at local colleges and universities.

Previous to the 1988 reform, it was often very difficult for faculty in local colleges and universities to work with Chicago schools. An unwieldy centralized review and clearance process discouraged such initiatives. Area faculty frequently turned instead to nearby suburban school systems, which were more welcoming. In contrast, four years into reform, significant changes had occurred. By 1993, virtually every local college and university had a center of activity focused on school reform and improvement in Chicago. The actively restructuring schools that we studied were quite knowledgeable about these new institutional resources and sought them out.

Strategic Use of Discretionary Financial Resources

Last, but not least in importance, are the new monies provided to schools as part of PA 85-1418. They played a key role in initiating change in each of the six EARS sites.[28] By transferring increased amounts of state Chapter 1 funds to local schools to spend at their own discretion, a significant resource was made available to advance improvement efforts. These new state monies supplemented federal Chapter 1 dollars and other categorical funds, which also increased in many Chicago schools during the first four years of reform.

Depending primarily on the number of low-income students served, the six schools varied considerably in the proportion of their budget derived from discretionary resources. (See Figure 6.1.) Spry, with 100 percent low-income students, received the highest proportion: Almost 40 percent of its budget came from federal, state, and other categorical sources. Ebinger, in contrast, with only 44 percent of its students classified as poor, received the least (about 10 percent). Translating these percentages into per-pupil expenditures, Ebinger and Hoyne received a little more than $400 per pupil in 1993; Field received $700; Bass and Hefferan obtained about $1300; and Spry netted more than $1600 per student.

Although this level of discretionary funding was substantial, on balance, schools had to dip into some of these monies to meet basic education costs.[29] Even so, EARS sites still experienced a net increase in local funds during the first four years of reform, and these new resources were key in supporting the organizational changes documented in this chapter.[30]

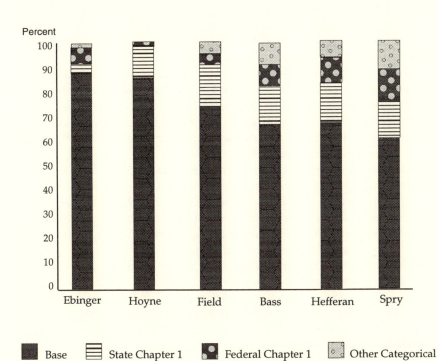

FIGURE 6.1 Percent of 1993 Budgets from Base and Discretionary Funds

In order to better understand the impact of these school-financing changes, we analyzed the budgets and spending plans in the six EARS schools from 1991 through 1993. We focused our attention on the use of discretionary monies coming from federal Chapter 1, state Chapter 1, and other categorical funds (including Project CANAL, bilingual, and desegregation money).

Use of Federal Chapter 1 Funds. These funds, a major discretionary resource in three of the six schools, continued to be used as they were prior to reform—primarily for staff salaries for pull-out programs and self-contained remedial classes. Little reallocation of funds occurred to advance school improvement efforts initiated under reform. Principals complained that the central office had not been supportive of whole-school Chapter 1 programs and that this greatly constrained their ability to use these resources in more effective ways.[31]

On balance, it is not clear that simply removing the external constraints on federal Chapter 1 funding would automatically have resulted in a different use of these funds. Most of these monies paid for staff and purchased programs that had been in schools for a long time. Reallocating these funds, therefore, would entail redefining staff roles, perhaps making some personnel changes, and abrogating some long standing institutional ties. None of these changes would be particularly easy to effect.

Use of State Chapter 1 and Other Categorical Funds. The most striking feature about the use of state Chapter 1 and other categorical funds was the amount devoted to expanding human resources. (See Figure 6.2.) For the three budget years that we examined, each school allocated at least half of its state Chapter 1 and other categorical funds for this purpose. At Bass School, nearly all state Chapter 1 and other categorical money was spent on new staff, with much of this money going for additional teachers and teacher aides to reduce class sizes.

In addition to expanding human resources, most of the EARS schools also allocated significant portions of their state Chapter 1 and other categorical budgets for equipment and textbooks. In 1992, 14 percent of the state Chapter 1 money at Field School was budgeted for math and reading textbooks. Similarly, in 1991, Hoyne budgeted roughly 20 percent of its discretionary money for computer equipment.

While the total amount of discretionary money used during this three-year period for staff development was relatively small, EARS schools were gradually directing more resources to this area. For example, Ebinger increased allocations annually beginning in 1992. In 1993, more than $19,000 was set aside for this purpose.

Strategic Allocations to Meet School Goals. More important than the general patterns in allocating discretionary resources were concerns about the strategic use of these funds: whether there was a clear link between

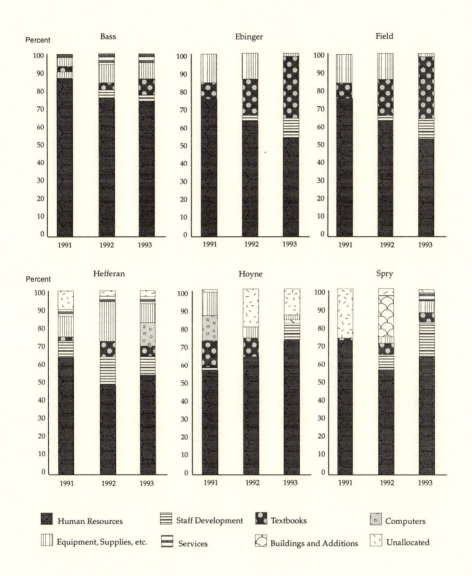

FIGURE 6.2 Percent of State Chapter 1 and Other Categorical Money
Allocated to Various Categories

budgeting and school improvement planning. We explored this question through a coordinated analysis of school budgets and improvement plans for the first four years of reform in each of the EARS schools. The results from Hefferan and Ebinger, presented below, illustrate our findings.

Between 1991 and 1993, Hefferan received more than a quarter of a million dollars from Project CANAL. Of this, more than half (approximately $150,000) was budgeted for purchasing a schoolwide computer-assisted instruction network. Hefferan implemented this network as a central part of its school improvement plan to raise student achievement in reading, writing, mathematics, and higher order thinking. In addition, Hefferan sought to address increased student achievement through staff development activities. According to the school's 1992 SIP, "The staff will be involved in extensive staff development activities to strengthen their ability to provide adequate instruction in (reading, writing, mathematics, and higher-order thinking)." Approximately $80,000 of the 1992 and 1993 CANAL money was budgeted for this purpose. These dollars supported in-service programs on writing across the curriculum (the Illinois Writing Project), whole language development, classroom management, assertive discipline, cooperative learning, and the IBM Write to Read program. Some monies were also used to create a collection of professional literature in the school library, including periodicals for teachers.

Similarly, Hefferan dedicated its state Chapter 1 money to pay primarily for the school's new instructional initiatives. These funds, for example, supported the teaching positions for the science laboratory and the creative arts program. In addition, state Chapter 1 funded a human relations specialist, a Japanese language program, and an assistant principal who functioned as a teacher facilitator and financial officer. Some state monies were also used for "basic services." In 1993, for example, $37,000 was spent on painting rooms inside the school; $8,000 was budgeted for blinds in classrooms; and $5,000 was set aside to replace furniture for teachers.

Our analysis at Ebinger also confirmed a strong connection between the School Improvement Plans and local budgeting decisions. In 1990 and 1991, Ebinger allocated a substantial portion of its state Chapter 1 funds for material needs at the school. As the principal described it, the increasing amounts of state Chapter 1 funding "directly parallels the development of the school over the last four years. Our immediate concern was, let's get more goodies. By goodies I mean bookshelves, tables, chairs, computers, those kinds of things." In 1991, more than half of all state Chapter 1 money was allocated for such equipment, with nearly 70 percent ($22,750) of it used to purchase computers. Like Hefferan, Ebinger bought computer-assisted learning programs in reading, writing/language arts, math, and reasoning skills.

In 1992, however, there was a marked shift away from purchasing equipment and toward purchasing instructional materials which would address the School Improvement Plan. For example, 37 percent of all state Chapter 1 funds that year were allocated for textbooks: $5,000 for recreational reading materials for classrooms; $10,000 for mathematics instruction manipulatives; and $11,726 for social studies maps, globes, and manipulatives. It was also in 1992 that the school decided more money should be spent on staff development. As the principal said: "After we took care of the little needs that everybody wanted physically around the building, then we moved into more training and development of skill."

In 1993, the evolving shift in allocation was even more pronounced at Ebinger. While more than 19 percent of state Chapter 1 funds were allocated for staff development and 42 percent were allocated for learning materials, only 2 percent of the money was used on equipment. Most of the learning materials money was used to support new instructional initiatives, including a Great Books Reading Enrichment Program, math manipulatives and textbooks, and resources and materials for teaching thinking skills.

In general, we found a strong connection in each EARS site between annual budgeting decisions and School Improvement Plans. Moreover, we observed a highly strategic pattern of allocating discretionary resources to finance improvement efforts. The immediate emphasis during the first two years of reform was on improving the environmental order of the school and replenishing basic material supplies. As noted earlier, these allocations played an important role in regenerating the school's image and renewing a sense of agency among local participants. After addressing some of these "basic needs," EARS schools shifted more attention toward instructional materials and staff development to support their efforts at systemic improvement.

Tying It All Together

Each EARS school gained citywide recognition for its initiative during the first four years of reform. This acknowledgment further empowered principals and extended the collective sense of self-esteem and efficacy among teachers, parents, and community members. Principals spoke proudly about how far their schools had come; but they were also realistic about where they still had to go, and what it would take to get there. None believed that the job was done or even nearly done. When asked about their future priorities, each spoke in his or her own way about staff development, improving instruction, creating a more humane and caring environment, and further strengthening ties to parents and the community.

The work at Bass had begun prior to reform, and in some ways this school was furthest along in the process. They had a stable professional community that worked well together. The increased autonomy and extra monies made available as part of reform made it easier to pursue improvement efforts that, prior to reform, might have demanded "creative insubordination" to sustain.[32] At the other end of the spectrum, Field, Hefferan, and Spry were among the most troubled schools in the system prior to reform. The organizational changes in these schools in just a few years were quite remarkable. Our independent judgments in this regard were amply supported by extended testimony from many local participants, including parents, teachers, and students. Reform had been a very positive experience.

Figure 6.3 on pages 252-253 summarizes the common features of the change process found in EARS schools. In most general terms, the development in these schools was a multifaceted endeavor demanding effective political processes, institutional leadership, broad and sustained attention to improving professional activity, and adequate technical and fiscal support.

Transformative principal leadership was the most significant common feature in the development of these six schools. Virtually all of the constructive activity that we observed had begun under the direction of the current principals. All were helping to guide their school organizations in the transition from central control to collective democratic enablement both within the school-based professional community and in relation to the local external community. The visions-in-outline articulated by these principals grew richer over time through accumulating school experiences. These ideas also broadened some as others came to embrace them. Nonetheless, even as these visions became collectivized, they still anchored local efforts. They defined appropriate boundaries for future schoolwide initiatives as well as individual work. A distinctive rhetoric—"This is for the children"— undergirded a shared commitment in each school and created a base of moral authority for collective action.

While principal leadership appeared key, no one person can transform a school alone. Many parents and local community members, both individually and through the LSC, supported and encouraged these improvement efforts. A number of teachers also assumed important new leadership roles. Overall, the collective social and human resources for improvement expanded in each school community.

Many activities occurred simultaneously at each site, and the connections among them sometimes appeared vague even to participants. Some initial steps were clearly missteps. Others were chosen because they were expedient now, with the hope of a favorable redress at a later time. Nonetheless, there was a strategic quality to this action. Schools were clearly moving in constructive directions even if they did not neatly follow models of planned change. Finally and also of key significance, these schools made creative and effective use of their discretionary resources. It is hard to envision how the progress we observed in EARS sites could have occurred without the supplemental discretionary funds provided under reform.

The Mechanisms at Work: How Expanded Local Participation Sustains a Focus on Systemic Restructuring

Our examination of the experiences of these actively restructuring schools identified several common strands of activity shared by schools which have taken best advantages of the opportunities provided by PA 85-1418. These include: an active local school council that supported local improvement efforts; a facilitative, inclusive principal who together with parents, community, and school staff articulated a vision for the school and drew local actors into the process of enabling it; a sustained focus on strengthening the professional core; an expanded access to external ideas and expertise that helped school staff to work more productively and cooperatively; and a strategic use of school resources, especially the new discretionary dollars provided under reform.

With this as background, we now return to the question which motivated this chapter: "What role did local democratic participation—the prime lever chosen by Chicago reformers to catalyze change—really play in schools that were making significant progress?" Chapter 5 offered considerable statistical evidence linking the emergence of a strong local democratic practice, sustained attention on systemic school restructuring, and instructional innovation. Thus, we know that these processes are interconnected; but through what mechanisms did this occur?

As we consider the key elements in the successful unfolding of Chicago school reform identified in this chapter, two of them—strengthening the professional core, and strategic use of discretionary resources—represent central features in the formal organization of schools and would be a prime concern in any systemic restructuring. Neither of these two developments appears to be a direct consequence of the expanded local participation in school affairs. Rather, both can be traced to other specific provisions in PA 85-1418 that granted principals control over the hiring of new teachers and required annual school improvement plans to guide the allocation of expanding discretionary resources. It seems likely that these reform provisions would have similar consequences even under alternative school-based management initiatives where there might be less commitment to local democratic enablement. At best, the effects of expanded participation here are indirect, by motivating school leadership to sustain attention to these core improvement issues.

We note that the nature of a school's politics and its improvement efforts are deeply intertwined, so much so that efforts to firmly establish cause and effect can be quite illusive. For example, local participation was

**Figure 6.3 Key Elements of Successful School Development
under Chicago School Reform**

I.   ACTIVE LOCAL SCHOOL COUNCIL ROLE

- Select a principal committed to students and parents
  and then support this principal's efforts.
- Take an active role in efforts to improve parent and
  community involvement, to enhance physical plant, and to
  improve order and safety.
- Endorse initiatives by principal and teachers for instructional
  improvement.

II. FACILITATIVE, INCLUSIVE PRINCIPAL LEADERSHIP

- Reach out to both parents and staff to get more involved.
- Articulate a vision-in-outline of how "this can be a good
  school for **our** kids and **our** families."
- Encourage sustained conversations and activity among
  both parents and faculty that further develop the vision.
- Commit to quality standards and be willing to engage
  conflict to advance them.
- Derive moral authority from public rhetoric: "Everything
  we do is for the kids."

III. PRINCIPALS' KEY FIRST STEPS: A NEW IMAGE FOR THE SCHOOL
     AND A RENEWED SENSE OF AGENCY

- Become highly visible in the school and in the community.
- Focus on identifying pressing problems that can
  be solved quickly.
- Use new symbols (e.g., school logo, stationery, uniforms) to
  distinguish the "new school" and mark individual membership.
- Offer a distinctive voice, a broader conception of the school's
  responsibility for children, their families, and the
  local community.
- Frequently remind both parents and teachers, "Look at what we
  have accomplished . . . together we can make this place better."

IV.   LONGER-TERM FOCUS: STRENGTHENING THE TECHNICAL CORE

- Hire quality new faculty.
- "Encourage" some teachers to leave.
- Build a team compatible with the evolving vision of the school.
- Support individual teacher initiative on instructional improvement.
- Move toward more sustained, schoolwide staff development.
- Promote professional community among the faculty (providing time and place to meet, committee structure for offering input, access to resources, authority to act, and support for effective group process).

V.   STRONG EXTERNAL CONNECTIONS TO SUPPORT SCHOOL DEVELOPMENT

- Principals have ties to professional networks and key associates to support their work.
- Teachers have numerous connections to local colleges and universities for staff development and instructional improvement.
- Schools have established institutional ties to support their development including ties to local social services, recreation facilities, and businesses.

VI.   STRATEGIC USE OF DISCRETIONARY RESOURCES

- Strong coupling of budget and School Improvement Plans.
- An initial focus on environmental order (e.g., improving safety and cleaning up the school), replenishing basic school supplies and instructional materials, and some add-on programs.
- Over time, increase allocations for core instructional improvement.

surely stimulated by the fact that school communities had significant authority to exercise, including new resources to allocate for staff and programs. The real opportunities given LSCs to change their schools helped catalyze local initiative. In contrast, had LSCs been primarily advisory groups with little real authority, like the school improvement councils that they replaced, it is unlikely that we would have seen as much local involvement as we found in the six EARS schools. Quite simply, it is hard to maintain voluntary participation in organizations that do not sustain significant work.

More generally, it is important to remember that PA 85-1418 was a complex piece of legislation that included a number of provisions to directly promote school improvement, in addition to establishing local school governance arrangements. Some of these school improvement provisions may also have had the effect of expanding local participation. In this sense, one might be tempted to reverse the "causal arrow" in the logic of Chicago of school reform set out earlier in Figure 5.7. That is, an improving organization might actually promote more participation. Nonetheless, in at least three important ways as detailed below, the "causal arrow" seems clearly to run in the direction originally specified: the expanded local participation sought by PA 85-1418 leveraged sustained attention to fundamental organizational change.

A Recasting of the Principalship to Promote Entrepreneurial Behavior

First in this regard is the transformation wrought by PA 85-1418 in the role of the principal. In order to vitalize local control while at the same time curtailing the direct administrative control of the central office and sub-districts, PA 85-1418 sought to make principals locally accountable. It advanced this goal by removing principals' tenure and placing them on four-year performance contracts subject to LSC review.

The reshaping of the principalship that ensued from this policy initiative is a key factor in fostering democratic localism. As documented in Chapter 2, an inclusive and facilitative principal leadership style was a salient feature in schools where strong democratic practices emerged. We also see in the six schools analyzed in this chapter that such leadership was central to systemic change. In each EARS school, the principal was the direct and immediate link through which the expanded local participation influenced school activity. The beliefs and actions of these persons provided the necessary conduit for the school community's political activity to enter the formal school organization and redirect its efforts. These principals were not just neutral bureaucratic actors carrying out decisions formally made by the local council. Rather, they actively supported the work of the council, personally embodied its aims, and sought to enact the commitments which undergirded them.

In most general terms, by making principals accountable to local constituents—not only parents and community members but also teachers—the system of sanctions and incentives affecting the principalship was fundamentally altered. The traditional orientation of Chicago principals—looking up into the bureaucracy for guidance and career advancement—had promoted widespread conservatism. Leading change at the school building level could be dangerous to one's career.

Under reform, the basic incentives changed. Principals became local entrepreneurs of values, ideas, and money.[33] Increasingly, this behavior was publicly endorsed not only in school communities but more generally around the city. Innovative schools received considerable public attention through both print and electronic media.[34] Perhaps the most significant indicator of the value of entrepreneurial behavior is this: One year after our first local report on the EARS schools, three of the six principals had moved on to more responsible professional positions.[35] In the past, risk taking in the interest of promoting school change often demanded a measure of heroism and was mainly supported by the psychic rewards of "doing the right thing" for children. With the advent of local control, tangible extrinsic rewards also now accrued.

It is important to emphasize that while the six principals in the EARS sites were strong committed school leaders, they were not unique, charismatic figures. These six schools were selected out of a larger group of seventy-two nominated elementary schools. In this selection process, we deliberately excluded several schools from the study which had already received substantial media coverage. Further, in order to obtain a diverse set of schools in terms of student composition, size, resources, and location around the city, we also excluded several other notable sites. Thus the six sites discussed in this chapter were good examples of schools actively pursuing improvement, but they were not necessarily the very best in the city.

More generally, both the case-study synthesis and indicator analyses presented in Chapter 2 suggest that entrepreneurial principal behavior became widespread across the system. In short, this is not just a story about a small number of extraordinary school leaders. Rather, the extant evidence indicates that, by fundamentally changing the incentives and sanctions affecting the principalship and by supporting new school leaders to operate in different ways,[36] it is possible to attain very different principal behavior than we have witnessed in the past.

Social Support for Fundamental Change

As we noted in the introduction to Chapter 3, considerable animus was expressed by parent and community leaders toward principals and teachers during the mobilization for reform in Chicago. The schools were distant institutions, unresponsive to local needs. Even more critical were their comments about the central office. The agency of the Chicago Public Schools was seriously questioned. While much of this criticism was clearly justified, it left local school professionals with a very uncertain basis for action—neither supported locally by parents and community nor from above by a strong central office.

In schools with strong democratic politics, however, sustained discussions emerged among local participants about the need for fundamental change. Moreover, initial actions by principals and other school professionals toward these ends were locally backed and encouraged. In the past, principals might have taken refuge behind some central office mandate or rule, even if it were dysfunctional. In contrast, after reform local control made it more likely that principals would challenge such external constraints in the interest of moving their schools forward.

In most general terms, PA 85-1418 expanded the moral authority of local professionals to act in a school community's interests. The reform created processes and structures that encouraged interactions among parents, community members, and local professionals, all of whom had been silenced previously within a highly centralized bureaucracy. To the extent that these groups sustained a positive engagement around shared concerns, the reform tapped a powerful mobilizing agent that resides in such public conversations. At base here is the moral force of a social movement.[37] As local professionals drew in other local constituents, they recognized that they were not alone. In conversations with parents and community members, a nucleus of school leaders emerged who shared a deep dissatisfaction with current affairs. In this collective solidarity, they found strength to act.

More generally, many of the problems of urban schools are not strictly contained within the school walls and under the exclusive authority of professionals to redress. For example, the concerns about safety and disorder, which are widespread in urban schools, begin in the communities where these schools are located.[38] Such problems need simultaneous address both inside and outside of school. The school-community partnerships formed around Chicago's democratic localism facilitated action on just such problems, as the examples from both Spry and Field schools recounted in this chapter amply demonstrate.

The destructive social and economic changes in many urban neighborhoods during the last two decades have created much more problematic environments for rearing children. The basic fabric of supportive social relationships between parents, other community adults, and school staff have greatly weakened. While urban schools have profound needs to strengthen instructional programs and improve the pedagogy of teachers, it is also clear that repairing the social fabric of the school community is critical. If local professionals in urban schools do not reform their relationships with parents and community members to build a stronger foundation of trust, it is hard to envision how these schools can improve fundamentally, or how communities can better support the education of their children.[39]

Opening Up the Flow of Ideas

A major tenet of the school restructuring movement is that schools must become more commitment-oriented learning organizations. It is argued that such developments are essential if schools are to reach and maintain the levels of teaching practice necessary to afford all students sustained opportunities to engage challenging academic subject matter. An enormous amount of individual and organizational learning must take place to transform a school like Beacon, described in the Prologue, into the kind of instructional environment described in the opening section of Chapter 4. For this to occur, schools must have much greater access to outside ideas and expertise than ever in the past. Four years into reform, it was clear that Chicago's efforts had truly opened up schools in this regard.

It is an established adage that information is power. Limiting access to information in highly centralized bureaucracies has historically been a major device for maintaining control. Central office administrators formulated rules and plans which were then passed down to schools to implement. Similarly, at the school building level, principals tended to maintain close control over the ideas and options made available to teachers to change their practice. The end result was an overall school environment that was not particularly conducive to organizational learning.

By weakening central office control over schools and legitimizing the participation of parents, community, and local professionals in school-based decision making, PA 85-1418 transformed these processes. The embrace of democratic localism promoted an expanded equality whereby teachers, parents, and community members could bring improvement proposals to the table. As a result, the number of channels by which new ideas might enter schools literally exploded. To be sure, principals remained the major conduit, but teachers, parents and community members were also active in this regard. Recall, for example, that it was a few teachers at Spry who became convinced through their outside course work that their school could be better, and they helped to bring Azcoitia into the school to lead that change.

In addition to legitimizing an expanded access to ideas, reform also created numerous forums, such as the LSC, PPAC, and other derivative committees, where ideas could be publicly discussed and collective understandings constructed. In the past, individual teachers might introduce innovations in their own classrooms and might even collaborate with a few close colleagues, but there were few structured opportunities for these initiatives to diffuse more broadly through the school. Contexts for meaningful cooperation of local professionals with parents and community members were even less common. As the EARS cases clearly document, these discussion contexts expanded substantially under reform.

Thus the two major components of organizational learning—access to outside ideas and internal structures that facilitate their diffusion through the school community—were both significantly influenced by Chicago's embrace of democratic localism. A major strength of the Chicago reform was that it legitimized this activity, created at least some initial structures through which it might develop, and accompanied this with a strong exhortation for local actors to "get involved."

Finally, by weakening central office control, the reform also indirectly supported efforts by numerous other local entities—community-based and citywide advocacy groups, colleges and universities, and a wide range of civic and business groups—to become more knowledgeable about urban education and more active in improving the city's schools. The actual supply of ideas and expertise—through colloquia, workshops, professional networks, and external development groups engaged in school restructuring activities—expanded dramatically. The highly centralized control over improvement efforts that characterized the CPS prior to reform tended to discourage both local university-based educators and national groups from focusing their efforts here. School improvement became an open marketplace in Chicago. Thus, the reform had a significant effect on the supply of ideas and expertise, as well as on the schools' demand for them.

* * * * *

In closing, we note that the mechanisms by which democratic localism helped to sustain attention on school improvement are not especially simple nor direct. Even when the reform "was working," its operations varied considerably across different school contexts. Improvement efforts also broke down at times, requiring schools in some cases to go backwards before they proceeded forward again. As a result, a casual examination of the Chicago experience could easily miss much of what we have described here.

This subtlety and complexity notwithstanding, we have amassed considerable evidence that supports the basic premise of the reform. Democratic localism can challenge dysfunctional school operations by generating a moral force for change, by encouraging commitment and entrepreneurial behavior on the part of local school professionals, and by opening up schools to new ideas and practices. Our analyses support the conclusion that weakening central-office control and promoting local democratic enablement is an effective lever for catalyzing basic organizational change. Although the case is still open about how much improvement in student learning this will ultimately produce, these first steps must be viewed as productive developments. When judged against the reality of schools like Beacon, and the label that they had acquired as the "Worst in America," this is a significant accomplishment.

7

Major Lessons from the Initiating
Phase of Chicago School Reform

As we began the research that culminated in this book, we knew all too well about the deep and expansive problems of major urban school systems. They have accumulated over several decades and require long-term redress. Past studies have taught us that even some of the most successful cases of change in individual urban schools have taken five or more years to culminate in comprehensive restructuring. To be sure, substantial changes in organizational operations were occurring two and three years into the process, and there was a logic to these changes, but "the bottom line" of student achievement was one of the last things to move. And for every success, there were surely many other attempts with less positive outcomes.[2]

In designing this study, it was tempting to argue that student achievement gains should be the primary evidence for making judgments about short term progress. Political demands for an immediate demonstration of such measurable improvements were present, reflecting genuine concerns about the dysfunctional status quo and longstanding frustrations over a seeming inability to do anything about this.[3] As a statement of purpose, as an expression of high aspirations, and as a symbol of serious commitment, we view this press for quick demonstrable improvement as laudable. As a realistic expectation for meaningful institutional change in a major urban school system, however, it is simply not sustainable. In our view, any large-scale reform, regardless of its merits, is likely to fail if judged primarily against this short-term standard.[4]

It is especially important that those engaged in research articulate realistic expectations for the reform endeavors whose progress they seek to evaluate, because our discourse helps to shape the larger climate of public opinion about such matters. Reasonable markers of progress to date and formative feedback on missteps, as well as steps well taken, can offer constructive guideposts for the next round of action. In contrast, to continue to reiterate that the ultimate aim has not yet been accomplished is only likely to undermine the long-term commitment needed to achieve genuine change.

For these reasons, we organized our study around articulating the logic of the reform and probing its critical assumptions. We sought to test this logic against evidence about what was actually happening in schools, and evaluated the observed changes based on past studies of individual school and system level development. Our work was framed around one overarching question: "What evidence exists that this initiative is evolving in ways that are likely to lead to major improvements in students' school experiences and learning?" At base, we have attempted to combine an empathetic orientation toward the espoused logic of the reform with an empirical perspective about its actual operations.

A Capsule Review of the Reform and its Initial Effects

The Chicago School Reform Act of 1988 launched an undertaking of enormous scope that was still very much in the process of developing five years later. The reform sought to weaken central decision making and to promote greater site-based control by devolving resources and authority to local schools. Reform gave principals greater control over the school budget, the physical plant, and the recruitment and hiring of new teachers. By removing their tenure and making them accountable to a Local School Council (LSC), principals were in turn encouraged to redirect initiative toward local constituencies and their concerns.

The reform also created a real voice for parents and community members through representatives on the LSC. These parent-majority councils have the power to hire and fire the school principal, and to approve the budget and the School Improvement Plan (SIP). To a lesser degree, teachers were also given an expanded voice. Through their two seats on the LSC, they have direct influence on school affairs, including the choice of principal, and through the teacher-elected Professional Personnel Advisory Committee (PPAC), they have advisory responsibility over school curriculum and instruction. Also important, new funds became available to

local schools to support improvements. Four years after the onset of reform, the typical Chicago elementary school was allocating approximately
a half-million dollars each year in such discretionary resources.

Taken as a whole, the Chicago School Reform Act was a complex and
ambitious piece of legislation. It unleashed a broad institutional restructuring, reaching well beyond the school system itself to include community organizations, business groups, local colleges and universities, and
labor unions. We know of no comparable institutional change in public
education that is currently under way in another major U.S. urban center.

At the heart of the reform was a simple idea. PA 85-1418 aimed to re-
claim initiative for local actors—parents, community members, teachers,
and principals. It was hoped that the new structures and roles established
by reform would create a political force strong enough to leverage the organizational changes needed to make schools more responsive to the communities, families, and students they were intended to serve. It envisioned
that by expanding local participation in school affairs, a collective responsibility for the schools' work would emerge. This would create a natural
social resource to advance significant changes in classroom instruction and,
ultimately, in student learning.

The analyses presented in this book have focused on the functioning of
these new governance arrangements, whether schools were using their
newfound autonomy to promote fundamental reorganization, and whether
this local activity sustained attention to improvements in teaching and learning. More specifically, our research examined both the political and organizational rearrangements under way in Chicago schools: to determine
whether the changes envisioned by PA 85-1418 were in fact occurring; to
identify places where this had and had not taken place (and why this may
be so); and to analyze whether new structures and norms were being established such that the ultimate aims of the reform—major improvements
in student learning—might be achievable. In the process, we have also
evaluated the central premise of the Chicago reform: that expanded local
participation in school affairs is an effective lever for organizational change
and instructional improvement.

A Story of "Three-Thirds"

The diverse array of statistical analyses and field study findings presented in this book documents three general patterns of school development. We found that an approximately equal number of elementary schools
fell into each group.

Self-initiating, Actively Restructuring Schools. Four years into reform,
about one-third of the elementary school communities most in need of
change (i.e., where student assessments were significantly below national

norms prior to reform) had developed strong democratic participation that focused on a systemic approach to school improvement. Significant changes were occurring: in the relationships of these schools to their parents and local communities; in the organization of teachers' work and their cooperative engagement around school improvement, and in classroom instruction.

These schools appeared headed in a productive direction. Substantial social resources had formed. Supportive relationships existed both within the professional staff and with parents and the local community. A palpable sense of both urgency and agency had emerged: "We can make a difference for our children and we must do this!" Better conditions had also been created for improvements in classroom teaching—long-needed instructional materials had been purchased, new ideas had been introduced, new strategies were being tried, and support for change was now being offered by school leadership and a wide range of outside organizations and individual agents. In essence, the table was set for the continued efforts that would be needed to significantly improve student learning. If these schools stayed the course, such results seemed likely.

Schools Engaged, but Struggling with Improvement. A second third of the schools shared some of the characteristics of the first group described above, but were not as far along. They were engaged in a change process, although sometimes they were struggling. While they often undertook worthwhile projects, they did not always attend to the quality with which these projects were implemented. Looking across the ensemble of activities in which these schools were engaged, it was often difficult to discern anything resembling strategic action. Very worthwhile new initiatives often stood alongside more dubious undertakings.

In fairness, service fragmentation and programmatic incoherence is arguably the most significant organizational problem confronting urban schools today. For almost three decades, educators have taken the view that improving opportunities for students meant adding more special programs. "Good schools" came to be synonymous with this aim. A variety of outside actors—in central offices, state and federal government, universities, foundations, and private enterprises—all developed ideas about how schools could be better, provided at least some marginal resources to implement their ideas, and often added another layer of rules and procedures to follow.[5] Each initiative tended to have a specific programmatic focus (e.g., dropout intervention, drug prevention, AIDS awareness, etc.), but few dealt directly with the ensuing issues of coordination and organizational integration. As a result, schools became very complex, but not robust, organizations. In principle, all of this could work well together, but frequently it just did not happen. Moreover, a higher density of this external activity focused on urban schools, which typically had the greatest needs but also the least local capacity to integrate these diverse efforts. Perhaps most troublesome of all, over the long term school-based actors gradually came to think that this is the way schools are *supposed to be run. Ironically, this is in fact the antithesis of organization.* Rather, it resembles an entropic end-state—an organizational equilibria of many disconnected, random activities.

Schools Left Behind by Reform. As for the final third of Chicago elementary schools, these places were largely unaffected by reform during the first four years. A fraction of the schools in this group had gotten stuck in very divisive adversarial politics that blocked significant improvement initiatives. Even here, however, we discerned a positive sign: At least there was energy in these communities focusing on schools. As we saw in the case of Spry school, strong local leadership can harness this energy and convert it into a resource for collective improvement. So there was some reason to hold out hope for these schools.

The overwhelming majority of the schools is this third group, however, were not so fortunate. In about a quarter of the elementary schools in the CPS, there was little indication that viable local governance arrangements had emerged four years into reform. Typically, the principal had consolidated power in these school communities and was using that power, albeit sometimes unintentionally, to maintain a dysfunctional status quo. With little operative accountability either to local constituents or external agents, existing arrangements appeared likely to persist. Although the extra local fiscal resources provided by reform were surely welcomed, there was no indication that a strategic planning and improvement process had begun.

How Should We Judge This?

From the standpoint of the mobilizing rhetoric in the late 1980s for Chicago's reform—a need to substantially improve educational opportunities for all children—the progress during the first four years certainly came up short. Some schools were unaffected, and others struggled. On balance, however, it is far from clear that any systemwide reform, regardless of its specific features, could produce results as quickly and as widely as promised by the reform rhetoric. While such rhetoric may be of great value in building support for change, it should never be confused with analysis, based on evidence from other districts, of what has actually been possible to achieve, even assuming reasonably good circumstances.

Viewed in the light of actual urban reform experiences, the developments in Chicago during the early 1990s were impressive. A dysfunctional status quo was challenged in many local schools, and leadership had emerged to promote change. Energy had been activated in a diverse cross section of schools, largely without regard to income, race/ethnicity and pre-reform achievement levels. Organizational capacity was being built to sustain fundamental change. Efforts to strengthen social relationships among local school professionals and parents were coupled with a focus on developing the knowledge and skill of faculties and their collective will to pursue improvement. Such changes struck us as much more important than experiences in some other districts that may have effected a short term boost in test scores but left the basic human, social, and technical resources of schools largely untouched.[6] Moreover, this was not a case of a few new schools or alternative schools or magnets. Rather, significant organizational changes had been catalyzed in many ordinary urban schools serving very disadvantaged populations.

We suspect that this story of "three-thirds" is likely to be a common theme in school decentralization. As we argued in Chapter 1, we should expect highly variable results from any reform that relies on local initiative to catalyze change. In the first phase of such a reform, we should expect that the variability among schools will grow, as some move forward and others are left behind. While we may not be able to predict very well at the outset which specific schools will progress, as was our experience in Chicago, we can be fairly confident that the first phase of decentralization will produce varied results overall.

On balance, we do not view such variability during the first phase of a large system change effort as especially worrisome. In essence, this is the price that must be paid for relying on a strategy of mobilizing local initiative. School-based actors need to know that they have the freedom to act— to try, to perhaps fail, and to try again. While some will do this well and others may not, to compromise this freedom, because we know it will not be used especially well in some places, would vitiate the local agency-building so necessary for collective action. Moreover, it is not clear that varied initial consequences can be avoided, even with much better planning and support than occurred in Chicago. Perhaps the percentages of schools in the three groups might shift a bit toward the more favorable side, but in the end we would still expect this to be a "tale of three types."

Some Larger Theoretical Observations

As schools seriously engage change, the mechanics of these processes, as well as more fundamental aspects of schools as organizations, open themselves up for observation. Because Chicago's experiences with democratic localism catalyzed major changes in many schools, our study also afforded an opportunity to learn more about the organization of schools and their processes of improvement. Some insights that we have gleaned from our research on the first four years of reform are sketched out below.

The Centrality of School Micro-Politics to Local Improvement

As noted in Chapter 2, there is growing recognition that the politics at the school building level can be a major impediment to reform. Many recent efforts at school restructuring have failed precisely for this reason.[7] Interestingly, the analyses presented in this book add further support to this argument about the significance of local school politics, but also suggest a more nuanced view of the effects. To be sure, collective political activity can be an impediment to change; but it can also be a resource. Specifically, we have documented how capable leadership in many Chicago schools used the institution of local governance to create opportunities for an extended discourse about school aims and the effectiveness of school operations. Over time, this discourse promoted a sense of shared purpose and fomented a moral force to advance improvement. This social movement in turn expanded the local mandate for change well beyond the formal authority granted LSCs and principals under PA 85-1418.

These experiences in Chicago suggest an important lesson for school improvement. In order to achieve reform on a broad scale, we must consider not only the instrumental initiatives that might directly strengthen school operations, teaching practice and instruction, but also how to mobilize the political life of the school community in support of such changes. That is, regardless of the quality of the reform ideas, significant educational improvements may not materialize unless the political life of the school creates and sustains authority for it. It is the latter which significantly mediates whether a school maintains attention over the long term for genuine change to develop fully.[8] While many weaknesses surely remain in Chicago schools, by drawing attention to this issue, Chicago's reform has made a significant contribution to the larger national discourse on educational improvement.

Strong Democratic Politics as a Transitional State

This book has offered a positive account of strong democratic politics as a lever for more responsive local elementary schools.[9] We have documented how such politics can foster collective activity among local school professionals, parents, and community members which challenges an unsatisfactory state of affairs in schools and mobilizes initiative for institutional change.

On balance, while we recognize that such politics is effective in catalyzing fundamental change, we are uncertain whether this political activity will continue to characterize the functioning of these institutions over time. While strong democratic practice may be highly effective during the transitional state of fundamental change, it may well be too time- and energy-consuming to be sustained inside a high-performing organization.

In this regard, it is necessary to draw a distinction between political activity occurring in a legislative context and decision making as carried out in schools. In a legislative context, deliberation about collective affairs is the principal work. In schools and other organizations, on the other hand, collective decision making is simply a component of their activity—something which must be satisfactorily resolved so that coordinated work can proceed. Not every aspect of operations can be up for extensive debate at every moment. This suggests that schools may evolve toward some compromise position that blends individuals' influence over decision making with a value for efficiency and organizational routine. On this point, it is important to recognize that professional staff in Chicago schools tend to regard democratic decision making as an additional responsibility on top of what is already a very demanding job.[10]

We suspect that a more consensual form of politics is needed to sustain schools beyond the transitional state. This concern draws our attention to another form of political practice—called unitary politics—not previously discussed in this book.[11] Although not directly observed in any of our field sites, we suspect that this form of communal activity may characterize stable high-performing schools.[12] At the core of unitary politics is a set of principles, held in common among organizational members, which provides the guiding framework for institutional life. This couples with a strong relational ethic, characterized by respect and trust, which nurtures a distinctly personal face to local efforts. Decision making inside such an organization is jointly shaped by the guiding force of the principles, by respect for strongly held views of individual participants, and by deference to leadership whose behavior most clearly embodies the principles. Some structural conditions facilitate the development and maintenance of this type of politics. It is more likely to thrive, for example, in a small, stable community where people have shared histories, a common view of the future, and ample opportunities to work together and get to know each other well. Ample opportunities for substantive talk and collective planning are also critical. These interactions may even carry over outside of school into members' social lives.[13]

Institutional leadership can directly promote the development of unitary politics by recruiting like-minded individuals into the organization and by aggressively socializing new members into established norms. On occasion there is also a need for an expulsion mechanism: When individuals' values and behavior are highly deviant from the group, they must leave. Interestingly, we documented in Chapter 6 that deliberate attention to faculty selection, socialization and "counseling out" were common characteristics of these actively restructuring schools. While none of the EARS sites had yet achieved the value consensus and cumulative density of positive social interactions that characterize unitary politics, at least some of these schools appeared pointed in this direction.

More generally, we note that much of the writing about high-performing organizations in the corporate world appears to assume this form of political activity.[14] We also note that the conditions identified in the literature for nurturing unitary politics are very similar to conditions documented in recent research on the organizational characteristics of successfully restructured schools.[15] Both strands of research suggest that unitary politics is the form of collective political activity that will primarily characterize the operations of commitment-oriented learning organizations.

For these reasons, unitary politics appears a more stable and efficient organizational alternative to strong democratic politics, and we posit that many improving Chicago elementary schools will likely evolve in this direction. To be sure, this does not mean that we expect the democratic local institutions at the heart of this reform (LSCs, PPACs, and other local school committees) will disappear. To the contrary, they will remain active contexts for continuing conversations about how the organizing principles of the schools should shape daily life. A wide zone of discretion, however, will be afforded school leadership whose actions would be broadly viewed as advancing the vision of the school. The basic presumption will be that leadership is doing the right things for the right reasons. Individuals will be free to speak their minds, but some issues simply will not arise. The social context will generally be characterized as respectful, trusting and to some degree deferent as well. Should operations seriously begin to go awry, however, local democratic institutions will still exist to check excessive action.

Interestingly, a common characteristic of both strong and unitary forms of democracy is that organizations have structures in place that encourage sustained discourse. In the "revolutionary stage" associated with strong democracy, discourse tends to focus on articulating the common principles that should come to dominate the organization. In contrast, emphasis shifts in a unitary politics to applying these "accepted" principles to organizational analysis and institutional improvement. Nevertheless, both conceptions of politics share the position that substantive public conversation is the lifeblood of political practice. Thus, both stand in contrast with a pluralist bargaining form of politics which, as discussed in Chapter 2, holds a diminished role for genuine discourse.

A Blending of Choice with Democratic Localism

Given the nature of the Chicago reform, we have quite naturally focused on its central element for change—democratic localism as a lever to catalyze initiative. We would be remiss, however, in not pointing out an important fact about the Chicago Public Schools. Extensive choice operates within this system alongside local control. More than 30 percent of the elementary school students do not currently attend their neighborhood school, and this percentage may well grow under the combination of an open enrollment policy and the further evolution of decentralization.

We view this element of choice as a productive, perhaps even a necessary complement to making democratic localism work in a complex and diverse urban context. Specifically, a key concern in any decentralization effort is how the interests of "minority students" within a school community are accommodated. (Minority should be read here as meaning students and families whose interests are different in any way from the dominant majority interests in the school.) Historically, the protection of minority interests has been a weakness in local democratic control, which typically has necessitated oversight and intervention from higher levels of government. While one could envision an activist Board of Education passing policies that regulate local action in this regard, such regulations might introduce distortions into school practice instead of supplying effective solutions to problems. Over time, such central action may simply re-create the complex bureaucratic state of affairs that the current reform sought to relieve.

Moreover, problems with students' lack of fit are likely to be exacerbated in a decentralized system where individual schools are philosophically and programmatically distinct. That is, if schools become truly different, there will be more reasons for some parents to want to choose something other than their local unit. While proximity to home is valued, especially at the elementary level, so is a school whose instructional content, pedagogy, and social norms are complementary to the home. Finally, if reform actually approaches its highest aspirations—a better informed and more educated citizenry around matters of schooling—we should expect to see more articulated differences in tastes about education and greater pressures on government to recognize and respond to these needs. In short, no matter how enamored one might be with democratic localism as an ideal, a pragmatic realist view of the American urban scene implies that "choice" must accompany "voice" as part of a comprehensive effort to create a system of schools.

The Necessity of a Theory of School Development to Guide Reform

There is considerable discussion today about standards-based education and how schools should become more outcome-oriented. Accompanying this is a move to develop common educational goals, and content and performance standards for student achievement. We believe that the absence of such standards was a weakness of the first phase of the Chicago reform. In our view, good external guidance here could have contributed to more productive local decision making.

On the other hand, an exclusive attention on outcome standards also has its down side, as this may well divert efforts away from the real structural changes needed to move productively in this direction. By analogy, imagine observing a high school track team that is learning to high jump. Suddenly, the coach tells the team that the bar is no longer at 5 feet, but 7 feet, 6 inches. The coach proclaims, "Now, it is your responsibility to figure out how to get there. I am just setting the standards." When the student athletes appear stunned, the coach repeats the message, this time saying it louder. In observing students' subsequent failures at the new standard, the coach then proceeds to decry their lack of enthusiasm and effort. This does not sound like effective coaching and it is not a productive strategy for school improvement either. Rather than promoting improvement, it is more likely to foster cynicism and undermine the hope and commitment necessary to sustain effort during the very uncertain process of individual and organizational change.

In short, we need more than just strong exhortations that schools be at some preferred state of operations. We also have to have an understanding of how they might realistically get there. The common rhetoric today, that states and districts set the goals and leave it up to schools to achieve these goals, glosses over the very real consideration that how to get there *is* the problem. We worry that without some integrative view of school development, educators are likely to maintain a fragmented approach to change that continues to reach out for the "hot new initiatives" without examining how these fit within larger organizational processes and long-term objectives. As we have documented in this book, disjointed decision-making is a common way of enacting reform in many schools.

Such a theory of school development would have to begin with a realistic assessment about the base conditions in schools, which we might call "state A." A school's capacity to pursue new standards, or other calls for reform, is grounded in the basic human, social, intellectual, and fiscal resources available in that specific school community. Within any large system, schools will vary as to their base capacity, and this will influence both the pace of progress and the likelihood of success. For example, schools with dedicated faculties, good leadership and a history of successful collective action are more likely to improve quickly than those with weak leadership, poor faculty commitment, and a long history of failure with earlier innovations. The path analysis results presented in Chapter 5 clearly support this contention.

In addition, we need to be able to envision in some detail how schools might realistically proceed from their current situation, "state A," to some preferred "state B." That is, if "state B" is to become common practice, what has to change and how do we expect this to come about? Such a theory of development entails: an identification of the major elements that must be engaged and how they interconnect; an acknowledgment of the problems that schools are likely to confront, and some alternative approaches to their redress; and a standpoint for articulating what counts as reasonable progress along the way. The analysis presented in Chapter 6 was our attempt to outline such a theory in the specific context of the Chicago reform. To recap, principals worked together with a supportive base of parents, teachers, and community members to mobilize initiative. Their efforts broadly focused along two major dimensions: first, reaching out to parents and community to strengthen the ties between local school professionals and the clientele they are to serve; and second, working to expand the professional capacities of individual teachers, to promote the formation of a coherent professional community, and to direct resources toward enhancing the quality of instruction. Improvement efforts involved a blend of strategic long term initiatives that might truly move the "bottom line" with an emphasis on "quick hits" that drew local attention and built agency. In terms of the technical core of teaching and learning, sustained attention was focused on enhancing the human resource base by recruiting good new people, emphasizing staff development, and actively pushing out resisters to change.

In more general terms, this development theory focuses attention on a small number of key areas: local managerial and leadership capacity; strengthening school-parent-community ties; human resource development; professional community formation; and local access and use of ideas, materials, and expertise to improve instruction. It also focuses attention on two broad processes: political mobilization of local actors to initiate and sustain attention to school improvement, and the strategic quality of cumulative decision making. On the first account, the reform process must achieve and maintain a sense of integrity that warrants a continued collective commitment to the school and its efforts to improve. On the second account, a school's improvement planning must be marked by an evolving direction over time that is anchored in a specific conception of improved performance. It should not be disjointed and fragmented.

In our view, school reform needs such a set of ideas to guide the work of local actors in their efforts to pursue a coherent program of school change. In addition, as we take up in the next section, reform also needs such a conceptualization to direct the restructuring efforts at the system center necessary to support school-based change. We simply note at this point that without such a framework to guide policy, neither the functions to be undertaken at the system level nor the key aims to be advanced through them are obvious.

On balance, any development model is just that: a model, and not a specific lockstep plan. Progress can advance along numerous viable paths, and no one course is obviously best for all schools. How development starts and proceeds in any specific context will largely depend on the base capacity of that school and the particular interests of the leadership group. Nonetheless, it is clear that sustained work must eventually emerge on each of the major elements within our development model. Stated somewhat differently, it is hard to envision improved student achievement in a school with poor leadership, weak parent-school ties, little professional commitment or learning, and no attention to the quality of the instructional materials. Similarly, it is hard to imagine a coherent program of local school development being sustained across these various areas without a process that collectively engages a major portion of the school community in a plan of strategic action. Quite simply, good schools do not just emerge by accident.

Similarly, it is important to recognize that this a working theory. Various components are likely to be modified over time, some may become more significant, others might diminish, and the salience of some features may remain unclear for a long time. For example, we remain uncertain about the precise function of Local School Councils within the Chicago reform. It is clear to us that they are important in several regards. First, the LSC has created a context and provided some good reasons for expanded interactions among school staff, parents, and the local community about the aims and operation of the school. In many instances this has opened up public discourse about how schools work and how they should work. Second, formalizing the LSC as a structure with genuine authority signals to local school professionals that they should pay attention to the needs of the parents, children, and the community that the school serves. This school renorming redresses an important problem, noted in Chapter 3, of the disconnect between too many urban schools and their clientele. Third, the LSC clearly gives parents and community members the potential to significantly redirect local operations. This constitutes an important check on local action. What still remains unclear to us, however, is whether LSCs must actually function as active legislative bodies that closely direct school operations. Our field evidence raises doubts in this regard. In improving schools, professional staff, parents, and community members have achieved a respectful and trusting relationship with each other. Parents and community members may often defer under such circumstances to professional staff about the design of improvement initiatives. Local school professionals, however, work under a set of norms which emphasizes being locally responsive, and are also cognizant of the real authority that LSCs can choose to exercise. In this regard, the primary influence of an LSC may well derive not so much from what it does, but from local actors' understandings of what it can do, and how this tends to reframe the collective responsibilities of school professionals to children, families, and the local community.

In short, a theory of school development, like any other theory, will evolve over time as evidence accrues and social discourse extends about the meaning of this evidence. Just because we do not know all of the nuances of such a theory as we begin a reform does not justify going to the other extreme of being totally agnostic about how school change might reasonably proceed.

Taking Stock: The Unfinished Business of Chicago School Reform

As our data collection and initial analysis work for this book drew to a close in late 1994, we suspected that Chicago had gotten about as much as could be expected out of local initiative. Major new policies seemed needed: to extend progress in actively restructuring schools; to better support improvement initiatives in struggling schools; and to catalyze change in those schools which had been "left behind."

Actively restructuring schools were poised to make major advances in student learning. They continued to operate, however, under remnants of the old centralized administrative control. It was often not until the middle of the academic year that the Board of Education made discretionary funds available to schools, impeding their ability to execute school improvement plans in a timely fashion. Although principals had authority to hire new staff, actually getting them on the payroll frequently required a personal visit to the central office at Pershing Road to track down paperwork gone awry. Procurement of supplies and materials was slow and cumbersome, and much-needed major capital improvements remained bogged down in a political process that produced few new buildings and school renovations even though money had been set aside for this purpose. Although central administrative problems affected the whole system, they seemed especially salient in actively restructuring schools because those schools were aggressively trying to move forward and often found that they lacked the full range of autonomy needed.

In addition, as acknowledged in Chapter 6, even actively restructuring schools had to pay more attention to enhancing the subject-matter knowledge and pedagogic expertise of individual teachers, and to developing as professional communities of practice. Unless schools became more supportive learning environments for adults as well as students, the potential of PA 85-1418 to advance student learning was unlikely to be reached. Some schools, like Bella in Chapter 3, had accessed external support and made major progress in this regard. If large numbers of schools, however, chose to move suddenly in this direction, there was not nearly enough capacity around the city to offer quality assistance.

Concerns about instructional improvement seemed even more salient for the second "third" of the schools described earlier. While actively restructuring schools had been able to assemble and integrate the necessary resources for continued development, we were less sanguine about this second group. Although the goal remained the same as for the first group—each school as a self-guided, responsive and effective local institution—a more organized and sustained form of external assistance would probably be needed to move these school communities forward. How to create such comprehensive support within a decentralized system posed some new problems.

As for the third group, those not yet touched by reform, major problems of leadership confronted these schools. None of the three local sites of power—the LSC, the principal, or the faculty—had managed to challenge a clearly dysfunctional status quo. Left to their own devices, these schools seemed unlikely to improve. To respond here, external accountability had to be organized in order to identify non-improving schools, and a local assistance capacity assembled to jump-start change. At a minimum, these schools needed help to develop active LSCs. Principals needed mentoring on improvement planning, operations management, and school community leadership. Also, more collective faculty effort had to focus on advancing student learning and welfare.

Unfortunately, the problems in many of the school communities left behind by reform were both more extensive and deep-seated than in the second group. Moreover, the human and social resources available to sustain change were also typically less.[16] Even with substantial external assistance, many of these schools might not succeed. Some probably should just be closed and then reopened with new leadership, new faculty, and a new educational program. In short, another new function—school reconstitution—was emerging for the decentralized system, and another new capacity had to be assembled.

As noted in Chapter 1, several specific provisions had been incorporated into PA 85-1418 to reform "Pershing Road," but virtually none of these had been implemented four years later. Although the name had been officially changed from the "Central Office" to a "Central Service Center," neither the organizational culture nor structure of operations had shifted much. The system center was still trying to perform the same functions as it had pre-reform, but with fewer people and resources. While a rhetoric of "service to schools" had emerged, little in the day-to-day operations reflected this.[17] Central action was still largely driven by a control ethic that maintained a deep distrust of local actors. Much of the relations from the system center to the schools still reflected the old "patron-client" world view.

Clearly, a major new infrastructure to support school development, including reconstituting the worst of the schools, had to be built. Moreover, if Chicago was truly to become a system composed of a diverse set of schooling options, the old centralized forms of curriculum, staff development, and instructional guidance would have to give way to an entirely new and unprecedented alternative. Nothing, however, in the past work experiences of anyone in the Chicago central office had prepared them for this unique task. Nor were there other obvious models to draw upon, at least in terms of other major urban U.S. school systems. Something extraordinary would have to be created in Chicago.

Similarly, a "systemic" accountability component had to be grafted onto democratic localism. Again, this need had been recognized in the original 1988 legislation, but nothing was ever implemented. Local democratic accountability was not working in some communities because the intended political institutions had never materialized. Further, even in some sites where a viable local governance had emerged, sufficient attention was not focusing on improving academic achievement. Some central push was needed.

More generally, the school system was still bound up with layers upon layers of policies, work rules, regulations, and arbitrary administrative decisions. The central administration needed to become more of an advocate for local improvement—weeding out existing impediments, rethinking future policies to create incentives to promote local improvement, and developing effective sanctions against those who might act to block change.

In short, the onus of the reform was shifting from local schools to the system center. Much had been accomplished through local initiative, but to move further forward would require coherent central action. Reform had to come to Pershing Road if Chicago's efforts at improvement were to continue to build. A growing public awareness and an unexpected political turn of events opened up new possibilities in this regard.[18] In the spring of 1995, the Illinois legislature passed another major piece of legislation affecting Chicago schools. The fifteen member Board of Education was replaced with a five-member Reform Board of Trustees, directly appointed by the mayor. A corporate style management team, headed by a chief executive officer, was also mandated. Greater flexibility over use of state funds was provided to the Board and many work rules previously included in the state school code were stricken. Principals were allowed more control over building hours and service personnel. Although school-level governance by the LSC was not substantially altered, the new CEO was given authority to sanction non-improving schools, including the legal authority to reconstitute failing schools.[19]

In broad terms, the 1995 legislation opened up the possibility for major central reforms in response to many of the problems identified above. In fact an unprecedented array of new policy initiatives have come forth.[20] As we concluded our writing on this book, the new administration's plans were still unfolding and their theory of action continued to evolve. Consequently, it would be premature to attempt to evaluate the consequences of these efforts. Suffice it to say that some early initiatives, such as expanded training for LSCs, appear quite supportive of the 1988 reform; others, such as the peremptory removal of some principals, look more like an effort to recentralize the system.[21]

In concluding this book, we have chosen instead to lay out our own view of the system-level changes needed to better support educational improvement in a decentralized system of schools. We discuss the core educational functions that require redress and the new capacities that have to be built. While we elaborate on these ideas in some detail in order to clarify the scope of what is needed, nonetheless, this should be read only as a sketch or outline. It is primarily intended to flesh out the work that still remains in attempting to create an effective decentralized system of schools. In forming these concluding remarks, we have drawn both on the findings presented in this book and the direct experiences of two of the authors (Bryk and Easton) who became personally involved in efforts to reform Chicago's system center.[22] Because we are now looking to the future, rather than analyzing the past, and because we are heavily drawing on our own experiences as observing participants, the tone of the next section changes some, involving more of a blend of policy analysis and reform advocacy.

Reframing the System Center

This book has documented an extraordinary outburst of activity spawned by the 1988 reform. Nonetheless, it is also clear in retrospect that reformers underestimated the enormity of the transition required here, the vast new demands that it would place on schools, and the system's lack of capacity (in addition to occasional outright resistance) to support such radical change.

In fairness, even if Chicago reformers had sought in 1988 to address these concerns directly, local context greatly constrained their options. Remember that in the initial mobilizing for reform, a bloated central office bureaucracy and an unresponsive Board of Education were villainized as the primary reasons for the dysfunctional state of affairs. A populist rhetoric of "chop the top" (and channel these resources back to schools) dominated much of the conversation. Moreover, the reform legislation directly threatened the authority and social status of central office personnel at Pershing Road. PA 85-1418 promised to undo their power, and might even cost them their jobs! Given the nature of this legislation, it is not surprising that they were unenthusiastic supporters.

In short, reformers confronted a dilemma: Even if they recognized a need for central support, there was no legitimate institutional infrastructure to which such tasks could be safely delegated. The most obvious was the central office and the subdistrict offices, but their control was part of "the problem" that the reform sought to redress. These offices had broadly lost agency and were widely distrusted across the city. Much the same was true of the Chicago Teachers Union in 1988. Few expected them to advance the spirit of this reform. Beyond this, however, there really was no other extant infrastructure to which they could turn. The reformers could not realistically assign these tasks to themselves, as this would appear self-serving. And even if they considered doing so, there was insufficient capacity among the groups active in mobilizing for reform to support development in 550 schools. The local colleges and universities were another possible choice, but they had been little involved up to that point and were also viewed negatively by some reform leaders.

Against this backdrop, focusing attention instead on freeing local initiative as an engine for school change (and as a sustained force against an intractable central office) was a reasonable first point of attack. Given the circumstances, there was little reason to believe that much else might work. While central support would surely be needed to successfully operate a decentralized system of schools, the most effective short-term strategy might well be to deliberately disable the system center, which was largely responsible for the dysfunctional current state of affairs. At base here is an intriguing tactical issue. No central support might better catalyze reform than an empowered central administration that lacked capacity, motive, and vision. Eventually, however, restructuring of the system center would have to be addressed.

A Closer Look at the Central Office

The pre-reform caricature of the central office as a bloated bureaucracy was just that: a caricature. The central office of the Chicago Public Schools, like other large urban school districts, was not a bureaucracy in the formal sense of a hierarchically arranged set of offices with clear lines of reporting leading from schools to subdistricts into a central office and eventually up to a superintendent. Instead, the extra-school layers more resembled a congery of bureaucracies (special education, bilingual education, compensatory education, and a host of special programs such as dropout prevention, drug abuse, etc.) which at best were only loosely coordinated. Each of these organizational entities reached down into schools to guide and constrain the work of teachers and principals, and each typically maintained connections out of the district, to state and federal offices and sometimes the courts as well. In addition, behind each of these often stood a well-organized special interest group that remained ready to press on the Board of Education for its distinctive needs.[23] Taken together, these external connections provided both independent resources and authority for many central office actors. In addition, the actual functioning of these separate entities often more resembled feudal fiefdoms than bureaucracies. While each had its own rules and regulations, actual operations frequently exhibited a high degree of arbitrariness, depending on the particular persons in authority and the nature of their relationship to the supplicant (school or principal) in question.

Perhaps the clearest structural indicator of the significance of categorical programs is that the majority of funds for the educational operations of urban central offices typically come from set-asides attached to various categorical programs.[24] For example, in 1993 only 44 percent of the CPS central education budget was directly supported out of unrestricted district funds. In the case of the CPS's research and evaluation unit, with which we worked directly, only five positions out of eighty were locally supported; the rest were all covered by external funding. Quite literally, some aspects of the educational operations of a central office would virtually disappear were it not for categorical funds.

Given the combination of limited core budget commitment and substantial external regulatory control, superintendents are often at the mercy of their own assistants in terms of efforts to craft a "systemic agenda." Also, given that much of the resources and authority for many central office actors are externally derived, there is little incentive for these officials to coordinate work. Such coordination entails a sharing of resources and authority, which from a purely rational actor perspective would be tantamount to acting against one's self-interest. In short, absent strong institutional norms of collaboration (which certainly did not characterize activities at Pershing Road), and delimited central authority to command coordination, there is little reason to expect people to behave in this fashion. Not surprisingly then, it just did not happen during the first four years of reform.

The structure of the central office also had an impact on how administrative staff viewed their roles. Much like school-based actors, they too had come to think about their work as "running programs" rather than supporting systemic school development as described in Chapter 3. Instead of being a source of guidance to counter the fragmentation and incoherence in school life, central office actions often tended to further exacerbate this. At a minimum, one might think that at least some part of the central office would see its role as strengthening school operations in order to create a more responsive context for improvements in teaching and learning. As obvious as this may sound, nothing at Pershing Road as late as 1995 was deliberately designed to do this.

In short, categorical programs have profoundly affected both the structure and norms of the central office. These programs have placed central actors in the role of being control-oriented toward local schools. Like parents of potentially misbehaving children, central office staff must closely watch the schools and demand that school leaders seek their permission before acting. And, on balance, this orientation is bolstered by a legal reality—it is the district, and not the individual school, that ultimately is held responsible. This has especially important implications in the context of the extraordinary level of decentralization that now exists in Chicago. While local actors have substantial authority to act, the district is still responsible for any malfeasance, neglect, or otherwise injurious actions that local actors might commit. At base here is an important consideration: The individual school is not fully recognized in state and federal law as a legal entity. Only the district is. Unless this reality is eventually changed, it seems likely to become a factor pushing toward recentralization in the future.

Not surprisingly then, four years into reform the basic orientation of the central office remained focused on program compliance and emphasized control of local school practice through both regulation and direct line authority. Central office staff still felt pressure to regulate school activities based on the belief that they retained responsibility for everything that happened in 550 schools. The transformations that we documented in many local elementary schools, from command-oriented regimes to commitment-oriented learning organizations, had yet to reach Pershing Road. A reframing of the structure, functions and culture of the central office was still needed.

A New Vision of Central Action[25]

The simple turning of a phrase from "school system decentralization" to a "decentralized system of schools" has profound implications for how central actors should engage their work. As discussed in Chapter 2, past efforts to establish one best set of rules and programs to guide action in 550 schools with more than 40,000 employees typically proved unsuccessful. Especially in the context of the increasing diversity among schools deliberately fostered by Chicago's reform,[26] successful regulatory action would seem even harder to craft. Substituting a rhetoric that simply eschews regulatory control, however, is also insufficient. Rather, a new vision for constructive central action is needed.

Clarifying Responsibilities, Local and Central. The 1988 reform clearly sought to break from the tradition of absolute control by the district. Reframing the proper division of responsibility between the center and local schools, however, remains a lingering problem. Moreover, Chicago is not alone in this regard; this concern has also arisen in other districts attempting decentralization.[27]

A key premise of the Chicago reform was that responsibility for student learning primarily rests with the schools and not the central office. Central officials do not directly educate even a single child—only local professionals, working in conjunction with parents and community leaders, do. For local actors to be effective, they must have a broad base of authority and the resources to act. They also need access to a wide array of external assistance to support their work. If these capacities for local improvement are put in place, then it is quite reasonable—and in fact necessary—to hold schools rigorously accountable for their productive use in advancing student learning.

On the system-level side, decentralization entails a renorming toward becoming advocates for local schools rather than acting as their super-patrons. It also has major implications for the structures through which central responsibilities are best carried out. We detail below new systemwide capacities that are needed to further advance reform. These should not be read, however, as an endorsement for an expanded central bureaucracy. Rather, much of this might best be accomplished through an array of new quasi-public enterprises, whose development would be stimulated by Board action, but whose day-to-day activities would not be directly controlled by a central office. For these reasons, we refer to this capacity building as the *extra-school infrastructure* needed to promote improvement.

A Policy Responsibility for Making Decentralization Work. In Chapter 6 we documented the importance of principal leadership in local school development. Much the same can be said about the need for system level leadership. Similarly, the style for effective system level leadership, like good school community leadership, is also distinctly different under decentralization. The primary strategy of bureaucratic command and control is re-balanced toward a more facilitative and educative orientation. Central action focuses on helping local leaders better understand their roles and responsibilities, providing them with training to succeed, using the "bully pulpit" to stimulate local action, and focusing attention on the successes that have occurred in order to enhance agency systemwide. Complementing this is deliberate policy action toward creating an external environment for local schools that encourages continuous school improvement, ferrets outs impediments to improvement, and actively promotes innovation.

A Focus on Local Capacity Building. Our research has documented a broad base of efforts toward improvement in a sizeable proportion of school communities. Many local school staff, parents and community leaders are working hard and want to be productive, even though they may not be achieving the outcomes that they and we desire. To attain greater advances in student learning requires enhancing the basic human and organizational capacities of these school communities. One key is helping local actors—principals, teachers, parents, and community leaders—to better understand their own school situations and improve their abilities to plan, budget, and evaluate. Even more fundamental is a need for significant advances in the knowledge, skill, and dispositions of local school professionals, in their ability to work cooperatively together toward a more coherent school practice, and in their ability to effectively engage parents and the local community.

A Commitment to Rigorous Accountability. The system also maintains a responsibility to establish external accountability that tracks the progress of schools' improvement efforts and that can intervene in failing situations. It is critical, however, that this accountability operate in ways that advance, rather than undermine, local capacity building. Decentralization is based on the premise that the best accountability is not regulatory. While it may be necessary from time to time to use bureaucratic intervention in very troubled schools, the ultimate aim is a stronger base of professional norms of practice for educating all children well, coupled with supportive parent and community involvement toward the same ends.

We also note in passing that decentralization entails a more complex accountability relationship between the system center and schools. Replacing the one-directional reporting in a bureaucratic system is a reciprocal relationship between schools and the system center. Local schools are accountable to the system center for progress, while the system center is accountable to local schools for the effectiveness of its support efforts. Although we will not take up this topic further in this chapter, we simply point out that no opportunities for schools to evaluate central operations exist in Chicago, or for that matter in most any other school district. Yet, this is a logical consequence of the formal division of responsibilities defined under decentralization.

Stimulating Innovation. Even though a decentralized system of schools no longer mandates programs for every school to implement, it still maintains a strong interest in spawning innovations and diffusing effective improvement efforts. The experiences of actively restructuring schools, described in Chapter 6, document reasons to doubt that individual schools will invest sufficiently here. There is an understandable tendency for schools to use marginal resources for more programs and people, rather than to fund innovative developments. This may be quite sensible for individual schools, but it is bad policy for the system. Thus, we argue that support for innovation is an important system function under decentralization. We even envision in this regard, as we discuss later, a role for the judicious use of competition among schools as a goad to improvement.

To sum up, the division of responsibilities under decentralization gives local schools the authority to act, and must also provide the resources and assistance to use that authority productively in advancing children's learning. Schools in turn are held accountable to assure that serious efforts are made in this regard. The educational work of the system center focuses on policy making to support decentralization, maintaining an external assistance capacity for local schools, engaging rigorous external accountability for improvement, and stimulating innovation. These four functions constitute the major tasks for a reformed system center in a decentralized school system. We discuss each of these in more detail below.

Policy Action Toward a System of Schools

Decentralizing a school system creates a vast terrain for new policy action. Basically, every Board rule, every standard operating procedures, and all provisions in collective bargaining agreements should be open for reconsideration. Moreover, such reconsiderations are probably best pursued from a "zero-base" perspective. Rather than looking for rationales to maintain extant procedures or considering conditions under which waivers of these procedures might be granted, the conversation should instead begin with one simple question: "What do we need to make decentralization work?"

Invariably, much of the discussion will focus on unresolved issues of local autonomy. Although the Chicago reform devolved more resources and authority to schools than in any other major U.S. urban system, the domain of action for local leaders still remains constrained in significant ways. PA 85-1418, for example, called for lump-sum budgeting for schools, but this was never implemented because collective bargaining agreements specified class sizes and teacher slot allocations. Although principals did achieve control over the hiring of new teachers, removing problematic teachers from their buildings remains a very difficult task. Similarly, the length of the school day and the class period structure also remains constrained by collective bargaining agreement. While these constraints can sometimes be creatively resolved in individual schools, these resolutions are often time consuming and politically difficult. A system committed to decentralization should work to make solutions to such problems easier for local actors.

Stated somewhat differently, if we wish to hold schools accountable for success, it is only reasonable in return that they be able to leverage the key resources necessary to achieve that success. This implies, for example, that they control the bulk of their budget; that they be able to make key human resource decisions—hiring, compensation, evaluation, and firing—for all staff including food service and janitorial; and that they have authority to select instructional materials, adopt curriculum, and pursue distinctive educational strategies as appropriate for their clientele. Clearly, implementing decentralization entails quite radical changes in school district practice.

Constructive central policy action on a wide range of issues can provide a major assist to local efforts. The Board, for example, has an interest in restructuring the system of incentives and sanctions built into labor agreements in order to better advance local initiative. (See the discussion below on accountability consequences.) On some occasions the system needs to act as an advocate for local schools in pressing back on higher levels of government, both state and federal, whose policies might inadvertently undermine local efforts. It also has a role in enhancing the quality of the human resources available to schools. This may entail pressing on the colleges of education to improve the pool of new teacher candidates for schools to choose from; it may mean efforts to expand the pool of qualified principals from which LSCs choose.

In addition to enabling local action, the system center also maintains responsibility for making the overall system work. At base here are two general concerns: establishing the common boundaries for practice in all schools, and organizing the relationships among schools in the system. Key to the first issue is the core set of conditions held in common across all schools. Likely to be considered here are such concerns as basic academic standards for all students, due process considerations, and financial record-keeping requirements. In terms of the relationships among schools, the system center has a responsibility to assure an equitable and stable distribution of resources to schools and fair access for students to such resources. The system center also has to assure that options exist for individual families who find the orientation of their local school incompatible with their needs. (See the earlier discussion on Democratic localism and choice.) Also of concern are procedures for governing the flow of students across different schools and grade level structures (i.e., primary, middle, and high schools) that comprise the system.

We note that the reform view of central operations articulated here also implies a need to rethink how central initiatives actually become promulgated. A system of schools conjures up notions of an educational federalism where individual schools, operating as recognized legal entities, have a direct voice in crafting the rules by which the whole system runs. This would entail much greater consultation between the center and individual schools than has typically been the case in the past, where central actors assumed it was their right simply to tell schools what to do.

Similarly, a decentralized system of schools also has major implications for how members of the Board of Education think about their roles. Consonant with the notion of a system of schools, board members must shift from a paternalistic stance toward schools—where they feel responsible to intervene at any time, on any matter, in any school—toward acting more akin to a holding company, where in this case the holdings are a diverse portfolio of schools. When viewed through this lens, the Board obviously has an interest in what is happening in its schools but it does not run them on a day-to-day basis; this is left to local actors. The Board's primary interest is in strengthening its overall holdings. It can do this by supporting improvements in the operations of existing schools, promoting promising start-ups in the form of new and alternative schools, and eliminating its weakest units (i.e., ineffective schools).

We recognize that the changes implied here for system-level actors are enormous, and there is a natural inclination to fall back on control-oriented thinking. Moreover, as noted earlier, unresolved issues about the legal status of individual schools and district liability further reinforce such behavior. Not surprisingly, there is also a tendency to withhold autonomy from all schools, because some schools will surely not use it effectively. The solution, however, is not to move backwards toward recentralization, but rather to vitalize two other key extra-school functions: assistance to schools and school-based accountability. Unless these capacities become vitalized, effective decentralization seems unlikely.

Supporting School Development

The Chicago reform explicitly sought to institutionalize in each school community a continuous cycle of improvement. Annual school improvement planning and budgeting processes were key elements in the reform vision of individual schools as self-guiding local institutions. In addition, reform thrust down into schools a wide range of functions—including curriculum and instruction development, program evaluation, and analysis of operations—that previously had been done at the system center. Reformers argued that if schools were to become responsive local organizations, these functions had to be located at the school level. There was less awareness, however, of the vast implications that this had for changing the work of school-based professionals. Few of these tasks were part of the normal pre-service preparation programs for principals or teachers, and little in their past workplace experiences would have prepared them for this. Similarly, LSCs were an entirely new institution. Even if very good people were drawn into this work, supporting school development was a novel undertaking for them as well. While some school leaders figured out how to do this on their own, our analyses indicate that many schools require extra assistance here if they are to realize a more effective school practice.

Local School Councils. Although the 1988 law called for thirty hours of training, no infrastructure was ever put in place to effect this.[28] As a result, many councils were left to their own devices to orient themselves to their new roles, to organize their activities, and to identify the key problems on which they should focus. Moreover, the training of councils is not a one-time need. Elections occur every two years, and early experiences indicate that a substantial membership turnover accompanies each election. In addition, numerous vacancies occur between elections.[29] This implies that a standing capacity must exist to continuously train new LSC members.

Further, councils need at least some access to ongoing, independent technical support. Having no staff or budget, they are entirely beholden to a school principal. Sometimes council members just need a well-informed "second opinion." In other situations where conflicts arise between the school professionals and parent and community members on LSCs, outside facilitation and advice can be especially helpful. In our view, further expanding the impact of the Chicago reform seems unlikely without increased investments in ongoing training and support for its LSCs.[30]

Principal Leadership. We have documented that school reform brought many new individuals into the principalship who acted as catalysts for change in their buildings. It also significantly reshaped principals' roles and expanded their formal responsibilities. The Chicago principalship is now more complex, challenging, and stressful. Principals must both take on the task of political leadership in the school community and assume responsibility for strategic planning and action. They have to facilitate an inclusive local decision-making process that undertakes a systematic analysis of school operations, and which plans and implements effective action on a wide range of matters including staff development, curriculum, and instruction. In short, the aim of Chicago's reform—that each school should become a self-guided, responsive and effective local institution—had profound implication for the work of principals. In the past, principals were largely told to run programs that were designed somewhere else. Now they must assist other local actors to envision their own future and together chart a course toward it.

Most principals were unprepared for their new responsibilities. The pre-service professional preparation for principals needed revamping, and new programs of principal mentoring were needed to better support them, especially during the early years of their work. As was the case with LSC training and support, a number of independent centers around the city sought to address at least some aspects of these needs during the first four years of reform. As late as 1995, however, no comprehensive system response had yet emerged.[31]

Most troublesome, these additional new functions were not accompanied by any corresponding reductions in other aspect of principals' work. Rather they were simply added onto what had already been a very demanding role.[32] Of greatest irritation to principals, none of the time consuming administrative paperwork disappeared. Basic procedures for hiring staff, purchasing materials, and responding to central office requests for information remained as cumbersome as ever. In fact, in some ways the situation was made worse: As the central office shrunk in size and went through several reorganizations, it was no longer clear, even to veteran principals, how actually to get things done. Schools still often needed permission to spend money or hire new staff, but the bureaucratic operations for these functions were gradually disintegrating at Pershing Road. Not surprisingly, serious questions were raised about whether Chicago could sustain high quality principal leadership over the longer term needed to institutionalize change in a school community.[33]

Faculty Enablement. A similar account can be offered about efforts to support teacher engagement in reform. Of the various institutions created by PA 85-1418, the Professional Personnel Advisory Committee (PPAC) was among the weakest. No broad-based organizational support for developing teacher leadership at the school-site was established. Some private efforts did emerge: For example, an independent group of teachers formed the Teachers Task Force, and the Chicago Teachers Union spawned the Quest Center; but these groups covered only a modest portion of the system at best. Similarly, efforts to enhance greater teacher professional-ism around matters of curriculum, instruction, and assessment also lagged. Over the longer term, the latter may well be the most serious concern of all. Unless, teachers' practice improves dramatically, Chicago schools are unlikely to attain much higher standards of intellectual work from students.

Implications for Capacity Building. Clearly, an extensive multi-compo-nent program of professional development is essential to build up the tech-nical knowledge and skills among all school-based actors. This external support must focus directly on efforts to improve teaching and learning. Sustained attention is required to enhance teachers' knowledge of subject matter and pedagogy.

In addition, our analyses imply that a broader base of organizational de-velopment assistance is also needed. As we documented in Chapter 6, genu-ine school improvement entails both changes in basic school functions and a renorming of school culture. Human resource development is only one of the problems in transforming an urban district to a system of self-guided local institutions. Local professionals must also sustain cooperative efforts toward school improvement, with each other and with parents and community mem-bers. Similarly, parents and community members must have the capacity to be active partners in this enterprise. Our field observations demonstrate that many schools required help in this regard. Included here are a range of assistance needs with respect to team building, managing the change pro-cess, nurturing the development of high-performing work groups, and mediating conflict, local crises and breakdowns in decision-making pro-cesses. As school-based actors seek to turn the rhetoric of local democratic community into an operational reality, they need sustained support from people they trust, and who understand their particular circumstances.

Organizational development needs also arise around strategic analysis in local schools. As noted in Chapter 3, school improvement has commonly meant adding more programs. Many educators have little sense of the school as a social system where program coherence is a valued organiza-tional aim, and they have little experience with school improvement planning as an evolutionary process toward such a systemic end. Thus, a variety of circumstances point in the same direction: Schools need locally tailored organizational development support. Although this should be anchored in individual professional education, school needs reach well beyond individual learning.

A Sketch of How This Might Be Structured. During the first four years of reform, each CPS school operated within a diverse marketplace of staff and organizational development services. A substantial portion of EARS principals' time, for example, was spent brokering these various connec-tions and acting as entrepreneurs for their schools. Some services were purchased with discretionary funds from the for-profit market; others were subsidized in part or whole by foundation grants or core college and university funds. Responsibility for integrating these diverse offerings into a coherent system of instructional guidance and school development, however, fell entirely on the shoulders of local actors.

As we have shown in this book, some schools made good choices and were able to coordinate these resources in a coherent development plan. Many others, however, struggled. The educational marketplace provides highly varied services of uneven quality and for diverse purposes. Represented across the service landscape are conflicting assumptions about how students learn, how teachers' work is best organized, and what educational aims for children are worth holding. Moreover, the market itself bears no liability for the proper integration of these services into overall school operations. The responsibility for choosing wisely is thrust entirely upon the schools, as is the responsibility for creating coherent school improvement out of the many possibilities offered.

The clearest example of the weaknesses in this system are found in "Christmas tree schools" such as Travis, discussed in Chapter 3. Leaders in schools like Travis engaged in aggressive efforts to bring many new programs and services to their schools. Much less attention, however, focused on quality implementation of these initiatives or on how well each new option related to what was already in place. The overall effect was a proliferation of weakly implemented and unaligned programs that might make a school look good to a casual observer, but often left staff frustrated and discouraged by the failure to realize significant improvements in student learning.

We conclude that for a large number of schools struggling under this free market system of support, a more intensive and carefully coordinated strategy is needed. Chicago's initial free market approach appears neither robust nor particularly stable. The basic organizational infrastructure is just too happenstance. If more schools are to make significant gains through restructuring, and if those already in progress are to continue to develop, much more attention needs to focus on expanding the resources to support such development and strengthening the capacity for their delivery.

To the extent that school districts addressed such needs in the past, they did so through centrally developed plans that were typically delivered through regionally organized subdistrict offices. For example, the introduction of a new curricular or instructional approach in Chicago would have been developed at Pershing Road and implemented through required teacher training sessions at various subdistrict headquarters. This centralized approach, however, is clearly problematic in a decentralized system that allows individual schools to differ both in philosophy and in organizational form. Under such circumstances, schools have varying goals and confront distinct problems. Geographic proximity no longer provides much assurance of a commonality of school interests and needs.

We argue that an important unfinished aspect of Chicago school reform is the development of a new intermediate layer, between schools and the Board of Education, which can replace geographically based subdistricts to support school development. A more promising approach is to organize this external support around naturally occurring clusters of schools working in conjunction with external partners of their own choosing. The commonality of educational philosophy and practice, rather than geographic proximity, becomes the primary basis for association among schools in a decentralized system. Thus, clusters would form around distinctive pedagogies and problems of practice, drawing together the expertise of the intermediate organizations and the common needs and affinities of a set of schools. Correspondingly, schools should be allowed to associate with an intermediate organization that best fits their needs, and periodically should be able to revisit this decision.

Even without any central support, several networks of this type have already emerged in Chicago around a number of educational groups and area universities. A variety of national projects such as Accelerated Schools, Success for All, The Comer Project, and The Coalition of Essential Schools also serve some of these functions, and have the potential to evolve further in this direction. Similarly, some citywide school advocacy groups would be obvious candidates to build such networks, and a few have already begun to do so.[34] In principle, a cluster of schools could organize among themselves to learn from each other and provide necessary support.[35]

Unfortunately, most of these networks are fledgling enterprises, dependent largely on soft money and individual school contributions to survive. Moreover, since they exist outside of the system, central actions frequently undermine their efforts, albeit often unintentionally.[36] Here again, Board policy action is needed in order to expand this external activity and create a more robust infrastructure for the further development of intermediate providers.[37] The system should officially recognize that a regulated marketplace of intermediate organizations is its mechanism for supporting school development. It should develop basic standards for intermediate providers, act to stimulate the supply of such providers, and assure that accountability occurs through aggressive dissemination of information about the services provided by intermediate organizations and schools' experiences with them.

The system also needs to develop a stable funding mechanism for this work. In this regard, central action can moderate a weakness that we have detected in local school politics around improvement efforts. As we documented in Chapter 6, the overwhelming majority of discretionary funds, even among actively restructuring schools, has been used to expand school staff and purchase more materials. Only very small amounts have been allocated for staff and school development that aim to help professionals work smarter and more productively together. In this instance the rhetoric of more immediate services to children inadvertently undermines children's longer term interests. By centrally allocating some funds for staff and school development, this troublesome local issue is bypassed.[38]

Key to the effective operation of a system of external support is that each school remains free to choose among any certified provider. At the core of assisted school change is a helping relationship between a school and an external partner. A base of trust between these external agents and local actors is a key social resource for improvement, especially during the initial stages of work, when few face-to-face interactions have occurred and little direct evidence has accumulated about effectiveness. If school staff choose to work with a particular intermediate organization, they are more likely to bring positive predispositions to these activities. Similarly, external agents are more likely to feel that their presence is genuinely desired and that they can proceed without worrying too much about "earning entry."[39]

Finally, the presence of an external accountability system, as discussed below, can act as a positive assist. School development, like individual staff development, is often viewed as an "extra" that individuals may take on as they so choose. Typically, there are no real stakes attached to it. As a result, this leaves external school development agents with a weak authority base for action, since no consequences accrue to local actors who fail to engage seriously in school improvement. In the presence of rigorous accountability for improvement, however, the rules of the game change dramatically. While school based actors get to choose their intermediate providers, they are jointly accountable along with the intermediate organizations for the progress that occurs or fails to occur. This raises the stakes considerably on both sides, making shared participation in local improvement a much more serious business.

Building External Accountability

School accountability is a formal component of system governance. Under the traditional centralized control of schools, accountability functions primarily through hierarchical line reporting responsibilities embedded in the system bureaucracy. Extra-school officials monitor the performance of local actors against a set of rules and regulations specifically designed to constrain local discretion. Two common features of this system stand out: centralization of control, and regular administrative monitoring of local compliance.

As noted in Chapter 1, PA 85-1418 radically changed both of these. It established a decentralized governance system in which parents, community members, and local school professionals would have much more authority over school operations and would be locally accountable for its productive use. At the same time, the reform legislation deliberately constrained the direct line authority of the central office, thereby severing the normal accountability mechanism embedded in hierarchical organization control. Instead, reform banked on democratic localism as its first accountability principle. Consonant with democratic political theory, Local School Council members are accountable to their respective constituents and can be voted out of office if they fail to perform satisfactorily. Similarly, the principal is accountable to the LSC, which now has authority to hire, annually evaluate, and fire him or her if dissatisfied.

PA 85-1418, however, also recognized that all Chicago schools are accountable to a larger public. It articulated specific improvement goals for student learning against which all local schools should be judged. The legislation also recognized that some school communities might experience difficulty in the transition to self-governance and might be unable to take advantage of the opportunities for improvement. Consequently, it gave the central office responsibility to intervene in failing schools, in order to catalyze the necessary local initiative for improvement. Thus, PA 85-1418 simultaneously embraced a second principle of accountability: In addition to local democratic control, the system center should also hold schools accountable. Importantly, the emphasis of this external accountability is not process compliance, but school improvement.

These two approaches—democratic localism and system-level external evaluation—represent very different conceptions of accountability. If carefully crafted, external accountability for improvement at the system level can effectively complement democratic accountability at the local level. There is a great danger, however, that the blizzard of external process accountability which frustrated past school improvement efforts could easily transform itself into a new blizzard of external standards set by multiple audiences, each with its own vision of good schooling and criteria for judging effectiveness. Unless a coherent system of external accountability is specifically crafted to join with the democratic localism at the heart of the Chicago reform, the aim of this external accountability—substantial improvements in student learning—is not likely to occur.

We note that although the concerns raised here are set in the specific context of the Chicago reform, similar issues are likely to arise in any decentralized system of schools, regardless of the specifics of local control. At base, a fundamental tension exists between local control and external public accountability. We sketch out below a set of ideas that seek to respond rigorously to the need for external accountability, but that would also operate in a fashion that is likely to support local actors' efforts over the longer term to improve their schools. This approach is predicated on the view, noted earlier, that ultimately the best assurance that all children will be educated well rests in a stronger base of professional norms of practice coupled with well informed parent and community involvement pressing toward this end. Thus, the external accountability strand in a decentralizing system has itself a developmental objective. Can we craft this initiative in ways that, over time, would enhance the capacity and reframe the collective responsibility of those who most directly touch students—their teachers and parents?[40]

Aims for External Accountability. In a decentralized system of schools, the first aim of external accountability is to promote more effective local action. It can accomplish this by providing critical feedback to local actors about the effectiveness of their school improvement efforts, and more generally, about the provisions they are making for the education and care of children.[41] In so doing, external accountability shapes the terms of the discussion in which local school professionals engage with their parents and local community. The intent is to strengthen the knowledge and expertise available to all local actors—school professionals, parents and community members—and through this to promote a more informed and reflective local practice. This approach is based on a longstanding observation about democratic practice: Effective decision making depends upon broadly shared understandings or a social intelligence among the community about matters under public consideration.[42] In the case of local school governance, these matters are the core issues of schooling: What educational goals for children are worth holding; what quality instruction looks like; and how overall school operations might be structured to create environments more conducive for student learning.

Thus, advancing local understandings about the core matters of good schooling is central to the first aim of external accountability. In this way, aggressive external accountability can make local accountability work better, and thereby advance the system's overall aim of promoting continuous improvement in all schools. This is another instance where productive central strategy turns first to an educative tool, rather than direct regulation, to influence local action. External accountability, however, must also serve two other aims. By identifying exemplary sites of practice, and making it easy for people to learn more about them, the system center can influence the improvement planning decisions in many schools.

Such a quality school recognition process represents still another important mechanism through which central actors can promote local school development. This also represents a significant component of the "consequences" within the accountability system, when school success is publicly acknowledged and rewarded.[43]

Thus, the second aim of external accountability is to create a credible base of information for recognizing local school accomplishments, acknowledging those responsible, and making these effective practices accessible to others. We emphasize, however, that for this activity to promote genuine improvements across the system, it is essential that these school evaluations be conducted in a rigorous and fair manner. This should not result in just a superficial endorsement of a favored projects of central office leaders or their close associates. Each school recognition must be anchored in a solid base of evidence about good practice and program effectiveness. Integrity in the accountability system is the coin of the realm in this regard.

This concern is even more strongly manifest in a third aim of external accountability—identification of non-improving schools. When local initiative is not undertaken and external assistance fails, consequences must ensue. An administrative intervention process which might include vacating an LSC, hiring a new principal, imposing a school improvement plan, and even closing and reconstituting a school, makes real this possibility. This is the "hard edge" in the system's overall strategy to promote school improvement.[44] While the system's primary thrust should be to provide resources and assistance to schools, local school leaders must also know that there are consequences for failure to use these opportunities.

To serve this purpose, the accountability system must also establish a credible information base that can be accessed by system officials to identify schools that have been unable either to improve on their own or to sustain an effective working relationship with an intermediate school development unit. Clearly, real stakes in the accountability process place a high premium on the content and quality of the information collected, and on the integrity of the office or agency engaged in this work. This has important implications for how the accountability activity is organized and its work controlled.

The Technical Core. Accountability concerns are often expressed in terms of demands for higher test scores and other indicators of improved student performance. This tendency to equate accountability with student outcomes, however, is unfortunate. It obscures the fact that school accountability and student outcomes are both important, but also distinct and different, albeit related, concerns. Specifically, accountability focuses on questions about the efficiency and effectiveness of individual organizational units, in our case schools. Student outcome data are an important, but also only partial, information source to inform these judgments about unit operations.

In general, designing a formal accountability system requires that we consider several questions:[45]

- Who is to be held accountable to whom?

- What are they to be held accountable for?

- How will information be assembled to inform judgments about the proper execution of these responsibilities?

- Are there consequences for good and bad performance?

(i.) The who, what, and how of accountability. From the perspective of external school accountability,[46] each school is viewed as an agent of the state and local government. Under Chicago reform, each local school community, through its elected Local School Council and its chief administrative officer (the school principal), is accountable to the larger public which funds their activities and maintains a stake in their productivity. We note that this notion of a school as an agent is a direct consequence of viewing the school as a self-guided organization. It must now be directly accountable for what it does or fails to do. Thus, in answer to the first question, we view the individual school as the primary unit accountable to the district (and state) for school improvement.

As for the second question—What are they to be held accountable for?—this directs our attention toward the standards by which schools' efforts are judged. Standards for student learning are obviously a prime consideration here; but so are concerns about the quality of improvement efforts, and the efficiency and propriety of school expenditures. Each of these represents a broadly valued public objective that we can and should reasonably ask of schools.

As for the third question, about the information base, this focuses on the data system to be established and the mechanisms by which information will be collected and maintained, so that credible judgments can be made about the relative effectiveness of each organizational unit in terms of the established standards. This is where specific data about student outcomes, such as standardized test scores, enter the process.

(ii.) The role of test scores in accountability schemes. We note that an adequate address to the second and third questions above is more complex than it may seem at first. The most obvious solution—to judge each

school in terms of annual reports about student achievement as measured by standardized test scores—is deeply problematic on both practical and philosophical grounds.[47] First, on the practical side, standardized tests were never developed with this aim in mind, and as a result are poor indicators when used for this purpose. The content of such tests is deliberately designed to sample broadly from a subject domain in order to provide a basis for global comparisons of how students in any school or district compare with a national sample of children who took the same test. That is, the tests are purposefully not aligned with any one curriculum or instructional strategy, so as to be useable across a wide range of schools. As a result, they offer a rather blunt instrument for assessing increasing productivity in teaching a particular curriculum. Only a modest portion of any of these tests assesses what any particular school is actually trying to teach its students in a given grade.[48] If we want to use student assessment data to inform school accountability, at a minimum the tests should be aligned with specific curricular content and performance standards that have been established by the school, district, or state.

This concern is especially salient today in the context of the press for more challenging standards of academic work for all students. In contrast, the content of most standardized tests tends to focus heavily on basic skills, and does not address the kinds of student performance envisioned under these "New Standards."[49] Thus, holding schools accountable primarily on the basis of basic skills tests is likely to signal to schools that only low level attainments are really valued. If test data are used for external accountability and consequences are attached to good and bad performance, schools are likely to take notice and respond. In essence, we will have created a system that encourages local school professionals to value what we measure rather than a system where we seek to measure what we value.[50]

Even if we had better test content, however, the problems would be far from solved. Accountability uses of test data place a premium on charting progress over time: Are the test scores going up?[51] This requires that the different forms of tests used across different grades and years be equated in order to maintain a stable measurement ruler for purposes of making judgments about change. Put simply, if we measure two students of identical abilities but use different forms of a test for each student, we expect similar test scores to result. The same is true for schools. If we want to compare aggregate achievement across time for a school, we want to be sure that the particular forms of the tests taken at various times do not affect our inferences. None of this, however, is part of the routine psychometric practice in constructing standardized tests, because again they were not developed for this purpose.[52]

Moreover, even when more appropriate test construction proce'ures are used, such as those employed in the SAT and NAEP programs, anomalies in test score trends can still arise.[53] Although test scores are often described as "hard data," in fact these information sources are fallible, and substantial random variation characterizes assessment processes. This raises further doubts about the wisdom of designing an accountability system based exclusively on such information.

Next come concerns about the corruptibility of any statistical indicator system. Arguably, if major improvements in instruction are occurring, standardized test scores should also improve. Unfortunately, the reverse is not necessarily true. That is, once a school system places emphasis on a particular indicator, it introduces incentives to improve performance on the indicator, but not necessarily on the underlying systems that have generated past performance.[54] For example, high stakes accountability may drive teachers to redirect instructional time toward preparation for taking standardized tests, and divert attention away from other student work such as writing essays.[55] It may encourage schools to buy supplemental programs to improve test performance, even though these tend to be primarily of the drill-and-practice sort and not focused on more challenging academic standards.[56] It can also encourage schools to direct additional services to students whose scores might help on the accountability indicator and away from other students, who might be in more need but are less likely to improve a school's standing.[57]

We note that concerns such as these apply generally to quantitative indicators. Similar problems plague reports on attendance, disciplinary actions, course taking, and drop-out rates. Quite apart from simple outright cheating, the incidence of which is not likely to be trivial, rational actors will attend to what is measured and seek to modify their actions to improve these numbers. Thus, we are left with the bureaucratic nightmare of the numbers going up, but the practice deteriorating. These experiences should caution us about building an accountability system only around statistical indicators.

In sum, because of various logistical concerns about the validity of data information systems (i.e., our third question), we are not sanguine about creating and maintaining a credible accountability system based exclusively on quantitative indicators of student performance. If we place all the weight of accountability on these numbers, the system will almost surely collapse in use. To be sure, these data can be a valuable component in a larger accountability information system, but we should not ask them to carry the whole load.

(iii.) What other criteria should be considered? Turning attention back to the question of accountability standards, we are still left to consider whether student performance, taken alone, *should be* the appropriate basis

for judging school productivity. We need to ponder a bit more whether a move in this direction is likely to serve education well over the longer term. While in today's parlance student achievement is often spoken of as the "the bottom line" for education, it is important to recognize that teachers and schools do not directly produce achievement, just as a firm does not directly produce a profit.[58] More specifically, a firm develops and maintains a set of operations to produce an array of goods and services. A profit or loss is generated in the interaction with consumers in the marketplace around these goods and services. That is, "the bottom line" is jointly constructed in the interactions of suppliers and consumers. To the point, the production capacity of a firm may be absolutely first rate—high quality human resources, working efficiently together, with a superior technology, and producing a high quality product—but this does not assure a profit without a corresponding consumer response.[59] The situation is comparable for education's "bottom line." Student achievement is jointly constructed out of the efforts of school professionals, students, their parents, and the communities of which they are a part. A school may assemble a superior staff of educators who work well together and design a quality set of instructional experiences within a very positive learning environment. But good achievement will not occur unless appropriate student and parent support are forthcoming. Teachers, for example, need parents to help get students to school on time, encourage them to work hard, and support their school efforts more generally.

Completing this analogy, a school is like a production unit within a larger firm, and local school leaders are like plant managers. It is quite reasonable to focus attention on the quality of the human resources that a school has assembled, how well staff members work together and the adequacy of the technology they employ. All of this is key to what school "workers" directly produce—a set of instructional experiences and a larger organizational environment to support student learning. Formally, this is the product for which they can rightly be held accountable.[60]

At a minimum, this argument should offer reasons to pause and reflect a bit on the current dominant rhetoric about student outcome-based accountability. While we maintain that data on student attainment and engagement with schooling deserve a role in an external school accountability system, arguments such as those outlined above have convinced us that these indicators need to be complemented, on at least an equal footing, with direct assessments of the efforts that schools are making to improve the quality of teaching and learning and the operational elements needed to support this. Anything less is likely to create short-term incentives to improve the numbers while diverting attention away from core improvements needed to strengthen the overall educational system.[61] In this regard, the accountability system runs the risk of creating incentives for local actors to do the wrong things (i.e., short-term strategies to "get the numbers up") for the wrong reasons (i.e., to appease central officials rather than advance opportunities for children). If sustained over time, this is likely to vitiate the social trust among local school professionals and parents necessary to promote effective school operations.[62]

(iv.) The consequences. Finally, in terms of the fourth accountability question, we must emphasize that without consequences, there is no real accountability. Addressing this question in the context of an external school accountability system entails consideration of the rewards to be offered schools and sanctions imposed as a consequence of their activity. Formally, each school is provided by the district and state with a conditional warrant to act. This warrant can and should be removed under specific circumstances. Beyond obvious consideration about fiscal malfeasance and failure to maintain basic provisions for human safety, a local school should lose its warrant to operate under Chicago school reform if three conditions hold: 1) all the assembled indicators on student performance show no signs of improvement and perhaps signs of real decline; 2) there is evidence that the local school governance arrangements set out under PA 85-1418 have not been operationalized (i.e., the LSC is nonexistent or dysfunctional and there is little indication of significant faculty involvement); and 3) there is no evidence from an analysis of the implementation of school improvement plans and budgets that a serious effort at development is underway.[63] As noted earlier, the sanctions that might be applied in such cases might well include vacating the LSC, replacing the principal, and in the most serious cases, school closure and reconstitution.

The consequences for schools, however, must focus on more than just imposing sanctions. They must be counterbalanced with incentives and rewards for serious efforts at school improvement. The school recognition and reward program, mentioned earlier, would be a key element in this regard.

More generally, the basic system of remuneration for all school staff members needs to be reconsidered in terms of the extrinsic incentives it creates for local school professionals.[64] For example, the entrepreneurial principal behavior, which we noted in Chapter 6 as a positive aspect of reform, also has its negative side. Some incentives now exist for principals to make "their school look good quickly," because such activity often gains recognition which may afford an opportunity for career advancement to a non-school-based post. In this way, the basic system of professional status and remuneration for principals can work in opposition to the needs of reform. Although effective school restructuring is still largely an uncharted course, conventional wisdom suggests that such a process may easily require five to ten years before change becomes fully institutionalized. Given that our results clearly indicate that strong principal leadership is a key factor in such a process, it would be foolhardy not to structure an incentive system that encourages effective principals to make the long term commitments necessary to transform their schools.[65]

Similar issues must be raised about teachers' work as well. Teachers too had full time jobs prior to school reform. Serious engagement in a restructuring effort is a time-consuming and often conflict-laden endeavor. Consequently, it is quite sensible to ask, "Why should teachers do this?" While an ethical imperative to improve opportunities for children is part of a larger professional ethos for teachers, we find nothing in the existing system of extrinsic incentives that particularly supports this. In fact, in some important ways the current system of remuneration—advancements based on extra degrees and years of experience—runs counter to what is needed.[66] While improving instruction may demand advances in teachers' knowledge and skill, this individual development must be related to teachers' work responsibilities and integrated into a school's overall improvement efforts. That is, major advances in student learning are not likely to come about through idiosyncratic activity by various teachers in individual courses. At base here is a need for more cooperative, collective action across the school faculty. Unfortunately, nothing in the current system of teacher remuneration and work assignments encourages this either. [67]

A full discussion of how to properly structure an individual (i.e., for principals and teachers) and collective (i.e., schoolwide) incentive system would take us well beyond the scope of this final chapter. Our main point is that fiscal incentives are a potentially powerful policy tool for central actors in their efforts to promote improvement in a decentralized system of schools. To put this aside, as somehow beyond the scope of reform, significantly delimits the ability of central policy to influence local action.

A Sketch of the Operations of an External Accountability Agency. We outline below ideas for a quasi-independent accountability agency that would both gather extensive indicator information on each school and periodically undertake intensive school quality reviews. The combined information base from these two approaches should provide an adequate basis for addressing the core accountability aims of providing critical feedback to local actors and of creating the necessary documentation to identify both improving schools and schools left behind.

(i.) The indicator system. The heart of the indicator system is information about the school's productivity in advancing student achievement. Formally,

the school is responsible for the learning that occurs while students are in attendance. This directs our attention to the gains in achievement that students are making and whether these are improving over time or not. More specifically, the indicator system should focus on estimating the "value added" to students' learning while under instruction at a particular school. These "value-added" statistics might usefully be constructed in each subject matter for a set of grade groupings such as prekindergarten through third grade, fourth through sixth grade, seventh and eighth, ninth and tenth, and eleventh and twelfth grade.[68] We specifically note that this recommendation stands in sharp contrast to now-prevailing practice of judging schools based on average annual test scores regardless of how long students have been in the school or how much progress they have made while there.[69]

These school productivity indicators should be further supplemented with data on student experiences and engagement with schooling. Obvious candidates here include attendance, retention and drop-out rates. The indicator system might also track enrollments in key "gatekeeper" courses such as the percentage of students taking algebra in grade 8, taking two or more years of a foreign language in high school, and enrollments in advanced placement courses.

It would also be important to track whether the basic student inputs to each school, i.e., the background and experiences that students and families bring, are changing over time. This suggests attention to the percentage of students entering primary programs with pre-school experience. Similarly, a data baseline on students' readiness skills at school entry would be valuable. The mobility histories of new entrants is another potentially important indicator, because students who frequently change schools tend to show weaker patterns of academic development.[70] We note that it is quite possible for a school's productivity to be increasing while average annual test scores are declining, if the school's student population is becoming more disadvantaged over time.[71] Moreover, this is not just an academic point. There is ample evidence that urban school populations in at least some cities have become more disadvantaged over the last decade.[72]

Similarly, it would also be useful to track the stability of student enrollment, and assuming the school is not overcrowded, its "in-mobility rate" (i.e., the percentage of new students transferring into a school each year.) Taken together these two statistics constitute leading indicators of school improvement. That is, as parents begin to recognize that a school is beginning to improve, incentives are created for maintaining enrollment among current students (thereby improving the stability rate) and for attracting new students to the school (thereby increasing the in-mobility rate.)

We note that a *sine qua non* for indicators involves establishing a data baseline and maintaining rigorous and common standards for data collection (including adequate audit procedures on local record keeping).[73] Without this, it is impossible to make fair comparisons of progress or decline over time. Although this point may seem obvious, we specifically mention it because this generally has not been a priority for urban school districts. Their information systems are typically neither well-developed nor well-maintained. To do this properly will require both an infusion of expertise and significant new funds. This has to become a new policy priority for any system center that seeks to promote a decentralized system of schools.

(ii.) School quality reviews. Complementing the quantitative indicator system would be periodic external quality reviews of all schools. Such reviews would entail a combination of extensive field-based observations and interviews with a rigorous analysis of local documentation. These reviews should be centered on students' school experiences, and expanded out from there to consider the nature of the school's efforts to improve their learning outcomes. External reviews should begin in the classroom with the actual quality of student work, and then move from there to consider the schools' overall development efforts. To guide such analysis, the external reviews must be grounded both in standards for student learning and a larger framework of effective school organization and development. (See earlier discussion in this chapter about this topic.)

The actual conduct of the reviews must be deliberately bifocal. Under a decentralization initiative, such as in Chicago, each school is responsible for its own improvement planning and budgeting. In the spirit of supporting and complementing this local initiative, one part of the review should consist of a formative evaluation of the school's own efforts to improve. That is, if we are to take local control seriously, we must begin with the presumption that most local actors are engaged in rational action to improve their schools. Thus, this aspect of the review should start with their espoused improvement plans, trace them through to actual implementation and explore their consequences. What priorities have been established? How has the school programmed and budgeted to advance these? How well have these new initiatives been implemented, and what evidence has been assembled to examine their cost effectiveness? More generally, the overarching focus for this aspect of conversation with local school leaders is one of strategic planning and analysis: "How does the school envision its various improvment initiatives coming together to advance student learning?"

This school-specific analysis should in turn be located within a larger systemic framework of school organization and development. Such an analysis might begin with a school's documentation of the actual tasks that students are asked to take on and the quality of the work they produce.

(This in-depth, on-site analysis complements the more standardized data available in the quantitative indicator system.) Closely linked to this are observations of the instructional programs to which students are exposed and the materials used. Reviews might next consider the school's efforts to enhance the professional capacities of its teachers and the teachers' abilities to work cooperatively on improving school programs. The review might then move out to a broader set of issues necessary to create a more supportive context for teaching and learning.[74] This would entail scrutiny of such concerns as the nature of school leadership, the school's relationships with local community and parent body, and the overall character of the school climate. Is the school orderly and safe, for example, and do adults press all students toward academic work within an environment of personal concern and caring? [75]

The planning and execution of such reviews should be undertaken in close collaboration with school community leaders. This communication should begin prior to the review (as part of the local self-analysis process), run throughout the on-site activities, and continue during the preliminary report of results and after submission of the final school report. The primary audience for the school quality reports is both local school leadership (e.g., the principal, teacher leaders and the Local School Council) and the larger local school community. The intent again of these reports is to strengthen the knowledge and expertise available to local actors, and to promote a community-wide discourse about good schooling that enables more effective local democratic accountability over the longer term.[76]

Individual school reports would also subsequently be transmitted to the system superintendent and/or other designated senior administrative staff charged with carrying out the school recognition and administrative intervention processes described earlier. These reports should contain sufficient documentation to both identify improving schools and provide a basis for initiating administrative intervention in non-improving schools. While the accountability agency might offer a recommendation in these regards, final decisions should be made by the Board of Education.

In suggesting a formal separation of powers between the political actors on the Board of Education and the professional leadership in the quality review agency, we acknowledge longstanding concerns about the concentration and potential abuse of centralized power, particularly in large urban school districts. The design of governance for a decentralized system of schools must offer formal protections to local schools against arbitrary centralized action. The specific idea suggested here is that the meting out of consequences, both rewards and sanctions, remains under direct democratic control. The exercise of this control, however, would be bounded by the independent professional knowledge produced through the quality reviews. In essence, we seek a check and balance between political action and professional judgment.

We also note that, as a database of individual school reports builds up, we will have created a valuable information resource for local schools, and for systemwide analyses of central policy effects on local action. If the reports are maintained in an online database, staff in any individual school could easily identify other schools that may be especially effective in dealing with some aspect of practice that is problematic for them. Similarly, planned syntheses of school reports would provide much rich detail about the common problems faced by schools, and the effectiveness of various special programs and external sources of assistance. These synthesis reports would provide much more complex descriptions and analysis than are currently available, and thereby hold potential for stimulating organizational learning, both in schools and at the system level.

(iii.) Composition of agency staff. The quality review process described above builds partially on ideas found in school accrediting systems. The actual school visits envisioned here, however, would entail a much more intensive process, and the final public reports would be much more critically focused. While agency staff members would work to maintain collegial relations with school sites, their primary commitment is to advancing, both in local school communities and across the system, more challenging standards of school improvement and student learning. Clearly, since consequences will ensue from these school reviews, well-established professional standards must guide them, and processes must be maintained by the agency to moderate judgments within and across review teams. That is, if significant stakes are contingent upon the information generated in a school review, the validity of this information should not be dependent upon the particular team reviewing an individual school. In this regard, quality reviews must be subject to, and meet basic standards of, inter-reviewer reliability, at least in terms of their major findings.[77]

Considerations such as these place a special burden on staffing for school reviews. Specifically, we do not believe that quality reviews intended to address the purposes described above[78] can be accomplished with recycled central-office staff and voluntary contributions from others. There must be a permanent core of educators, committed to creating a serious accountability and quality review process, who establish the basic professional routines for school reviews and maintain the distinctive organizational norms necessary for this kind of agency. Complementing this core would be a larger cadre of additional, rigorously trained school reviewers (principals, teachers, university faculty, and school community leaders) on shorter term contracts, perhaps for two years. These individuals would help to assure that "new blood" continually cycled through the agency, and to expand the specific expertise available within the agency staff.[79]

Also important to consider is how individuals might be chosen to serve in the quality review agency. The viability of a school review process is highly dependent upon the personal integrity and professional expertise of its reviewers. As a result, it is important that a process be carefully designed for selecting these individuals, which engages both independent professional evaluation and opportunities for input from school communities. It is especially important to buffer this personnel process from the shorter-term political considerations that often tend to influence central office decision making.

(iv.) Governance arrangements: a quasi-independent agency. As noted earlier, in order to secure the integrity of the accountability system, the agents charged with undertaking the accountability reviews should be separated from the administrative agents who must make judgments about the consequences, if any, to be enacted. Otherwise there is the danger that the reports will be "shaded" by the very agents who might then initiate possible consequences for a particular site. Since administrative intervention is properly the responsibility of the general superintendent or chief executive officer, the director of the accountability agency should not be under the direct supervision of this official. By direct analogy, the fiscal auditor of a firm does not work under the direct supervision of the chief financial officer.

More generally, no Board of Education employee or individual Board member should be able to intrude into the day-to-day operations of the agency. Although the likelihood of this occurring may be small, even a rare event of this sort could undermine the agency's effectiveness and public trust in the process. It is imperative that the internal norms of the accountability and quality-assurance agency maintain a central focus on advancing challenging standards for school improvement and student learning.

To accomplish this will require special arrangements for establishing the agency's budget and the process of evaluating the agency effectiveness, in addition to the special arrangements already mentioned above regarding personnel selection. For the accountability agency to be effective, all of these processes must be shielded from the short-term political considerations that tend to buffet public bureaucracies, especially schools. At the same time, the basic work of the agency must maintain a public responsiveness and be publicly accountable. How best to establish a governance structure that accomplishes this requires considerations far beyond what is possible in this closing chapter. The overall aim, however, seems clear: The intent should be to structure the agency as "quasi-independent," with sufficient control over its internal budgets, personnel, and operations to assure maintenance of a quality staff, strong internal norms toward rigorous accountability, and external trust in the agency's credibility. This need for independence must in turn be balanced with an assurance of coordination and responsiveness to the concerns and efforts of state and local Boards of Education.

Yes, This Will Cost Money. A common reaction to a proposal for a school accountability agency is that this just adds new layers of bureaucracy and will cost more money. In fact, the accountability system outlined above is intended to replace and dramatically streamline how centralized control is executed in a decentralized system. Whereas in the past, an army of district and subdistrict bureaucrats was needed to closely monitor local compliance with centralized rules, now a much smaller cadre of educators would be engaged in sustained conversations with school- and system-level leadership about how best to foster school improvement and advance student learning.

In terms of costs, it is important to locate this discussion within the larger financial context of urban school districts. The typical urban district spends today between $5,000 and $10,000 per year educating each pupil. Yet, these same districts typically spend less than $10 per pupil per year to know how well they are doing. To raise this figure to perhaps $25 per pupil per year seems trivial if we are serious about quality improvement.[80] To be sure, there are many grounds on which the ideas suggested above merit debate, but opposing it purely on the basis of financial consideration raises doubts about whether policy actors are serious about improvement. Yes, some new funds will be needed, but the real question is: What is the alternative? How else are central actors to know about what is happening in the schools and to carry out their primary responsibilities to promote improvements across a decentralized system?

Stimulating Innovation

The two extra-school functions discussed above—support for school development and external accountability—provide the key mechanisms through which central actors can stimulate local initiative and nurture its development. When coupled with constructive policy action to support decentralization, a more coherent external environment can evolve for schools that both guides local action and provides incentives for significant improvements.

In addition, the system center also can directly stimulate school improvement by advocating for locally developed innovation and by supporting the introduction of promising external initiatives. To accomplish this, the school system needs a capacity to identify such promising initiatives and provide technical, logistical, and legal support in order to facilitate their broader implementation. For example, there is an ongoing effort in Chicago to create small schools. This initiative is highly consistent with the findings of this study, as well as a much larger body of research about the positive effects of small schools on both adults and students.[81] Some of these small schools are emerging in vacant space in existing school buildings, and others from efforts to subdivide very large schools into several smaller schools-within-schools. Central assistance is needed to help find appropriate space, establish the small schools as independent units with their own administrative authority, obtain waivers, give legal advice, and provide seed money and consultative services during the development phase. We note that a central office that supports local innovations such as this stands in marked contrast to typical practice, where schools must approach the center in a rather subservient fashion, ask permission, and often be told why they cannot do something.

In addition to facilitating initiatives that bubble up from schools, the system center also has an independent interest in externally stimulating innovation. The system might support a wide range of activities, including developing model curriculum frameworks, promoting exemplars of professional development tied to these curricular frameworks, and initiating special programs, such as child-parent centers and extended day programs. The online information base from the quality review process mentioned earlier, as well as access to other online educational information services, provide further examples of central support for local innovation. At base, here again is the notion of the central office as an educative agent that promotes best practices across school communities, rather than as a controlling agent telling schools what to do.

Similarly, the Board should encourage promising groups on the local, national, and international scene to start new schools. This support might entail waving regulatory constraints, providing seed money and venture capital, facilitating the location and renovation of appropriate space, and so on. For example, the system might sponsor the development of a network of Montessori primary schools or the expansion of the International Baccalaureate program at the secondary level. Similarly, Success for All, a widely recognized elementary school restructuring initiative, has only recently appeared in the city. In each of these cases, system policy might actively stimulate the development of networks of schools working within one of these frameworks, and simultaneously also help develop a local intermediate agent who could support program implementation within each network.

The system interest in new school development is part of a larger strategy for using competition among schools to improve the overall quality of the options available to parents. Specifically, by targeting development of new schools in neighborhoods where existing schools are not strong, the system expands opportunities for the students and families most disenfranchised by the current system. At the same time, such action sends clear signals to "dead in the water" schools that they can no longer remain complacent. If they continually fail to take advantage of the support opportunities provided by the system center, shrinking enrollments and weak school quality review reports should make it easy to identify and close these schools. The key idea here is to generally strengthen the holdings within the system's portfolio of schools, and more specifically to focus this activity on populations that are not well served currently.

Closing Perspective

We have sketched out in the previous section a very ambitious agenda for system-level reform. We have argued that coordinated developments must occur in four critical areas—policy making, assistance to schools, external accountability, and innovation support—in order to take Chicago's reform to a scale where it realizes its aims of improving significantly the learning opportunities afforded to *all* of Chicago's children. We want to emphasize that although we have explored some of these functions at length, this is still a sketch and not a blueprint. Many important details remain unaddressed. We have not, for example, considered the core educational administrative functions that would still have to be maintained by a system center. Nor have we examined the operations side of the school system—finance, facilities and non-educational services (transportation, food, janitorial, etc.). To be clear, the intent of this chapter has not been to propose a master plan for central reform. Rather, we have focused attention on several critical dimensions, suggested to us as we look out from schools into their external environment, and asked the question, "How could this environment better support the local initiative at the heart of Chicago's reform?" In responding to this query, we have tried to envision a bridge from the individual school successes that were achieved during the first four years of Chicago reform to a larger-scale realization of such progress.

In engaging this task we have switched roles from the systematic, empirically grounded analysis that characterizes the first six chapters of this book to one more akin to a policy advocate—in this case for reforming the system center. In the preceding pages, we have taken on the mantel of a reform architect—elaborating a sketch of several extra-school functions that need to be addressed and how the extra-school layer would have to be restructured and renormed to accomplish this. None of us is particularly sanguine that these new extra-school functions could be well executed within existing school system arrangements. Thus, we consciously sought to articulate a more hopeful set of alternative possibilities.

On the structural side, we have consciously looked for ways to break the link between the systemwide extra-school functions that need address and the routine assumption that this implies another central administrative department. A regulated market mechanism looked attractive to us as a way of expanding the quality and array of integrated support services available to schools. Such an arrangement would productively reframe the nature of the relationships between schools and their service providers toward a voluntary association among individuals who share a genuine interest in working together. Similarly, we looked to empower professionals to evaluate schools and take greater collective responsibility for their improvement. We are convinced that the Chicago Public Schools will not become fundamentally better over the long term unless greater professionalization occurs. Marginal changes can be effected in other ways, but the deep changes required to reach "world class standards for all" remain unlikely. Finally, we could even envision novel arrangements to support innovation such as a public-private fund for innovation that builds on notions about effective partnerships between government and private concerns. This seems especially useful to consider in addressing such public goods as research and program development.

Embedded in the various structural alternatives mentioned above are a diverse array of institutional control mechanisms including choice and markets, an increased reliance on professional norms, and a hybrid public-private enterprise. A critical question as we move ahead is how to best deploy such alternative mechanisms, along with enhanced bureaucratic control, to create a more productive decentralized system of schools.

At this point, we switch roles again, retreating from architect to engineer, and switch tasks from envisioning to a critical analysis of what we have just laid out. As we make this transition, the enormity of the changes entailed here comes quickly into focus. Even if we embrace the "architect's vision" of a new structure as good and worthy, we immediately confront immense organizational capacity and public leadership problems. As we have noted already, the intermediate assistance organizations to support schools would have to be developed, and this will take time. Around the external accountability function, procedures would have to be piloted and refined, individuals would have to be selected and trained, and a collective capacity built up to undertake this novel work. Similarly, a massive retraining of the remaining central staff would be required, and quite likely a substantial personnel turnover would be needed as well. The central office human resource problem in this regard is not unlike what we witnessed at the school level when new leadership sought to seriously engage the restructuring process. Finally, a major community education task is required to support all of these changes. It is essential to bring the public into this discussion and invite them to share in a vision of a school system quite different from the one they attended.

Deep normative changes are also required. Central actors have to acknowledge the primacy of schools over the system center. They need to reconceptualize their roles in more facilitative and educational terms, and then develop the capacity to act in these ways. While pressing for strong external accountability, central actors have to view this not as a throwback to their old role of controlling schools, but as part of a larger, longer term process to both enhance the professional capacity and standing of teachers and to expand the knowledge and skill of parents and community members around the meta-task of improving public education. All of this entails a huge shift from past routines of processing paperwork and monitoring compliance.

To be sure, we believe that urban school systems could make progress on these various capacity problems, given time and resources, but this in turn raises the second big concern: a need for stable, wise, prudential leadership to stay such a course. Unfortunately such leadership has been in short supply in urban districts. Moreover, as noted earlier in this chapter, the governance structure of school districts, with their multiple, dense, conflicting political interests, regularly undermine even the best of people and the noblest of intentions. We have a tendency to fall back on a comforting dream that the "right central leader" can remedy the current state of affairs. In reality, the problems that anyone who occupies this role confronts are deeply set in the institutional structure of school system governance and the interest group politics that swirls around this. A growing body of research suggests that without a significant change in the mechanism of direct democratic governance of school systems, it would be very difficult to sustain the systemwide organizational development envisioned above.[82]

In sum then, as Chicago's efforts to renew its schools push further forward, they point toward re-creating the entire system of democratic governance for its schools. The infusion of democratic localism jump-started initiative in many school communities. Truly reforming the system center requires even more major structural changes. So from a skeptic's point of view, yes, some remarkable things have happened in individual Chicago schools during the first four years of reform. Moreover, there has been an enormous growth of understanding in the multiple policy shaping communities that continue to press on the system. Discussions have moved rapidly forward to where many of the ideas presented in this chapter are publicly discussed and debated. While some reformers would surely disagree with many of the specifics proposed here, few would quarrel with the need to address the underlying concerns we have identified. Nonetheless, how to accomplish further progress remains quite a formidable task.

In some ways, this final chapter has become a colloquy with ourselves. In crafting a vision of reform for the system center, we express a deep hopefulness for more productive schools and improved opportunities for the city's children. A similar spirit moved Chicago in the mid-1980s and culminated in the original Reform Act of 1988. As we proceed, however, to consider the implementation of such system level changes, we begin to worry a lot more about the work that still lies ahead. Ultimately, this is the nature of meaningful reform. It entails a delicate mix of hopefulness and doubt. Ironically, too much of either is almost surely disabling.

In our view, Chicago's experience with decentralization is still an open book. Each of the authors was critical about some major aspect of the 1988 legislation as we began this research.[83] None of us were active in the original mobilizing coalition that advocated it. In the course of our study, however, we accumulated substantial documentation that important human and social resources have been cultivated in many school communities. We judge these developments quite significant and certainly worth trying to build on further. The 1988 reform was ambitious in setting up the basic structure of local control, but was thin in providing the necessary supports and policy actions to transform the CPS into a system of 550 effective, self-guided local institutions. The positive results that have emerged in many elementary schools appear even more impressive when viewed in this light. One can only wonder where Chicago might have been four years into reform had a comprehensive system of external supports and policy initiatives been put into place at the outset.[84] In recognizing the additional policy actions and organizational capacities needed to create an effective decentralized system of schools, however, we also acknowledge the great distance still to be traveled. This sense of genuine progress, coupled with an expanded sense of the work left undone, also distinctly marks the nature of meaningful reform.

Appendix

The specific questionnaire items that were employed to construct the indicators described in Chapters 2, 3, and 4 are detailed below. The information is organized by indicator clusters: first are the four clusters used to define the types of local school politics types; then the five clusters that delineate the school organizational change types; and finally two clusters that describe instructional innovations. Following the text of each questionnaire item is the source of the question (either principal or teacher survey) as well as the variable name from the public release data set. (See Bilcer, Luppescu, Sebring, and Thum, 1996.)

Indicators of Types of Local School Politics

Facilitative Principal Leadership

Priority Use of Time

"Approximately how many hours do you [principal] spend on average per week in each activity?"

1. "Principal's professional development (reading, conferences, etc.)" [principal, PPW073].
2. "Staff development (planning, conducting)" [principal, PPW049]
3. "Community (PTA, advisory groups, other organizations, etc.)" [principal, PPW067]

Participatory orientation

4. Composite measure which takes mean of 3 items: "I don't mind conflict if it helps people understand their values and beliefs better" [principal, LEADO05]; "Real school change often requires confrontation" [principal, LEADO16]; "I'm not afraid to provoke conflict in this school to address an important issue" [principal, LEADO25].

5. "I rely on committees to make decisions about conflictual matters" [principal, LEADO07].

6. Composite measure based on mean of 2 items: "I prefer to work with committees rather than work alone" [principal, LEADO02]; "Whenever I can, I rely on a consensus decision-making process in my school" [principal, LEADO20].

7. "Teachers should teach and leave the school administration to me" [principal, LEADO18] (Note: scale reversed for use as a positive indicator.)

Teachers' Roles

8. Combination of two items: "What role do you think faculty should play in each activity? Spending the school budget [principal, LEADO27]; Hiring personnel [principal, LEADO29]. (Note: indicator coded 1 if principal responds 'consensus of faculty 'needed' for budget and responds at least that the faculty 'should be informally consulted' for hiring personnel.)

Collective Faculty Activity

Teacher Voice

1. Composite measure based on mean of 2 items: "I feel comfortable voicing my concerns in this school" [teacher, GOV11]; "I feel that my ideas are listened to in this school" [teacher, GOV12].

Teacher Influence

2. Rasch measure: How much influence do teachers have over school policy in each of the areas below? "Determining student behavior codes" [teacher, GOV26]; "Determining the content of inservice programs" [teacher, GOV27]; "Establishing the school curriculum" [teacher, GOV29]; "determining the school's schedule" [teacher, GOV30]; "Hiring new professional personnel" [teacher, GOV31]; "Planning overall school budgets" [teacher, GOV32]; "Determining how money for staff development will be spent" [teacher, GOV33].

Collective Activity

3. "About how many hours outside of class do you spend during a typical <u>week</u> in each of the following activities?" "Working on other school committees" [teacher, TPW41].

4. "About how many hours outside of class do you spend during a typical <u>week</u> in each of the following activities?" "Working on LSC or PPAC committees" [teacher, TPW40].

5. Rasch measure: "The administration and teaching staff collaborate toward making this school run effectively" [principal, PPSC26]; "I have the support of teachers in enforcing school rules" [principal, PPSC04]; "Teachers at this school make a conscious effort to coordinate their teaching with what occurs at other grade levels" [principal, PPSC06]; "About how many teachers in this school cooperate well with each other?" [principal, PPW030].

Teachers Share Decision Making

6. Composite measure based on mean of teachers' responses: "I am familiar with most of the major points in our School Improvement Plan" [teacher, GOV14]; "I am involved in helping to implement our School Improvement Plan" [teacher, GOV15]; "The School Improvement Plan will help us make a better school over the next 5 years" [teacher, GOV17]; "I helped develop the School Improvement Plan for my school" [teacher, GOV25].

7. "The PPAC in this school plays an important role in developing new programs and ideas" [principal, PGOV37].

Active Local School Council

1. At least one LSC meeting per month - "Since January 1992, how many regular meeting has your LSC held?" [principal, PGOV50].

2. At least one subcommittee - "How many committees does your LSC have that meet regularly (more than twice a year)?" [principal, PGOV53].

3. An average of three or more guests per meeting - "What is the approximate average of adult guests in the audience at LSC meetings?" [principal, PGOV52].

4. Four or more stable parent/community members on the LSC since the second election (1991) [from LSC records].

5. More than 5 percent of parents voting in the second election [Chicago Public Schools election data].

6. At least as many parent/community candidates in the second election as positions available on the LSC [Chicago Public Schools election data].

7. Principal does not strongly agree with the statement "I am able to get the LSC to do what I want" - "I am generally able to get the LSC to do what I want" [principal, PGOV10].

Sustained School Conflict

Principal agrees that:

1. "In this school the LSC is dominated by conflict" [principal, PGOV12].

2. "In this school, the LSC is a cooperative group of people" [principal, PPSC29] (Note: scale reversed for use as a negative indicator).

3. "The relationship between the school and the community is good" [principal, PPSC17] (Note: scale reversed for use as a negative indicator).

4. "This school seems like a big family. Everyone is close and cordial" [principal, PPSC07] (Note: scale reversed for use as a negative indicator).

Teachers agree that:

5. "Since reform, there is more conflict in the school" [teacher, TWP02].

6. "In this school, the LSC is a cooperative group of people" [teacher, GOV19] (Note: scale reversed for use as a negative indicator).

7. "The relationship between the school and the community is good" [teacher, GOV02] (Note: scale reversed for use as a negative indicator).

8. "This school seems like a big family. Everyone is close and cordial" [teacher, PSC10] (Note: scale reversed for use as a negative indicator).

Indicators of School Organizational Change

Engagement of Parents and Community Resources

1. Rasch measure:" In this school, the LSC seeks advice from the PPAC on instructional programs and issues" [principal, PGOV29]; "In this school, the LSC does a good job communicating with the school community [principal, PGOV17]; "The PPAC represents the teachers' views" [principal, PPSC34]; "About how many teachers in this school express their opinions even if they are different from yours?" [principal, PPW034]; "The teacher members of the LSC fairly represent their colleagues' views to the rest of the LSC" [principal, PPSC28].

2. Rasch measure: "School participates in an external mentoring program, such as "I Have a Dream," which follow students for several years [principal, RESTR24]; "School offers adult education programs and recreational opportunities for the community" [principal, RESTR25]; "School has formal arrangements with institutions of higher education to assist with staff development and curriculum design" [principal, RESR26]; "School has a systematic program for parent involvement in the academic life of students that goes beyond the normal activities of PTA, parents' night, and attendance at extracurricular activities" [principal, RESTR22]; "School has formal mechanisms for coordinating with community agencies: for example, offering services dealing with child care, drug and alcohol abuse, and parental employment and training, etc." [principal, RESTR23]; School has formal parent and community volunteer programs [principal, RESTR27].

3. Composite measure based on mean of 2 items: "Since reform, more parents are involved in this school" [teacher, TPW06]; "Since reform, there are more informal occasions for parents and teachers to talk" [teacher, TPW07].

4. Composite measure based on mean of 3 items: "I receive a great deal of support from parents for the work I do" [teacher, PSC01]; "Parents respect teachers in this school" [teacher, PSC12]; "Teachers respect parents in this school" [teacher, PSC13]; "Parents support teachers' educational judgment" [teacher, IPG09].

Access to New Ideas

5 "What [educational] institutions have you had on-going contact with about school related matters?" Respondents wrote in names of organizations and frequency of contact. [principal, PPW124].

6. "Have you engaged in any of the following [professional development activities]?" Workshops or courses sponsored by the CPS; workshops or courses sponsored by professional organizations; courses at colleges or universities; none of these. [teacher, TPW44].

7. "About how many teachers have you hired of your own choice since reform?" [principal, PPW025].

Professional Community

8. "Participatory management is a trend that will eventually fade." [principal, PGOV06] (Note: scale reversed for use as a negative indicator.)

9. Rasch measure: "Teachers function in differentiated roles such as mentoring of novices, directing curriculum development, and supervision of peers" [principal, RESTR13]; "Staff participates in collegial planning, curriculum development and peer observation-reflection, with time scheduled for this during the school day" [principal, RESTR16]; "Staff functions in extended roles with students that involve advising and mentoring" [principal, RESTR14]; "Specific organizational incentives for teachers to experiment and to develop new programs and curriculum" [principal, RESTR18]; "Staff helps to design ongoing, on-the-job staff development based on local needs assessment" [principal, RESTR15]; "Teachers work with parents and human service professionals to meet student needs" [principal, RESTR19]; "School makes program decisions based on systematic analysis of student performance data" [principal, RESTR21].

10. Composite measure based on mean of 2 items: "Staff members support and encourage each other at this school" [principal, PSC11]; "There is a great deal of cooperative effort among staff members" [principal, PSC17].

11. Rasch measure: "About how many teachers in this school are willing to spend extra time to make the school better?" [principal, PPW029]; "About how many teachers in this school are eager to try new ideas?"

[principal, PPW028]; "Teachers in this school are continually learning and seeking new ideas" [principal, PPSC13]; "About how many teachers in this school take responsibility for improving the school?" [principal, PPW032]; "About how many teachers in this school can you count on to do what they say they will do?" [principal, PPW033]; About how many teachers in this school feel responsible that all students learn?" [principal, PPW031]; "Teachers in this school really care about their students" [principal, PPSC14]; "Teachers at this school work hard to help their students succeed" [principal, PPSC05].

12. Composite measure based on mean of principals' responses: "Goals and priorities for this school are clear" [principal, PSC16]; "Most of my colleagues share my beliefs and values about what the central mission of this school should be" [principal, PSC18].

Internalizing Responsibility for Change

13. Measure based on mean of teachers' responses: "Many of the students I teach are not capable of learning the material I am supposed to teach them." [teacher, IPG02] (Note: scale reversed for use as a positive indicator.)

14. Measure based on mean of teachers' responses: "The attitudes and habits my students bring to class greatly reduce their chances for academic success." [teacher, IPG04] (Note: scale reversed for use as a positive indicator.)

15. Measure based on mean of teachers' responses: "The changes made since reform have no effect on my classroom practices." [teacher, TPW26] (Note: scale reversed for use as a positive indicator.)

16. Measure based on mean of teachers' responses: "My instructional practices will change as a result of the School Improvement Plan." [teacher, GOV16].

Strategic Educational Planning

17. Rasch measure : "Basically, I developed the SIP" [principal, INPLN04] (Note: scale reversed for use as a positive indicator); "Teachers prefer that I write the SIP" [principal, INPLN10] (Note: scale reversed for use as a positive indicator); "The PPAC in this school played a major role in developing the SIP" [principal, PGOV42]; "SIP is just another form" [principal, INPLN13] (Note: scale reversed for use as a positive indicator); "In this school, the LSC participated in developing the school improvement plan." [principal, PGOV28].

18. Rasch measure: "I refer often to the SIP" [teacher, INPLN07]; "Students are benefiting from SIP initiatives" (teacher, INPLN06); "The SIP has already led to academic improvements in this school" [teacher, INPLN05]; "The SIP will help us make a better school over the next five years" [teacher, PPSC36]; "The SIP helps our school focus on common goals" [teacher, INPLN09].

19. Rasch measure: Since reform, I spend more time: communicating with parents [teacher, TPW19]; preparing for teaching [teacher, TPW13]; helping individual students [teacher, TPW15]; teaching in my classroom [teacher, TPW14]; working with the principal [teacher, TPW21]; working with other teachers" [teacher, TWP20].

Indicators for Human Resource Development
and Adoption of Instructional Innovations

Human Resource Development

Hiring New Faculty

1. "About how many teachers have you hired of your own choice since reform?" [principal, PPW025].

Active Staff Development

2. "Teachers are very active in planning staff development activities in this school." [principal, PPW021].

3. "We have an active professional development program for teachers." [principal, PPW020].

4. "There is adequate time for teacher professional development." [principal, 022].

Regular Contacts with External Educational Organizations

5. "What [educational] institutions have you had on-going contact with about school related matters?" Respondents wrote in names of organizations and frequency of contact. [principal. PPW124].

Adoption of Instructional Innovations

Adoption of Best Practices

6. "About how many students in your school are involved in each of these activities/programs? Hands-on math, hands-on science, cooperative learning, writing across the curriculum, and literature-based reading." [principal, INPLN16-24]. School is adopting best practices if half or more of the students are exposed to 4 out of 5 practices.

Emphasis on Authentic Instruction

7. Rasch measure: "Students have substantial influence in the planning, conduct, and evaluation of their work." [principal, RESTR12]; "Learning tasks emphasize 'multiple intelligences' and multiple cultures" [principal, RESTR05]; "Learning and assessment tasks that emphasize student production rather than reproduction of knowledge" [principal, RESTR03]; "Students serve as and have access to peer tutors" [principal, RESTR11]; "Learning tasks aim for depth of understanding rather than broad exposure" [principal, RESTR04]; "Academic disciplines integrated in the curriculum" [principal, RESTR06]; "Use of small group work in classrooms" [principal, RESTR01]; "Students extensively use computer technology" [principal, RESTR10]. Schools were considered to have an emphasis on authentic instruction if the principal reported having adopted all of these practices.

Notes

Prologue

1. *Chicago Tribune* (1988), p. x.

2. Beacon Elementary School is a pseudonym. Since we are sharing information collected by *Chicago Tribune* reporters, and did not carry out field work ourselves, we have assigned fictitious names to the school, the community, and the characters.

3. *Chicago Tribune* (1988), p. 2.

4. When Beacon still had a truant officer, Mac often accompanied him on his rounds. After the position was cut by the Board, Mac took over the role himself.

5. Inclusion became a CPS policy subsequent to the passage of the Chicago School Reform Act of 1988.

1
Framing Our Analysis

1. Advocacy for stronger high school graduation requirements began with *A Nation at Risk*, prepared by the National Commission on Excellence in Education (1983), and, like the emphasis on greater order and discipline, took root in effective schools research. For major reviews, see Smith & O'Day (1990) and Fuhrman (1993). Emphasis on higher order thinking and authentic instruction can be found, for example, in Sizer (1992) and Newmann & Associates (1996). See also the New Standards Project developed by the National Center on Education and the Economy (1995).

2. Major policy initiatives on reforming teaching include The Holmes Group, Inc. (1990), Lieberman (1989), and Darling-Hammond (1989).

3. See, for example, Carnegie Foundation for the Advancement of Teaching (1988). This report advocated ungraded primary schools and more humane and caring school environments. Ungraded primary schools were subsequently enacted as a core element in the Kentucky state school reform. See the Kentucky Education Reform Act of 1990.

4. This perspective is more fully detailed in Chubb & Moe (1990). It is worth noting that their specific empirical work and policy recommendations have been subject to intensive criticism. See, for example, Witte (1994), and Bryk & Lee (1992) about methodological concerns, and Elmore (1990) for a policy critique. However, their basic theoretical formulation of an institutional analysis for school failure is seminal. We are indebted to these ideas in shaping our own work on Chicago school reform.

5. For a detailed discussion of these developments, see Tyack (1974).

6. See Cremin (1988), Fass (1989), Peterson (1976), and Tyack & Cuban (1995).

7. See Wise (1979) and Hill (1992). See also Smith & O'Day (1990).

8. Chubb & Moe (1990), p. 21.

9. On this point, see Sarason (1990).

10. Chubb & Moe (1990) offer a detailed elaboration of these arguments about the interconnections between large-scale democratic control and centralized bureaucracies and how this combination has acted to stifle initiative and discourage accountability.

11. See Morris & Crowson (1984).

12. The impact of the profit motive is explicitly addressed in M. Lieberman (1986), and is more generally implied in most of the writings on choice that would include private schools in these plans. For a more general discussion of the arguments offered about the advantages of markets, see M. Lieberman (1989).

13. Bryk, Lee, & Smith (1990) raise this concern in their analysis of the likely effects of a market control mechanism on school organization.

14. See Elmore (1990).

15. See, for example, Wells (1993) and Willms & Echols (1993).

16. For a contemporary discussion of the democratic aims of education, see Gutman (1987) and Barber (1992). Lovin (1988) focuses on the social processes of values education. Similarly, Green (1985) argues that schools should stimulate the voices of conscience toward a sense of craft in one's work, social responsibility, and sacrifice. For a comprehensive treatment of the civic agenda of schooling, see Butts (1988). More generally, the socialization functions of schooling in a democratic society are a strong theme in the writings of John Dewey. See, for example, Dewey (1899, 1966).

17. For a discussion of these issues about education and the common good, particularly in the context of the education of disadvantaged students, see Chapter 12 of Bryk, Lee, & Holland (1993). More generally, see Boyer (1993).

18. For a more detailed discussion of systemic reform, see Smith & O'Day (1991). Also see Fuhrman (1994).

19. See, for example, the discussion in Smith & O'Day (1990) on "systemic barriers to educational change," p. 236 ff.

20. For evidence on this point, see Newmann & Wehlage (1995). In their intensive research and study of twenty-four schools in the United States that had been deliberately organized to promote more challenging academic work for all students, the most effective of this subset were either new schools, charters, or magnets. Not a single restructured school (i.e., one that had been "ordinary" and was eventually transformed over time) appeared in their top group. Although this is a "small sample" finding, at a minimum it does signal caution about how quickly schools might transform themselves toward new and more rigorous standards.

21. Lewis (1995). In urban contexts, there is deep suspicion about performance standards among some minority leaders. See Poinsett (1995).

22. For a detailed discussion of these ideas, see Tyack (1974). See also Chapter 2 of Katz (1987).

23. For a discussion of the historical alternatives to centralized bureaucracies, see Chapter 2 of Katz (1987). On how these developments lead to the

"privatization" of Catholic and other religious schools, see Chapter 1 of Bryk, Lee, & Holland (1993).

24. For a further elaboration of these arguments, see Katz (1992).

25. See, for example, the analysis by Cuban (1984, 1990) on the failure of past efforts to improve teaching.

26. See Moore (1990), p. 193.

27. See Wong & Rollow (1990). For a detailed historical treatment of democratic localism and educational governance, see Katz (1987).

28. For a detailed historical treatment of democratic localism and educational governance, see Katz (1987).

29. For a specific account with regard to Chicago school reform, see Katz (1992). For more general treatments of this idea, see Boyte (1980) and Evans & Boyte (1992).

30. See, for example, Chicago United (1981). Chicago United is a coalition of business and civil rights leaders that enlisted the aid of numerous executives from business, universities, and civic groups to develop the report. The report called for decentralization of authority from the central office and strengthening talent at the school and district level.

31. See Hess & Lauber (1985).

32. See Hess, Lyons, Corsino, & Wells (1989).

33. See Designs for Change (1985).

34. See *Chicago Tribune* (1988), p. x.

35. For a detailed discussion of the role of the Chicago business community in school reform, see Shipps (1995). Her thesis research chronicles the activities of the Civic Committee and its satellite organizations, Chicago United and Leadership for Quality Education, in the mobilizing for reform. She draws out the historical links between this current activity and a larger, century-long effort by this elite organization of business leaders to shape public education in the city.

36. *Chicago Tribune* (1988), p. 40.

37. Certainly some local schools had relationships with universities, but in a blue collar city like Chicago, where intellectuals are viewed with some suspicion, this was the exception rather than the rule.

38. An analysis of Council membership reveals the extent of its populist influence. Of the fifty-four members, 19 percent were professional educators, 4 percent were clergy, 22 percent came from business, 6 percent came from unions, 24 percent were from community organizations, and 20 percent were CPS parents. These last two groups—parents and representatives of community organizations—comprised 44 percent of the total membership.

39. Wong & Rollow (1990).

40. Supernumeraries are teachers who lose their current position and are not hired by a new school. This provision commits the CPS to employ these teachers, even though no school may want them. The controversy surrounding the School Finance Authority primarily centered around how its chair should be appointed: by the Democratic mayor, the Republican governor, or jointly.

41. Katz, Simon & Fine (1993).

42. See, for example, Poinsett (1990).

43. When PA 85-1418 was first passed, many Chicago teachers viewed it negatively. See Easton, Bryk, Driscoll, Kotsakis, Sebring, & van der Ploeg (1991), for further discussion. On the national scene, Chicago's reform is under scrutiny because it is at odds with national efforts to promote school improvement through teacher professionalism. See A. Lieberman (1989) and Johnson (1990). The Chicago School Reform Act is also contrary to efforts to strengthen the instructional leadership skills of principals. See Leithwood & Montgomery (1982, 1986). It also departs from attempts to bolster the technical core of instruction in urban schools. See Slavin (1989).

44. Moore (1990), p. 193.

45. Moore (1990), p. 194.

46. The impetus for community control in New York was somewhat different than the push for reform in Chicago. In Chicago, as noted earlier, parents argued that the schools were failing their children academically. While these same issues were raised in New York, parents were also concerned about the socialization of their children and the role of school personnel in that development. They did not want "outsiders"—white, Jewish education professionals—to have undue influence. See Fantini & Gittel (1973) and Fantini, Gittel, & Magat (1970).

47. Wong & Rollow (1990) detail the formal powers of the central office in the period leading up to the reform. See also Hess (1991), O'Connell (1991), and Kyle & Kantowicz (1992). Each discusses the failings of the central office in the period leading up to the drafting of Chicago school reform.

48. Bryk, Easton, Kerbow, Rollow, & Sebring (1993a).

49. When the legislation was first passed, school staff elected two teacher representatives. This procedure has since been changed such that the staff "nominates" their representatives, who then are "officially appointed" by the Board of Education. Additionally, in high schools, students elect a representative who can vote on everything except personnel issues.

50. This is true, for example, in school-based management initiatives in Miami/ Dade County, Los Angeles, and Hammond, Indiana. See Malen, Ogawa, & Krantz (1990).

51. Yanguas & Rollow (1996).

52. Malen & Ogawa (1988).

53. Moore (1990) and Hess (1991).

54. Material emanating from the Citywide Coalition for Chicago School Reform, of which both Designs for Change and the Chicago Panel were members, made frequent reference to this literature. See, for example, Chicago Training Task Force (1989).

55. Wong & Rollow (1990).

56. See remarks by Moore (1990).

57. Anecdotal information suggests that most principals still find this procedure time-consuming and cumbersome and, consequently, continue to rely on less formal means to persuade teachers that they would be happier elsewhere. At Beacon, for example, Mac assigned an incompetent teacher to a third-floor classroom even though she was overweight and walked with a cane. In 1995, the law was modified to shorten this process.

58. Cited in Putnam (1993).

59. Michael Madigan, Speaker of the House, worked to keep the teachers' union at the table as the legislation was being formulated by honoring their demand to protect supernumeraries. See Kyle & Kantowicz (1992).

60. Descriptions of restructuring efforts that focus on the work of teachers, such as career ladders and merit pay, include Darling-Hammond (1989) and A. Lieberman (1989). See also, for example, the professionalization initiatives in Rochester, described in Wohlstetter & Odden (1992). Also see a review of these professionalization efforts by Smylie (1994).

61. This provision remains controversial. Principals in Chicago must evaluate their faculties annually. Most teachers are tenured. Since it is very difficult to remove incompetent teachers, a negative evaluation often does little more than exacerbate an existing personnel problem. Under reform, two members of the faculty have an opportunity every four years to influence whether that principal's contract will be renewed, thus complicating the situation even further. Many principals find this aspect of the reform legislation highly objectionable.

62. See Hess (1993), for a further discussion of the reallocation of funds under Chicago school reform.

63. Louis & Miles (1990).

64. Shipps (1995).

65. In fact, Chicago has always benefited from activist community-based and citywide organizations that focus on educational improvement. Historically, there has been a split over leadership, representation, and motives between the neighborhood-based community organizations, influenced by Alinsky, and more affluent citywide reform groups. For more discussion of this history, see Alinsky (1971), Herrick (1971), Hogan (1985), and Wrigley (1982). See Poinsett (1990) for a viewpoint on this controversy in Chicago's current reform.

66. McKersie (1993).

67. A good example of influential media coverage was *Chicago Schools: Worst in America.* See *Chicago Tribune* (1988). A research report that had a substantial effect on conversations in the city is a *View from the Elementary Schools: The State of Reform in Chicago* by Bryk et al. (1993a).

68. In a letter to the editor of the *Chicago Tribune*, Katz, Fine, & Simon (1991) suggested that reform in Chicago is "more than educational change. . . In Chicago school reform is a social movement that embraces and reflects the city's diversity." It is "one of the great adult education movements in American history" that has "rekindled optimism, unleashed energy and activated coalitions across race, class, gender and politics."

69. In spring 1995, the Illinois state legislature passed a second major Chicago school reform bill. The act ceded vast powers and responsibilities for control over the school system to the city's mayor, including direct appointment of the Chicago School Reform Board of Trustees. It created a new administrative structure that vested substantial powers in a chief executive officer, who also is directly appointed by the mayor. The CEO post replaces the position of superintendent.

The 1995 act also extended budget and accounting flexibility to the school system. It struck down numerous provisions on collective bargaining that previously were secure in state law. (Some of these provisions, however, became part of the contract between the teachers' union and the school system.)

A key element of the law was stronger central authority to identify and intervene in non-improving schools. Specific language was incorporated to permit school reconstitution. This included: vacating a Local School Council, terminating a principal's contract, and revoking teacher tenure in these schools. A new accountability council also was established and charged with developing and implementing a plan of periodic review of all Chicago public schools. Taken together, these provisions created substantial new degrees of freedom for policy and administrative activity by the new Chicago School Reform Board of Trustees and chief executive officer.

At the same time, the new law sustained and strengthened the democratic localism of the earlier school reform law. To improve LSC functioning, for example, the law assured that new LSC members would receive training. Principals' powers were extended to include supervision and personnel evaluation of all school staff. A cumbersome process for removing incompetent staff, which had been a major complaint of principals, also was further streamlined. Finally, schools were assured that their primary source of discretionary funds, state Chapter 1 dollars, would not be cut for purposes of balancing the system budget.

70. Louis & Miles (1990), for example, provide accounts of high school improvement efforts. Comer (1980) reports that it took a minimum of five years to effect measurable improvements in the New Haven, Connecticut schools in which he worked. The now highly touted alternative schools in District 4, New York City, evolved over a period of ten to twenty years. Thus, even in these "best cases," organizational change took many years to materialize fully.

71. Although schools were required to generate their first School Improvement Plans in 1989-90, there was neither time nor guidance for this process, and the resultant documents had little real content. See Chicago Public Schools, Department of Research, Evaluation, and Planning (1990) for the analysis of the content of School Improvement Plans. See Easton & Storey (1990) for a description of first-year Local School Councils.

72. On the past failures of urban school reform see, for example, Tyack & Cuban (1995) and Katznelson (1985).

73. Until recently, this aspect of the school reform legislation has not been vigorously pursued by the Chicago Public School system. There has been widespread dissatisfaction with the existing standardized testing system, the Iowa Tests of Basic Skills, but only recently have efforts begun to find an acceptable substitute.

74. For an advocate's statement about the success of this program, see Finn & Walberg (1994). Contrast this positive report with the actual research on achievement gains documented in Witte (1994).

75. This comment was made by Smith (1994).

76. See Smith & O'Day (1990), for this specific exhortation aimed at school district officials.

77. This is a general character of change in all organizations that is formally referred to in systems theory as the principle of equifinality. For an exposition on equifinality in the business sector, see Kimberly, Miles, & Associates (1980).

78. See, for example, Comer (1980), which describes a five-year plan of work to successfully restructure a New Haven elementary school. He notes that, in addition to this documented success, they had also begun work in a second school at about the same time. This project, however, did not progress as successfully.

79. See Fullan (1991), A. Lieberman (1995), and Louis & Miles (1990).

80. Formally, this was defined as schools with a composite average on the Illinois Goals Assessment Program (IGAP) in reading and mathematics at grades three, six, and eight (or whatever subset of these were present in the school) of less than 235 in the year prior to school reform. When the IGAP program was established, the state average was set at 250 with a test standard deviation of 100. For any typical Chicago elementary school, with approximately 100 students per grade, a composite score of 235 or less, averaged over multiple grades in reading and math, is several standard errors below norms.

81. Grounded theory requires that the findings of relevant literature(s) be tested against the observations of field work. The theory gives researchers a framework to help them make sense of their observations in the field. The new empirical work also tends to reconceptualize and extend existing theory. For more discussion of this methodology, see Glaser & Strauss (1967).

82. Some of the major resources on school politics considered here include: Ball (1987), Blase (1991), Wong (1992), and Katz (1987, 1992). We also considered more general scholarship on enhanced democratic participation: see Barber (1984), Bellah, Madsen, Sullivan, Swidler, & Tipton (1991), Bowles & Gintis (1986), Dewey (1929), Evans & Boyte (1992), and Mansbridge (1980). Some of the major resources on school restructuring and improvement include Louis & Miles (1990), Fullan (1991), Comer (1980), and preliminary observations from colleagues in the Center on Organization and Restructuring of Schools at the University of Wisconsin-Madison. The latter were subsequently formalized in Newmann & Wehlage (1995).

83. For more details about the design and conduct of the CSI study, see Bryk, Bertani, Rollow, Moultrie, & Schneider (1992). For details of the Chicago Panel's study, see Easton & Storey (1990).

84. Bryk and Rollow had conducted field work through the CSI project, and Easton had organized and done field work as part of the Chicago Panel's study. Susan Flinspach, who had been involved in the Panel's research, also participated in the consensus process. The actual field notes on which they drew represented observations from more than fifteen different field workers. Thus, multiple perspectives entered into both the original data collection and the final analysis.

85. All but sixty of the low achieving schools participated in at least one of the two surveys. Moreover, the response rates reported here are somewhat conservative because we used only teacher surveys from schools where at least 50 percent or more of the faculty participated. We actually have some teacher surveys from another forty-nine elementary schools, but the response rates were too low in our judgment to include them in the analysis. The fact that so many schools responded to at least one, if not both, of the surveys suggests a very low likelihood of unmeasured systematic errors in these data.

2
Politics as a Lever for Organizational Change

1. See Easton et al. (1991); Bennett, Bryk, Easton, Kerbow, Luppescu, & Sebring (1992).

2. See Rollow & Bryk (1994).

3. While there is some ambiguity about what is meant by the concept of decentralization, virtually all definitions involve some increase in resources, authority, and responsibility to the school. See Hill (1991).

4. See Wong (1992). Ball (1987) also makes the point that decentralized resources and authority stimulate school politics.

5. Evaluative case studies by the Coalition of Essential Schools suggest a failure, on the part of both external supporters and the initial core group of school proponents, to attend to the political dynamics of change. Also, stakeholders' need to develop strategic political skill has undermined attempts to restructure. See Muncey & McQuillan (1992).

6. See Cremin (1988), Tyack (1974), Cohen (1988).

7. Cuban (1988) distinguishes between "first order" reforms that are directed at core operations and "second order" reforms that focus on the margins or peripheral programs of the school.

8. In fact, many reformers argue that without a fundamental change in school governance, structural change was unlikely to occur on a wide scale. See, for example, Chubb & Moe (1990) and Moore (1990) who make the same argument but from very different sides of the political spectrum.

9. See Etzioni (1988), p. 1.

10. Ibid, p. 10.

11. Ibid, p. 6.

12. See Peterson (1976).

13. Sarason (1990) suggests that these institutional features have proven intractable to most reform efforts. One of the distinctive aspects of the current restructuring movement is that many of these seemingly intractable practices are now being questioned. This is suggestive of a new political practice that develops both to challenge institutional features and bring restructuring to fruition.

14. Negotiations between the federal, state, and local municipalities to fund schools are also a part of this educational politics literature. For example, Peterson (1981) contends that beginning in the late 1960s, urban school politics were changing because financing was in jeopardy. The Great Society era of big spending was ending, and the power of cities, relative to the suburbs, was diminishing. This forced Chicago and other big city school districts to compete with their growing metropolitan rings for federal, state, and local resources.

15. See Peterson (1976).

16. The machine politics that Peterson (1976) describes is, in essence, maintenance politics. The negotiating of interest politics responsive to specific complaints, pressures, individuals, and interest groups forestalls fundamental challenges to the status quo.

17. Also described in Peterson (1976) is the use of patronage jobs to reward allies and co-opt potential enemies. This created an ethnic and racial succession in the city's school system that correlates with waves of new groups coming into the city's neighborhoods and being assimilated into Chicago's politics.

18. See Ball (1987) and Blase (1989, 1991).

19. See Powell, Farrar, & Cohen (1985).

20. Ball's (1987) analysis of British secondary schools in the 1970s was the pathbreaking work. Ball examined the politics that developed in different schools when the following changes occurred: Efforts were made to increase enrollment; a new headmaster was named to replace a retiring headmaster; and mixed ability grouping and other "innovations" to teaching practice were introduced. See also Blase (1991).

21. Ball (1987) observes that principals also bring in "experts" to solve some of their problems—those that they do not wish to tackle themselves nor want the faculty to have jurisdiction over. He suggests that this reliance on experts diminishes teachers' opportunities to develop expertise. For more discussion of the expert role in democratic practice, see also Bellah et al. (1985, 1991), Etzioni (1988), MacIntrye (1984), and Lindblom (1990).

22. Ball (1987) believes that a more democratic politics would be desirable. However, he suggests that the ability to envision alternatives is difficult because "thinking [in schools] is constrained by existing beliefs and values and crucial issues do not emerge" (p.128). In concluding his book, Ball suggests that the institutional "definition of the school"—its value system, goals, and mission—could be opened to debate (p. 267). He conceives of a school micro-politics that focuses on a struggle over values and definitions rather than merely the distribution of resources. He ends with a question:

> Is the form of organizational life presented here the only possible form for running schools? The answer must be "no" and as I see it the alternative lies in the direction of school democracy. But that, as they say, is another story (p. 280).

23. J. Mansbridge, personal communication (December 1993). See, as well, Mansbridge (1980) where she argues that successful politics are able to access the needs of the community on an issue-by-issue basis. Moreover, decision makers have a repertoire of strategies that they can utilize in different situations.

24. The schools that Ball (1987) studied were perceived in this way, and the reforms that they implemented were peripheral ones.

25. The Midwest Training Academy, a school that trains community organizers in the Alinsky tradition, is also located in Chicago. See Knopfle (1990).

26. We borrow the term "strong democracy" from Barber's book (1984) of the same name.

27. See Bellah et al. (1985, 1991).

28. See Evans & Boyte (1992), pp. xix and 198.

29. See Barber (1984), p. 126.

30. Barber (1984) calls this a "liberal" or "thin democracy." Anchored in the rational choice theory described earlier, it is predicated on an "ideology of radical individualism" that regards individual freedom and private choices as paramount (p. 110). He suggests that American democracy has become synonymous with representative government. Elected representatives vote on contested issues, and decisions are made by majority rule. Much negotiation takes place in private, behind the scenes. In representative democracy there are winners and losers, accountability functions primarily through the electoral process, and the interests of the voters are perceived to be static and unchanging. Between elections, substantive issues are rarely discussed publicly, and ties among citizens and their representatives tend to be weak. Special interest groups hire lobbyists to represent them, and experts are brought in to solve problems. Further, as the population has increased in size and much governmental activity has migrated to the state and federal levels, citizens are left with less and less say about politics, and their local public institutions are weakened.

31. See Barber (1984), p. 119. Similarly, Barber says:

Decision making without common talk always falls short of judgment and cannot be the basis of strong democratic politics. The test of legitimacy is whether an individual value has been changed in some significant way to accommodate larger, more common, or public concerns. If a value emerges from this process unchanged, then it is either a private value masquerading as a public norm or it denotes a prior consensus that has been revealed by the political process. There can be no strong democratic legitimacy without ongoing talk. (p.136)

It is important to note, however, that Barber discounts the kind of talk that occurs around pluralist bargaining, as the substantive focus of this talk is about individual or group interest, rather than the public good.

32. See Peterson (1976).

33. Bowles & Gintis (1986) suggest that this transportation of practices is not limited to ideas and understandings, but extends to well-learned skills and ways of doing things that have developed from their experiences in other sites of power as well.

34. See Bowles & Gintis (1986) for further discussion of the "history of the liberal discourse of rights," (p. 25). The authors suggest that:

In society meanings are not fixed, they are prizes in a pitched conflict among groups attempting to constitute their social identity by transforming the communicative tools that link their members together and set them apart from others (p. 157).

Thus, the words "become [themselves] the object of social struggle," p. 161.

35. *Chicago Tribune* (1988). See also Wong & Rollow (1990).

36. Here we seek to distinguish between parents who lobby on behalf of their own biological children and parents who strive to represent the concerns of "all

children." In operation, the former type of parent may not function differently from any other interest group. The latter parent, in contrast, is articulating a concern for the common good.

37. As noted earlier, a main reason for democratic localism in nineteenth-century rural America was that parents should control the socialization of their children. See Katz (1987). Community control carried these same themes into New York City's more modern-day conversations. See Fantini & Gittel (1973), Fantini, Gittel, & Magat (1970), Fein (1970).

38. See Boyd (1976).

39. As noted earlier, the legislation relied on both a carrot (increased resources and authorities) and a stick (the loss of tenure) in its effort to encourage principals to work with parents on a common mission of school improvement.

40. See Bellah et al. (1985, 1991).

41. See Ball (1987) for discussion of an "authoritarian" leadership style.

42. See Weber (1947).

43. See Rollow & Bryk (1994).

44. A provocative corollary to the lawlessness of some present-day urban communities might be found in Putnam's (1993) description of feudal Italy. His research suggests that those regions wracked most by crime and anarchy in the dark and middle ages are the same regions where the Mafia and the institutional Catholic Church gained and maintained their strongest footings. Both of these institutions were hierarchical and paternalistic, much like the description of consolidated principal power schools offered here.

45. In a report on Local School Councils, Easton, Flinspach, O'Connor, Paul, Qualls, & Ryan (1993) describe the LSC activity in consolidated principal power schools as a "limited governance" type.

46. The magnet schools and "good" schools in this group are unlikely to receive large amounts of discretionary funding because they enroll fewer low-achievement and poor children. Still, they do get some, and even minimal amounts become a point of negotiation for the principal. In contrast, some of the "weak" schools that fall into this category may receive larger amounts of discretionary money. In maintenance politics, the principal typically has a great deal of say about how this money is divided and spent.

47. "Council Wars" is a reference to the fighting that occurred among aldermen in Chicago's city council during Mayor Harold Washington's first term in office.

48. For more discussion of the historical tension between direct and representative democracy, see Morone (1990).

49. In Chicago it takes seven council votes to hire a new principal. If parents and community members on the LSC are, indeed, factionalized, it is likely that none of the factions will have the requisite votes to make a new appointment. Each faction can, however, block the appointments of its rival.

50. Positive reports from teachers and principals about LSC functioning did not differentiate case-study schools with strong LSCs from schools with relatively weak LSC involvement. We have concluded that responses to questions (particularly by principals) such as "Does the LSC contribute to academic improvement?" are very dependent on the perspective of the respondent and on the context of the school.

For example, an autocratic principal might respond positively to such a question if the LSC does not "interfere" with his or her decisions. Conversely, a principal attempting to initiate sustained discussion with the community would have a very different standard for judging a contribution. As a consequence of these contextualized responses, we were unable to develop a set of indicators that tapped what might be described as a strong or activist LSC.

51. Various approaches to calculating the classification error-rate are available. The classification criteria can be derived from a subsample of the identified schools and then applied to the remainder of schools. The error-rate is then the proportion of the remaining schools that were misclassified (i.e., a school identified as strong democracy by field observations but assigned to the consolidated principal power type by the classification criterion). Due to our relatively small sample size, this approach was not advisable.

Instead, we chose a cross-validation approach. Cross-validation treats n-1 of the schools as a training set. It determines the discriminant functions based on these n-1 observations and then applies them to classify the one observation left out. This is done for each of the n training observations. The misclassification rate is then the proportion of sample observations that are assigned to an incorrect political type. This method achieves a nearly unbiased estimate.

52. The sustained conflict indicator cluster score was not used in this discriminant analysis because theoretically it should not discriminate among these two types of politics. Rather, it functions as a direct measure of adversarial politics. Based on the observations from the case-study synthesis sites, when a high level of sustained conflict over institutional power is present in a school, this factor dominates over any other form of political activity.

53. Discriminant analysis can take both parametric and nonparametric forms. With this data set, the assumption of multivariate normality is plausible; thus, we adopted the parametric approach. The discriminant function (or classification criterion) is determined by a measure of generalized squared distance. In our case, the classification criterion is based on the pooled covariance matrix, yielding a linear function.

The linear functions for each school political type take the following form:

$$\text{Coefficient vector} = S_p^{-1} \, \overline{X_j}$$

where X_j is the mean vector of cluster scores for schools in political type j (either consolidated principal power schools or strong democracy schools) and S_p is the pooled covariance matrix of the cluster scores.

For the political types analysis, the linear discriminant functions are:

	Consolidated	Democratic
Principal leadership	.379	2.638
Faculty activity	-.744	.987
Active LSC	-1.583	.223

If each cluster score variable is functioning as hypothesized, the coefficients for consolidated principal power schools should be consistently smaller than the strong democracy schools. This is clearly the case above.

The posterior probabilities are derived from a measure of generalized squared distance and a type-specific density estimate. We define the squared distance for a school with a vector of cluster scores x to type j as:

$$d_j^2(x) = (x - \overline{X_j})'S_p^{-1}(x - \overline{X_j})$$

The type-specific density estimate at x from type j is then given by:

$$f_j(x) = (2\pi)^{-1/2}|S_p|^{-1/2}\exp(-.5d_j^2(x))$$

Using Bayes' theorem, the posterior probability of x belonging to type j is:

$$p(j|x) = \frac{q_j f_j(x)}{\sum_u q_u f_u(x)}$$

The denominator is the sum of the density functions from each political type, weighted by q where q is the prior probability of the school being in type j. In our analysis, we do not have any evidence of the proportion of schools in each political type. Thus, we assume equal proportions for priors. It should be noted that this does not dramatically affect the final results. For example, when priors are set to the proportion of schools in each type for the case studies, the classifications remain largely unchanged.

54. Easton et al. (1991) and Bennett et al. (1992) found small school effects.

55. For the purposes of this section, a probability of .82 (the midpoint between .75 and .90) was used in the discriminant analysis to classify each school in its appropriate type. Thus, range percentages are not presented.

The statistics reported here are odds ratios. Technically, they are the conditional probability that a school is a particular political type given that the school is in a particular low-income group divided by the unconditional probability that the school is in that political type. In equation form:

$$\Pr[type_i | lowincome_j] / \Pr[type_i]$$

For example, the proportion of adversarial schools in the relatively advantaged income category (less than 50 percent low-income) is computed by dividing the percentage of adversarial schools that have less than 50 percent low-income students by the percentage of adversarial schools in the population. Thus, ratios greater than one imply over representation, that is, a higher percentage within the type than in the population. Ratios less than one imply under representation.

56. Even though the integrated schools do not typically have a majority of white students, whites still act as the leadership elite. The best evidence of this is results reported by Bennett et al. (1992) on new principal selection. Where principals were replaced in an integrated school, over 90 percent of them were white. Councils in

racially isolated African-American schools chose African-American principals over 90 percent of the time.

57. See Coleman (1988).

58. See Putnam (1993).

3
Catalyzing Basic Organizational Change
at the Building Level

1. It has been argued that civic education and the development of community leadership can ensue from such forms of participation, and that this is particularly important for disadvantaged neighborhoods. See Evans & Boyte (1992) and Katz (1992). From this perspective, PA 85-1418 can be viewed as a model to address broader concerns about renewal of urban community life.

2. This argument about who gains and who loses in school decentralization is detailed in Elmore (1991). For a further analysis of the hypothesized links between restructuring and instructional improvement, see Elmore, Peterson, & McCarthey (1996).

3. See the review of this literature by Malen, Ogawa, & Krantz (1990).

4. Hess (1991), p. 193.

5. Moore (1990), p. 194.

6. In addition, numerous associations among the city's business and professional leaders have emerged to provide technical and financial assistance to schools. See, for example, Shipps (1995), for an analysis of the active role played by the business community through two of its major organizations, the Civic Committee and Leadership for Quality Education. Similarly, the local philanthropic community committed substantial new funds to support local reform. See McKersie (1993). New research, development, and professional education centers, focusing on Chicago school reform and improvement, have also emerged at most local universities.

7. Wilson (1987) has provided a seminal analysis of the problems of truly disadvantaged communities in Chicago. This analysis applies most forcefully to racially isolated, poor, African-American neighborhoods in the city. Other minority neighborhoods in the city, although often quite poor, still tend to have a stronger institutional base. For an elaboration of the themes raised by Wilson, see Jencks & Peterson (1991).

8. The role of social capital and the importance of functional communities to the work of schools is developed in Coleman & Hoffer (1987) and Coleman (1988). Closely related ideas can also be found in Comer (1980).

9. See the introduction to Comer (1980) for a more thorough articulation of this argument.

10. See Kotlowitz (1991) for a poignant ethnographic account of the harrowing lives of Lafayette and Pharoah growing up in the Henry Horner Homes on the west side of Chicago.

11. See Comer (1980).

12. *Chicago Tribune* (1988), p. 52.

13. Ogbu (1974) articulated these concerns about minority parents' and teachers' perceptions of each other. These ideas have been further elaborated in Ogbu (1986, 1988).

14. This is the fundamental premise of James Comer's school development model. In Comer's early work (1980), he maintained that if you reform the social relationships of local school professionals with parents and their communities, improvements in student learning would follow without any special consideration. More recently, he has added an instructional/curricular component. Nonetheless, concerns about social misalignment remain central to his analysis of the problems of urban schools.

For an earlier treatment of these arguments about the special needs of urban students and the demands that misalignment makes on the methods and aims of urban schools, see Janowitz (1969). In this essay, Janowitz distinguishes between the specialization and aggregation model for change in educational institutions. The specialization model envisions school improvements through technical solutions, including increased specialization of teachers' work. In contrast, the aggregation model focuses on the larger organizational environment and improving the overall quality and density of the human relations that occur there. While not denying the importance of direct efforts to enhance student learning, Janowitz argues that such efforts are likely to fail unless embedded within sustained attention to these larger aggregative concerns.

15. See, for example, Gage (1978).

16. On the continuing controversy over a knowledge base for teaching, see Wang, Haertel, & Walberg (1993). They articulate a knowledge base for school learning that received critical reactions from eleven different authors.

17. For classic treatments of this theme, see James (1899) and Dewey (1929). For a more contemporary discussion, see, for example Lampert (1984, 1985), Richardson-Koehler (1987), Kliebard (1993), and Kerdeman & Phillips (1993).

18. This argument is made by Cohen (1988). Supportive evidence about teachers' needs for social and professional support can be found in the research of Rosenholtz (1985, 1989) and also in the work of Little (1982), and Bird & Little (1986). More specifically in terms of parent-school relations, Bryk, Lee, & Holland (1993) note that many urban Catholic high schools benefit from being organized as voluntary communities. The trust relations that are established in these schools constitute an important social resource for professionals and afford a base of moral authority that substantially extends the relatively weak technical authority of school professionals in poor communities.

19. This is one of the key factors identified by Louis & Miles (1990), in their research on effective efforts at improving urban high schools.

20. See Heath, McLaughlin, & Wallin (1987), for a discussion of the problems of service coordination in urban communities with a particular focus on schools.

21. For analyses of the hyper-bureaucratization of schools and its impact on teachers, see Wise (1979) and Hill (1992).

22. The history of mastery learning in Chicago as recounted by Johnson (1991) in the pages of *Substance* is a very good example of this.

23. See, for example, the case study accounts of Louis & Miles (1990). For a specific discussion of the idea of a school's "deep history" and its effects, see pp. 185-187.

24. See, for example, Wilson (1987) for an account of the emergence of truly disadvantaged neighborhoods within our major urban centers.

25. Bilcer, Luppescu, Sebring, & Thum (1996), report that the average Chicago public school teacher has seventeen years of experience in the system. Much of the workforce in Chicago when school reform began had been hired in the 1960s and early 1970s.

26. For some of this rhetoric, see Moore (1990). This is also the reason behind the Consortium's decision to undertake a teacher survey as its first major research activity. We carried out this study as a critical early test of the status of reform. If the evidence were to show that, two years into the reform, teachers were not engaging the basic structures and processes of the reform, then the reform was likely to be in serious trouble.

27. See, for example, Graham (1993) for an historical account of the shifting demands on the U.S. educational system toward higher levels of skill attainment for all. The recent changes in the "returns to education" (i.e., the link between the amount of education and personal income) have been documented by Murnane & Levy (1993). Smith (1994), noted that his earlier research reported in Jencks, Smith, Acland, Bane, Cohen, Gintis, Heyns, & Michelson (1973), about the weak role of education in attenuating inequality, no longer holds. Lack of access to a quality education is now a much larger factor in forming social inequality.

28. Cohen, McLaughlin, & Talbert (1993).

29. The idea of loose coupling has been noted by such organizational theorists as Bidwell (1965), Weick (1976), and Meyer & Rowan (1978).

30. For a general discussion of Taylorism, see Part One of Weisbord (1991). In the specific context of education, see Callahan (1962).

31. The process-product tradition of research on teaching is rooted in this scientific management theory. See Brophy & Good (1986). The direct instruction curriculum also reflects this orientation. Teacher observational procedures developed by Madeline Hunter are another exemplar of this general approach. See Hunter & Russell (1981). In principle, these materials and techniques define acceptable teaching that can be used with any subject matter at any grade level.

32. Edmonds (1979) emphasized strong principal control, frequent testing, and close observation of teachers' work. Currently, Sizemore argues for an emphasis on basic skills which will prepare minority students to do well on standardized tests. In her view, poor performance on such tests has been a major impediment for minority and poor children in gaining entry to competitive colleges and universities. See Poinsett (1995).

33. Rowan (1990).

34. See, for example, Burns & Stalker (1961) or Weisbord (1991).

35. See, for example, Lampert (1985), and Cohen, McLaughlin, & Talbert (1993). Also see Darling-Hammond (1993).

36. These arguments draw extensively on ideas from the corporate restructuring movement. For a relatively early account of the basic principles of high commitment work systems, see Walton (1980), p. 266.

37. Darling-Hammond has written extensively on the notion of teacher professionalism. See, for example, Darling-Hammond (1989). On the moral dimensions

of a profession, see Bellah et al. (1985), and specifically as this applies to teaching, see Goodlad, Soder, & Sirotnik (1990) and Purpel (1989).

38. For further detail on these arguments about the contextual nature of teacher development, see Hargreaves & Fullan (1992). For a more general review of the research on the relationship between organizational change and teacher practice, also see Fullan (1991, 1993).

39. See Lortie (1975), Little & McLaughlin (1993), and Smylie (1994).

40. For further discussion of a school as a professional community and the structural, social, and human factors necessary to sustain this, see Kruse, Louis, & Bryk (1994).

41. For a further discussion of the distinctions between a control-oriented and commitment-oriented approach, see Rowan (1990). The analysis presented in this section draws extensively on his work.

42. For a general account of the centrality of principal leadership to school improvement, see Sergiovanni (1992).

43. See Weisbord (1991), p. 98, for further discussion of the legitimate and non-legitimate uses of power in democratic work places.

44. Evidence from the case study research at the Center on Organization and Restructuring of Schools at the University of Wisconsin-Madison tends to support this argument. The main activity of this center was to identify and study twenty-four of the most restructured schools in the United States. The most successful cases tend to have a strong transitional leadership figure, either currently or in their recent past history. In one instance, a restructured school that is now run collectively by a faculty had a strong principal leader who actively facilitated the emergence of this faculty collectivity.

45. Katz (1992) is a notable exception. His analysis of Chicago school reform focuses attention on the role of "alternative experts," based in advocacy groups, new institutes, and universities, whose ideas supported the development and implementation of this reform.

46. See Tyack & Cuban (1995).

47. See, for example, Berman & McLaughlin (1974).

48. See March & Olson (1986). On the idea of "muddling through," see Lindblom (1959). On balance, there is considerable validity in the way schools ordinarily manage much of their day-to-day affairs. At times of major structural change, which is the explicit intent of school restructuring, however, these approaches may no longer apply, at least with quite the same force.

49. See Louis & Miles (1990).

50. See A. Liebermann (1995).

51. In a mathematical modeling sense, the process of school change is both nonlinear and sometimes chaotic. Nevertheless, it is not without reason. See Fullan (1993).

52. Again, the names of these schools, key individuals, and organizations have been changed and some ancillary details blurred in order to protect confidentiality. Some of these descriptions include composites of events from more than one school within the same category.

53. Subsequent studies have shown a strong correlation between students' ratings of school safety and the crime rates in the neighborhoods surrounding their schools. See Sebring, Bryk, Roderick, Camburn, Luppescu, Thum, Smith, & Kahne (1996).

54. The five types described in the case-study synthesis are quite distinct and readily identifiable through field observations. Making some of the more subtle distinctions among these categories (e.g., peripheral academic changes versus "Christmas tree" schools) on the basis of survey and administrative data proved difficult, because the teacher and principal surveys were not specifically designed to measure this. Thus, the number of relevant items was very limited. We eventually chose to focus our analysis on the major distinction between emergent restructuring and more incremental, unfocused forms of change.

55. A sixth characteristic that clearly stood out in our case-study synthesis was a distinctive form of principal leadership. A "transformational" leadership was critical at Bella school, for example, in the emergence of its restructuring efforts. Mrs. Greeley combined an inclusive, facilitative orientation, discussed in the previous chapter, with a conscious aim to reframe the basic assumptions about her school that were held by parents, community, and school staff. (For a further discussion of transformational leadership, see Sergiovanni (1992), Bartunek (1984), and Tushman & Romanelli (1985). Since principal leadership has already been identified in the previous chapter as a key feature of local school governance, we have not included it here. In reality, principal leadership is central to both the nature of the political practice and organizational restructuring that emerges within a school community. However, since in Chapter 5 we use the nature of school politics to predict the type of organizational change occurring, we deliberately decided to keep these two analytic frameworks non-overlapping. In an earlier descriptive report on this work, principal leadership was included in both frameworks. See Bryk et al. (1993a).

56. The notion of "client orientation" is a key characteristic of teacher professionalism, as contrasted with a "working to rules" orientation. See, for example, Darling-Hammond (1993).

57. The concept of the learning organization, which has been made popular by Senge (1990), builds on a considerable body of earlier work in organizational development including Daft & Huber (1987). For a specific treatment of this topic in the context of educational change, see Louis (1994).

58. Louis (1994) underscores the importance of these communication networks and the ready access to new ideas during school restructuring. She argues that unless schools can identify the problems in their current operations, learn about alternative approaches, and adapt them through experimentation, restructuring will come to nothing.

59. For a more detailed elaboration of the concept of a school as a professional community, see Kruse, Louis, & Bryk (1994).

60. On the importance of internalizing responsibility for change, see Schon (1979).

61. The conceptualization of professional community employed here drew on our understanding of this domain, at the time of the survey data collec-

tions in 1991 and 1992. We have subsequently engaged in a further elaboration of these ideas and developed an expanded set of survey indicators. For
further detail, see Bryk, Camburn, & Louis (1997).

62. In this standardized metric, the zero point is the average response in the
sample schools. Each unit above or below zero corresponds to a standard deviation
in this sample for each variable.

63. The linear discriminant functions and the posterior probabilities were
computed in a similar fashion as those described in Chapter 2. The discriminant functions took the following form:

	Unfocused	Systemic
Engagement of community resources	-.348	.733
Access to new ideas	2.762	4.893
Professional community	1.401	2.175
Internalization of responsibility	-.239	.068
Strategic educational planning	.947	2.809

Again, as anticipated, each coefficient displays relatively wide differences
between schools with unfocused change approaches and those with systemic
organizational change approaches.

4
Instructional Change

1. See Fullan (1991), p. 22.

2. Firestone, Bader, Massel, & Rosenblum (1992).

3. This argument has been put forth in numerous commission and panel reports that call for substantial increases in academic achievement of all students,
with special emphasis on higher order thinking and problem solving abilities. See,
for example, the National Council of Teachers of Mathematics (1989); American
Association for the Advancement of Science (1989); the National Council on Education, Standards, and Testing (1992); see also the National Research Council (1989).
In 1994 Congress passed legislation authorizing grants to states and local schools
to support work aimed at implementing the National Education Goals.

4. See Graham (1993).

5. See Murphy (1991).

6. See Elmore, in Murphy (1991), p. 58. See also McLaughlin & Talbert (1993),
who also argue that reformers today have a vision of educational practice that departs considerably from what is usually seen in classrooms. According to this vision, students are actively involved in exploring knowledge and constructing their
understandings of the world. Instead of being the center of classroom activity, teachers act as guides and coaches, leading students to examine complex questions and
to consider ideas and relationships, and challenging them to think more deeply.

7. For a review of the student as worker, see Murphy (1991).

8. See Sizer (1984), p. 89. See also Goodlad (1984).

9. See Graham (1993).

10. See Murnane & Levy (1993).

11. See Porter, Kirst, Ostoff, Smithson, & Schneider (1993). For research on the effectiveness of Catholic schools with at-risk students, see Bryk, Lee, & Holland (1993).

12. See a seminal essay on this point by Green (1981).

13. See National Council of Teachers of Mathematics (1989); American Association for the Advancement of Science (1989); the National Council on Education, Standards, and Testing (1992). See also the National Research Council (1989).

14. See Gutmann (1987).

15. See Barber (1993).

16. See Gutmann (1987).

17. See Dewey (1929), pp. 27-29.

18. See Tanner & Tanner (1975).

19. Moreover, insights gained through recent research on how students learn and years of professional experience in putting these ideas into practice, have added more fuel to this movement. For a compendium of such developments, see Zemelman, Daniels, & Hyde (1993).

20. See Delpit (1986).

21. Ibid., p. 384.

22. Ferguson (1991) offers perhaps the most powerful evidence on the effects of teacher quality. He reports that 40 percent of the variation on student achievement in Texas schools is attributable to teacher background.

23. See Cohen (1990) for a case study of Mrs. O, who attempts to implement a new mathematics curriculum.

24. See Cohen & Barnes (1993). Cuban (1993) also claims that the failure to address teachers' needs and provide adequate time and support for their development was a major cause for the collapse of progressive reforms in the past.

25. Extant research suggests that it can easily take four or five years of sustained development for teachers to fully alter their pedagogy in these ways. The typical staff development program—a day or two of in-service—is ineffective in this regard. See, for example, Cohen & Barnes (1993). See also Cohen (1990).

26. See Bennett et al. (1992).

27. We did not ask teachers about their reasons for taking new positions, but we can surmise that some of these teachers replaced those who left to retire, who changed schools, who stayed at home to raise their own children, and so forth. From budget information, we also know that some principals used discretionary funds to hire new teachers, thus increasing the overall size of the faculty.

28. During the 1994-95 school year, the number of in-service days was increased to three and one-half days.

29. In 1990, a group of Chicago area faculty—Steve Zemelman, Harvey Daniels, and Art Hyde—published the first tabloid, *Best Practices I*, which was a compilation of the national consensus on best practices in the traditional academic subjects: reading, writing, mathematics, social studies, and science. This was followed by three additional issues and finally a book. Their work helped to direct the attention of Chicago educators to these practices. See Zemelman, Daniels, & Hyde (1993).

30. For a further elaboration on the ideas behind challenging intellectual work and the pedagogy to advance this, see Newmann & Associates (1996).

31. Other researchers have found discrepancies between principals' responses to questionnaire items and results from interviews, where the researchers can probe more deeply about the actual implementation of change efforts. See Berends & King (1994).

32. During the first four years of reform, there were extensive cutbacks in the central office, especially in the area of curriculum and instruction. As documented by Wong & Sunderman (1994), Instructional Services lost 320 people between August 1992 and November 1993. Those who remained were demoralized, with few resources to promote new school-based initiatives.

33. Unfortunately, the topics considered in this chapter were not a central focus in the CSI or Chicago Panel case-study projects. As a result, there was insufficient information, especially about classroom practice, to directly validate the survey reports about classroom instruction, as we did in Chapters 2 and 3. On a more limited level, however, we did check these data against field observations from the six EARS schools, discussed in detail in Chapter 6. We found consistency between survey reports and field data in these six sites.

34. The twelve cases from the CSI study included a limited number of classroom observations. The Chicago Panel study had none. Thus, one of the prime reasons for adding EARS was to examine the issue of instructional improvement in places that were most likely to be making progress—i.e., schools that were taking best advantage of the opportunities afforded by reform. By studying schools we expected to be further along in the process, we assumed we would gain a good sense of the best that has been accomplished to date and, by inference, a sense of what still needed to be addressed.

35. To preserve the confidentiality of teachers, pseudonyms are used, and there is no mention of the school name. To further protect the anonymity of teachers, at times we incorporated aspects of more than one classroom in the description.

36. Evidence of instructional change in the EARS schools comes from interviews with forty teachers whose classes we observed.

37. To gather students' perceptions of their teachers, their schools, and changes during the first four years of reform, we interviewed small groups of sixth and eighth graders from the classes we observed. We talked with approximately seventy-five students of varying academic ability levels.

38. These responses were evident as early as 1991. In our first teacher survey, a solid majority of respondents gave positive marks to reform and the opportunities it afforded for school improvement. Even stronger evidence emerged in our 1994 follow-up survey. When asked about recent changes in their schools on some thirteen different dimensions, the most positive reports emerged for "professional growth opportunities" (ranked second), "teachers learning from one another" (ranked third), and "my commitment to the school" (ranked fifth). In each case, a majority of teachers indicated that the situation had "gotten better" and less than 10 percent checked that it had "gotten worse." The remainder indicated "no change." See Sebring et al. (1995), p. 4.

39. We deliberately interviewed EARS principals about views of their school's progress in improving academic achievement. Each acknowledged that there was still much more to do and none was satisfied with the status quo. For their personal statements, see Bryk, Easton, Kerbow, Rollow, & Sebring (1993b), p. 87.

5

Testing the Basic Logic of the Chicago School Reform Act

1. These areas were originally discussed in Bennett et al. (1992). The section which follows draws heavily from this report.

2. A general caveat about this section is required. It is important to emphasize that all information contained here is based on principal reports. In prior research with items of this type, principals have tended to over-report the scope of restructuring activity actually occurring in their schools. See Berends & King (1994). Thus, the reports offered by the principals are probably more positive than precise factual description. They are useful, nonetheless, in indicating the relative amount of attention being devoted to various initiatives, and provide reasonable indicators of the relative amount of effort across schools.

3. A two-step Rasch analysis was utilized to develop the restructuring measures for schools in each of the three topical areas: reorganizing teachers' work, school community ties, and authentic classroom practices. The Rasch model is one of the family of latent trait models. It produces instrument-free person measures and person-free measures of item difficulty on the same interval scale. The scale units are logits (log odds units) which, unlike raw scores, are linear and thus suit able for calculations and statistics. The analysis produces two useful measures: for each restructuring practice, a measure of its prevalence (or difficulty, in Rasch terminology); for each school, a measure of the extent of restructuring in that area. The Rasch model is more fully explicated in Wright & Masters (1982).

In the first stage of the analysis, measures of "current restructuring" activity were developed. These measures were based on a dichotomization of principals' responses to each item. The response was coded "1" if the activity was "characteristic of most of my school" and "0" if it was not. Thus, the intent was to determine if the school was currently involved in a particular restructuring activity, regardless of whether the restructuring began prior to or since reform. The resulting measures for each school indicate the amount of restructuring that was reported at the time of the survey. In the second stage, an additional measure was developed to capture the *timing* of the restructuring. Principals' responses were coded "1" if the restructuring activity was "characteristic of most of my school, and was *initiated prior to reform*" and "0" otherwise. The item calibrations from the first stage of the analysis (when both scoring categories are used) were employed to "anchor" the scale of the second measures. The anchoring provides a consistent interpretation across both the restructuring-prior-to-reform and subsequent restructuring measures.

In each restructuring area, the practices scale was divided into four categories as follows. A pivot activity that represented the central concept for each restructuring area was determined based on the substantive centrality of the practice as well as the statistical properties of the item's calibration. Two additional values were calculated 1.1 logits above the pivot item (which implies a 75 percent probability of a school engaging in the pivot activity) and 1.1 logits below the pivot (which implies only a 25 percent probability of the school engaging in the pivot activity). These three points demarcate the boundaries for the four categories that we term "extensive," "moderate," "limited," and "minimal" school restructuring. Schools classified as minimal are likely to have the practices in the first category, the practices which are most prevalent in the school system. However, they are less likely to have those in other categories. Schools classified as limited are likely to have implemented the practices of the first and second categories but not those of the third and fourth. Similarly, the moderate group is likely to have initiated the practices in categories 1, 2, and 3 but not 4. The extensive group is likely to have the activities in all four categories.

The item difficulties and fit statistics for each measure as well as their reliabilities follow. Pivot items for each scale (i.e., where the "0" value is set) appear in italics.

Reorganizing teachers' work (reliability: 0.72)

Item text	Difficulty	Fit
Teachers function in differentiated roles such as mentoring of novices, directing curriculum development, and supervision of peers.	1.17	.90
Staff functions in extended roles with students that involve advising and mentoring.	.57	.93
Specific organizational incentives for teachers to experiment and to develop new programs and curriculum.	.49	1.12
Staff participates in collegial planning, curriculum development, and peer observation-reflection, with time scheduled for this during the school day.	.42	.99
Staff helps to design on-going, on-the-job staff development based on local needs assessment.	-.73	.88

Item Text	Difficulty	Fit
Teachers work with parents and human service professionals to meet student needs.	-.77	1.05
School makes program decisions based on systematic analysis of student performance data.	-1.16	1.11

School-community ties (reliability: 0.67)

Item Text	Difficulty	Fit
School participates in an external mentoring program, such as "I Have a Dream," which follows students for several years.	2.32	1.00
School offers adult education programs and recreational opportunities for the community.	1.13	.96
School has formal arrangements with institutions of higher education to assist with staff development and curriculum design.	.12	1.09
School has a systematic program for parent involvement in the academic life of students that goes beyond the normal activities of PTA, parents' night, and attendance at extracurricular activities.	-.47	.92
School has formal mechanisms for coordinating with community agencies: for example, offering services dealing with child care, drug and alcohol abuse, and parental employment and training, etc.	-.61	.98
School has formal parent and community volunteer program.	-2.49	1.03

Authentic classroom practice (reliability: 0.74)

Item Text	Difficulty	Fit
Students have substantial influence in the planning, conduct, and evaluation of their work.	3.58	1.06
Learning tasks emphasize "multiple intelligences" and multiple cultures.	.22	.91

Learning and assessment tasks emphasize student production rather than reproduction of knowledge.	-.10	.82
Students serve as, and have access to, peer tutors.	-.10	1.17
Learning tasks aim for depth of understanding rather than broad exposure.	-.22	.80
Academic disciplines are integrated into the curriculum.	-.51	.97
Small-group work occurs in classrooms.	-1.33	1.04
Students extensively use computer technology.	-1.55	1.27

4. Actually we had a further hypothesis about maintenance politics being at least moderately linked to unfocused initiatives. However, because we were unable to develop a measure of maintenance politics, we could not test this directly. Many of the mixed politics schools had some features of both consolidated principal power and strong democracy. In terms of the statistical connections between "mixed politics" and the organizational change types, 41 percent showed systemic improvement strategies with another 31 percent showing features of both unfocused and systemic efforts.

5. A Chi-squared test of independence was significant at the .0001 level. Thus, there was strong evidence of a general relationship between the type of political activity at the school and the school's organizational change efforts.

6. That these schools were in transition is at least partially supported by our data. In this sub-group of schools, a disproportionate number of principals (more than 50 percent) were new hires, who were at their school three years or less. Thus, many of these schools were experiencing a leadership transition and, perhaps, a change in their political and organizational arrangements as well. In contrast, for schools classified as having consolidated principal power and an unfocused organizational approach, only 38 percent had hired principals since reform.

7. Each comparison of unfocused to systemic schools with regard to use of various instructional practices resulted in Chi-squared statistics which were significant at the .05 level, except literature-based reading, which had a p-value of .09.

8. Technical details about the derivation of this probability are provided in Chapter 2. A logit transformation was taken of the probability in order to create a ratio scale measure for use in the path analysis.

9. As in the probability for strong democracy, this variable is the posterior probability derived from the discriminant analysis. A logit transformation was performed for use in the path analysis model.

10. In a preliminary analysis, we attempted to use them separately. A colinearity problem resulted, however. The use of the composite solved this problem. The

composite is the standardized sum of Rasch measure of reorganizing of teachers' work *prior to reform* and of the extent of school-community ties *prior to reform*.

11. Information on "best instructional practices" prior to reform was not available.

12. The descriptive statistics and correlations among the basic school characteristics are presented in the table below.

Correlation Matrix of Basic School Characteristics

	1	2	3	4	5	6	7	8
1 - Percent low income								
2 - High student mobility	.192***							
3 - Hispanic schools	.138**	.011						
4 - African-American schools	.346***	-.058	-.299***					
5 - Racially mixed schools	-.178**	.056	-.093	-.347***				
6 - Minority schools	.145*	.169**	-.118	-.441***	-.137*			
7 - Small schools	-.218***	-.052	-.037	.024	-.103	.022		
8 - Pre-reform IGAP	-.593***	-.135*	.007	-.471***	.247***	-.016	.154**	
Mean	84.72	.248	.074	.527	.098	.148	.090	187.45
Standard deviation	21.36	.432	.263	.500	.297	356.	286	23.91

* - significant at .05 level; ** - significant at .01 level; ***- significant at .001 level

13. A dichotomous dummy variable was created to indicate schools with high student mobility rates, i.e., in excess of 45 percent per year.

14. Dichotomous variables were created for each category. Integrated schools are used as the comparison group in the analysis. That is, the resulting "path coefficients" represent differences between the integrated schools and each of the four other categories.

15. Again, a dichotomous variable was created for school size. Schools with less than 350 students were coded "1"; others were coded "0."

16. The following table contains the full statistics for the path analytic model that appears in Figure 5.8.

Complete Path Model
Standardized Regression Coefficients

	Model 1 Strong Democracy	**Model 2** Systemic Restructuring	**Model 3** Innovative Instruction
Percent low income	.008	-.101	.102
High student mobility (>45%)	-.025	-.004	-.015
Racial Composition			
Predominately Hispanic	.190*	.020	-.080
Predominately African-American	.023	-.053	-.147
Racially mixed	-.096	-.098	-.175**
Predominately minority	-.021	-.020	-.181*
Small school (<350)	.050	.123*	-.023
Pre-reform achievement (IGAP)	.036	-.139	.115

	Model 1 Strong Democracy	**Model 2** Systemic Restructuring	**Model 3** Innovative Instruction
Pre-reform restructuring of teachers' work and community relations	.145*	.131*	-.056
Pre-reform authentic classroom practices	—	—	.566***
Likelihood of strong democracy	—	.381***	.061
Likelihood of systemic restructuring	—	—	.297***
R-squared	.068	.210	.461

N=269, schools in the analysis.

* - significant at .05 level; ** - significant at .01 level; *** - significant at .001 level

Models that regressed the endogenous variables of basic characteristics on the pre-reform restructuring measures were also run. Only two statistically significant relationships emerged. The percentage of low-income students was predictive of restructured school relations (at the .05 level, standardized coefficient =.235). A school's pre-reform achievement was statistically associated with the adoptions of authentic instructional practices (at the .05 level, standardized coefficient = .215).

17. Although we found a weak to moderate relationship between school size and strong democracy in Chapter 2, this association diminishes when other school characteristics were considered simultaneously.

18. The variable for the likelihood of a school being strongly democratic was included in the final equation. However, it was not statistically significant, even at the .01 level. The standardized regression coefficient for this variable in predicting innovative instruction was only .061. See the complete table in note 15 above.

19. The correlation between pre-reform authentic classroom practices and pre-reform achievement is .112 which is significant at the .05 level.

20. The achievement level of a school prior to reform also has a marginally significant relationship (at the .1 level with a standardized coefficient of .115) with the introduction of innovative practices. Schools with higher average test scores prior to reform were more likely to report classroom innovation. Schools with lower achievement scores prior to reform, however, made significant changes in their instructional practices under reform. For example, prior to reform, 21 percent of the higher-achieving schools (with average IGAP scores between 200 and 235) reported extensive use of authentic classroom practices. The comparative percentage for lower-achieving schools (with less than 150 on the IGAP) was only 10 percent. After reform, this percentage rose to 39 percent for higher-achieving schools and to 25 percent for the lower-achieving schools. This relationship was also evident for "best" instructional practices. At the outset of the reform, the higher-achieving schools had more of these practices in place. Nevertheless, lower achieving schools reported significant movement in this direction since reform. Thus, although a gap still remained, the proportional gains for lower-achieving schools were, in fact, greater.

6
A Closer Look at Actively Restructuring Schools

1. These are the actual school names; no pseudonyms are used here. Unlike the case-study synthesis project which promised anonymity to the individual schools, in the EARS study confidentiality was promised only to individual teachers, parents, and LSC members. Both the schools, and by implication the names of their principals and LSC chairs, are public information.

As part of negotiating access to each school, we guaranteed anonymity to individual teachers and students. As a result, we have decontextualized teacher and student quotes and descriptions of classroom practices. Our decision not to identify individual teachers and students by name reflects these confidentiality agreements; it should not be read as implying lesser value to their contributions to their schools or the significance of their ideas.

2. The *New York Times* article abstracted in this section was written by Isabelle Wilkerson and appeared on March 9, 1990. For a closely related story, also see Wilkerson, March 2, 1990.

3. Legally, the Local School Council was not required to give a reason not to terminate the pre-reform principal. This course of action, however, often inflamed opposition, as was the case at Spry.

4. The characterization offered here is based on conversations and events observed in some of the case-study synthesis school sites. It refers to how reform was initially interpreted and discussed in some schools. For a more detailed account of the views of key reformers, see Chicago Training Task Force (1989). These training materials were used by twenty-five different reform groups.

5. For evaluations by teachers and principals, see Easton et al. (1991), pp. 3-7, and Bennett et al. (1992), pp. 3-10. For the views of Local School Council and Professional Personnel Advisory Committee chairs, see Williams (1993). In each of these studies, respondents were asked a number of overlapping survey items about their LSC and local governance arrangements. Depending on the particular item, positive endorsements ranged from about 50 percent to more than 80 percent; most came in around 65-75 percent.

6. As noted in Chapter 1, the field work in the EARS sites was conducted during spring 1993. The information reported here involves retrospective accounts by the participants still remaining in the school two or three years later. This implies the possibility of some "revisionist history." In response to this concern, we sought to cross-validate these accounts wherever possible with local documents and news reports. In addition, the general patterns of behavior reported in the EARS sites are similar to those observed in the case-study synthesis project that involved a longitudinal study of school communities since the onset of reform. Thus, we are reasonably confident about the validity of these accounts.

7. No systematic analysis has been undertaken of the original principal evaluation/selection process by Local School Councils. Both the Chicago Panel on School Policy and Center for School Improvement case-study projects observed situations where teachers played a central role in removing a principal or "encouraging a principal to leave." These results suggest that teachers may have been more empowered by PA 85-1418 than originally recognized. By organizing politically at the school level, teachers could force out an unsatisfactory principal and choose someone more to their liking. This represents a radical departure from traditional practice.

8. See Yanguas & Rollow (1996) for a more detailed case-study account of another Chicago school community which was initially plagued by adversarial politics but eventually overcame them.

9. This phenomenon of shared influence or "balanced councils" is described in more detail in Easton et al. (1993).

10. The EARS study did not focus explicitly on the LSC role since extensive documentation already existed from the case-study synthesis sites. The main thrust of the EARS project was institutional improvements and the factors contributing to them. For a more general treatment of high-performing councils and the full range of their contributions to school improvement, see Easton et al. (1993).

11. Bennett et al. (1992), in a major study of Chicago principals, reported that the majority of Chicago Public Schools principals were spending much more time after reform working with parent and community groups, including the Local School Councils. Moreover, they also believed that they should be spending even more time on these matters. They also felt that they had not received enough professional development to carry out this new role.

12. See our discussion in the opening section of Chapter 2 on school politics and the emphasis on individuals and interest groups bargaining for marginal resources. For an insightful analysis of this behavior at the school building level, see Ball (1987).

13. For a further discussion of the interconnections between interpersonal trust, social capital, and moral authority, see Putnam (1993). This theme is also taken up in Schneider & Bryk (1995).

14. See Bryk & Driscoll (1988) for a discussion of the important role that symbols play in the communal organizational of a school. For a popular discussion of the symbolic dimensions to transformational leadership, see Sergiovanni (1992). See Bolman & Deal (1984) for a more general discussion about the role of symbols in organizational life.

15. There are significant commonalities between the reform efforts in the Chicago and Denver public schools. Both involve the creation of local school councils and both provide more discretion at the school-building level over selection of new faculty. Murphy & Emerson (1995) also report in their study of actively restructuring Denver schools that considerable attention was paid to recruiting new faculty who were committed to the emerging vision for improvement at the school.

16. In a case discussed by Rollow & Bryk (1994), none of the faculty in this CPS elementary school had taken a course at a local college or university in the ten years before school reform. Although there are obviously many other ways that teachers can pursue professional development, this fact is nonetheless a significant indicator of the parochial character of school practice in many Chicago schools prior to reform.

17. For discussion of engaging broader participation in systemic change, see, for example, Weisbord (1991) and Tafel & Bertani (1992). See also Darling-Hammond (1989), Smith & O'Day (1990), Cohen, McLaughlin, & Talbert (1993), and Little & McLaughlin (1993).

18. A longer-term organizational development perspective helps to illuminate the value even of this uncoordinated activity. There is evidence from past research on urban school improvement that successful school development has an evolutionary quality and rarely follows textbook formulations of strategic planning. See Louis & Miles (1990) and Fullan (1991). Thus, during the initial mobilizing for school change, individual professional development activity may be viewed as positive behavior, in that it is preparing the school for more intensive, schoolwide, coordinated activity. If a school maintains this random individual activity over the longer term, however, it would no longer be considered a positive indicator.

19. This was a widely shared complaint among Chicago principals. In a major survey of Chicago principals, they ranked "difficulty in removing poor teachers" as the second most troublesome roadblock to school improvement. Lack of time for

teacher professional development was ranked first, just slightly ahead. See Bennett et al. (1992).

20. Since much of this activity occurred before and after school and on weekends, some of the discretionary fiscal resources provided by Project CANAL were used to pay teachers stipends for this extra work, to keep the school open for extended hours and to support off-site meeting expenses, such as for retreats. This is another instance when supplemental fiscal resources appear to have played an important role in stimulating organizational change.

21. PA 85-1418 offers modest endorsement for faculty participation in school affairs. Less than one page of the 100-plus pages in the act focused on the creation of Professional Personnel Advisory Committees at each school. Both the organization and operation of these committees were left largely to individual schools to decide.

22. This critique of teachers' work applies more generally to elementary schools than high schools, where both the structure of the day and the organization of the high school into departments creates more opportunities for collegial exchange. See, for example, McLauglin, Talbert, Kahne, & Powell (1990) and Bidwell & Bryk (1994). These limits are especially severe in Chicago elementary schools, many of which are on a "closed campus" schedule. Typically, teachers meet their students at 9:00, remain with them in their classrooms through lunch, and then go home at 2:30. The only structured out-of-class time is between 8:30 and 9:00, before school begins.

23. Moves to deprivatize teacher practice and to create more opportunities for reflective dialogue are two important components of school restructuring. See, for example, Newmann (1991). The basic outline for this section draws heavily on the conceptual framework for professional community developed in Kruse, Louis & Bryk (1995).

24. For a further elaboration of teachers' views about the effects of reform in these schools, see Bryk et al. (1993b), p. 79.

25. The idea of a whole school faculty forming as a professional community has attracted considerable attention of late. Our analysis in this section draws heavily on the key features of a whole-school professional community developed by the Center on Organization and Restructuring of Schools at the University of Wisconsin-Madison. See Kruse et al. (1995) for a theoretical elaboration of these ideas and an analysis of several cases of emergent professional community.

26. In formal sociological terms, these schools were experiencing an expanding social capital; see Coleman (1988). The communication network among the faculty had become much more dense and professional as the normative influence was expanding. This is a very important organizational resource for schools. Prior to the development of the concept of social capital, however, this factor has gone largely unrecognized in the formal literature on school organization.

27. Although PA 85-1418 detailed a number of very specific roles for the central office in supporting reform (e.g., creating a training capacity for new LSC members), most of these were either never implemented or implemented so poorly (or so late) that few schools found them of value. For example, after the 1991 elections, the central office sponsored two citywide training sessions. By 1995, the newly

formed Chicago Association of Local School Councils began to offer conventions and trainings. See Weismann (1994) and Williams (1994).

The only significant exception to this were the schools affiliated with Project CANAL. Although this Chicago-Public-Schools-supported initiative began about the same time as reform, its genesis was entirely independent of reform (i.e., a result of a federal consent degree concerning racially isolated city schools). It operated largely as a free-standing enterprise within the CPS during this time period. None of its more progressive organizational elements had much impact on the larger system.

Although it is too early to tell, there may be an irony in all of this. From one perspective, the failure of the central office to fully support the reform in its early years certainly impeded, and in some cases undermined, the ability of local school communities to develop further. On the other hand, this central-office reticence created opportunities for many other organizations to fill this void. A substantial external capacity to support urban school change grew from almost nothing during the first five years. This may serve the city well in the future.

28. We wish to thank G. Alfred Hess, Jr., former executive director of the Chicago Panel on School Policy, for his valuable contribution to this section. In formulating the background on finance reforms associated with the Chicago School Reform Act of 1988, we drew heavily upon Hess (1993).

29. In this regard, it is instructive to compare base funding in EARS schools to two different standards for minimum per-pupil funding. The first is the 1992-93 General State Aid (GSA) per-pupil foundation of $2,600, which is the amount guaranteed for each public school student in Illinois. The second is the minimum level of per pupil spending needed for a basic education—$3,898—as established by the Illinois Task Force on School Finance. The base funding at both Field and Spry did not reach the $2,600 standard, and only Ebinger and Hoyne had enough base funding to surpass the Illinois Task Force's minimum level. Thus, four out of six of these schools needed to draw on their discretionary funds for basic school purposes, such as textbooks and art and music programs. Most troublesome was Field School, where even with its discretionary funds, the school's budget did not reach the level recommended by the Illinois Task Force.

30. At the start of reform, state funds represented 47 percent of all CPS revenues. Just four years later, the amount had declined to 37 percent. This change forced the school system to cut back on some services previously provided by the base budget, leaving local schools to use at least part of their new state Chapter 1 funds to support these programs.

31. The Hawkins-Stafford Act of 1988 permitted schools with high proportions of low-income students to use federal Chapter 1 as general programmatic support, rather than tying the funding to targeted students as in the past. Subsequent reauthorization of Chapter 1 further expanded this authority. The Chicago central office, however, moved very slowly to embrace these changes, and whole-school programs were generally not approved until much later.

32. See Morris & Crowson (1984).

33. Deal & Peterson (1994) argue that entrepreneurship has both an instrumental and symbolic dimension. Such behavior involves both gathering resources and

expertise for the school (instrumental) as well as articulating the values and ideas that can anchor and motivate a common agenda for change (symbolic). The six EARS principals were clearly entrepreneurial in both of these regards.

34. In addition to periodic feature reports on individual schools in Chicago's major daily newspapers, the *Sun Times* and the *Chicago Tribune*, the monthly periodical on Chicago school reform, *Catalyst: Voices of Chicago School Reform*, received wide circulation and brought considerable attention to individual schools that were actively seeking to reform. Several specials on both public radio and television highlighted individual schools and heralded the leadership of their principals.

35. Pat Harvey and Carlos Azcoitia moved into the central office as Executive Assistant to the Superintendent and Assistant Superintendent for Reform Implementation, respectively. Don Anderson at Ebinger took a principalship in a Chicago suburb. Moreover, these are not unique cases: Several other Chicago Public Schools principals who received attention because of their innovative efforts since reform also moved to more responsible positions both inside and outside the system. (Both Marcie Gillie and Nelda Hobbs took advantage of an early retirement offer extended by the CPS as part of its continuing efforts to reduce costs.)

On balance, it is unclear whether this increased career visibility and attendant mobility is a good thing for schools. Deep organizational changes need time to develop, and it is uncertain that any of these school leaders stayed long enough for change to be institutionalized in their respective buildings. In this regard, the book is still open on the longer-term effects of their leadership.

36. During the first four years of reform, this support mainly came from outside advocacy and university-based groups. The system itself provided little centralized support for the new roles that principals assumed. Five years into reform, more organized support from the system itself began to take form.

37. For a further discussion of Chicago school reform as a social movement, see Katz (1992).

38. Sebring et al. (1996) found that the strongest predictor of students' reports about school safety is the crime rate in the neighborhood surrounding the school. This was much more important than any demographic characteristics of students or the local community.

39. In this regard, these early results from the Chicago reform tend to support the basic contention of Comer (1980), who views the misalignment of relations among these three parties as a fundamental impediment to student learning. Although the Chicago case is still open in this regard, we note that it took several years in Comer's initial New Haven site before measurable gains in student achievement occurred.

7
Major Lessons from the Initiating Phase of Chicago School Reform

1. Much of this chapter was written somewhat later than the preceding chapters. As a result, it benefits from two additional "data sources" not available during the main body of work. First, from July 1, 1994, through June 30, 1995, Anthony Bryk was on leave from the University of Chicago working as a

special advisor to the Superintendent of the Chicago Public Schools, Argie Johnson. In this capacity, he became actively involved in a major effort to fundamentally restructure the education side of the central office. Thus, this chapter benefits from his experiences as an observing participant. Also beginning on July 1, 1994, and extending through June 30, 1997, John Easton served as Director of the Department of Research, Evaluation, and Planning for the CPS. He has brought the perspective of an inside actor to this effort. Second, another Consortium project, sponsored by the Annie E. Casey Foundation, assembled a group of researchers from several major urban centers to engage in a cross-site comparative analysis of decentralization reforms. We are especially indebted to the contributions of Paul Hill, who has been a co-principal investigator on this project with Anthony Bryk. The fruits of this collaboration are reflected in the section of this chapter which focuses on the restructuring of the central office.

2. See, for example, Comer (1980) which describes a five-year-plus plan of work to successfully restructure a New Haven, Connecticut elementary school. He notes that in addition to this documented success, they had also begun work in a second school at about the same time. The project in the second school, however, failed.

3. To date, this aspect of the school reform legislation has not been vigorously pursued by the Chicago Public School system. Because of widespread dissatisfaction with the existing standardized testing system, the Iowa Tests of Basic Skills, and an absence of sustained activity toward finding a more acceptable substitute, little has happened on this account.

4. For example, the much simpler and smaller school voucher initiative in Milwaukee, though hailed as successful by its advocates, did not demonstrate achievement gains in its first three years. See the third year report from Witte (1993). Similarly, advocates for systemic reform increasingly describe their work as a "generation's effort," and specifically caution against a project orientation demanding "get improvements quick." See, for example, the comments offered by Marshall Smith (1994) in a Joyce Lecture at the University of Chicago on "Systemic Reform and Urban School Improvement."

5. This topic has been taken up extensively by David Cohen. See, for example, Cohen (1982; 1990b; 1996a) and Cohen & Spillane (1992) .

6. There is a growing body of case evidence documenting that it is possible to raise standardized test scores quickly under high stakes accountability systems based on these standardized tests. Such results have been reported by a variety of school systems and state agencies including Charlotte-Mecklenburg, Dallas, and in the last year Chicago as well. However, there is also some evidence that these effects may not generalize beyond the specific accountability instruments and may not persist over time. See Koretz, Linn, Dunbar, & Shepard (1991). These results suggest that it is possible to achieve short-term test score improvements without undertaking the fundamental change necessary to achieve effects that are more likely to persist over time.

7. See, for example, Muncey & McQuillan (1992) for an ethnographic account of the difficulties encountered in efforts to develop "Essential Schools." For a more general discussion of the increased importance of school micro-politics during school restructuring, see, for example, Louis & Miles (1990).

8. We believe that this need for more attention to the political conditions needed to sustain school change also apply to the city and state levels. Although we did not study this as part of our work, support for this conclusion can be found in related studies by Hill (1992, 1994).

9. It is important to emphasize that the results reported here are limited to elementary schools. More recent studies have not found the same effects in high schools. While the Chicago reform stimulated considerable change at the elementary level, it appears to have been too weak of a treatment to catalyze similar changes at the high school level. On this point, see Sebring, Bryk, Easton, Luppescu, Thum, Lopez, & Smith (1995) and Sebring et al. (1996). In fairness, urban high schools appear much harder to improve than their elementary counterparts. Major structural features, such as larger school size, programmatic complexity, and density of external regulation, interact with the fact that principals are less able to control day-to-day activity directly, and parents also typically have less influence to support this kind of reform in high schools.

10. See Bennett et al. (1992).

11. For a fuller treatment of unitary politics, see Mansbridge (1980). For a critique of this, see Barber (1984). Barber is specifically concerned that unitary politics can deteriorate into a narrow parochialism where certain ideas can remain unchallenged and unchallengeable. Ironically, while a unitary politics may sustain an effective organization over the long term, it may also make an organization ill-equipped to engage a radical change in its environment. It is precisely at such a time when new ideas should be considered and prevailing practices challenged.

12. For an actual urban school case study of unitary politics, see Raywid (1995).

13. We note that this description of unitary politics resembles field accounts of decision making in Catholic high schools (Bryk, Lee, & Holland, 1993). We also note that on the surface, similarity exists between unitary politics and principal domination (i.e., consolidated power.) In both cases, considerable deference is afforded school leadership in the operation of day-to-day affairs. The differences, thus, are not so much manifest in how individual decisions are made but rather in the larger intellectual life of the organization and how individuals judge the exercise of leadership. Under a unitary politics, we expect to find ample social discourse about the organizing premises to the school, and frequent referral to these as individuals rationalize the conduct of their daily affairs. We would also expect that most participants would characterize the leadership's exercised authority as legitimate, good. and moral (i.e., consistent with the guiding principles of the organization.)

14. See, for example, Mohrman, Lawler, & Mohrman (1992), Hammer & Champy (1993), Senge (1990), and Peters & Waterman (1982).

15. See Newmann & Wehlage (1995) and Newmann & Associates (1996).

16. For supporting evidence on this point, see the organizational analysis of low-achieving Chicago schools in Sebring et al. (1996).

17. Evidence supporting this appeared in a study by Oberman (1997) of principals who left the system between May 1994 and November 1995. (Approximately one-third of the principalships turned over during this period.) While Oberman

had expected to find that the new demands of the restructured principalship (working with local constituencies and strategic planning) had "worn people out," in fact this was only a minor reason given by principals for the decision to depart. An attractive early retirement offer from the CPS played a big role, as did continued complaints about excessive paperwork, interference, and lack of support from the central office.

18. Some Consortium researchers contributed to this increase in public awareness, including Bryk et al. (1993a), who first raised the issue of the need for more local autonomy, a coherent assistance system, and centralized accountability. This work eventually led to an invitation to Bryk and Easton by Argie Johnson, the Superintendent of Schools, to assist in the restructuring of the central office. Many of the efforts that she began in 1994 finally found fruition either directly in the 1995 reform legislation or in the priority initiatives of the new Vallas-Chico administration.

The unexpected political turn of events was the fall 1994 election, in which both houses of the Illinois legislature became Republican in the presence of a sitting Republican governor. This unexpected shift of power opened up opportunities for Chicago reform that previously had not been possible under split Democratic-Republican control. Business leadership in the state had an unusual opening to promote change. For a further discussion of the important role of the business community in Chicago reform, see Shipps (1997).

19. For a further discussion of the 1995 legislation, see Shipps (1997).

20. To date, no published account of these efforts has yet appeared. Most, however, have been covered by local media. See the online search capacity for the *Chicago Tribune*, http://www.chicago.tribune.com.

21. Most of these new initiatives and the controversies surrounding them have been taken up in the pages of *Catalyst: Voices of Chicago School Reform*—a monthly publication that reports on and analyzes recent developments in Chicago school reform. See *Catalyst's* web site at: http://www.catalyst-chicago.org.

22. During the 1994 and 1995 school year, both Bryk and Easton joined the central office staff. Easton headed the Department of Research, Evaluation and Planning, and Bryk became a special advisor to Superintendent Johnson. In addition to working directly on efforts to build a data and policy analytic capacity within the central office, both became deeply involved in a larger effort guided by a major corporate consulting firm, CSC Index, to restructure the central operations. While Bryk returned to the University of Chicago in July 1995, Easton continued to assist the new administration through June 1997.

23. See Cohen (1982, 1990b).

24. Data for this were drawn from the 1992-1993 Chicago Public Schools Budget. We wish to acknowledge the assistance of Todd Rosenkrantz at the Chicago Urban League for the specific data presented here. To be sure, considerable unrestricted core district funds are allocated to the central office. These, however, primarily support budget, finance, and basic operations (space, janitorial services, etc.).

25. The discussion in this chapter focuses on the education side of the central office. We consider the extra-school functions and capacities that must be assembled to promote more extensive educational improvements in schools. We note that

important changes are also required on the operations side of the central office. Included here are transportation, food services, janitorial and building maintenance, legal services and personnel, payroll, purchasing, budgeting, and accounting. Local schools had many complaints about these services as well during the first four years of reform. In fact, much of the negative commentary about Pershing Road emphasized the slow, cumbersome, and unresponsive nature of central actors in these areas. Clearly, a major restructuring was needed.

26. We note important differences among current efforts at school system decentralization. Some initiatives are administrative decentralizations. While some resources and responsibilities are devolved to schools, the intent is to maintain common core operations. Curriculum, instruction, support services, and assessment systems remain centrally driven, and systemwide educational goals greatly constrain local initiative. This is quite different from the intent of PA 85-1418, that Chicago become a system of schools at least some of which might be organized around different philosophies and approaches to instruction. Under PA 85-1418, even goal setting was, at least partially, a local school responsibility.

27. See Bryk, Hill, & Shipps (1997) for a report on the problem of implementing decentralization in six major urban districts.

28. Considerable foundation money supported council training in 1990 and less so in 1992, and a variety of organizations around the city tried to respond to this need. See McKersie (1993). No central support or funding for this was forthcoming. This problem was finally redressed in the 1995 Chicago School Reform legislation that vested responsibility for LSC training with the University of Illinois at Chicago.

29. See data in Chapter 2 on LSC activity.

30. The Vallas-Chico administration has increased system capacity in this area since 1995. All new LSC members are required to receive a minimum of eighteen hours of training that is now centrally provided. Similarly, an expanded Office of Community Relations provides some support services to LSCs. Whether these resources are of sufficient quality and scope, however, remains unclear.

31. The Vallas-Chico administration has also made a significant investment in this area. They have committed a substantial amount of Board funds to the Chicago Principals and Administrators Association to develop a comprehensive array of professional development initiatives for potential principals, new principals, and senior members.

32. See the Bennett et al. (1992) study of the Chicago principalship. Oberman (1997) found that administrative burden from the central office remained a major factor cited by individuals in choosing to leave the principalship.

33. See Bennett et al. (1992) for an early account on this point.

34. We note that this network development is the central focus of the Chicago Annenberg Challenge. For a further discussion of the theory of action of these networks and their early implementation, see Hall (Forthcoming).

35. The idea of schools initiating their own network to support improvement is a natural extension of the Chicago rhetoric of local control. While it is an engaging idea, it is not clear that it is a very realistic strategy, at least in the near term. While this might work well in a situation where there are many good schools,

some outstanding ones, and a few that are very troubled, we have instead in Chicago many troubled schools, some good ones, and a few outstanding ones. The extant expertise and organizational capacity within schools to support the development in other schools is quite limited. In the near term, it seems necessary to draw in outside expertise from colleges, universities, other local groups, and various national groups and associations that are supporting school restructuring. Over the longer term, the vision of school-centered networks remains attractive, and presumably some of the externally centered networks might eventually evolve in this direction.

36. The most obvious problems emerge around scheduling professional development time. Since the amount of such time is highly constrained by union contract, external agents seek to make the best use of what is available. System-level actors, however, also make demands on this time, often making it very difficult for networks to maintain momentum in their work with schools. More generally, every time the system promulgates a new policy, it potentially undermines constructive improvement efforts occurring in some networks. A group might be working, for example, on developing performance-based assessments only to learn that the system intends to mandate retention in grade based exclusively on standardized test scores. Similarly, schools might be developing a project-centered curriculum only to learn that the new district policy on mandated homework conflicts with their efforts. In general, so long as the district continues to see itself as a direct agent of school improvement, conflicts between local initiative and central actions are inevitable. Unless the center vacates this realm (or repudiates decentralization), productive local action will be frustrated.

37. Recently, the Board of Education has contracted with a number of external groups to provide support services to schools placed on probation. This central initiative is highly consistent with the ideas developed in this section. The way in which this has been pursued, however, is problematic on two accounts. First, the Board assumes that these organizations have reserve capacity to serve large numbers of new schools. In fact, most of these enterprises are relatively new and still in the process of developing their own approaches to supporting schools. Many of these intermediate organizations, as a result, are struggling under the demands of a rapid scale up coupled with expectations for rapid progress. The further development of this intermediate layer could easily get undermined in the almost inevitable public disillusionment that is likely to accompany the failure to achieve quick results.

Moreover, because system accountability focuses exclusively on raising the percentage of students above national norms on the ITBS, it tends to divert the attention of both schools and their intermediate partners away from the longer term changes needed (e.g., increasing teachers' knowledge and skills) toward a shorter term focus on specific programs and materials that will raise ITBS scores, especially for those students just below national norms. This is a good example of the troublesome case where the accountability signals undermine the longer term development needs of the system.

38. Even here, however, allowance could be made based on the results of the school quality reviews discussed in the accountability section. Any school judged

to be "at or above standards" or making "substantial progress on their own" would not be subject to this budget restriction. In essence, this restricted funding set aside is the first signal that the center sends to schools about the need to improve, i.e., saying to the schools, "You should be spending more resources on this activity."

39. This principle of local choice has emerged as a central feature of several national school development organizations including Accelerated Schools and Success for All.

40. We are indebted for this observation to David Cohen. See, for example, Cohen (1996a).

41. This notion of teachers' responsibilities for the provisions that they make to educate all children well was a central norm in the British school inspection system. See Wilson (1996).

42. For a classic reference on this point, see Dewey (1954). These same themes are central to the work of Lindblom (1990).

43. This focuses on the school community as an agent that is externally accountable. Within the school community, questions about rewards, incentives, and sanctions for the internal agents—teachers and principals—also need to be raised. This directs our attention to a careful reconsideration of how collective bargaining agreements influence their work. While the latter is beyond the scope of this book, it is an essential aspect of "consequences" within the overall accountability system.

44. The capacity of the CPS to initiate reconstitution was clarified in the 1995 legislation. This was used for the first time in the summer of 1997, when seven high schools were designated for reconstitution that fall.

45. For a similar framing of the external accountability questions, see Newmann, King, & Rigdon (1997).

46. Our focus here is the external accountability of schools to the state for which a formal system must be built. We note that in a decentralized system like Chicago, these same questions can also be addressed internal to each school community. At this level at least the principal, and to some lesser extent teachers, may be viewed as agents of that local community and responsible to them for educating "their children." Under the democratic localism in Chicago, principals are held directly accountable to a Local School Council, and teachers in turn are indirectly accountable through the principals' oversight and evaluation of their work. Similarly, we can ask about the standards applied by LSCs in evaluating principals and the information sources used to ground specific judgments. In contrast to external accountability, which has more formal system features, in most cases, local accountability is likely to be less so. Since LSC members typically live close to the school, are frequently on campus, and have extensive interactions with other parents and community members, these informal social interactions will largely shape the way accountability works at this level.

47. For an analysis of these problems in the context of the Chicago Public Schools testing program, see Bryk, Thum, Easton, & Luppescu (1998).

48. For a discussion of the content overlap between standardized tests and common classroom texts, see Freeman, Kuhs, Porter, Floden, Schmidt, & Schwille (1983).

49. See, for example, the New Standards Project (1995). In part, the problem

here stems from limitations imposed by the multiple choice format of standardized tests. To pose more challenging academic tasks for students typically requires more open-ended formats where students show their work and explain their thinking. See, for example, the sample assessments from New Standards. Again, this is not to be overly critical of standardized tests. They were intended to be a cost effective device for simple national comparisons. They were not intended for the kinds of school accountability purposes for which they are now being used.

50. For a review and critique of extant accountability systems that rely exclusively on test scores, see Darling-Hammond (1997).

51. In principle, we can hold a school accountable only for the learning that occurs while students are under instruction in that school. From this perspective, a simple comparison of annual test scores is inappropriate for drawing accountability judgments since such test reports are about students' current status and not what they have learned over some recent period of time (say the last academic year or two). In contrast, an appropriate indicator of school productivity should assess the value added to student learning while students are under instruction in a particular school. See Meyer (1996), Bryk et al. (1993a), Bryk, Thum, Easton, & Luppescu (1998). (Such indicators required repeated measures on student learning over time in the same school.)

We note that this concern is especially problematic in urban school contexts, given the high levels of student mobility. Kerbow (1995) has shown that in the typical Chicago elementary school, only 75 percent of the students tested in a given year were present in that school a year earlier. In some schools, the percentage falls below 50 percent. In such situations, school staff may be engaged in very productive efforts at improvement that might never show up in a status-based accountability indicator, because the students whose status we are assessing keep changing.

52. In this regard, the development of the grade equivalent metric for standardized tests is very unfortunate in that it implies that such a metric exists when in fact it does not. When standardized tests are subject to item response theory scaling, i.e., the scaling techniques used in testing systems such as NAEP and SAT where a stable measurement ruler is valued, these anomalies become readily apparent. A specific student ability measure, as developed through IRT scaling, will translate into different grade equivalents depending on the form and grade level of the test taken. Bryk et al. (1998) document and illustrate these problems with the ITBS series used in Chicago.

53. On the trend anomalies in NAEP, see NAEP Technical Review Panel (1989) and Beaton, Zwick, Yamamoto, Mislevy, Johnson, & Rust, (1990). Also see Wright, Linacre, & Thum (1996) on the reading tests used as part of the state testing program in Illinois.

54. Koretz et al. (1991) documents a very compelling example of this. In the case studied, a district shifted from one form of a test, "Form A," to an alternative "Form B," which they then used for several years. During that period of time, the test scores appeared to be going up. When they subsequently returned to Form A a few years later, test scores dropped all the way back to the base level. Thus, the ob-

served improvements were totally specific to a particular form of a particular test; as soon as the form changed, the results did also.

55. We note that Chicago teachers already spend considerable time on these activities. In 1991, about 40 percent of elementary school teachers reported spending twelve hours or more of class time preparing for standardized tests. See Easton, et al. (1991). By 1994, 52 percent reported twelve hours or more of test preparation activity. See Bilcer, Luppescu, Sebring, & Thum (1996).

56. We have witnessed numerous examples of this in field sites for related research conducted by the Consortium.

57. Bryk encountered examples of this in the Charlotte-Mecklenburg district, which has a high stakes accountability plan linked to test scores. One of the school indicators used is the percentage of students scoring above 3 (on a four point scale) in a writing assessment. Since movement from category 1 to 2 is not valued under the accountability system, he observed instances where schools were specifically focusing their compensatory education programs on students at level 2, in the hope of moving them to level 3.

58. We are indebted to a conversation with Phil Schlecty about appropriate standards for school accountability. In discussing our concern about achievement being co-constructed, he pointed out the analogy to profit and loss in a firm.

59. The General Motors Saturn plant is a corporate example of what is generally regarded as a quality production operation, but one that is not generating the kinds of profits expected. See Stern (1994).

60. As novel as this idea may sound to most American audiences, it has a longstanding tradition in other countries. As Wilson (1996) points out, the primary standpoint for the English system of school inspections has traditionally been of the "provisions" that local professionals make for the education and care of children (given the resources provided to them and the particular needs of the community they may serve). Ours is basically an argument about the provisions local school leaders are making for the education of children.

61. Extending the analogy to the firm a bit further, corporate actors can also positively affect their short term bottom line through efforts such as cutting back on research and product development and under-funding human resource and organizational development. While these savings might well improve the current bottom line, over the longer term, such actions would greatly weaken the future capacity of the firm to compete in the marketplace.

62. For a further elaboration of this argument about the centrality of social trust to school effectiveness and empirical data supporting this point, see Bryk & Schneider (1996). Additional empirical evidence can also be found in Sebring et al. (1996).

63. Our remarks here are directed to the approximately one-third of the schools that we have characterized as "left behind by reform." While school problems may be highly visible in a fraction of these places, our analysis suggests that the majority of these schools would not immediately catch the attention of a casual observer. Principals have established control, and on the surface at least, there is no visible opposition from parents, teachers, or the community. (Unfortunately,

not much is actually going on in terms of a broad-based, meaningful improvement.) Test score trends and other quantitative indicators, will also look like many other schools—generally flat—and by themselves will not be likely to trigger external scrutiny. It is only on the basis of an intensive quality review that such schools will likely come to light.

64. For a more thorough discussion of these issues, see Odden (1996).

65. To be clear, we are not suggesting that fiscal incentives and concerns about career advancement are primary motivating factors for school principals. On the other hand, two years after we completed our study of the six EARS sites, only one of these principals still remained in her building. Two had moved on to significant promotions at Pershing Road, one to a better paying position in the suburbs, and two took early retirement. Although this is a small sample, it does offer support for the concern raised here.

More generally on this point, see Mohrman & Lawler (1996), who argue for extrinsic incentives to complement intrinsic incentives embedded in a redesign of work to create greater individual influence and more social cohesiveness.

66. To the point, the interim Board of Education in Chicago entered into a collective bargaining agreement with the Chicago Teachers Union that provided fiscal incentives for teacher-initiated professional development. No requirement was made that such activities connect to the local school improvement plan. While our data suggest that a substantial number of teachers took advantage of this, we found little evidence in our field work that this random individual activity culminated in collective instructional improvements.

67. In this regard, we were impressed during field work in the Charlotte-Mecklenburg district at the ways in which school teachers responded to the school-based financial incentives in their accountability system. If a school met the goals set for it for the year, all staff received a bonus. The presence of schoolwide goals and schoolwide bonuses for teachers appears to have created an incentive for professional collaboration at the school-building level. See Bryk, Shipps, Hill, & Lake (1997). Staff know that bonuses are unlikely unless most classes improve, and so real incentives exist for teachers to help each other. This provides a reason both for more competent staff to help those experiencing difficulty and for the latter to accept that help. We note that this is a very different consequence from what is likely to ensue from individual teacher bonuses (i.e., performance pay). The latter would tend to introduce competition among teachers within schools, thus and work directly against collaboration on improvement (i.e., if someone else improves, it might well reduce my chance of a bonus.)

68. The overall school is probably too gross a unit, as it will tend to mask improvements in subunits within the school. In contrast, the grade level is probably too fine. The amount of data available may be too limited to generate reliable estimates of trends and may encourage across-grade competition rather than coordination. A logical division into grade level grouping could stimulate both within- and across-grades articulation of curriculum and collective responsibility for student learning. Such an indicator system signifies that a group of faculty will be held responsible for what they jointly accomplish.

69. To be sure, there are other purposes for which average annual reports are useful, such as judging whether the overall level of attainment in a school system is improving or declining. Similarly, each student must be held to the same standards of performance, and so judging "distance from an external standard" is also important. In our application, however, we seek to build indicators to judge school productivity, and these should be value-added. For a further discussion of the theory and use of value-added indicators, see Meyer (1996) and Bryk et al. (1994). For a specific application see Bryk et al. (1998).

70. See Kerbow (1995).

71. See Meyer (1996).

72. See Storey, Easton, Sharp, Steans, Ames, & Bassok (1995).

73. As stakes are attached to the accountability system, the incentives to cheat on the indicator data rise dramatically. School districts typically have weak or nonexistent audit and control procedures in this regard. For example, standardized tests are distributed by classroom teachers who proctor their administration and then are responsible for the submission of test score forms to the central office. The same tests are often reused year after year, and few procedures are rigorously followed to keep them secured. In short, it is very easy to cheat if one is so inclined.

74. The sequence described here is intended to provide a conceptual plan for the field visit, not a specific organization for the conduct of the work while on-site.

75. The Chicago Public Schools have already adopted a document, called the "Five Essential Supports for Student Learning," that could serve this purpose. The "Five Essential Supports" emerged out of a process that involved both: 1) a synthesis of Consortium research on the progress of school reform in Chicago and findings from other studies of successful urban school improvement efforts, and 2) extensive local stakeholder consultation and piloting by school and community-based leaders. This reference guide is offered to schools by the CPS to assist them in their self-analysis of local practice. It also provides the basic framework for the required annual School Improvement Plans. Thus, to extend its use as a framework for school quality reviews would be quite natural. See Chicago Public Schools (1995).

76. The centrality of community education in school decentralization is taken up by Strike (1993). He argues that promoting this conception of democratic activity in local school communities, in contrast to an emphasis on the political sovereignty of local legislative bodies, is key to effective site-based management.

77. Much like fiscal audits, one could envision a two-part report. The first part would consist of core findings about the quality of the school and its improvement efforts. The second part might take the character of an educational opinion about possible improvement practices that the school might consider in the future. The field data to support the first part of the report would have to meet some standards of reliability. The second part might be more interpretive.

78. In this regard, we intend specifically to distinguish the school reviews envisioned here from school visits based around the notion of "critical friends." This latter type of school review might better be characterized as a school development strategy. It may serve formative evaluation purposes quite well, but seems less well suited for the summative purposes also envisioned here.

79. We note that a two-year term in the accountability agency is likely to constitute a very significant professional development experience for those involved. It
may well become the training ground for future system leadership.

80. These cost figures are based on the research, evaluation, and planning expenditures for the Chicago Public Schools in fiscal 1995. The projected costs for a
quality review system obviously depend on the specific details of the system implemented. The estimates here are based on five-day school visits by a five-person
team of paid staff. In addition to the on-site time, supplemental staff time was also
budgeted for pre-visit planning and post-visit report writing and consultation with
school leaders. This proposed system would review all schools on a four-year cycle
with more frequent reviews for schools deemed especially problematic.

81. On the effects of school size on student achievement, see Lee & Smith (1997).
More generally on this topic, see Bryk, Lee, & Smith (1990).

82. For a further discussion of the linkage between direct democratic control of
systems and bureaucratic failure see Chubb & Moe (1993). On the more specific
topic of how the governance of American schools has undermined efforts to construct more coherent instructional guidance for schools, see Cohen & Spillane (1993).

We note that the early experiences post-1995 of reform in Chicago offer a con-
firming case in this regard. The new governance structure of a Chief Executive
Officer and Reform Board of Trustees, all appointed by the mayor, has created a
much more unitary voice around central policy making. An impressive array of
new policy initiatives has resulted over the past two years. This affords a case proof
that changing institutional governance can facilitate central action. On the other
hand, we do not believe that the particular governance design adopted in Chicago
is a "silver bullet." Much of its implementation success is directly tied to the particular structure of the city's politics, where the mayor also maintains a similar
level of policy control over the City Council. Were policy making more actively
contested at the city level, we would also expect this to happen for schools.

83. See, for example, the critique of parental involvement in school governance
in Bryk, Lee, & Smith (1990).

84. It is instructive to consider the research by Smylie, Lazarus, & Brownlee-
Conyers (1996) on school restructuring efforts in the Glenview, Illinois, school
system. In contrast to Chicago, Glenview experienced stable leadership, funding, and considerable external support for their decentralization. Smylie documents that significant improvements in student learning emerged after seven
years. Virtually none of the external conditions that supported local improvements in Glenview characterized Chicago during its first four years of reform.

References

Alinsky, S. (1971). *Rules for radicals: A pragmatic primer for realistic radicals.* New York: Vintage.

American Association for the Advancement of Science. (1989). *Science for all Americans: A Project 2061 report on literacy goals in science, mathematics, and technology.* Washington, DC: Author.

Ball, S. J. (1987). *The micro-politics of the school: Towards a theory of school organization.* London: Metheun.

Barber, B. R. (1984). *Strong democracy: Participatory politics for a new age.* Berkeley: University of California Press.

_____. (1992). *An aristocracy of everyone.* New York: Oxford University Press.

_____. (1993, November). America skips school. *Harper's, 287,* (1722), 39-46.

Bartunek, J. (1984). Changing interpretive schemes and organizational restructuring: The example of a religious order. *Administrative Science Quarterly, 29,* 355-372.

Beaton, A. E., Zwick, R., Yamamoto, K., Mislevy, R. J., Johnson, E. G., & Rust, K. F. (1990). Disentangling the NAEP 1985-86 reading anomaly. Report No. 17-TR-21. Princeton: National Assessment of Educational Progress, Educational Testing Service.

Bellah, R. M., Madsen, R., Sullivan, W. M., Swidler, A., & Tipton, S. M. (1985). *Habits of the heart.* New York: Knopf.

_____. (1991). *The good society.* New York: Knopf.

Bennett, A. L., Bryk, A. S., Easton, J. Q., Kerbow, D., Luppescu, S., & Sebring, P. A. (1992). *Charting reform: The principals' perspective.* Chicago: Consortium on Chicago School Research.

Berends, M., & King, M. B. (1994). A description of restructuring in nationally nominated schools: Legacy of the iron cage? *Educational Policy, 8* (1), 3-27.

Berman, P., & McLaughlin, M. W. (1974). *Federal programs supporting educational change: Vol. I. A report prepared for the United States Department of Education.* Santa Monica, CA: RAND Corporation.

Bidwell, C. E. (1965). The school as a formal organization. In J. G. March (Ed.), *Handbook of organizations* (pp. 972-1022). Chicago: Rand McNally.

Bidwell, C. E., & Bryk, A. S. (1994, April). *How teachers' work is organized: The content and consequences of the structure of the high school workplace.* Paper presented at the annual meeting of the American Educational Research Association, New Orleans, LA.

Bilcer, D. K., Luppescu, S., Sebring, P. B., & Thum, Y. M. (1996). *The Charting reform survey series: Public use data.* Chicago: Consortium on Chicago School Research.

Bird, T., & Little, J. W. (1986). How schools organize the teaching occupation. *Elementary School Journal, 86*(4), 493-511.

Blase, J. J. (1989). The micropolitics of the school: The everyday political orientation of teachers toward open school principals. *Educational Administration Quarterly. 35*(4), 377-407.

Blase, J. J. (1991). *The politics of life in schools: Power, conflict and cooperation.* Newbury Park: Sage.

Bolman, L. G., & Deal, T. E. (1984). *Modern approaches to understanding and managing organizations.* San Francisco: Jossey-Bass.

Bowles, S., & Gintis, H. (1986). *Democracy and capitalism: Property, community, and the contradictions of modern social thought.* New York: Basic Books.

Boyd, W. L. (1976). *Community status and conflict in suburban school politics.* London: Sage.

Boyer, E. L. (1993). Foreword. In E. Rassell, & R. Rothstein (Eds.), *School choice: Examining the evidence* (pp. xi-xiv). Washington, DC: Economic Policy Institute.

Boyte, H. C. (1980). *The backyard revolution: Understanding the new citizen movement.* Philadelphia: Temple University Press.

Brophy, J. E., & Good, T. L. (1986). Teacher behavior and student achievement. In M. C. Wittrock (Ed.), *Handbook of research on teaching* (3rd ed.) (pp. 328-375). New York: Macmillan.

Bryk, A. S., Bertani, A., Rollow, S. G., Moultrie, L., & Schneider, B. (1992). *A workshop on Chicago school reform: A discussion of research in progress.* Paper presented at the annual meeting of the American Educational Research Association, San Francisco.

Bryk, A. S., Camburn, E., & Louis, K. S. (1997). Professional community in Chicago elementary schools: Facilitating factors and organizational consequences. Occasional Paper, Consortium on Chicago School Research.

Bryk, A. S., Deabster, P. E., Easton, J. Q., Luppescu, S., & Thum, Y. M. (1994, May). Measuring Achievement Gains in the Chicago Public Schools. In Hess, G. A. (Ed.). *Education and Urban Society,* 26(3), pp. 306-319.

Bryk, A. S., & Driscoll, M. E. (1988). *The school as community: Theoretical foundation, contextual influences, and consequences for teachers and students.* Madison, WI: National Center for Effective Secondary Schools.

Bryk, A. S., Easton, J. Q., Kerbow, D., Rollow, S. G., & Sebring, P. A. (1993a). *A view from the elementary schools: The state of reform in Chicago.* Chicago: Consortium on Chicago School Research.

_____. (1993b). *A view from the elementary schools: The state of reform in Chicago. A technical report.* Chicago: Consortium on Chicago School Research.

Bryk, A. S., Shipps, D., Hill, P. T., & Lake, R. (1997). *Decentralization in practice: Toward a system of schools.* Final report to the Annie E. Casey Foundation, Baltimore, MD.

Bryk, A. S., & Lee, V. E. (1992). Is politics the problem and markets the answer? An essay review of "Politics, markets, and America's schools." *Economics of Education Review.* 2(4), 439-451.

Bryk, A. S., Lee, V. E., & Holland, P. E. (1993.) *Catholic schools and the common good.* Cambridge, MA: Harvard University Press.

Bryk, A. S., Lee, V. E., & Smith, J. (1990). High school organization and its effects on teachers and students: An interpretive summary of the research. In W. Clune, & J. Witte (Eds.), *Choice and control in American education: Vol. 1* (pp. 135-226). New York: Falmer.

Bryk, A. S., & Schneider, B. (1996). *Social trust: A moral resource for school improvement.* Chicago: Consortium on Chicago School Research.

Bryk, A. S., Thum, Y. M., Easton, J. Q., & Luppescu, S. (1998). *Assessing school productivity using student achievement: The Chicago public elementary schools.* Chicago: Consortium on Chicago School Research.

Burns, T., & Stalker, G. M. (1961). *The management of innovation.* London: Tavistock.

Butts, R. F. (1988). The moral imperative for American schools . . . Inflame the civil temper. *American Journal of Education, 96*(2), 162-194.

Callahan, R. E. (1962). *Education and the cult of efficiency; a study of the social forces that have shaped the administration of the public schools.* Chicago: University of Chicago Press.

Carnegie Foundation for the Advancement of Teaching. (1988). *Imperiled generation: Saving urban schools.* Princeton, NJ: Author.

Chicago Public Schools, Department of Research, Evaluation and Planning. (1990). *The school improvement plans of 1990: What the schools will do.* Chicago: Author.

_____. (1995). *Children first: Self-analysis guide.* Chicago: Author.

Chicago School Reform Act, Public Act 85-1418. (1988).

Chicago Training Task Force. (1989). *Kids first: Leadership guide for school reform. Participant's resource materials.* Chicago: Author.

Chicago Tribune. *Chicago Schools: 'Worst in America': An examination of the public schools that fail Chicago.* (1988). Chicago: R. R. Donnelley and Sons.

Chicago United. (1981). *Report of the special task force in education: Chicago school system.* Chicago: Author.

Chubb, J. E., & Moe, T. M. (1990). *Politics, markets and America's schools.* Washington, DC: The Brookings Institution.

Cohen, D. K. (1982). Policy and organization: The impact of state and federal educational policy on school governance. *Harvard Educational Review, 52*(4), 474-499.

_____. (1988). Teaching practice: Plus que ça change . . . . In P. W. Jackson (Ed.), *Contributing to educational change* (pp. 27-84). Berkeley: McCutchan.

_____. (1990a, Fall). A revolution in one classroom: The case of Mrs. Oublier. *Educational Evaluation and Policy Analysis, 12*(3), 311-30.

_____. (1990b). Governance and instruction: The promise of decentralization and choice. In W. H. Clune, & J. F. Witte (Eds.), *Choice and control in American education, Vol. 1* (pp. 337-386). Philadelphia: Falmer.

_____. (1996a). Rewarding teachers for student performance. In S. H. Fuhrman, & J. O'Day (Eds.), *Rewards and Reform* (pp. 60-112). San Francisco: Jossey-Bass.

_____. (1996b). Standards based school reform: Policy, practice and performance. In H. Ladd (Ed.), *Holding schools accountable* (pp. 99-127). Washington, DC: Brookings.

Cohen, D. K., & Ball, D. L. (1990, Fall). Policy and practice: An overview. *Educational Evalution and Policy Analysis,12*(3), 233-40.

Cohen, D. K., & Barnes, C. A. (1993). Pedagogy and policy. In D. K. Cohen, M. W. McLaughlin, & J. E. Talbert (Eds.), *Teaching for understanding* (pp. 207-239). San Francisco: Jossey-Bass.

Cohen, D. K., McLaughlin, M. W., & Talbert, J. E. (1993). *Teaching for understanding.* San Francisco: Jossey-Bass.

Cohen, D. K., & Spillane, J. P. (1992). Policy and practice: The relations between governance and instruction. In G. Grand (Ed.), *Review of Research in Education* (pp. 3-49). Washington, DC: American Educational Research Association.

Coleman, J. S. (1988). Social capital in the creation of human capital. *American Journal of Sociology, 94,* 95-120.

Coleman, J. S., & Hoffer, T. (1987). *Public and private high schools: The impact of communities.* New York: Basic Books.

Comer, J. (1980). *School power: Implications of an intervention project.* New York: The Free Press.

Cremin, L. A. (1988). *American education: The metropolitan experience, 1876-1980.* New York: Harper & Row.

Cuban, L. (1984). Transforming the frog into a prince: effective schools research, policy and practice at the district level. *Harvard Educational Review, 54*(2), 129-151.

_____. (1988). *The managerial imperative and the practice of leadership in schools.* New York: State University of New York Press.

_____. (1990). Reforming again, and again, and again. *Educational Researcher. 19*(10), 3-13.

_____. (1993). *How teachers taught.* New York: Teachers College Press.

Daft, R. L., & Huber , G. P. (1987). How organizations learn: A communication framework. In N. DiTomaso, & S. Bacharach (Eds.), *Research in the Sociology of Organizations: Vol. 5* (pp. 1-36). Greenwich, CT: JAI.

Darling-Hammond, L. (1989). Teacher professionalism: Why and how? In A. Lieberman (Ed.), *Schools as collaborative cultures: Creating the future now* (pp. 25-50). New York: Falmer.

_____. (1993, June). Reframing the school reform agenda: Developing capacity for school transformation. *Phi Delta Kappan, 74*(10), 752-761.

_____. (1997). Toward what end? The evaluation of student learning for the improvement of teaching. In J. Millman (Ed.), *Grading teachers, grading schools* (pp. 248-263). Thousand Oaks, CA: Corwin Press.

Deal, T. E., & Peterson, K. D. (1994). *The leadership paradox: Balancing logic and artistry in schools.* San Francisco: Jossey-Bass.

Delpit, L. (1986, November). Skills and other dilemmas of a progressive Black educator. *Harvard Educational Review, 56*(4), 379-385.

Designs for Change. (1985). *The bottom line: Chicago's failing schools and how to save them. Report No. 1.* Chicago: Author.

Dewey, J. (1899). *The School and Society.* Chicago: University of Chicago Press.

_____. (1929). *My pedagogic creed.* Washington, DC: Progressive Educational Association.

_____. (1954). *The public and its problems.* Chicago: Swallow.

_____. (1966). *Democracy and education.* New York: MacMillan.

Easton, J. Q., Bryk, A. S., Driscoll, M. E., Kotsakis, J. G., Sebring, P. A., & van der Ploeg, A. J. (1991). *Charting reform: The teachers' turn.* Chicago: Consortium on Chicago School Research.

Easton, J. Q., Flinspach, S. L., O'Connor, C., Paul, M., Qualls, J., & Ryan, S. P. (1993). *Local school governance: The third year of Chicago school reform.* Chicago: Chicago Panel on Public School Policy.

Easton, J. Q., & Storey, S. L. (1990). *Local school council meetings during the first year of Chicago school reform.* Chicago: Chicago Panel on Public School Policy.

Edmonds, R. (1979). Effective school for the urban poor. *Educational Leadership, 37,* 15-24.

Elmore, R. F. (1990). Choice as an instrument of public policy: Evidence from education and health care. In W. H. Clune, & J. F. Witte (Eds.), *Choice and control in American education: Vol. I* (pp. 285-317). London: Falmer.

_____. (1991). *Restructuring schools: The next generation of educational reform.* San Francisco: Jossey-Bass.

Elmore, R. F., Peterson, P. L., & McCarthey, S.J. (1996). *Restructuring in the classroom: Teaching, learning, and school organization.* San Francisco: Jossey-Bass.

Etzioni, A. (1988). *The moral dimension: Toward a new economics.* New York: The Free Press.

Evans, S. M., & Boyte, H. C. (1992). *Free spaces: The sources of democratic change in America.* Chicago: University of Chicago Press.

Fantini, M. D., & Gittel, M. (1973). *Decentralization: Achieving reform.* New York: Praeger.

Fantini, M. D., Gittel, M., & Magat, R. (1970). *Community control and the urban school.* New York: Praeger.

Fass, P. S. (1989). *Outside in: Minorities and the transformation of American education.* New York: Oxford University Press.

Fein, L. J. (1970). Community schools and social theory: The limits of universalism. In H. M. Levin (Ed.), *Community control of schools.* Washington, DC: The Brookings Institution.

Ferguson, R. F. (1991, Summer). Paying for public education: New evidence on how and why money matters. *Harvard Journal on Legislation, 28,* 465-498.

Finn, C. E., & Walberg, H. J., (Eds.). (1994). *Radical reforms: The series on contemporary educational issues.* Berkeley: McCutchan.

Firestone, W. A., Bader, B. D., Massel, D., & Rosenblum, S. (1992, Winter). Recent trends in state educational reform: Assessment and prospects. *Teachers College Record. 94*(2), 254-77.

Frank, K., Hermanson, K., & Camburn, E. (1991). *User's manual. Charting reform: The teachers' turn.* Chicago: Consortium on Chicago School Research.

Freeman, D. J., Kuhs, T. M., Porter, A. C., Floden, R. E., Schmidt, W. H., & Schwille, J. R. (1983). Do textbooks and tests define a national curriculum in elementary school mathematics? *Elementary School Journal, 83,* 501-513.

Fuhrman, S. H. (1994). *Challenges in systemic education reform.* New Brunswick, NJ: Consortium for Policy Research in Education.

Fuhrman, S. H. (Ed.). (1993). *Designing coherent education policy: Improving the system.* San Francisco: Jossey-Bass.

Fullan, M. G. (1991). *The new meaning of educational change.* New York: Teachers College Press.

_____. (1993). *Change forces: Probing the depths of educational reform.* Philadelphia: Falmer.

Gage, N. (1978). *The scientific basis for the art of teaching*. New York: Teachers College Press.

Glaser, B. G., & Strauss, A. L. (1967). *The discovery of grounded theory: Strategies for qualitative research*. New York: Aldine De Gruyter.

Goodlad, J. I. (1984). *A place called school*. New York: McGraw-Hill.

Goodlad, J. I., Soder, R., & Sirotnik, K. A., (Eds.). (1990). *The moral dimensions of teaching*. San Francisco: Jossey-Bass.

Graham, P. A. (1993, February). What America has expected of its schools over the past century. *American Journal of Education, 101*, 83-98.

Green, T. F. (1985). The formation of conscience in an age of technology. *American Journal of Education, 94*, 1-32.

Green, T. F. (1981). Excellence, equity and quality. In L. S. Shulman, & G. Sykes (Eds.), *Handbook of teaching and policy* (pp. 318-341). New York: Longman.

Gutman, A. (1987). *Democratic education*. Princeton, NJ: Princeton University Press.

Haertel, E. W. (1994). Theoretical and practical implications. In T. R. Guskey (Ed.), *High stakes performance assessment: Perspectives on Kentucky's educational reform* (pp. 65-75). Thousand Oaks, CA: Corwin Press.

Hall, K. (Forthcoming). *Annenberg networks: Partners in improving Chicago schools*. Unpublished report. Chicago: Consortium on Chicago School Research.

Hammer, M., & Champy, J. (1993). *Reengineering the corporation: A manifesto for business revolution*. New York: Harper Collins Publishers.

Hargreaves, A., & Fullan, M. G. (Eds.). (1992). *Understanding teacher development*. New York: Teachers College Press.

Heath, S. B., McLaughlin, M. W., & Wallin, M. (1987). A child resource policy: Moving beyond dependence on school and family. *Phi Delta Kappan. 68*(8), 57680.

Herrick, M. (1971). *The Chicago schools: A social and political history*. Beverly Hills, CA: Sage.

Hess, G. A. (1991). *School restructuring, Chicago style*. Newbury Park, CA: Corwin.

_____. (1993, April). *Buying or aiding teachers? The reallocation of funds under Chicago school reform*. Paper presented at the annual meeting of the American Educational Research Association, Atlanta, GA.

Hess, G. A., & Lauber, D. (1985). *Dropouts from the Chicago Public Schools: An analysis of the classes of 1982-1983-1984*. Chicago: Chicago Panel on Public School Policy and Finance.

Hess, G. A., Lyons, A., Corsino, L., & Wells, E. (1989). *Against the odds: The early identification of dropouts*. Chicago: Chicago Panel on School Policy.

Hill, P. T. (1992). Urban education. In J. D. Steinberg, D. W. Lyon, & M. E. Vaiana (Eds.), *Urban America*. Santa Monica, CA: RAND Corporation.

_____. (1994). *Reinventing public education*. Santa Monica, CA: Rand Corporation.

Hill, P. T., & Bonan, J. (1991). Decentralization and accountability in public education. Santa Monica, CA: RAND Corporation.

Hogan, D. J. (1985). *Class and reform: School and society in Chicago, 1880-1930*. Philadelphia: University of Pennsylvania Press.

Holmes Group, Inc., The. (1990). *Tomorrow's schools: Principles for the design of professional development in schools*. East Lansing, MI: Author.

Hunter, M., & Russell, D. (1981). Planning for effective instruction. In *Increasing your teaching effectiveness*. Palo Alto, CA: The Learning Institute.

James, W. (1899). *Talks to teachers on psychology and to students on some of life's ideals*. New York: Henry Holt and Co.

Janowitz, M. (1969). Models for urban education. In J. Burk (Ed.). (1991), *On social organization and social control*. Chicago: University of Chicago Press.

Jencks, C., & Peterson, P. (1991). *Urban underclass*. Washington, DC: The Brookings Institution.

Jencks, C., Smith, M., Acland, H., Bane, M. J., Cohen, D., Gintis, H., Heyns, B., & Michelson, S. (1973). *Inequality: A reassessment of the effects of family and schooling in America*. New York: Basic Books.

Johnson, C. (1991, September). New reading program: Now it's CMLR [Letter to the editor]. *Substance*, pp. 1, 6.

Johnson, S. M. (1990). *Teachers at work: Achieving success in our schools*. New York: Basic Books.

Katz, M. B. (1987). *Reconstructing American education*. Cambridge, MA: Harvard University Press.

_____. (1992). Chicago school reform as history. *Teachers College Record, 94*(1), 5672.

Katz, M. B., Fine, M., & Simon, E. (1991, March 7). School reform: A view from the outside. *Chicago Tribune*, p. 27.

Katz, M. B., Simon, E., & Fine, M. (1993, June). You could be beacon, you must not fail. *Catalyst: Voices of Chicago School Reform, 4*(9), 14.

Katznelson, I. (1985). *Schooling for all: Class, race, and the decline of the democratic ideal*. New York: Basic Books.

Kentucky Education Reform Act of 1990, PA 940.

Kerbow, D. (1995). *Pervasive student mobility: A moving target for school improvement*. Chicago: Chicago Panel on School Policy.

Kerdeman, D., & Phillips, D. C. (1993). Empiricism and the knowledge base of educational practice. *Review of Educational Research, 63*(3), 305-313.

Kimberly, J. R., Miles, R. H., & Associates. (1980). *The organizational life cycle*. San Francisco: Jossey-Bass.

Kliebard, H. M. (1993). What is a knowledge base and who would use it if we had one? *Review of Educational Research, 63*(3), 295-303.

Knoepfle, P. (Ed.). (1990). *After Alinsky: Community organizing in Illinois*. Springfield, IL: Sangamon University Press.

Koretz, D. M., Linn, R. L., Dunbar, S. B., & Shepard, L. A. (1991). *The effects of high stakes testing on achievement: Preliminary findings about generalization across tests*. Paper presented at the annual meetings of the American Educational Research Association and the National Council on Measurement in Education, Chicago.

Kotlowitz, A. (1991). *There are no children here*. New York: Doubleday.

Kruse, S. D., Louis, K. S., & Bryk, A. S. (1994, Spring). Building professional community in schools. *Issues in Restructuring Schools, 6*, 3-6.

Kruse, S. D., Louis, K. S., & Bryk, A. S. (1995). An emerging framework for analyzing school-based professional community. In K. S. Louis, & S. D. Kruse (Eds.), *Professionalism and community: Perspectives on reforming urban schools* (pp. 23-42). Thousand Oaks, CA: Corwin.

Kyle, C. L., & Kantowicz, E. R. (1992). *Kids first: Primero los niños.* Springfield, IL: Sangamon State University Press.

Lampert, M. (1984). Teaching about thinking and thinking about teaching. *Journal of Curriculum Studies, 16*(1), 1-18.

———. (1985). How do teachers manage to teach? Perspectives on problems in practice. *Harvard Educational Review, 55*(2), 178-194.

Lee, V., & Smith, J. (1997). High school size: Which works best and for whom? *Educational Evaluation and Policy Analysis, 19*(3), 287-249.

Leithwood, K., & Montgomery, D. (1982). The role of elementary school principals in program improvement: A review. *Review of Educational Research, 52*(3), 309339.

———. (1986). *The principal profile.* Toronto: OISE.

Lewis, A. C. (1995). An overview of the standards movement. *Phi Delta Kappan, 76*(10), 744-750.

Lieberman, A. (1989). *Schools as collaborative cultures: Creating the future now.* New York: Falmer.

———. (1995). *The work of restructuring schools: Building from the ground up.* New York: Teachers College Press.

Lieberman, M. (1986). *Beyond public education.* New York: Praeger.

———. (1989). *Privatization and educational choice.* New York: St. Martin's.

Lindblom, C. E. (1959). The science of "muddling through." *Public Administration Review, 12*(2), 79-88.

———. (1990). *Inquiry and change.* New Haven, CT: Yale University Press.

Little, J. S. (1982). Norms of collegiality and experimentation: Workplace conditions of school success. *American Research Journal, 19*(3), 325-340.

Little, J. W., & McLaughlin, M. W. (Eds.). (1993). *Teachers' work: Individuals, colleagues, and contexts.* New York: Teachers College Press.

Lortie, D. (1975). *Schoolteacher.* Chicago: University of Chicago Press.

Louis, K. S. (1994). Beyond "managed change": Rethinking how schools improve. *School Effectiveness and School Improvement, 5*(1), 2-24.

Louis, K. S., & Kruse, S. D. (1995). *Professionalism and community: Perspectives on reforming suburban schools.* Newbury Park, CA: Corwin.

Louis, K. S., & Miles, M. B. (1990). *Improving the urban high school: What works and why.* New York: Teachers College Press.

Lovin, R. W. (1988). The school and the articulation of values. *American Journal of Education, 96*(2), 143-161.

MacIntyre, A. (1984). *After virtue.* Notre Dame, IN: University of Notre Dame Press.

Malen, B., & Ogawa, R. T. (1988). Professional-patron influence on site-based governance councils: A confounding case study. *Educational Evaluation and Policy Analysis, 10*(4), 251-270.

Malen, B., Ogawa, R. T., & Kranz, J. (1990). What do we know about school-based management? A case study of the literature—A call for research. In W. Clune & J. Witte (Eds.), *Choice and control in American education: Vol. 2. The practice of choice, decentralization and school restructuring* (pp. 289-342). Philadelphia: Falmer.

Mansbridge, J. J. (1980). *Beyond adversary democracy.* Chicago: The University of Chicago Press.

March, J., & Olsen, J. (1986). Garbage can models of decision making in organizations. In J. March & R. Weissinger-Baylon (Eds.), *Ambiguity and command: Organizational perspective on military decision making* (pp.11-35). Marshfield, MA: Pitman.

McKersie, W. (1993, Summer). Philanthropy's paradox: Chicago school reform. *Educational Evaluation and Policy Analysis, 15*(2), 109-128.

McLaughlin, M. W., & Talbert, J. E. (1993). Introduction: New visions of teaching. In D. K. Cohen, M. W. McLaughlin, & J. E. Talbert (Eds.), *Teaching for understanding* (pp. 1-12). San Francisco: Jossey-Bass.

McLaughlin, M. W., Talbert, J., Kahne, J., & Powell, J. (1990). Constructing a personalized school environment. *Phi Delta Kappan, 72*(3), 230-235.

Meyer, J. W., & Rowan, B. (1978). The structure of educational organizations. In M. W. Meyer & Associates. *Environments and organizations* (pp. 78-109). San Francisco: Jossey-Bass.

Meyer, R. H. (1996). Value-added indicators of school performance. In E. Hanushek, & D. W. Jorgensen (Eds.), *Improving the performance of America's schools* (pp. 197-223). Washington, DC: National Academy Press.

Mohrman, S. A., Lawler, E. E., & Mohrman, A. M. (1992). The performance management of teams. In W. J. Bruns (Ed.), *Performance measurement, evaluation, and incentives*. Boston: Harvard Business School Press.

Mohrman, S. A., & Lawler, E. E. (1996). Motivation for school reform. In S. H. Fuhrman, & J. O'Day (Eds.), *Rewards and reform* (pp. 115-143). San Francisco: Jossey-Bass.

Moore, D. R. (1990). Voice and choice in Chicago. In W. H. Clune, & J. F. Witte (Eds.), *Choice and control in American education: Vol. 2: The practice of choice, decentralization and school restructuring* (pp.153-198). Philadelphia: Falmer.

Morone, J. A. (1990). *The democratic wish: Popular participation and the limits of American government*. New York: Basic Books.

Morris, V. C., & Crowson, R. (1984). *Principals in action: The reality of managing schools*. Columbus, OH: Merrill.

Muncey, D. E., & McQuillan, P. J. (1992). The dangers of assuming a consensus for change: Some examples from the Coalition of Essential Schools. In G. A. Hess (Ed.), *Empowering teachers and parents: School restructuring through the eyes of anthropologists* (pp. 47-69). Westport, CT: Bergin & Garvey.

Murnane, R. J., & Levy, F. (1993). Why today's high school educated males earn less than their fathers did: The problem and the assessment of responses. *Harvard Educational Review, 63*(1), 1-19.

Murphy, J. (1991). *Restructuring schools: Capturing and assessing the phenomena*. New York: Teachers College Press.

Murphy, M. J., & Emerson, K. R. (1995). *Decentralization in the Denver public schools: The first three and one-half years*. A paper presented at the annual meeting of the American Educational Research Association, San Francisco, CA.

National Commission on Excellence in Education. (1983). *A nation at risk: The imperative for educational reform*. Washington, DC: United States Government Printing Office.

NAEP Technical Review Panel. (1989). *Report of the NAEP technical review panel on the 1986 reading anomaly. CS 89-499.* Washington, DC: U. S. Department of Education, Office of Educational Research and Improvement.

National Council on Education, Standards, and Testing. (1992). *Raising standards for American education.* Washington, DC: Superintendent of Documents.

National Council of Teachers of Mathematics. (1989). *Curriculum and evaluation standards for school mathematics.* Reston, VA: Author.

National Research Council. (1989). *Everybody counts: A report to the nation on the future of mathematics education.* Washington, DC: National Academy Press.

New Standards Project. (1995). *Performance standards. Volume 1: Elementary school. Consultation draft.* Pittsburgh, PA: National Center on Education and the Economy.

_____. (1995). *Performance standards. Volume 2: Middle school. Consultation draft.* Pittsburgh, PA: National Center on Education and the Economy.

_____. (1995). *Performance Standards. Volume 3: High school. Consultation draft.* Pittsburgh, PA: National Center on Education and the Economy.

Newmann, F. M. (1991). Linking restructuring to authentic student achievement. *Phi Delta Kappan, 72,* 458-463.

Newmann, F. M., & Associates (1996). *Authentic achievement: Restructuring schools for intellectual quality.* San Francisco: Jossey Bass.

Newmann, F. M., King, M. B., & Rigdon, M. (1997, Spring). Accountability and school performance: Implications from restructured schools. *Harvard Educational Review, 67*(1), 41-74.

Newmann, F. M., & Wehlage, G. G. (1995). *Successful school restructuring: A report to the public and educators.* Madison, WI: Center on Organization and Restructuring of Schools.

Oberman, G. (1997). A study of principal turnover in the Chicago Public Schools. Paper presented at the annual meeting of the American Educational Research Association, Chicago.

O'Connell, M. (1991). *School reform Chicago style: How citizens organized to change public policy.* Chicago: Center for Neighborhood Technology.

Odden, A. (1996). Incentives, school organization, and teacher compensation. In S. H. Fuhrman, & J. O'Day (Eds.), *Rewards and Reform* (pp. 226-256). San Francisco: Jossey-Bass.

Ogbu, J. U. (1974). *The next generation: An ethnography of education in an urban neighborhood.* New York: Academic Press.

_____. (1986). The consequences of the American caste system. In U. Niesser (Ed.), *The school achievement of minority* children (pp. 19-56). Hillsdale, NJ: The Lawrence Erlbaum Association.

_____. (1988). *Community forces and minority educational strategies: A comparative study.* Proposal summary prepared for the Russell Sage Foundation.

Peters, T. J., & Waterman, R. H., Jr. (1982). *In search of excellence: Lessons from America's best run companies.* New York: Harper & Row.

Peterson, P. E. (1976). *School politics Chicago style.* Chicago: University of Chicago Press.

_____. (1981). *City Limits*. Chicago: The University of Chicago Press.

Poinsett, A. (1990). School reform, Black leaders: Their impact on each other. *Catalyst: Voices of Chicago School Reform, 1*(4), 7-11.

_____. (1995). Sizemore aims to neutralize the new "lynching tool." *Catalyst: Voices of Chicago School Reform, 7*(4), 13-15.

Porter, A. C., Kirst, M. W., Ostoff, E. J., Smithson, J. L., & Schneider, S. A. (1993). *Reform up close: A classroom analysis*. Madison, WI: Wisconsin Center for Education Research and the Consortium for Policy Research in Education.

Powell, A. G., Farrar, E., & Cohen, D. K. (1985). *The shopping mall high school: Winners and losers in the educational marketplace*. Boston: Houghton Mifflin.

Purpel, D. E. (1989). *The moral and spiritual crisis in education: A curriculum for justice and compassion in education*. Granby, MA: Bergin and Garvey.

Putnam, R. D. (1993). *Making democracy work: Civic traditions in modern Italy*. Princeton, NJ: Princeton University Press.

Raywid, M. A. (1995). Professional community and its yield at Metro Academy. In K. S. Louis, & S. D. Kruse (Eds.), *Professionalism and community: Perspectives on reforming urban schools* (pp. 45-75). Newbury Park, CA: Corwin.

Richardson-Koehler, V. (1987). What happens to research on the way to practice? *Theory in Practice, 36*(1), 38-43.

Rollow, S. G., & Bryk, A. S. (1994). Catalyzing professional community in a school reform left behind. In K. S. Louis, & S. D. Kruse (Eds.), *Professionalism and community: Perspectives on reforming urban schools* (pp. 23-45). Thousand Oaks, CA: Corwin.

Rosenholtz, S. J. (1985). Effective schools: Interpreting the evidence. *American Journal of Education, 93*(2), 352-389.

_____. (1989).*Teachers' workplace: A social organization of schools*. New York: Longman.

Rowan, B. (1990). Commitment and control: Alternative strategies for the organizational design of schools. In C.B. Cazden (Ed.), *Review of Research in Education: Vol.16* (pp. 353-389). Washington, DC: American Educational Research Association.

Sarason, S.B. (1990). *The predictable fortune of educational reform*. San Francisco: Jossey-Bass.

Schneider, B., & Bryk, A. S. (1995). *Trust as a moral resource: Constructive social relations in urban school communities*. Paper presented at the meeting of the Invitational Conference on Social Capital, University of Wisconsin-Madison, Madison, WI.

Schon, D., (1979). Public service organizations and the capacity for public learning. *International Journal of Social Science, 31*, 682-95.

Sebring, P. B., Bryk, A. S., Easton, J. Q., Luppescu, S., Thum, Y. M., Lopez, W., & Smith, B. (1995). *Charting reform: Chicago teachers take stock*. Chicago: Consortium on Chicago School Research.

Sebring, P. B., Bryk, A. S., Roderick, M., Camburn, E., Luppescu, S., Thum, Y. M., Smith, B., & Kahne, J. (1996). *Charting reform in Chicago: The students speak*. Chicago: Consortium on Chicago School Research.

Senge, P.M., (1990). *The fifth discipline*. New York: Doubleday Currency.

Sergiovanni, T. J. (1992). *Moral leadership: Getting to the heart of school improvement*. San Francisco: Jossey-Bass.

Shipps, D. (1995). *Big business and school reform: The case of Chicago, 1988.* Unpublished doctoral dissertation, Stanford University.

_____. (1997, Fall). The invisible hand: Big business and Chicago school reform. *Teachers College Record, 99*(1), 73-116.

Sizer, T. R. (1984). *Horace's compromise: The dilemma of the American high school.* Boston: Houghton Mifflin.

_____. (1992). *Horace's school: Redesigning the American high school.* Boston: Houghton Mifflin.

Slavin, R. E. (1989). What works for students at risk: A research synthesis. *Educational Synthesis, 46*(5), 4-18.

Smith, M. S., & O'Day, J. A., (1990). *Systemic school reform: Politics of education yearbook.* Washington, DC: Falmer.

_____. (1991). Systemic school reform. In S. Fuhrman, & B. Malen (Eds.), *The politics of curriculum and testing* (pp. 233-267). Bristol, PA: Falmer.

Smylie, M. A. (1994). Redesigning teachers' work: Connections to the classroom. *Review of Educational Research: Vol. 20* (pp. 129-178). Washington, DC: American Educational Research Association.

Smylie, M. A., Lazarus, V., & Brownlee-Conyers, J., (1996, Fall). Instructional outcomes of school-based participative decision making. *Educational Evaluation and Policy Analysis, 18,* 181-198.

Stern, G. (1994, October 5). GM puts Saturn in new group for small cars; unit is pushed to cut costs in shakeup of operations across North America. *The Wall Street Journal.* See World Wide Web site: http://www.wwnorton.com:81/wsj/varian/10-05-94/10-05-94.htm

Storey, S., Easton, J. Q., Sharp, T. C., Steans, H., Ames, B., & Bassuk, A. (1995). *Chicago's public school children and their environment.* Chicago: Chicago Public Schools with Chicago Urban League and the Latino Institute.

Strike, K. A. (1993). Professionalism, democracy, and discursive communities: Normative reflections on restructuring. *American Educational Research Journal, 30*(2), 255-275.

Tafel, L., & Bertani, A. (1992, Fall). Reconceptualizing staff development. *Journal of Staff Development, (13)*4, 42-45.

Tanner, D., & Tanner. L. N. (1975). *Curriculum development: Theory into practice.* New York: MacMillan.

Tushman, M., & Romanelli, E. (1985). Organizational evolution: A metamorphosis model of convergence and reorientation. In *Research in Organizational Behavior, Vol. 7* (pp. 171-222). Greenwich, CT: JAI.

Tyack, D. (1974). *The one best system: A history of American urban education.* Cambridge, MA: Harvard University Press.

Tyack, D., & Cuban, L. (1995). *Tinkering toward utopia: A century of public school reform.* Cambridge, MA: Harvard University Press.

Walton, R. E. (1980). Establishing and maintaining high commitment work systems. In J.R. Kimberly, R.H. Miles, & Associates (Eds.), *The organization life cycle: Issues in the creation, transformation, and decline of organizations.* San Francisco: Jossey-Bass.

Wang, M. C., Haertel, G. D., & Walberg, H. J. (1993). Toward a knowledge base for school learning. *Review of Educational Research, 63*(3), 249-294.

Weber, M. (1947). *The theory of social and economic organization.* New York: Oxford University Press.

Weick, K. E. (1976). Educational organizations as loosely coupled systems. *Administrative Science Quarterly, 21*(1), 1-10.

Weisbord, M. (1991). *Productive workplaces: Organizing and managing for dignity, meaning, and community.* San Francisco: Jossey-Bass.

Weismann, D. (1994, February). Updates. *Catalyst: Voices of Chicago School Reform, 5*(5), 22.

Wells, A. S. (1993). The sociology of school choice: Why some win and others lose in the educational marketplace. In E. Rassell, & R. Rothstein (Eds.), *School choice: Examining the evidence* (pp. 29-48). Washington, DC: Economic Policy Institute.

Wilkerson, I. (1990, March 2). Fate of principals splits some Chicago public schools. *The New York Times,* p. A2.

———. (1990, March 9). Democracy divides Chicago schools. *The New York Times,* p. A12.

Williams, D. (1993, May). LSCs great or not so great? It depends on whom you ask. *Catalyst: Voices of Chicago School Reform, 4*(8), 10-13.

———. (1994, December). Comings . . . and goings. *Catalyst: Voices of Chicago School Reform, 6*(4), 30.

Willms, J. D., & Echols, F. H. (1993). The Scottish experience of parental school choice. In E. Rassell, & R. Rothstein (Eds.), *School choice: Examining the evidence* (pp. 49-68). Washington, DC: Economic Policy Institute.

Wilson, T. A. (1996). *Reaching for a better standard. English school inspection and the dilemma of accountability for American public schools.* New York and London: Teachers College Press.

Wilson, W. J. (1987). *The truly disadvantaged: The inner city, the underclass, and public policy.* Chicago: University of Chicago Press.

Wise, A. (1979). *Legislated learning: The bureaucratization of the American classroom.* Berkeley: University of California Press.

Witte, J. F., Bailey, A. B., & Thorn, C. A. (1993). *Third-year report: Milwaukee parental choice program.* Madison, WI: Wisconsin Department of Public Instruction.

Witte, J. F., Thorn, C. A., Pritchard, K. M., & Claibourn, M. (1994). *Fourth year report: Milwaukee parental choice program.* Madison, WI: Wisconsin Department of Public Instruction.

Wohlstetter, P., & Odden, A. (1992). Rethinking school-based management policy and research. *Educational Administration Quarterly, 28,* 529-549.

Wong, K. K. (1992). The politics of urban education as a field of study: An interpretative analysis. In J. G. Cibulka, R. J. Reed, & K. K. Wong (Eds.), *The politics of urban education in the United States: The 1991 yearbook of the politics of education association* (pp. 3-26). Washington, DC: Falmer.

Wong, K. K., & Rollow, S. G. (1990). *The rise and fall of adversarial politics in the context of Chicago school reform: Parent participation in a Latino school community.* Madison, WI: Center on Organization and Restructuring of Schools.

Wong, K. K., & Sunderman, G. L. (1994). *Redesigning accountability at the system wide level: The politics of school reform in Chicago.* Paper prepared for delivery at the Federal Reserve Bank of Chicago Symposium, Midwest Approaches to School Reform, Chicago.

Wright, B. D., Linacre, J. M., & Thum, Y. M. (1996). *Technical report for the Illinois State Board of Education. IGAP reading tests, 1993-1995: Re-equating and disaggregating analyses.* Chicago: University of Chicago, MESA Psychometric Laboratory.

Wright, B., & Masters, G. N. (1982). *Rating Scale Analysis.* Chicago: Mesa.

Wrigley, J. (1982). *Class politics and public schools: Chicago, 1900-1950.* New Brunswick, NJ: Rutgers University Press.

Yanguas, J., & Rollow, S. G. (1996). *The rise and fall of adversarial politics in the context of Chicago school reform: Parent participation in a Latino school community.* Madison, WI: Center on Organization and Restructuring of Schools.

Zemelman, S., Daniels, H., & Hyde, A. (1993). *Best practice: New standards for teaching and learning in America's schools.* Portsmouth, NH: Heinemann.

Index